SIXTH EDITION

1998/1999 CUMULATIVE SUPPLEMENT

Nonprofit Corporations, Organizations, & Associations

HOWARD L. OLECK

Professor of Law, Emeritus
Stetson University College of Law
and Cleveland State University
College of Law

and

MARTHA E. STEWART

B.S., University of Miami
J.D., Stetson University

PRENTICE HALL

Library of Congress Cataloging-in-Publication Data
(Revised for 1998/1999 supplement)

Oleck, Howard Leoner
    Nonprofit corporations, organizations & associations
    Kept up to date by supplements.
    Includes bibliographic references and index.
    1. Nonprofit organizations–Law and legislation
–United States. 2. Unincorporated societies–United
States. I. Stewart, Martha E. II. Nonprofit
corporations, organizations & associations.
III. Title.
KF1388.044   1994   346.73`064   93-47544
                  347.30664

Printed in the United States of America

10 9 8 7 6 5 4 3 2 1

ISBN 0-13-911090-9

This publication is designed to provide accurate and authoritative information in regard to the subject matter covered. It is sold with the understanding that the publisher is not engaged in rendering legal, accounting, or other professional service. If legal advice or other expert assistance is required, the services of a competent professional person should be sought.

. . . From the Declaration of Principles jointly adopted by a Committee of the American Bar Association and a Committee of Publishers and Associations.

ATTENTION: CORPORATIONS AND SCHOOLS

Prentice Hall books are available at quantity discounts with bulk purchase for educational, business, or sales promotional use. For information, please write to: Prentice Hall Career & Personal Development Special Sales, 240 Frisch Court, Paramus, NJ 07652. Please supply: title of book, ISBN number, quantity, how the book will be used, data needed.

PRENTICE HALL
Paramus, NJ 07652

A Simon & Schuster Company

On the World Wide Web at http://www.phdirect.com

Prentice-Hall International (UK) Limited, *London*
Prentice-Hall of Australia Pty. Limited, *Sydney*
Prentice-Hall Canada, Inc., *Toronto*
Prentice-Hall Hispanoamericana, S.A., *Mexico*
Prentice-Hall of India Private Limited, *New Delhi*
Prentice-Hall of Japan, Inc., *Tokyo*
Simon & Schuster Asia Pte. Ltd., *Singapore*
Editora Prentice-Hall do Brasil, Ltda., *Rio de Janeiro*

ABOUT THE AUTHORS

HOWARD L. OLECK, the leading authority on nonprofit organization law and management since his treatise on the subject appeared in 1956, was Distinguished Professor of Law (and Dean) Emeritus of Cleveland State University College of Law and Professor of Law Emeritus of Stetson University College of Law, and had also been law professor at Wake Forest University and New York Law Schools. An active member of the New York, Ohio, and Federal Bars for 57 years, he had served as Special Master of Federal Courts on complex corporate cases, Consultant for Congressional Committees, several state legislatures, foreign nations, and many organizations worldwide, and as Counsel and Organizer and Officer of many kinds of nonprofit organizations. He was the author of many books and articles, including *Modern Corporation Law* (6 volumes) and (with Green) *Parliamentary Law and Practice for Nonprofit Organizations* (Amer. Bar Assn.– Amer. Law Inst.) and had been listed in *Who's Who in America* since 1950. Professor Oleck passed away in June, 1995.

MARTHA E. STEWART is an attorney specializing in nonprofit organizations cases. She is licensed to practice in Florida. As colleague, researcher, teaching fellow, editor, cocounsel, and coauthor, she worked with Professor Oleck for eight years at Stetson University College of Law on Nonprofit Organizations Law and Practice courses, seminars, cases, and problems, and on Advanced Torts Law seminars, following 16 years of service in biologic scientific environmental research worldwide. She has been chief researcher for several years and was coauthor of the Sixth Edition. She is the sole author of this supplement, and will be the author of future supplements and editions. She resides in Hartford, Wisconsin.

HOW TO USE THIS SUPPLEMENT

This *1998/1999 Cumulative Supplement* adds many new (additional) case decisions and agency rulings, as well as changes of rules and practices adopted since the publication of the sixth edition. The *index* to this supplement is vitally important; more important in some cases than the main-volume index, because of the many changes. Thus, in using this supplement:

- Identify the key words or terms that apply to the subject you would like to learn about;

- Use several possible approaches; thus, the same matter may be a "Members' rights" matter, or a "Voting" matter, or a "Parliamentary law" matter, and so on. Look under each appropriate term or word in the index.

- You have two indexes in one here: (a) supplement index and (b) the main volume index.

- The supplement references are indicated by **S** before the (supplement) page numbers, and the appropriate main volume pages are shown with no **S** before the page number.

- Read *more* than one or two case or ruling report items on the topic or matter. If time permits, read the entire chapter (or several pages) about the subject, if you want a fairly wide understanding of it. The more you read about it, the more you are able to deal with its nuances and variations.

PREFACE TO THE
1998/1999 SUPPLEMENT

Nonprofit organizations—voluntary associations—provide the sense of "belonging" and group "acceptance" that humans instinctively need. Millions of people spend the best parts of their lives in their churches, clubs, societies, and professional associations. Political, constitutional, religious, and ethical questions and rulings have greatly outnumbered other kinds of developments for nonprofits—including tax exemption law changes—in recent years.

Joint nonprofit and for-profit business operations have multiplied. Continuing government cutbacks in funding have caused more mixing of profit and nonprofit activities as social service agencies struggle to meet the increasing needs of the homeless, elderly, and unemployed. As a result we find that court and administrative agency rulings have dealt mainly with constitutional, ethics, and values issues in the nineties. Hundreds of such case decisions, regulations, and code enactments are set forth in this supplement.

During the past few years, tax-exempt organizations have been facing threats to their very existence. They've had to look to their roots to find legitimacy in their enormous power in the economy. Nonprofit and charitable institutions are woven into the fabric of this country.

State regulation of nonprofit institutions is becoming more far-reaching. Attempts are being made to require state registration of Internet solicitation. More and more class action lawsuits are being filed against nonprofits, when donors think the organizations aren't using donations properly. Such suits can ruin a medium-to-large organization. Many states are enforcing their unfair trade practice laws against nonprofits. Unfair trade practice acts often allow individuals to bring action under a private right of action provision. These acts result in a pool of virtually unlimited plaintiffs, many also allow suing for damages.

Spurred by the National Child Protections Act of 1993 and Violent Control and Law Enforcement Act of 1994, volunteer background checks are becoming routine at every nonprofit institution.

Continued reports of misconduct by officers, directors, and managers demonstrate the need for Director's and Officer's Insurance (D&O Insurance). Mismanagement at the American Red Cross is being investigated as this supplement goes to press. The first disbursements made to organizations that invested in the fraudulent Foundation for New Era Philanthropy were ordered by Arlin Adams, the federal bankruptcy trustee.

Nonprofit managers are turning to new technologies to streamline management techniques and find donors. Some of the software programs available for fundraising and management are described in this supplement. Nonprofits are increasingly finding donors in foreign countries. The President's Summit for America's Future was held in April of 1997, featuring former Presidents Bush and Ford, and President Clinton. The Summit's goal was to encourage volunteerism; volunteer numbers have been decreasing for years.

Academic centers for the study of nonprofit organizations are multiplying rapidly. There are now 75 graduate education programs that include three or more courses specifically focusing on nonprofit organizations. Another 42 universities offer one or two graduate courses, usually financial management and generic nonprofit management. In 1990, there were only 17 universities offering a graduate concentration in the management of nonprofit organizations.

Colorado voters overwhelmingly rejected an attempt to remove the property tax exemptions for nonprofits in Colorado. The Taxpayer Relief Act of 1997 will have a tremendous impact on nonprofits. The Act contains provisions for excise tax reporting requirements, intermediate sanctions abatement, stock contributions to private foundations, corporate sponsorship, gift tax filing requirements, and excise tax due date changes. A new provision states that if a nonprofit controls 50 percent or more of the votes or stock of the taxable subsidiary, income passed from the subsidiary to the nonprofit in the form of interests, rents, royalties, and annuities is subject to Unrelated Business Income Tax (UBIT).

With the challenge coming from every sector, nonprofit institutions in 1998/1999, need to focus on ethics within their organizations. Recent breaches of ethics and acts of criminal nature by nonprofit managers have eroded public trust. Only through ethical, efficient, and lawful management, can nonprofits continue to be an important factor in the economy of the United States. Criticism and attacks result from a bad public image. And, as we all know, nonprofit organizations rely mainly on donations from the public. It's obvious that the key to financial health of nonprofits is a return to the ethical, legal, and moral principles that led to their creation. The public is demanding ethical nonprofits.

CONTENTS

TABLE OF FORMS

1

NATURE OF NONPROFIT ORGANIZATIONS

§1. IMPORTANCE OF NONPROFIT (VOLUNTARY) ORGANIZATIONS

Charitable Contributions Data

<u>1997 Report</u>

The American Association of Fund Raising Counsel's Trust for Philanthropy (AAFRC) reported, in 1997, that totals for charitable giving increased, in 1996, by 7.3 percent compared to 1995. Total charitable contributions, in 1996, were $150 billion, up from the $140 billion contributed in 1995. The increase in giving can be associated with a 5.5 percent increase in personal income and a double-digit hike in the stock market indexes. Giving by individuals has remained at 2 percent of a personal income since 1972.

Health organizations, including hospitals, showed the strongest growth with an increase of 10.35 percent. Giving to art, cultural, and humanities organizations increased by 9.7 percent in 1996. Environmental and wildlife organizations raised only 1.6 percent more (a loss when inflation is factored in). International affairs organizations fell by 4.6 percent in 1996—continuing the trend of 1995, when giving to these causes fell by 6.6 percent.

The $150 billion figure for giving does not reflect the value of volunteer labor, worth more than $200 billion according to a study by Independent Sector. The $150 billion figure also does not reflect contributions to unchartered voluntary organizations that are not officially registered charities.

Religious organizations, as usual, received the most donations, with 69.44 billion or 46.1 percent of all giving. Educational organizations received the next largest revenue, at $18.81 billion, or 12.5 percent of all contributions. Health organizations garnered $15.03 billion or 9.2 percent of all contributions. Human services organizations brought in $12.16 billion or 8.1 percent of the total. Arts, cultural, and humanities organizations received $10.92 billion or 7.2 percent of the total. Gifts to foundations totaled $8.27 billion or 5.5 percent of giving dollars. Public/society benefit organizations brought in $7.57 billion or 5 percent of total giving dollars. Environmental and wildlife organizations took in $4.04 billion or 2.7 percent of giving, a decline of 0.1 percent in 1996. International affairs received $1.89 billion or 1.3 percent, a market share decrease of 0.1 points. Unallocated giving amounted to $2.57 billion or 2.4 percent of all contributions. Unallocated giving was significantly down in both actual donors ($4.01 billion) and percentage (3.6 percent) when compared to 1995.

Individual donors in 1996, gave the most at $119,92 billion or 79.6 percent, an increase of 6.9 percent over 1995. Foundations were a distant second place with $11.83 billion or just 7.8 percent of giving. Bequests made up 6.9 percent at $10.46 billion. Corporate giving was, as usual, in last place with $8.5 billion or 5.6 percent of all giving.

> *Giving USA 1997*, American Association of Fund Raising Counsel, copies available from AAFRC for $49 (plus $4.50 for shipping and handling, 1-800-462-2372), Clolery, Paul, (article), 11 *NonProfit Times* (8) 1, 47 (June, 1997).

Top Ten Nonprofit Organizations (By Revenue)

The top ten organizations in 1996 were: The YMCA of the USA ($2.4 billion); Catholic Charities of the USA ($2.1 billion); American Red Cross ($1.8 billion); Salvation Army (estimated by the *NonProfit Times* staff and consultants at $1.5 billion); Goodwill Industries ($1.2 billion); Shriners Hospital for Children ($1.04 billion); Boy Scouts of America ($533 million); YMCA of the USA ($510.8 million); American Cancer Society ($510.6 million); and Planned Parenthood Federation of America ($504 million).

> Clolery, Paul, (article), 11 *NonProfit Times* (14) 31–32 (November, 1997).

Harvard Nonprofit Study Program

Harvard, in 1997, received a gift to enable it to establish a center for the study of the nonprofit sector. The donation reflects the increasing influence of nonprofit organizations.

> Miller, Judith, *Gift Enables Harvard to Establish Center for Study of Nonprofit Sector, The New York Times*, April 12, 1997.

General Trends in 1996–1998

In 1996, nonprofits received more contributions. However, most nonprofits had to defend themselves against assaults from everyone, including radical citizens and a more radical Congress.

Most nonprofits looked to their roots and found that events have been signaling that the sector has enormous power in the economy and is woven into the fabric of this country.

More states will be pushing for charitable solicitation laws in 1997. The Internet will possibly come under attack. For example, if an organization solicits contributions on the Internet, must the organization register in the state where the solicitation occurs? If 1996 foretells what will continue into 1997, there will probably be more class action lawsuits by individuals against nonprofits that donors think aren't using donations properly. Such suits can ruin a medium-to-large organization. Many states are enforcing their unfair trade practices law against nonprofits. Such acts often allow individuals to bring action under a private right of action provision. The acts may also allow for damages.

Clolery, Paul, (article), 10 *NonProfit Times* (12) 24–25 (December, 1996).

Foundations and Social Change

In 1997, foundations are becoming much bigger and influential due to shrinking of government and the rise in the stock market since 1980. Foundations, with their new-found power, are attempting to influence political and social change. An example of such foundations is the Heritage Foundation, which played a major role during the Reagan-Bush era.

Lemann, Nicholas, *Citizen 501(c)(3): An Increasingly Powerful Agent in American Life Is Also One of the Least Noticed, The Atlantic Monthly*, February, 1997.

The PECTS System of Solving Social Problems

Social problems are most easily solved by teamwork among social institutions led by schools. The PECTS (Politics, Economy, Culture, and Third Sector) system allows these several elements to interact and come up with real solutions. Coordination of these institutions are politics under constitutional democracy and the economy under mixed capitalism. The cultural institutions are composed of families, communities, churches, and schools. The Third Sector is composed of nonprofit and voluntary groups.

Til, John Van, *Facing Inequality and the End of Work. Educational Leadership,* March, 1997.

Altruism and Economics

Nonprofits exist because they allow people to support an ideology or belief through altruistic acts. Since nonprofits are founded on nonselfish motives, nonprofits gain the trust of society. Only nonprofit organizations can solicit or attract donations, even if the services they provide are available from private firms. At the same time, donors are motivated to give money since these amounts are tax deductible.

> Rose-Ackerman, Susan, *Altruism, Nonprofits and Economic Theory, Journal of Economic Literature,* June, 1996.

Money/Power-Seeking NPOs

Unless money and power seeking become too blatant, an NPO does not lose its privileged status; some such seeking is inevitable in almost any human activity. Nonprofit does not mean "saintly." Charges of fraudulent use of nonprofit status are sometimes politically inspired, as in the Republican Party charges against the thirty-three-million member AARP (American Association of Retired Persons) in 1994, because of AARP's leaning toward Democratic Party programs. AARP paid $135 million to the Internal Revenue Service that year when accused of hawking insurance and other products to senior citizens for profit rather than nonprofit purposes.

> D. Dahl, *AARP at center of struggle for power, money, St. Petersburg (FL) Times,* pp. 1, 18, 19 (Oct. 9, 1994): a lengthy survey/analysis of this nonprofit organization's senior citizen advocacy.

Nonprofit Crime Victims Services

Though the crime rate in New York City is down, nonprofit Victims Services still receives a high volume of calls.

> *See,* Haberman, Clyde, *For a Victim, Any Crime Is Too Much, The New York Times,* April 4, 1997.

Decline in NPO Participation/Volunteers

Declining civic engagement by Americans had become serious by 1995. Since 1973 attendance at public meetings on town and school affairs had dropped over a third. Union membership had fallen from 35% to 15% of the non-agricultural work force in 1953–1995. PTA attendance fell from 12 million in 1964 to 7 million in 1995. Volunteers' numbers for the Boy Scouts and Red Cross for 1970–1995 fell off 26% and 61%, respectively.

> *George F. Will* column, Bowling leaguer decline is bad news for democracy,
>   *Washington Post Writers Group* (Jan. 5, 1995).

The number of volunteers is still shrinking in 1997, according to a study by the Community Resource Exchange.

> Foderaro, Lisa W., *Few Volunteers Sighted, The New York Times*, May 16, 1997.

§3. DEFINITIONS OF "NONPROFIT"

For more information about nonprofit purposes and the character that warrants the creation of a nonprofit corporation, *see* 16 ALR 2d 1345.

Affiliations; Joint Programs; Sponsorship

Cooperation by a city or county office may be had for the asking in some places. For example, St. Petersburg, Florida, offers "joint operation" to NPO programs that have some general public interest. Application forms for requesting cofinancial sponsorship must be filed well before the city's fiscal year; and a ($15) processing fee is charged. For details, call (813) 893-7494.
See also, Chapter 40.

§4. CHARITY—ORGANIZATION STANDARDS

Accreditation

Wise Giving Guide, current issues, issued intermittently, by National Charities Information Bureau, Inc., 19 Union Sq. W., New York, NY 10003-3395.

To check on local or state charities call your county Charitable Solicitations Officer; in Florida call the C.S. Section of the Dept. of Agriculture and Consumer Services, (800) 435-7352.

In 1995, many local affiliates of the Council of Better Business Bureaus (BBB) (17% of them) monitored and reported activities of local charities. The National Charities Information Bureau and the BBB's Philanthropic Advisory Service (PAS) evaluated 700 of the estimated 400,000 charities in the United

States. The local BBBs used a list of 22 standards, including program service expenditure ratios, board governance, and fund raising to evaluate charities. According to PAS, 69 percent of the national charities monitored met the standards while 31 percent failed to meet one or more of the standards. The PAS guide can be ordered from: PAS at (703) 276–0100, $14.95.

See Mehegan, Sean, (article), 9 *NonProfit Times* (2) 1, 5, 10 (February, 1995).

Accreditation Authority Rules

Accreditation of America's over 170 major law schools is done by the American Bar Association (ABA) [and Association of American Law Schools (AALS)] and the bases of such accreditation were being attacked in 1994. *Massachusetts School of Law v. ABA,* 93–6206 (E.D. PA) (N.L.J. 12–6–93). MSL charged violation of antitrust law and that ABA inflates the cost of legal education, and challenged salary levels, limits on teaching hours, use of standardized tests, law library guidelines, prohibition of bar exam courses, and limits on students' outside employment. A note of the judge hearing a preliminary motion said that the schools' managers were being charged with inflating their employees' wages. But the ABA (Section of Legal Education) meanwhile chose a committee to review the accreditation process and standards.

Ken Myers, Law Schools (column), *Natl. L. J.,* p. A16 (July 25, 1994).

Slander of Accrediting Officer

Slander of an accrediting officer (inspector) by a religious college [falsely calling him incompetent and a homosexual] is actionable tort; a program evaluator for the Missouri Department of Education had a cause of action for such defamation.

Nazeri v. Missouri Valley College, #75201 (MO Supr. Ct., Aug. 17, 1993).

Public or Private Charity

Private charity, by voluntary associations, is healthier than public charity by governmental authorities. Alexis de Tocqueville pointed this out in his 1835 *Memoir on Pauperism.* Public charity demeans the recipients, while private charity elevates the hearts of the givers and establishes a bond—a social contract that the recipient will in turn help others.

The trouble is that private charity is haphazard and public charity politicizes. One solution is to encourage organizations that give charity in ways that build community, in *volunteer centers* that combine individual support with group organization machinery.

William Raspberry, column, *Washington Post* Writers Group (Oct. 5, 1994).

Business vs. Government Problem Solving

According to a survey done by the Points of Light Foundation, at its National Community Service Conference in the summer of 1996, of 250 people responding, the government is rated below the private sector and the nonprofit sector in aiding with society's ills. The private sector (business) was rated most effective by 62 percent of the participants at solving problems while the volunteer-based nonprofit sector was rated as second most effective by about 20 percent of the participants. About 10.5 percent said that government is third on the list when it comes to problem-solving. No opinion was registered by the remaining respondents.

Holton, Carlotta, (article), 10 *NonProfit Times* (10) 5 (October, 1996).

Privatization of Kansas's Child-Welfare Services

Kansas's system to privatize its child-welfare services could become a model for other states attempting to reform these programs. Kansas's managed-care approach to children's services features a capitated fixed-priced papy system and promotes a competition between nonprofit providers. The privatized system has also set strict performance standards in revamping foster care and adoption service expectations. Kansas has faced very little opposition in turning to private providers for these services and has realized a number of efficiencies.

Eggers, William D., *There's No Place Like Home. Policy Review,* May–June, 1997.

Privatized Welfare Reform in Texas

A five-year $2 billion contract will replace the existing welfare system in Texas with one that will automate application for welfare benefits, possibly using something similar to a bank's automated teller machine (ATM). The current system in Texas costs more than $550 million to administer. The millions that an automated system would save reportedly will go toward children's health care coverage. While no contract for a welfare eligibility system has been awarded yet, and the corporate groups that will bid have not disclosed how their systems would be designed, many nonprofits fear the worst. For example, will only naturalized citizens be eligible? Welfare recipients will only contact a nonprofit when a crisis occurs, instead of an organization helping them as they change their lives. Texas's privatization of its welfare system will be difficult and complicated.

Sinclair, Matthew, (article), 11 *NonProfit Times* (7) (May, 1997).

Nonprofit Hope for Foster Children and Parents

Hope Meadows is a subdivision of 13 homes built at the former Chanute Air Force Base in Rantoul, Illinois. Families, comprised primarily of foster children and parents, live there rent-free. The Hope for Children nonprofit program is responsible for the development of the subdivision.

Henry, Ed, *Homes for Foster Children. Kiplinger's Personal Finance Magazine*, May, 1997.

"Social Safety Net" Needs Government to Do More

Representatives of 50 of the nation's largest nonprofits warned government welfare reformers that voluntary health and human services agencies can't single-handedly maintain the "social safety net" supporting the needy. Government must continue to have a responsibility for the homeless, the hungry, the jobless, the elderly poor, and children at risk. Though the Clinton Administration predicted that charities would close any "safety net" gaps created by government cutbacks, nonprofit sector leaders at the conference raised serious questions about Clinton's assumption.

Rankin, Ken, (article), 11 *NonProfit Times* (14) 1, 11 (November, 1997).

Recognition—Education Societies/Conventions

By the late 1800s there were many trade/professional/recognition/educational societies in America; for example, over 1,200 agricultural societies. As early as 1807 there were "exhibitions" (and soon "county fairs") to (first) market products and then to educate and entertain the public. [*See, Reader's Digest* (R.L. Scheftel, ed.), *Discovering America's Past,* 186 (1993).]

Today's vast *convention business* in America and worldwide is the direct descendant of those county fairs. Today it appears to be the *Number Two employer* and *Number Three retail industry* in the U.S., often involving travel and tourism. [*See* Chapter 24, Section 240, on the *Meetings Industry.*]

§5. ETHICS IN NONPROFIT ORGANIZATIONS

Ethics of Professional Associations

Erosion of the ethical standards of whole professions (let alone their "associations") is becoming dangerous today (1994). For example, a severe critique of the legal profession faults the bar associations. It criticizes not the "mouthpiece" but the big firms and bar associations that have created/tolerated a "legal services industry" that turns a *public*-service profession into "an increasingly unprincipled business." It is said (and this actually *is* being *done*) that law schools must teach more about ethics, and "the construction of *a formal code of ethics*." The same might be said of the profession of medicine.

> Sol M. Linowitz (with Martin Mayer), *The Betrayed Profession* (Charles Scribner's Sons, New York, NY, 1994) esp. c. 7, The Job for the Bar Associations (pp. 138–166).

ABA Standards: Religious Corporations v. Constitution: Standards of Conduct

Confusion as to ethics is made worse by the American Bar Association proposed statutes, such as those proposed for religious organizations. "If religious doctrine governing the affairs of a religious corporation is inconsistent with the provisions of this Act [model NPC Act] on the same subject, the religious doctrine shall control to the extent required by the Constitution of the United States or the constitution of his state or both." Model Nonprofit Corp. Act, subchapter H, §1.80 (adopted 1989). Also, Subchapter C §8.30 states: "General Standards for Directors," and subd. (e) says that "director shall *not* be deemed a trustee . . ." This sets the standards of an ordinary businessperson as the standard for directors.

Codes of Ethics

United Way of America approved a new *Code of Ethics* for the organization in early 1994. For a copy of this five-page code see 11 *Leadership I.S.* (4) 1–5 (Summer 1994) [Independent Sector].

National Society of Fund Raising Executives Code of Ethical Principles and Standards of Professional Practice, (adopted 1991, added to 1992) (2 pages), is set forth in the same issue of Independent Sector's periodical (above) pp. 35–36.

That same issue also contains a series of other statements and analysis of ethical principles and standards for various kinds of NPOs.

Ethics: State Control

It has long been recognized that NPOs "are considered by Parliaments as being part of the social structures in a wide sense, namely, of the society organized in the state . . . "

"Therefore, if individuals and groups tend to obtain for certain reasons the intervention and also the facilities of the state, it must be agreed that the organizations of persons and assets created by them be subjected to state control (by way of appropriate statutory and administrative means) aimed at ensuring both the correctness of their functioning and the adequacy of their purposes and activities to the needs and purposes of society in the light of their social responsibility . . ."

> Piero, Verrucoli, *Non-Profit Organizations. (A Comparative Approach)*, p. 111 (Conclusion) (Dott. A. Giuffre, Editore, S. p. A, Milano, Italy, 1984, based on American, English, French, Belgian, German, Italian, and Spanish law).

Ethics Versus Politics

Globalization has put the needs of shareholders at the top of the business priority list, along with an intensified drive towards pure profit. However, some businessmen oppose this idea and would like to inject some nonprofit and ethical elements into business practices.

> Lloyd, John, *Ethics Man? Perhaps . . .*, New Statesman (1996), March 27, 1997.

Ethics and Public Image

In January of 1996, The National Board of Visitors of the Indiana University Center on Philanthropy convened a meeting in New York City to determine whether philanthropy is in a crisis. A gathering of more than 100 of the most influential leaders in the nonprofit sector rejected a plan to form a commission to study the sector (a rejection of a commission similar to the 1975 Filer commission, which set the initial tone for the sector with its pioneering work "Giving in America"). The leaders present concluded that the sector has plenty of work to do to restore the public's image of nonprofits as a reliable provider of services and advocacy. A commission, "Filer II" will not be used to do that work.

> Clolery, Paul, (article), 10 *NonProfit Times*, (12) 24 (December, 1996).

Building Your Organization's Ethics Program

The Ethics Resource Center (ERC) recommends a 20-step process divided into three manageable phases to develop an ethics program—Phase 1: Needs analysis; Phase 2: Implementation; and Phase 3: Project continuation. Phase 1 includes building leadership consensus, identifying issues for the needs analysis, employee survey and self-assessment, data analysis and commitment to action.

Daigneault, Michael G., (article), 11 *NonProfit Times* (14) 64–65, 67 (November, 1997).

Ethics Bibliography Additions

Braybrooke, David, *Ethics in the World of Business,* Rowman & Allanheld, Totowa, N.J., 1983.

Business & Professional Ethics Journal, Human Dimensions Center, Rensselaer Polytechnic Institute, Troy, N.Y., 1981.

Deshpande, Satish P., "The Impact of Ethical Climate Types on Facets of Job Satisfaction: An Empirical Investigation," *Journal of Business Ethics,* June, 1996.

Deshpande, Satish P., "Ethical Climate and the Link Between Success and Ethical Behavior: An Empirical Investigation of a Non-Profit Organization," *Journal of Business Ethics,* March, 1996.

The Ethics of Corporate Conduct, Prentice Hall, Englewood Cliffs, N.J., 1977.

Frederick, William C., (editor), *Empirical Studies of Business Ethics and Values,* JAI Press, Greenwich, Conn., 1987.

Hess, J. Daniel, *Ethics in Business and Labor,* Herald Press, Scottdale, Pa., 1977.

Hoffman, W. Michael, [et al.], (editors), *Corporate Governance and Institutionalizing Ethics: Proceedings of the Fifth National Conference on Business Ethics,* Lexington Books, Lexington, Mass., 1984.

Jones, Donald G., (editor), *Business, Religion, and Ethics: Inquiry and Encounter,* Oelgeschlager, Gunn & Hain, Cambridge, Mass., 1982.

Manley, Walter W., with Shrode, William A., *Critical Issues in Business Conduct: Legal, Ethical, and Social Challenges for the 1990s,* Quorum Books, New York, 1990.

Mazliah, Sandra, *Vicarious Disqualification: Government and Nonprofit Agencies,* (Current Developments in Legal Ethics), *Georgetown Journal of Legal Ethics,* Summer, 1991, 5 n1 pp. 95–97.

Piper, Thomas R., Gentile, Mary C., and Parks, Sharon Daloz, *Can Ethics Be Taught?: Perspectives, Challenges, and Approaches at Harvard Business School,* Harvard Business School, Boston, Mass., 1993.

Windt, Peter Y., [et al.], *Ethical Issues in the Professions,* Prentice Hall, Englewood Cliffs, N.J., 1989.

§6. POTENTIAL ABUSE OF NONPROFIT STATUS

Standards of Ethics

Drafting of a written set of *Ethical Standards* by every NPO is now a growing trend. In 1994, for example, the Associated Press Managing Editors published a Media Draft Code (Declaration of Ethical Standards) for newspapers, journals, reporters, editors, freelance writers, and so on. A carefully worded, detailed set of rules of ethical practices was put before various "experts" for analysis and recommendations.

Watchdog Organizations/Rating of Charities

In 1996, the dispute between Boys Town and the American Institute of Philanthropy (AIP) and its president Daniel Borochoff settled when the publishing company agreed to a revision in its format. There was no cash settlement. AIP had given Boys Town an "F" rating for holding a large trust fund. However, Boys Town argued that the fund assured that it would be able to help children in the future.

Swarden, Carlotta, (article), 10 *NonProfit Times* (7) 4 (July, 1996).

In a suit by pension plan watchdog committees, the U.S. Court of Appeals for the Ninth Circuit held that plan administrators must disclose the names and addresses of plan participants to retiree groups that want to monitor the administration of the plan.

Hughes Salaried Retirees Action Committee v. Administrator of the Hughes Non-Bargaining Retirement Plan, CA 9, No. 93–55384, Nov. 7, 1994.

A commercial publisher of scientific journals sued nonprofit scientific societies for false advertising after the societies published surveys of scientific journals that rated nonprofit journals as superior. The court held that publication of the surveys was actionable under the comparative advertising theory. The publication of the surveys was not commercial advertising or promotion under the Lanham Trade Mark Act. However, the distribution of preprints of the survey at a librarians' conference was commercial advertising or promotion under the Lanham Act.

Gordon and Breach Science Publishers S.A., STBS v. American Institute of Physics, 859 F. Supp. 1521 (S.D. NY, 1994).

Abuse of Charitable Status

Too-high self-serving "overhead," salaries, and so on of charities are being attacked by attorneys-general, despite Supreme Court decisions barring interference by government authorities. Use of fraud and deception statutes and use of the media to broadcast warnings are major devices to get around the Supreme Court view.

Bush, article, *NonProfit Times*, p. 1 (Nov., 1993).

NPO Abuse Punishment

A former president of United Way of America, accused of stealing over a million dollars from the organization and spending much of it on personal luxuries, was indicted by the federal authorities (grand jury, Alexandria, Virginia) in September 1994. He was also accused of fraud, conspiracy, and money-laundering. He denied the charges. The indictment was the result of part of a broad review by the Department of Justice's tax division into potential abuse of NPCs. UWA has "cleaned house," adopting strict financial controls and ethics codes.

In 1995, former United Way President, William Aramony, received a seven-year prison term for fraudulently diverting $1.2 million of United Way funds to his personal use. Two Aramony associates were also sentenced in the case. The former United Way chief financial officer was sentenced to 55 months and three years' probation. The former financial officer of a United Way affiliate, the Partnership Umbrella, received 30 months in prison and one year of probation.

Aramony's conviction on fraud and conspiracy charges makes it doubtful that he will receive an estimated $3 to $4 million pension settlement from the United Way. United Way's general counsel plans to oppose the payment based on Aramony's breach of fiduciary duty and crimes against the organization.

See 9 *NonProfit Times* (6) 4 (June, 1995); 9 *NonProfit Times* (7) 5 (July, 1995), *St. Petersburg (FL) Times,* p. 1 (Sept. 14, 1994).

United Way Works to Avoid Scandal

In 1996, Elaine L. Chao, outgoing president and chief executive officer of the United Way of America (UWA), declined to accept a departure payment of $292,500 from members of the board. Though such payments are legal, Elaine

Chao responded to criticism and comparisons of the payment with the financial scandals at the United Way under the guidance of William Aramony.

Sinclair, Matthew, (article) 10 *NonProfit Times* (7) 1, 10 (July, 1996).

United Way Audited Again

The firm of KPMG Peat Marwick has been hired to do "an outside review . . . of United Way's procedures . . . to ensure that they meet the highest ethical standards and to make any recommendations to improve them." This, after it was revealed in 1996 that former president W. Douglas Ashby, while receiving a $141,960-per-year salary, was allegedly spending significant time building a private consulting business using United Way equipment and employees to do work for his private business (some without pay and on United Way time). There are also other allegations of misuse of funds for travel involving Ashby and his wife.

Breton, Tracy, (article), 10 *NonProfit Times* (10) 38, 40 (October, 1996).

Mismanagement of Funds

Mismanagement of funds, at the local or international level of an organization, can result in disasterous losses. For example, the United Nations Children's Fund (UNICEF) lost an estimated $10 million (one quarter of the Kenyan office's budget) in 1993 and 1994 due to personal fraud by staff members and mismanagement in its Kenyan office. Eight staff members were dismissed and 15 have been suspended and charged with serious misconduct, including two former directors. A 1995 audit indicated the funds were lost through fraud, overstaffing, and overspending.

See 9 *NonProfit Times* (7) (July, 1995).

A former head of a Baptist college (Mississippi College) after 25 years as president was indicted under 20 counts on charges that he stole $1.7 million in college donations to buy stocks and pay for prostitutes and lavish gifts. He was also accused of violation of the Mann Act, which bars transportation of a woman across state lines for immoral purposes. The former president pled "not guilty" to the charges. After officials of the college filed a lawsuit against him accusing him of embezzling over $3 million, the F.B.I. conducted a year-long investigation of the former president, resulting in the indictment in U.S. District Court in Jackson, Mississippi.

St. Petersburg (FL) Times, p. 4 (Sept. 23, 1994).

Board review of loans and expenditures is important for all nonprofit organizations. In response to a 1995 audit, the United Jewish Community (UJC) in Bergen County, New Jersey announced that it had received hundreds of thousand of dollars in improperly authorized loans and had made large expenditures on executive salaries without board approval. In response, the UJC will set up formal procedures for review of loans, write-offs, salaries, and benefits by a 25-member executive board.

See Sinnock, Bonnie, (article) 9 *NonProfit Times* (7) 5 (July, 1995).

The Taxpayer Bill of Rights Act

The Taxpayer Bill of Rights, retroactive to Sept. 13, 1995, now enables the IRS to levy fines up to $10,000 on board members for misdeeds of the nonprofit. The IRS will be looking for "excess benefits," which can be embezzlements, a big salary, or other illegal perks or alliances.

No More Sweetheart Deals, Forbes, Sept. 23, 1996. *See also,* Sections 273 and
     284.

New Era Grant Money

Three schools have returned grant money given to them through the New Era Ponzi scheme which promised organizations they could double their money through investments in six months. The University of Pennsylvania, Harvard University and Princeton University have agreed to return money, in response to a request from the U.S. Bankruptcy Court, that they received from the bankrupt Foundation for New Era Philanthropy

Swarden, Carlotta, (article) 10 *NonProfit Times* (7) 36 (July, 1996).

A $536 million lawsuit filed against John G. Bennett, founder of the Foundation for New Era Philanthropy, has been successful. Bennett has surrendered the $1 million of his assets which include his house, car, company stocks, retirement savings and other assets of Bennett Group International Inc.

Gattuso, Greg, *New Era Head Surrenders Assets, Fund Raising Management,*
     March, 1996.

In 1996, the New Era trustee filed a refund plan for fraud victims. *See* Stecklow, Steve, *The Wall Street Journal,* June 26, 1996.

Thirty nonprofit groups are suing Prudential Securities, as a "co-conspirator" over the fraud perpetrated by the Foundation for New Era Philanthropy.

Bulkeley, William M., *Nonprofits Sue Prudential Over New Era, The Wall Street Journal,* May 9, 1996.

John G. Bennett Jr., head of the fraudulent Foundation for New Era Philanthropy, plead no contest in the 1997 fraud contest against him.

Man in Charity Fraud Case Pleads No Contest, The New York Times, March 27, 1997.

Tobacco Association Investigated

In 1996, a criminal investigation has been reopened by federal prosecutors, looking into whether the Council for Tobacco Research misled the government about the purpose of nonprofit research funded by the tobacco companies.

Cohen and Geyelin, *Probe Reopens into Nonprofit Tobacco Group, The Wall Street Journal,* Feb. 8, 1996.

§7. PRIVILEGES OF NONPROFIT STATUS

Postage Privilege

On October 1, 1995 postal rates were raised in accordance with the Revenue Forgone Reform Act of 1993, which mandates a "phase up" in the institutional costs contribution of mail by the fiscal year of 1999. The new rate is 12.4 cents for letters and 17.5 cents for nonletters. Those rates represent a three-percent increase.

Swarden, Carlotta, (article), 9 *NonProfit Times* (9) 4 (September, 1995).

Nonprofit second-class, third-class, and fourth-class library mailing rates will continue to increase every year through 1998 as a result of the Fiscal Year 1994 Revenue Forgone Reform Act. Restrictions will also increase on advertising in third-class nonprofit mailings.

See Denton, Neal, (article), 9 *NonProfit Times* (10) 34–35 (October, 1995).

As of July 1, 1996, the post office began offering worksharing discounts for commercial bulk mailers to customers using automated mail. Nonprofits will also be affected on October 6, 1996. However, nonprofit mailers are having problems catching up with the first phase postal reclassification, which went into effect July 1. Many of the new software programs designed to aid with the transition are either not ready or contain serious bugs.

10 *NonProfit Times* (9) 20 (September, 1996).

In 1996, the U.S. Postal Service declared three mailings (two in Minnesota and one in Oklahoma), which included information about Charitable Gift Annuities (CGA), to be ineligible for nonprofit standard postage rates. The Postal Service ruled that the mailings promote a product or service, in this case, insurance, which is excluded from nonprofit eligibility. The National Federation of Nonprofits (NFN) is battling the rulings. For information, call (202) 628-4380.

10 *NonProfit Times* (10) 4 (October, 1996).

Lower Paper, Printing, and Mailing Costs for Nonprofits

Hart Press has formed a printing coalition to lower paper, printing, and mailing costs for nonprofit magazines. Its PowerPrint program requires magazines to adhere to strict print schedules and is designed for small, standard-frequency titles. PowerPrint magazines are printed, bound, labeled, and presorted en masse to maximize cost savings.

Sucov, Jennifer, *Short-Run Pubs Get in Line, Folio: The Magazine for Magazine Management,* Sept. 15, 1996.

Labor & Unemployment Compensation Privilege

Under Colorado's unemployment compensation exemption for employment with an organization operated primarily for religious purposes, the type of activity actually engaged in, not the motivation and impetus for the activity, determines the exemption status.

Samaritan Institute v. Prince-Walker, 883 P. 2d 3 (CO, 1994).

Where an employer is not a church and a large percentage of its support comes from the private sector, it is not entitled to an exemption from unemployment compensation, in Pennsylvania, as an organization operated primarily for religious purposes, operated, supervised, controlled, or principally supported by a church or convention or association of churches.

Pittsburgh Leadership Foundation v. Unemployment Compensation Board of Review,
    654 A.2d 224 (PA Cmwlth., 1995); 43 P.S. Section 753(1)(4)(8).

In Louisiana, an injured volunteer fireman is not entitled to workers' compensation benefits. His services are in the nature of gratuity. Benefits cannot be calculated where a worker neither expects nor receives financial compensation.

Genusa v. Pointe Coupee Volunteer Fire District No. 4, 644 So. 2d 851 (LA App. 1
    Cir., 1994).

Per diem workers, who prepare a fair site for a charitable organization once each year for one month prior to the fair, are "workers" under Oregon's workers' compensation statute, subjecting the organization to the payment of workers' compensation premiums to its insurance carrier. However, workers who perform services during the charity fair itself fall within the exemption.

Oregon Country Fair v. National Council on Compensation Insurance and SAIF, 877 P.
    2d 1207 (OR App., 1994).

Immunity from Tort Liability

See also Chapter 17, §§178–180.

In Pennsylvania, local agencies are immune, under the Political Subdivision Tort Claims Act, from tort liability. A volunteer fire company that was sued for an injury incurred at a company picnic is a "local agency" if it is created pursuant to relevant law and is legally recognized, in its articles of incorporation and through local ordinances as the official fire company for a political subdivision.

Kniaz v. Benton Borough, 642 A. 2d 551 (PA Commonwealth, 1994).

Favored Status

In New York, a housing facility that is operated "exclusively" for charitable purposes, in order to secure lodging and meals on a nonsectarian basis to working women of modest means, pursuant to a charitable bequest, is exempt from Rent Stabilization Law under the Emergency Tenant Protection Act. This is true even where there are religious services provided by the residents and there is an occasional operating surplus.

Salvation Army, Inc. v. Cruz, 615 N.Y.S. 2d 805 (Sup., 1994). *See also, Jones v. Division of Housing and Community Renewal,* 621 N.Y.S. 2d 71 (A.D. 1 Dept., 1995); Rent Stabilization Code, Section 2520.11(f).

§10. SELF-DESIGNATION AS TEST OF STATUS

An Indian tribe constitution that describes the tribe as being "in the nature of a nonprofit corporation," did not establish the tribe as a "corporation" for purposes of diversity jurisdiction in a suit for damages involving injuries received by a plaintiff at a tribe-operated ski resort. The tribe's constitutional, rather than corporate, entity operated the resort.

Gaines v. Ski Apache, 8 F. 3d 726 (10th Cir. [NM], 1993).

§11. KINDS OF NONPROFIT ORGANIZATIONS' STRUCTURES

Alter Ego Corporations

A corporation formed for enabling a defendant to avoid a trial court's orders and judgment is an *alter ego* corporation. Its corporate status may be disregarded if so doing will prevent fraud or injustice to creditors.

Envirotech Corp. v. Callahan, 872 P. 2d 487 (UT App., 1994).

2

STATISTICS AND BIBLIOGRAPHY*

§12. STATISTICS

*[The 1997 Report figures are summarized in Supplement §1.]

§14. GOVERNMENTAL SUPERVISION

Business Corporation Law Application

In 1993, Florida specifically provided that the Business Corporation "statute shall NOT apply to any corporations not for profit."

Fla. Stat. Section 617.1908, amended by Laws 1993, c. 93–281, Section 76, eff. May 15, 1993.

§16. BIBLIOGRAPHY OF NONPROFIT ORGANIZATIONS

Bibliography Additions

Association Internship Directory, a list of 55 internships with 150 associations (1994), the Greater Washington Society of Association Executives Foundation, Elizabeth Farasy, (202) 828–4643.

Associations Yellow Book (semiannual) lists officers, addresses, boards, budgets, employee numbers, and so on for NPOs (about 1150) with budgets over 1 million. (Monitor Leadership Directories, New York, NY.)

Bachmann, Steve, *NonProfit Litigation: A Practical Guide with Forms and Checklists,* John Wiley & Sons, Inc., New York, 1992.

Bakal, C., *Charity USA,* Times Books, NY, 1979, 498 pp.

Bennett, James T., and DiLorenzo, Thomas J., *Unhealthy Charities,* Basic Books, New York, NY.

Blazek, Jody, *Financial Planning for Nonprofit Organizations,* John Wiley & Sons, Inc., New York, NY, 1996.

Brenner, A.J., *Expression by Association,* 33 *Santa Clara L. Rev.* 467–517 (Spring 1993).

Brilliant, Eleanor L. *The United Way: Dilemmas of Organized Charity.* New York, Columbia University Press, 1990. 382pp.

Brimson, James A. and John Antos, *Activity-Based Management for Service Industries, Government Entities, and Nonprofit Organizations,* John Wiley & Sons, Inc., New York, NY.

Broce, T.E., *Fund Raising,* University of Oklahoma Press, Norman, OK, 1974, 254 pp.

Bryce, Herrington J., *Financial and Strategic Management for Nonprofit Organizations, 2d ed.,* Prentice Hall, Englewood Cliffs, NJ, 1992.

Burger, E.M., and M.N. Wilke, *Director Liability in NPC: What is it? How to avoid it,* 34 *New Hampshire Bar J.* 57–67, Dec. 1993 (Director Liability).

Caldwell, C., *Developing Ethical Standards for Charitable Fundraising,* 133 *Tr. and Est.* 56–63 (F. 1994).

Chronicle of Philanthropy, 1255 23rd St., N.W., Washington, D.C. 20037, biweekly.

Clotfelder, Charles T., ed., *Who Benefits from the Nonprofit Sector?,* Chicago and London, University of Chicago Press, 1992.

Collins, Sarah, and Charlotte Dion, editors, *The Foundation Center's User-Friendly Guide,* 39 pages, The Foundation Center, New York, NY, (800) 424–9836.

Colvin, Gregory L., *Fiscal Sponsorship: 6 Ways to Do It Right,* Study Center Press, San Francisco, CA, 1993.

Computer Software, an extensive list of computer software sources including computerized fund accounting, fund raising, and letter service systems can be obtained by writing to or subscribing to the *NonProfit Times,* 190 Tamarack Circle, Skillman, NJ 08558.

Connors, Tracy Daniel, *The Nonprofit Management Handbook,* John Wiley & Sons, Inc., New York, NY, 1993.

Consumers Should Know-How to Buy a Personal Computer (checklist of questions to help buyers), Electronic Industries Association's Product Services Department, (202) 457–4986.

Consumers Should Know-How to Choose, Use, and Care for Personal Computers (outlines uses for home and office, software, peripherals, and accessories), Electronic Industries Association's Product Services Department, (202) 457–4986.

Corporate 500: Directory of Corporate Philanthropy, 1994–95, 13th Edition, Public Management Institute/DataRex Corp., 358 Brannan St., Suite 302, San Francisco, CA 94107, (415) 896–1900.

Corporate and Foundation Grants 1995, Volumes 1 and 2, Romaniuk, Bohdan R., and DeAngelis, James (editors), The Taft Group, Washington, D.C., (800) 877–TAFT.

Corporate Foundation Profiles, Eighth Edition, Foundation Center, 79 Fifth Ave., New York, NY 10003, (800) 424–9836.

Corporate Giving Directory, 15th Edition, Taft Group, 835 Penobscot Building, Detroit, MI 48226, (800) 877–8238.

Corporate Giving Yellow Pages, 10th Edition, Taft Group, 835 Penobscot Building, Detroit, MI 48226, (800) 877–8238.

De Luca, M.J., *Nonprofit Personnel Forms & Guidelines,* Aspen Publications, Frederick, MD 21701, 1994.

De Mott, D.A., *Self-Dealing Transactions in NPCs,* 59 *Brooklyn L. Rev.* 131–147. Spring 1993, (Abuse of Privileges).

Directory of Computer and High Technology Grants, Second Edition, Research Grant Guides, Dept. 98, P.O. Box 1214, Loxahatchee, FL 33470.

Directory of Corporate Affiliations, 1991, Reed Reference Publishing Co., P.O. Box 31, New Providence, NJ 07974, (800) 323–6772.

Directory of Corporate and Foundation Givers, 1992, Taft Group, 835 Penobscot Building, Detroit, MI 48226, (800) 877–8238.

Directory of Grants in the Humanities 1994/95, Eighth Edition, Oryx Press, Phoenix, (800) 279–6799.

Directory of Grants for Organizations Serving People with Disabilities, (previous title *Handicapped Funding Directory*), 8th ed., Aug. 1993, Research Grant Guides, P.O. Box 1214, Loxahatchee, FL 33470.

Directory of International Corporate Giving in America and Abroad, Sixth Edition, Taft Group, 835 Penobscot Building, Detroit, MI 48226, (800) 877–8238.

Directory of Operating Grants, First Edition, Research Grant Guides, Dept. 98, P.O. Box 1214, Loxahatchee, FL 33470.

Drucker, P.F., *Managing the Nonprofit Organization,* HarperCollins, NY, 1990.

Duca, Diane J., *Nonprofit Boards: Roles, Responsibilities & Performance,* John Wiley & Sons, Inc., New York, NY, 1996.

Eckstein, Richard M. (editor), *Directory of Grants for Organizations Serving People with Disabilities, Eighth Edition,* Research Grant Guides, Inc., Loxahatchee, FL, (407) 795–6129.

Elliott, C. (ed.), *Board and Administrator* (newsletter, monthly), Aspen Publishers, P.O. Box 990, Frederick, MD 21705.

Energize, Inc. of 5450 Wissahickon Ave., Philadelphia, PA 19144 offers catalogs, training, and consulting assistance for NPO volunteers. See *Volunteer Energy* Resource Catalog 1994–1995.

Events Magazine, Ideas & Resources for Fundraising Events, PO Box 19284, Cincinnati, OH 45219-0284.

Federal Support for Nonprofits 1994, Spomer, Cynthia Russell (editor), The Taft Group, Washington, D.C., (800) 877–TAFT.

Fishman & Schwartz, *Nonprofit Organizations: Cases, Materials and Problems,* Foundation Press, 1995. (Law School casebook.)

The Foundation Directory, 1994 Edition, The Foundation Center, 79 Fifth Ave., Dept. CZ7, New York, NY 10003–3076.

Foundation News and Commentary, Council on Foundations, 1828 L Street, NW, Washington, D.C. 20036.

Foundation Reporter 1995, Romaniuk, Bohdan R., and DeAngelis, James (editors), The Taft Group, Washington, D.C., (800) 877–TAFT.

Garner, William C., *Accounting and Budgeting in Public and NonProfit Organizations: A Manager's Guide.* Jossey-Bass, San Francisco, CA, 1991.

Gerla, H.S., *Federal Antitrust Law and Trade and Professional Association Standards and Certification,* 19 *U. Dayton L. Rev.* 471–531, Winter 1994, (Antitrust).

Gershen, H., *A Guide for Giving,* Pantheon NY, 1990.

Gidron, Benjamin, Kramer, and Salamons, eds., *Government and the Third Sector: Emerging Relationships in Welfare States.* Jossey-Bass, San Francisco, CA, 1992.

Gies, Ott, and Shafritz, eds., *The Nonprofit Organization: Essential Readings.* Pacific Grove, CA, Brooks/Cole, 1990.

Gift Givers Guide, by Florida Department of Agriculture & Consumer Services, published December 1993, lists 1954 charities registered to show amounts (percent) each one spent on administration and program service as a guide to contributors to charities. The American Association of State Troopers was reported to have spent $2.6 million in its fiscal year, 44 percent for administrative costs, 43 percent for fund raising, and 13 percent for program services.

A Yoemans report, Associated Press, *St. Petersburg (FL) Times,* p. 4B, Dec. 21, 1993.

Gilbert, C.B., *Health Care Reform and the Nonprofit Hospital: Is Tax Exempt Status Still Warranted?,* 26 *Urban Law* 143–176, Winter 1994 (Tax Exemption).

Gladstone, D.J., *New Lobbying Expense Disallowance Rules . . . ,* 25 *Tax Advisor* 297(2) (May 1994).

Goldstein, D.L., *NPOs Can Be Profitable,* 41 *Canadian Tax J.* 720–723, Oct. 1993 (Canadian NPOs).

Grantsmanship Center Magazine (formerly *The Whole Nonprofit Catalog*), 1125 W. 6th St., Los Angeles, CA 90017. Current issues.

Greenfield, James M., *Fund-Raising Cost Effectiveness: A Self Assessment Workbook,* John Wiley & Sons, Inc., New York, NY, 1996 (includes disk).

Greenfield, James M., *Fund-Raising Fundamentals,* John Wiley & Sons, Inc., New York, (800) CALL–WILEY; 416 pages.

Guide to Corporate Giving in the Arts, 1987, American Council for the Arts, 1 East 53rd St., New York, NY 10022, (212) 223–2787.

Guide to Greater Washington D.C. Grantmakers 1994–1995, The Foundation Center, New York, (800) 424–9836.

Guillery, Joanne, and Lathan, Virginia, *Needs Assessments: A Manual for Community Action,* Vincente Publications, Inc., 2375 Wesley Chapel Rd. 3–298, Decatur, GA 30035.

Harris, J.E., *The Nonprofit Corporation Act of 1993 . . . (New Law and Old Corporations),* 16 *U. Ark. Little L.J.* 1–25, 1994.

Hect, Bennett L., JD. CPA, *Developing Affordable Housing: A Practical Guide for Nonprofit Organizations,* John Wiley & Sons, Inc., New York, (800) CALL–WILEY; 500 pages.

Hecht, Bennett, and Stockard, James, *Managing Affordable Housing,* John Wiley & Sons., Inc., New York, NY, 1996.

Heise, M., *Public Funds, Private Schools, and the Court,* 25, Tex. Tech. L. Rev. (1) 137 (1993).

Hodgkinson, Weitzman, Toppe, and Noga, *Nonprofit Almanac: 1992–1993, Dimensions of the Independent Sector, 4th ed.,* Jossey-Bass, San Francisco, CA, 1992.

Hopkins, Bruce R., *The Law of Fund-Raising,* John Wiley & Sons, Inc., New York, 1991.

Hopkins, Bruce R., *The Law of Tax Exempt Organizations,* John Wiley & Sons, Inc., New York, NY, 1992.

Hopkins, Bruce R., *The Legal Asnwer Book for Nonprofit Organizations,* John Wiley & Sons, Inc., New York, NY, 1996.

Hopkins, Bruce R., *A Legal Guide to Starting and Managing a Nonprofit Organization,* J. Wiley, New York, 1993.

Hopkins, Bruce R., *Nonprofit Law Dictionary,* John Wiley & Sons, Inc., New York, NY, 1994.

How to Find Information About Companies, Washington Researchers, Ltd., P.O. Box 19005, 20th St. Station, Washington, D.C., 20036, (202) 333–3499.

How to Form a Nonprofit Corporation, Nolo Press, Berkeley, CA, 1990.

Ivers, G., *Religious Organizations as Constitutional Litigants,* 25 *Polity* 243–266, Winter 1992 (Litigation).

Jankowski, Katherine E. (editor), *Inside Japanese Support 1994,* The Taft Group, Washington, D.C., (800) 877–TAFT.

Jeavons, Thomas H., *When The Bottom Line is Faithfulness,* Indiana University Press, Bloomington and Indianapolis (812) 855–4203.

Jones, Francine, Katie Lewis, and Georgetta Toth, *Corporate Foundation Profiles, 8th Edition,* 716 pages, The Foundation Center, New York, NY, (800) 424–9836.

Jordan, R., and Quynn, Katelyn L., *Planned Giving: Management Marketing, and Law,* John Wiley & Sons, Inc., New York, NY, 1994 (includes disk).

Karoff, H.P., *The Advisor's Role in Philanthropy: A New Direction,* 133 *Tr. & Est.* 47–50 (April 1994).

Kearns, K.P., *Strategic Management of Accountability of NPOs,* 54 *Public Admin. Review* 185–192.

Kleinfeld, A.J., *Politicization: From the Law Schools to the Courts,* 7 *Academic Questions* (1) 9–19 Winter 1994 (Politicking by Schools).

Kovacs, Ruth and Ben McLaughlin, editors, *Who Gets Grants/Who Gives Grants, 2nd Edition,* 1,580 pages, The Foundation Center, New York, NY (800) 424–9836.

Krancweide, B., and Z., *Reporting and Substantiation Requirements for Charitable Contributions,* 72 *Taxes* 14–18, Jan. 1994.

Landskroner, Ronald A., *The Nonprofit Manager's Resource Directory,* John Wiley & Sons, Inc., New York, NY, 1996.

Lynch, Richard, *Lead!,* 419 pages, Jossey-Bass Publishers, San Francisco, CA, (415) 433–1767.

Macintosh and Windows Fund-Raising Software, Campagne Associates, 491 Amherst Street, Nashua, NH 03063–1259, or (800) 582–3489.

Maloney, H., and B., *Tax Aspects of Lobbying by Public Charities,* 25 *Tax Advise* 36–41, Jan. 1994.

Master Software Corporation, Fund-Master, donor and fund-raising management, 5975 Castle Creek Pkwy. N. Dr., Suite 300, Indianapolis, IN 46250, (800) 950–2999, fax (317) 849–5280 for a free demo disc.

Matching Gift Details, 1994, CASE, Matching Gifts Dept., 11 Dupont Circle, Suite 400, Washington, D.C., 20036, (800) 554–8536.

Mazliah, Sandra, *Vicarious Disqualification: Government and Nonprofit Agencies,* (Current Developments in Legal Ethics), *Georgetown Journal of Legal Ethics,* Summer 1991, 5 n1.

McKinney, Jerome G., *Effective Financial Management in Public and Nonprofit Agencies: A Practical and Integrative Approach.* Quorum Books, New York, 1986.

McLeish, Barry J., *Successful Marketing Strategies for Nonprofit Organizations,* John Wiley & Sons, Inc., New York, NY, 1995.

National Directory of Corporate Giving, Third Edition, Foundation Center, 79 Fifth Ave., New York, NY 10003, (800) 424–9836.

National Directory of Corporate Public Affairs, Columbia Books, Inc., 1212 New York Ave., N.W., Washington, D.C.

Nichols, Judith E., *Pinpointing Affluence,* CFRE, 293 pages, Precept Press, Chicago, IL, (800) 225–3775.

Nielsen, W.A., *The Golden Donors,* E.P. Dutton, NY, 1985, 468 pp.

Nonprofit Legal and Tax Letter (newsletter), 18 issues/year, Organization Mgmt., Inc., Fairfax, VA.

Not-for-Profit Organizations: The Challenge of Governance in an Era of Retrenchment, April 9–10, 1992, Santa Monica, CA: ALI-ABA course of study materials, ALI-ABA, 4025 Chestnut St., Philadelphia, PA, 1992.

The NonProfit Times, 240 Cedar Knolls Road, Suite 318, Cedar Knolls, NJ 07927, (201)734-1700; Fax: (201)734-1777.

O'Connell, B., *Our Organization,* Walker & Co., NY, 1987, paperback, 142 pp.

O'Neill, Michael, *The Third America: The Emergence of the Nonprofit Sector in the United States.* Jossey-Bass, San Francisco, CA, 1989.

Orentlicher, D., *The Influence of a Professional Organization on Physicians' Behavior,* 57 *Alb. L. Rev.,* 583–605 (1994) (Association Effect).

Overton, George W., ed., *Guidebook for Directors of Nonprofit Corporations.* Chicago: American Bar Association, Section of Business Law, 1993.

Paul, Mary Eileen, *Organizational Development Tools,* Resource Women, Washington, D.C., (202) 832–8071.

Paul, Mary Eileen, and Linda Clements, editors. *Religious Funding Resource Guide,* Resource Women, Washington, D.C., (202) 832–8071.

Powell, Walter (ed.), *The Nonprofit Sector.*

Prince, Russ Alan, and File, Karen Maru, *The Seven Faces of Philanthropy,* Jossey-Bass Inc., San Francisco, CA, (415) 433–1740.

Rados, David L., *Marketing for Non-Profit Organizations,* Auburn House Pub. Co., Boston, MA, 1981.

Ready to Respond, manual for volunteer centers that handle natural and man-made disasters, Points of Light Foundation, (202) 223–9186.

Repars, L., and C., *Coping With the Lobbying Deduction Disallowance,* 177 *J. of Accountancy* 70 (4) May 1994.

Reynolds, Joe, *Out Front Leadership,* Mott & Carlisle, Austin, TX, (800) 945–3132.

Rietz, Helen L. and Marilyn Manning, *The One-Step Guide to Workshops,* Irwin Professional Publishing, Burr Ridge, IL, (800) 634–3966.

Salamon, Lester M., *America's Nonprofit Sector: A Primer,* New York, The Foundation Center, 1992.

Salamon, L.M., *The Rise of the Nonprofit Sector,* 73 *Foreign Affairs* (4) 109–122 July–Aug. 1994.

Sanders, Michael I., Esq., *Partnerships and Joint Ventures Involving Tax-Exempt Organizations,* John Wiley & Sons, Inc., New York, NY, (800) CALL–WILEY.

Schiller, Lewis A., *Limitations on the Enforceability of Condominium Rules,* XXII *Stetson L. Rev.* No. 3, 1133–1168, Summer 1993.

Schlachter, Dr. Gail Ann, *Directory of Financial Aids for Minorities,* TGC/Reference Service Press, 1100 Industrial Road, Suite #9, San Carlos, CA 94070.

Schlachter, Dr. Gail Ann, *Directory of Financial Aids for Women,* TGC/Reference Service Press, 1100 Industrial Road, Suite #9, San Carlos, CA 94070.

Seldin, S.F., *Three Years After the New Lobbying Regulations: What All Charities Should Know,* 47 *Tax Law* 43, Fall 1993.

Shenson, Howard L., *How to Develop and Promote Successful Seminars and Workshops,* John Wiley & Sons, Inc., New York, NY, 1996.

Smith, Bucklin, & Associates, Inc., *The Complete Guide to Nonprofit Management,* John Wiley & Sons, Inc., New York.

Standard & Poor's Register of Corporations, Directors and Executives, 1994 and 1995, Standard & Poor's 25 Broadway, New York, NY 10004 (800) 221–5277.

State and Local Taxes on NPOs (Symposium), 22 *Capital Univ. L. Rev.,* 321–372 (Spring 1993).

State Liability Laws for Charitable Organizations and Volunteers, Nonprofit Risk Mgmt. and Insurance Institute, 1990.

Successful Meetings (magazine) as to current hotel and other meeting facilities, supplies, services, and so forth, 355 Park Ave., So., New York, NY 10010, (212) 592–6403 (Editorial Office).

Taylor, K.W., *How to Prepare Loan Proposals for Not-For-Profit Clients,* 177 *J. Accountancy* 68 (4) Jan. 1994 (Accountancy for NPOs).

Teitell, Conrad, *Charitable Contribution Tax Strategies,* White Plains, NY, 1995.

Trenbeth, R.P., *The Membership Mystique,* Fund Raising Inst., Ambler, PA, 1986 paperback.

Ward, S.L., *Tort Liability of Nonprofit Governing Boards,* Garland Pub., New York, 1993.

Ward, Ralph, *21st Century Corporate Board,* John Wiley & Sons, Inc., New York, NY, 1996.

Warwick, Mal, *How to Write Successful Fundraising Letters,* Strathmoor Press, Berkeley, CA, (800) 217–7377.

Wave, Alan, *Between Profit and State* (1989).

White, Douglas E., *The Art of Planned Giving,* John Wiley & Sons, Inc., New York, NY, 1995.

White, V. (ed.), *Grant Proposals That Succeeded,* Plenum Press, NY, 1983, 240 pp.

Whole Nonprofit Catalog, issued frequently by the Grantsmanship Center, 1125 W. 6th St., Los Angeles, CA 90017; (213) 482–9860. (In 1995 titled *Grantsmanships Center Magazine.*)

Wise Giving Guide, current issues, issued intermittently, by National Charities Information Bureau, Inc., 19 Union Sq. W., New York, NY, 10003–3395.

Wolfers and Evansen, *Organizations, Clubs, Action Groups,* St. Martin's Press, NY, 1980.

Zeff, Robbin, *The Nonprofit Guide to the Internet,* John Wiley & Sons, Inc., New York, NY, 1996.

Zick, Kenneth A., *A Selected Bibliography of Study and Reading Materials: Officers Powers and Duties in Non-Profit Organizations,* ALI-ABA Course of Study, November 14–15, (1975), Wake Forest University, School of Law, Winston-Salem, NC.

3

MIXTURE OF PROFIT AND NONPROFIT ACTIVITIES

§17. MIXTURE OF PROFIT AND NONPROFIT PURPOSES

Mixture of NPC and Business and Government

Canada Gives Management of the St. Lawrence Seaway to a Nonprofit

Canadian Transport Minister, David Anderson, has signed a letter of intent handing over management of the St. Lawrence Seaway to a nonprofit corporation comprised of Canadian users of the waterway. Canada will retain asset ownership and oversee major repairs and upgrades. U.S. officials fear that ownership of a Canadian consortium could compromise U.S. shipping on the seaway.

> Freudmann, Aviva, *Canada Moves Closer to Privatizing Seaway, Journal of Commerce and Commercial,* July 22, 1996. *See also, St. Lawrence Seaway to be Administered by Nonprofit Group, The Wall Street Journal,* July 18, 1996.

Saskatchewan REDAs

Saskatchewan has developed a model for economic development strategic planning, which provides for grassroots initiative and regionalism and emphasizes business development. The resulting Regional Economic Development Authorities (REDAs) are nonprofit corporations owned by community economic development organizations. REDAs coordinate the cooperation of cities, suburbs, and rural communities.

> Conte, Andrew, *Saskatchewan's REDAs: Bottom-up Economic Development, Government Finance Review,* August 1996.

Museum Joint Venture

An exhibit project (museum style) of treasures of imperial Russia was planned for January 1995 in St. Petersburg, Florida. A joint venture was formed to carry out the project in 1994, based on a nonprofit corporation operated by a board of business leaders, with only one employee, its CEO, and a business corporation with the owner's family as principals, and his sons as employees of the museum project. The city contributed part of the museum funds and also promised public funds if the project flopped. The business corporation paid the employees working at the NPC.

St. Petersburg (FL) Times, p. B1 (Sept. 2, 1994).

Delegation of Government Authority to NPOs

A township may fund and *delegate authority* to the director of a nonprofit child advocacy corporation, to make determinations about child sexual abuse, without violating the rights of an arrestee charged with that offense. The township may rely on the director's stated qualifications and the recommendation of social services providers that administer the nonprofit center. Such reliance is not "deliberate indifference to the rights of the arrestee."

Fittanto v. Children's Advocacy Center, 836 F. Supp. 1406 (N.D. IL, 1993).

For-Profit Corporations and Community Involvement

Many corporations are implementing community involvement programs. For example, at United Parcel Service of America Inc. (UPS), diversity training is integrated with community service through its Community Internship Program (CPI). CPI was created in 1968 in response to intense civil unrest. The program allows companies to contribute to the community by offering its managerial experience to local organizations. Under CPI, senior managers work as interns at nonprofit institutions, and perform tasks based on their skills and the needs of the organization. Personal care products manufacturer, Tom's of Maine, allows employees to do community service 5 percent of their paid work time. Tom's employees teach illiterate people to read, do volunteer work in schools, and donate blood.

McCune, Jenny C., *The Corporation in the Community*. (includes related articles on managing corporate community involvement programs), *HRFocus*, March, 1997.

Government, Private, and Nonprofit Collaboration in Housing Projects

In the city of Colorado Springs, Colorado, residents from the vicinity, city, and utilities departments, local lenders, neighborhood associations, private business owners, nonprofit groups, and federal and state agencies all chipped in to complete an initiative to successfully transform old houses into affordable homes.

The project involved the relocation of 10 abandoned houses to a discarded parcel of land and the renovation of the homes. Then, the homes were sold to qualified low-income to moderate-income first-time buyers. The resulting home-ownership program has been warmly welcomed by the neighboring community.

> Warhola, Debbie, *Community Cooperation Turns Old Houses into New Dreams,*
> *Journal of Housing and Community Development*, March–April, 1997.

Hospital Joint Ventures

A joint venture between Michigan Affiliated Healthcare System (MAHSI) and Columbia Healthcare, which was to have allowed Columbia/HCA to manage the MAHSI acute care facilities, while MAHSI would use funds received to retire debt, was held by the court to break state prohibitions against transferring charitable assets to for-profit joint ventures.

> Carson, Marlis L., "Health Care Organization Stopped from Joining Venture for Profit," *Tax Notes,* Sept. 30, 1996.

Hospital Mixtures

Recently, a Michigan judge blocked a Columbia/HCA move into Michigan. Under Michigan law, nonprofits, like Lansing Hospital, can not co-mingle with for-profits, like Columbia/HCA Healthcare Corporation.

> Tomsho, Robert, *Columbia HCA Move into Michigan Blocked by Judge, The Wall Street Journal,* Sept. 9, 1996.

Health Care

See, Overview of the Tax Treatment of Nonprofit Hospitals and Their For-Profit Subsidiaries: A Short-Sighted View Could Be Very Bad Medicine. Andrea I. Castro. *Pace Law Review,* Wntr 1995 15 n2.

"Shell" Hospital Joint Operations

The new IRS training manual (September, 1996) tells federal auditors that a nonprofit joint operating company, formed by two or more hospitals, must play a significant part in hospital operation to keep its tax-exempt status. The joint company must provide vital, relevant services to the hospitals and function as a parent company would, in a for-profit arrangement. Hospitals in noncompliance could have their funding taxed as unrelated business income.

> Burda, David, *IRS Rules Against "Shell" Joint Entities, Modern Healthcare,* Oct. 7, 1996.

Health Associations and Drug Companies

Nonprofit Groups and drug makers are increasingly, in 1996, using tie-in deals to add marketing muscle for the drug companies and raise needed money for the health associations.

> *See,* Freudenheim, Milt, *Marriage of Necessity: Nonprofit Groups and Drug Makers, The New York Times,* August 20, 1996.

Financial Mixtures

A nonprofit corporation may enter into a mortgage loan transaction, with a union pension plan, even where it is the alter ego of the union which is a party in interest to the plan. Such plans are not explicitly prohibited as party in interest transactions under ERISA.

> *McLaughlin v. Compton,* 834 F. Supp. 743 (E.D. PA, 1993).

Business-Like Revenues

The American Association of Retired Persons (AARP) was called before the Senate finance Subcommittee on Social Security and Family Policy in 1995 to justify its financial practices. There was, in 1995, a move to strip federal tax exemption from 501(c)(4) organizations in Washington by calling attention to the vast "business-like" revenues garnered by tax exempt organizations from sources other than contributions and dues. In 1994, the AARP received $102 million from its health insurance program, $189.4 million from its licensing and royalty agreements, $133.77 million from advertising in AARP publications, plus state and federal grants. Only $145.7 million of its $468.8 million of 1994 revenues was raised from dues. Other 501(c)(4) organizations were also mentioned in the hearings, including the National Rifle Association (NRA).

Townsend, William, (article) 9 *NonProfit Times* (8) 1, 14, 16 (August, 1995); *Simpson Accuses AARP of Misusing Tax Exemptions.* (Sen. Alan Simpson; American Association of Retired Persons) Fred Stokeld. *Tax Notes,* June 19, 1995 67 n12 1573–1575; *The Business Activities of Nonprofit Organizations.* Hal Katen. *Los Angeles Lawyer,* Sept 1995 18 n6 p24(6); *Simpson Grills AARP, Considers Restrictions on Some Tax-Exempts.* (Alan K. Simpson; American Association of Retired Persons) Fred Stokeld. *Tax Notes,* June 26, 1995 67 n13 p1710–1711.

On-Campus Restaurants

After students protested, Iowa State University administrators rejected an attempt to open a second McDonald's Corp. outlet on campus, reversing preliminary permission in 1995, issued to the nonprofit corporation Memorial Union Foodservice.

See, Iowa State Students Protest Plan to Add Second McDonald's, Nation's Restaurant News, Oct. 7, 1996, v30 n39 p31(1).

Tax-Exempt Spinoff Arrangements

Even though the US Supreme Court had denied Bob Jones University its tax exemption because of its racial policies against interracial dating and marriage, the museum and art gallery at Bob Jones University, a spinoff arrangement, was found to be tax-exempt by the Tax Court in 1996. The Tax Court decision holds the gallery to be a separate organization from the university, despite overlapping boards of directors. The decision provides nonprofit tax planning benefits, even though the IRS will continue to monitor such arrangements closely.

Carson, Marlis L., *IRS Finally Frowns on an EO Spin-Off, but Loses in Tax Court, Tax Notes,* June 10, 1996.

Ubit and Taxable Subsidiaries

Many nonprofits are avoiding unrelated business income taxation (UBIT) by diverting the UBIT activity into for-profit, taxable subsidiaries. "Second-tier subsidiaries," a taxable subsidiary set up by the nonprofits's first existing taxable entity have been recognized by the IRS in private letter rulings as taxable entities whose activities do not affect the parent organization's exempt status. However, the second-tier subsidiary has to be set up for legitimate purposes and the ex-

empt organization must not be involved in the day-to-day activities of the secondary subsidiary. The exempt organization transfers its for-profit interests from
Subsidiary 1 to Subsidiary 2. Subsidiary 1 pays the exempt organization rents
and interest, but all Subsidiary 1 stock is owned by Subsidiary 2. Thus, Subsidiary 1 becomes a wholly owned subsidiary of 2, and hence a second-tier subsidiary of the parent exempt organization with no direct link to it. The National
Geographic Society is an example of one organization that uses such a system.

> Sanker, Sheri Warren, (article), 10 *NonProfit Times* (9) 33, 40 (September,
> 1996).

> *See also,* Sanders, Michael I., *Partnership and Joint Ventures Involving Tax-Ex-
> empt Organizations,* John Wiley & Sons, Inc., New York, NY, 1994.

The Internal Revenue Service (IRS) has issued two Private Letter Rulings
(PLR) demonstrating how a tax-exempt organization can create taxable subsidiary corporations without affecting exempt status. Both rulings rely on the
general rule that a corporation and its stockholders—including a parent corporation holding 100 percent of the stock—are considered separate entities for tax
purposes. The PLRs also serve to illustrate how tax-exempt corporations can ensure that the rule applies to them.

> Harnon, Gail, (article), 11 *NonProfit Times* (14) 66–67 (November, 1997).

4

SPECIAL ORGANIZATIONS

§25. CLASSIFICATIONS, GENERALLY

Building and Loan Associations

Resolutions Trust Corporations may repudiate claims of tenants as *"burdensome,"* under the Federal Deposit Insurance Act §2 (11) (e) (1) (B) and N.Y. Rent Control Laws.

> *Resolution Trust Co. v. Diamond,* 18 F. 3rd 111 (C.A. 2 (NY) 1994). *See also Herring v. Chicago Housing Authority,* (N.D. IL) #90-C-3797; 1994 WL 159849 (April 7, 1994).

§26. NONPROFIT ORGANIZATIONS AS "PUBLIC" [CONSTITUTIONAL LAW]

See also, Chapter 17, §§180–184; Chapter 44 §449.

Public Purpose and Open Meetings Laws

A public body (state university) does not have to comply with the Alabama Sunshine Law in discussions between it, and its attorney, concerning pending litigation. However, once discussion begins among the members of the public body, about what action to take based upon the advice of counsel, the discussion must be open to the public.

> *Dunn v. Alabama State University Bd. of Trustees,* 628 So. 2d 519 (AL, 1993).

Nonprofits can use open meeting laws in order to challenge the decisions of government if those laws are violated. For example, a statutory committee, that provided the Governor with a list of names of candidates for the position of Commissioner, is a "public or governmental body" subject to the requirements of open meeting statutes.

> *Common Cause of Montana v. Statutory Committee to Nominate Candidates for Commissioner of Political Practices,* 868 P. 2d 604 (MT, 1994).

In Alabama, the state or other public entities may donate public money and other things to private nonprofit corporations if those corporations serve a "public purpose." Donations to organizations like volunteer fire departments and rescue squads benefit the general public because the organizations are not engaged in private enterprise. Even a private nonprofit organization that promotes stewardship among private landowners and protects their property rights by confronting "environmental and political extremism," is a proper "public purpose" in Alabama.

Slawson v. Alabama Forestry Commission, 631 So. 2d 953 (AL, 1994).

In Minnesota, good faith is not a defense to city council members' violation of the state's open meeting law. In a 1994 case, council members engaged in at least three separate, intentional, and unrelated violations and had to be removed from office.

Claude v. Collins, 518 N.W. 2d 836 (MN, 1994).

Advocacy Societies

See also Chapter 39, §405.

Advocacy for the Handicapped

Nonprofit action organizations often play an important role in enforcing compliance with antidiscrimination laws. In a 1994 case, a nonprofit organization sued to challenge a landlord's refusal to show apartments to African-Americans. The court held that a landlord and its agent may be liable for Title VIII housing discrimination if the landlord decides not to show an apartment to African-American individuals posing as prospective tenants.

Cabrera v. Jakabovitz, 24 F. 3d 372 (2nd Cir. [NY], 1994).

Under the Individuals with Disabilities Education Act (IDEA), a handicapped student who follows a regular curriculum, meets the goals of the Individualized Education Plan (IEP), passes mainstream classes, and receives a high school diploma is not eligible for further special education services under IDEA. Such a program, completed, is "adequate free, appropriate public education (FAPE)."

Chuhran v. Walled Lake Consol. Schools, 839 F. Supp. 465 (D.C. MI, 1993).

A society of disabled individuals prevailed in its attempt to compel a city to install curb ramps to comply with regulations promulgated under the Americans with Disabilities Act (ADA). The ramps were required because the city street was "altered" when "resurfaced." Thus, the city could not rely on the fact that the streets were "existing facilities," subject to the undue burden defense of the ADA.

Kinney v. Yerusalim, 9 F. 3d 1167 (3rd Cir. [PA], 1993).

The federal government has a list of commodities that the government must procure solely from workshops for the blind and handicapped. For a commodity to be added to the list, the committee for purchase for the blind and other severely handicapped must prove that the blind would be able to produce the requisite quantities of the commodity at a fair market price.

McGregor Printing Corp. v. Kemp, 20 F. 3d 1188 (DC Cir., 1994).

A nonprofit corporation, whose purpose is to protect and advocate the rights of developmentally disabled people, has standing to intervene in a proceeding for the sale of real estate in the estate of an incapacitated and disabled person.

Estate of Witt, 880 S.W. 2d 380 (MO App. W.D., 1994).

Under the Individuals with Disabilities Education Act (IDEA), the state must participate in a hearing to compare the placement of a handicapped child in a local school district with referral for placement at a state school, in order to provide the child's parents due process under Section 1983 of the U.S. Constitution. The state must also require local school districts to consider the least restrictive environment, and can remove children from regular education only if supplementary aids and services do not allow satisfactory education. Local schools must provide documentation of why they are unable to provide appropriate local placement.

Hunt v. Bartman, 873 F. Supp. 229 (W.D. MO, 1994).

Advocacy for Paternal Rights

When a nonprofit corporation, P.O.P.S., sued to challenge the constitutionality of a Washington state law which provided presumptive child support awards in divorce cases, the court held that the statute was valid.

P.O.P.S. v. Gardner, 998 F. 2d 764 (9th Cir. [WA], 1993).

A school district may close neighborhood schools without violating parents' right to equal protection absent a showing of any intent on the part of the school board to discriminate against ethnic students or to pursue a hidden improper agenda, especially where there are numerous detailed studies to support the decision.

Villanueva v. Carere, 873 F. Supp. 434 (D. CO, 1994).

Advocacy for Free Speech

Does the government have the right to restrain or regulate the actions of nonprofits that advocate social causes and policy changes? There are basically four schools of thought on this question. (1) Government has no right to regulate such advocacy charities because nonprofits are usually more humane and cost-effective than government agencies. (2) Only organizations that advocate views contrary to the prevailing views of society should be curbed. (3) Nonprofits advocating unpopular causes are crucial to level the playing field for unpopular causes and should not be regulated. (4) Government should regulate the activities of special interests so that the needs of the few don't frustrate the desires of the majority.

Jon Van Til, (article), 8 *NonProfit Times,* (4) 9, 10 (April, 1994).

Some decisions of some state courts run counter to the U.S. Constitution as interpreted by the Supreme Court. For example, Arizona ruled that a city ordinance was not valid as a time/place regulation when it forbade demonstrators to block access to a health care facility. [This is a "political," not a "reasonable" decision in our opinion. Physical blockade is not "free speech."]

Sabelko v. City of Phoenix, 846 F. Supp. 810 (D. [AZ], 1994).

The Massachusetts Bay Transportation Authority may not ban, from its trolleys and subways, AIDS-related condom advertisements featuring sexual innuendo and double entendre while allowing movie advertisements that include both.

AIDS Action Committee of Massachusetts v. Massachusetts Bay Transportation Auth.,
    CA 1, No. 94–1116, Nov. 9, 1994.

See also, Section 449.

Nonprofit Monitors Waste in Federal Spending

The nonprofit Citizens Against Government Waste listed 241 pork-based projects or expenditures in its annual 1997 report. The organization also distributes "Oinker" awards to extravagant members of Congress. More reason for taxpayers to be angry when they file their income tax returns.

Wackerman, Daniel T., *Mind's Eye. America,* April 19, 1997.

Television Rating Organizations

The Parents Television Council, a nonprofit group project by the Media Research Council, has released its own analysis of content ratings for prime time network television. The Council questions the new voluntary ratings system. The Council objects to works like "suck" and "bastard" appearing in shows rated TV-PG, and such discussions of teenage sex in a show rated TV-G. The group also believes that programs, such as "Promised Land," have undeserved TV-PG ratings when they contain no sexual innuendo or vulgar language.

Rice, Lynette, *Group Finds Fault with TV Ratings: Parents Television Council Lists G and PG Shows with Sexual References, Broadcasting & Cable,* January 27, 1997.

Health Groups and Tobacco Companies

In 1997, nonprofit health groups demanded a role in negotiating settlement proposals in lawsuits against tobacco manufacturers. The nonprofit organizations object to the settlement offers extended by the tobacco industry.

Cushman, John H., Jr., *Health Groups Demand Role in Negotiating Tobacco Deal. The New York Times,* April 24, 1997.

Immigration Advocacy

An association of housekeepers and child-care workers does not have a legally protected interest in the ability to work, necessary to assert a violation of procedural or substantive due process claims to challenge an immigration statute, that reallocated the availability of employment-based visas in favor of skilled workers. The ability to work in the United States, before permanent residence, is not a fundamental right.

Aliens for Better Immigration Laws v. United States, 871 F. Supp. 182 (S.D. NY, 1994).

The state of California, consistent with federal law, may require applicants for restricted health benefits under Medi-Cal to disclose their immigration status and social security numbers, as long as satisfactory immigration status is not a condition of eligibility for the restricted benefits.

Crespin v. Coye, 34 Cal. Rptr. 2d 10 (CA App. 1 Dist., 1994).

A citizens group and sponsors of Vietnamese immigrants in Hong Kong have standing, as adversely affected or aggrieved parties, to bring action under the Administrative Procedure Act for declaratory and injunctive relief against the U.S. Department of State for refusal to process visas based on nationality-based discrimination in visa processing. Such discrimination violates the Immigration and Nationality Act.

Legal Assistance for Vietnamese Asylum Seekers, 45 F. 3d 469 (DC Cir., 1995).

Environmental Societies

Open Space for Municipalities

Land use regulations are not the only or the best way to gain open spaces for a municipality. Environmentalists, who seek to preserve open space, always face competition from many interests such as affordable housing and new business development. Leasing or purchase of open space by nonprofit groups is among the tips for gaining more open space for municipalities.

> Heacock, Craig, *Creativity Is Vital in Efforts to Preserve Open Space.* (includes tips on acquiring open spaces) (Parks and Grounds), *American City & County,* April, 1997.

Preserving Traditional Technology

See, Bragg, Malara P., *Learning from the Land: Preserving Traditional Technology at Tillers International.* (15-year-old institution near Kalamazoo, MI: includes a schedule of 1997 classes and activities) (Country Skills), *Mother Earth News,* June–July, 1997.

Gardening and Recycling

The nonprofit organization San Francisco League of Urban Gardeners (SLUG) began to link its gardening education efforts with solid waste management in 1989 in response to a growing public interest in recycling and reducing solid waste disposal. SLUG posted home composting brochures, held workshops, started a telephone hotline, and set up a home composting education center. Since then, the program has grown and the interest in home composting across the U.S. has increased.

> Sherman, Steven, *Home Composting Around the Bay, BioCycle,* March, 1997.

International Environmental Action

Actions brought by public interest organizations to compel government agencies to comply with bans under the Marine Mammal Protection Act (MMPA), are actions under an "embargo" law. The Court of International

Trade has exclusive jurisdiction over such actions. The MMPA involves a governmentally imposed quantitative restriction of zero on importation of merchandise.

Earth Island Institute v. Brown, 17 F. 3d 1241 (9th Cir. [CA], 1994).

Environmental organizations are increasing their involvement in international affairs. A statutory "governmental embargo," against the importation of shrimp from countries that ignore the protection of sea turtles, falls into the exclusive jurisdiction of the Court of International Trade (CIT). Negotiations with foreign nations about treaties to protect sea turtles are under the exclusive treaty power of the President.

Earth Island Institute v. Christopher, 6 F. 3d 648 (9th Cir. [CA], 1993).

The Endangered Species Act

When a group of nonprofit citizens' groups, trade associations, and lumber companies challenged regulations under the Endangered Species Act, the court held that the regulation defining "harm" to an endangered species as habitat modification was not void for vagueness. The regulation could be extended to all "threatened" species.

Sweet Home Chapter of Communities for a Great Oregon v. Babbitt, 1 F. 3d 1 (DC Cir., 1993).

Environmental/Freedom of Information Act

An environmental organization prevailed in its suit, under the Freedom of Information Act (FOIA), to compel the United States Department of Agriculture (USDA) to release data obtained through informational surveys submitted to the USDA by state agencies, after the state agencies agreed to waive their confidentiality interests. However, the organization was denied attorney's fees because the USDA had a reasonable basis for withholding survey data (i.e., confidentiality).

Chesapeake Bay Foundation, Inc. v. U.S. Department of Agriculture, 11 F. 3d 211 (DC Cir., 1993).

Clean Water Act Actions

For more information regarding the control of interstate pollution under the Clean Air Act as amended in 1977 (42 USCS §§7401–7626), *see* 82 ALR Fed. 316, §21.

Environmental groups have continued to bring suit under the Clean Water Act (CWA). Any pollutant discharged to navigable waters from a point source is a violation. A dam used to collect acid mine drainage from an abandoned mine site requires a National Pollutant Discharge Elimination System (NPDES) permit to discharge pollutants.

Committee to Save Mokelumne River v. East Bay Mun. Utility Dist., 13 F. 3d 305
    (9th Cir. [CA], 1993).

Citizens may bring suit to enforce water quality standards under a discharge permit even where those standards aren't translated into end-of-pipe effluent limitations. For example, the standards may include not only numeric effluent criteria but also narrative standards.

Northwest Environmental Advocates v. Portland, Ore., CA 9, No. 92–35044, 6/7/95;
    PUD No. 1 of Jefferson County v. Washington Department of Ecology, 62 LW
    4408 (1994).

Citizens' groups may sue under the Clean Water Act (CWA) to enforce "effluent limitations" even where a state National Pollutant Discharge Elimination System (NPDES) permit program operates in lieu of a federal program. Mine tailing ponds are "point sources" under the CWA. Discharges that migrate through groundwater are discharges of pollutants into "navigable waters."

Washington Wilderness Coalition v. HECLA Mining Co., 870 F. Supp. 983 (E.D.
    WA, 1994).

A federal citizen suit may not be brought to enforce state environmental regulations. Polluters may discharge pollutants that are not specifically listed in the state or national pollutant discharge elimination system (SPDES) (NPDES). However, polluters must report the discharge and abide by any new limitations imposed.

Atlantic States Legal Foundation, Inc. v. Eastman Kodak Co., 12 F. 3d 353 (2nd
    Cir. [NY], 1993).

An oil refinery violates its National Pollution Discharge Elimination System (NPDES) permit if it discharges chemicals in excess of the numeric standard set forth in the company's NPDES interim permit.

California Public Interest Research Group v. Shell Oil Co., 840 F. Supp. 712 (N.D.
    CA, 1993).

Nonprofit groups composed of residents who use a river for recreational, religious, and other purposes and individuals who own land adjoining a river are aggrieved persons, who are entitled to judicial review of an agency finding that a National Pollutant Discharge Elimination System (NPDES) permit modification is a "minor construction activity" so that an environmental assessment is unnecessary.

Save Our Rivers, Inc. v. Town of Highlands, 440 S.E. 2d 334 (NC App., 1994).

Environmental Impact Statements

The National Park Service cannot, under the National Environmental Policy Act (NEPA), transfer jurisdiction over portions of a national park for development of a theme park without the preparation of an environmental impact statement (EIS) or an environmental assessment (EA).

Anacostia Watershed Society v. Babbitt, 871 F. Supp. 475 (D. DC, 1994).

The Department of Fish and Game, rather than a lake recreation and park district, is responsible for determining whether an environmental impact report (EIR) should be prepared for a local duck hunting season in California. Thus, the conduct of a lake recreation and park district, in adopting implementation plans for the season, is not an approval of the season without a prior EIR, in violation of the California Environmental Quality Act (CEQA).

Friends of Cuyamaca Valley v. Lake Cuyamaca Recreation and Park District, 33 Cal. Rptr. 2d 635 (CA App. 4 Dist., 1994).

A nonprofit community organization brought action for declaratory and injunctive relief and to challenge a decision of the Federal Highway Administration (FHA) approving a toll road. The court held that the FHA did not, under the National Environmental Policy Act (NEPA), have to prepare a supplemental environmental impact statement (SEIS) to address the effect of wildfires which broke out after the EIS was approved. A university's ecological reserve was held not to function as a publicly owned park land, recreation area, or wildlife and waterfall refuge of national, state or local significance, where FHA projects are prohibited.

Laguna Greenbelt, Inc. v. U.S. Department of Transportation, 42 F. 3d 517 (9th Cir., 1994).

The U.S. Forest Service must consider "connected" and "cumulative" actions in determining whether an Environmental Impact Statement (EIS) is necessary. An access road and its associated timber management activities are connected activities. Seven access road permit applications are cumulative in nature and must be considered together.

> *Alpine Lakes Protection Soc. v. U.S. Forest Service,* 838 F. Supp. 478 (W.D. WA, 1993).

When a Native American nation sued to challenge the adequacy of an environmental impact statement (EIS), concerning the approval of a county solid waste management plan, the court held that review should be *de novo.* The adequacy of the EIS refers to the legal sufficiency of the environmental data contained in the impact statement. The EIS is tested under the "rule of reason." There must be a reasonably thorough discussion of the significant aspects of the environmental consequences of the agency's decision. Procedural errors may be harmless. Administrative decisions will only be overturned if the court is left with a definite and firm conviction that a mistake has been committed.

> *Klickitat County Citizens Against Imported Waste v. Klickitat County,* 860 P. 2d 390 (WA, 1993).

Actions Under CERCLA

A party, who holds indicia of ownership of land primarily to protect its security interest and who does not participate in the management of the property, can seek to invoke the security interest exemption to the strict liability scheme of the Comprehensive Environmental Response, Compensation and Liability Act (CERCLA). A defendant who financed a construction project through the sale and leaseback of land is not a responsible party under either CERCLA or the New Jersey Spill Compensation and Control Act.

> *Kemp Industries, Inc. v. Safety Light Corp.,* 857 F. Supp. 373 (D. NJ, 1994).

Cleanup Costs

Citizen suit provisions of the Resource Conservations and Recovery Act give private individuals a restitutionary remedy to recover environmental cleanup costs even if the site in question no longer poses a contamination threat at the time the suit is filed.

> *KFC Western Inc. v. Meghrig,* CA 9, No. 92–56597, March 1, 1995.

Clean Air Actions

Citizen suits can be brought, under the federal Clean Air Act, to compel the state to comply with the terms of a state implementation program and scheduling order for the reduction of ozone emissions from consumer and commercial products. Lack of expertise and the cost of compliance of the scheduling order are not justification for the state's delay.

American Lung Association v. Kean, 856 F. Supp. 903 (D. NJ, 1994).

Coastal Reserve Statute

When an environmental conservation group sued for judicial review of a Coastal Reserve Commission's (CRC) approval of a major development, allowing the drilling of wells on the coastal reserve for the operation of a public water supply, the court held that the drilling of public water wells is not a permissible "other public use" under the Coastal Reserve Statute.

Friends of Hatteras Island v. Coastal Resources Commission of the State, 452 S.E. 2d
    337 (NC App., 1995).

Credit Unions

Credit Unions Expansion

Five cases of banks challenging credit unions' rights to expand in several states were set for trial in late 1994 in federal court in Washington, D.C., led by the American Bankers Association. These were appeals stemming from the 1993 decision allowing C.U.s to enlist members outside their geographical, employment, or age limits: *First Natl. Bank and Trust v. Natl. Credit Union Administration,* 988 F. 2d 1272 (D.C., Cir. Ct. App., 1993).

Bank Suits, *Natl. L.J.,* p. B. 1 (Aug. 15, 1994).

State regulations that restrict a federally insured credit union from enrolling new members from an adjoining state are constitutional if the restrictions bear a rational relation to legitimate state interest. Such restrictions do not violate the commerce clause or the privileges and immunities clause. A credit union does not have standing to assert the claims of its members because the union's interest is business-related while the members' interests are related to assuring that deposits and loans are administered securely. A credit union has no constitutionally protected property interest in servicing new customers.

N.B.A. Credit Union, Inc. v. Hargrove, 846 F. Supp. 387 (E.D. PA, 1994).

Credit Unions Deposit Accounts

Terms and conditions for credit union members' deposit accounts usually are spelled out in detail in the handouts distributed by their CU organizations. A detailed example would be the one used in 1994 by the St. Anne Credit Union of New Bedford, Massachusetts. It is copyrighted, and can be obtained on request from 93 Union St., New Bedford, MA 02740–6361, (508) 993–0011. (10 pages of fine print.)

The National Credit Union Administration Board may, under provisions of the Federal Credit Union Act (FCUA), repudiate contracts which were entered into prior to its appointment as conservator. A union lacks standing to assert claims on behalf of its members under ERISA where it is not a participant under ERISA and makes no claim that it is designated as a beneficiary or that it possessed or exercised any authority concerning the ERISA plan.

> *International Union v. Auto Glass Employees Federal Credit Union,* 858 F. Supp. 711
> (M.D. TN, 1994).

A credit union, municipal employee annuity and benefit fund, and its trustee may require a municipal employee to execute a power of attorney, permitting the credit union to collect any balance due on a loan–from amounts to be refunded to the employee from the fund at the time of his separation from service–without violating the Illinois statute governing municipal employee annuity and benefits funds.

> *Wright v. Chicago Municipal Employees Credit Union,* 639 N.E. 2d 203 (IL App. 1
> Dist., 1994).

Credit Union Financial Disclosure

There is no private right of action provided for credit union members, under federal regulations requiring that their financial statements provide full and fair disclosure. Under New York law, a credit union treasurer does not commit fraud or a breach of fiduciary duty if he/she acts in good faith, even where financial statements are inaccurate, if the board of directors is indifferent to the impending management crisis.

> *Grand Union Mount Kisco Employees Federal Credit Union v. Kanaryk,* 848 F. Supp.
> (S.D. NY, 1994)

Protection of Agricultural Producers

An association of Idaho farmers brought action for declaratory and injunctive relief against the Fish and Wildlife Service after the service waited seven and one half years from the time of a proposal to list a snail species as endangered before issuing a final rule, withheld from the public a report which served as a basis for the listing, allowed only 10 days for final public comment on the proposed listing, and failed to respond to critical comments received during the final comment period. Such action is arbitrary and capricious.

Idaho Farm Bureau Federation v. Babbit, 839 F. Supp. 739 (D. ID, 1993).

The Secretary of Agriculture is required to consider the statutory factors listed in the Agricultural Marketing Agreement Act of 1937 (AMAA) in a decision to retain the existing structure for class I milk pricing. If the Secretary's decision is not supported with explicit findings regarding the factors, the decision is arbitrary and capricious.

Minnesota Milk Producers Ass'n v. Yeutter, 851 F. Supp. 1389 (D. MN, 1994).

Art Societies

Funding for the National Endowment for the Arts

Both houses of Congress agreed to a conference committee's recommendation of a $98 million budget for the embattled National Endowment for the Arts (NEA). President Clinton, however, may not sign the bill because of a provision unrelated to the agency, which restricts the implementation of statistical sampling in the next census.

Sinclair, Matthew, (article), 11 *NonProfit Times* (14) 5 (November, 1997).

Art Museum Revisionists

Revisionists claim that they hope to create a museum that is more inclusive and audience-centered by changing the building and modifying its programs. That claim is arguable. It often seems that the primary objective for such renovations is profit, which is not in the interest of the museum's patrons. The traditional idea of evolution of artistic achievement is distorted. Most revisionist museum visitors complain of overcrowded exhibitions and overpriced museum paraphernalia.

Munson, Lynne, *The New Museology. The Public Interest,* Spring, 1997.

Nonprofit Support for Music Education

VH1 launched the nonprofit fund Save the Music at the fourth annual "VH1 Honors" event on April 10, 1997, at the Universal Amphitheatre in Los Angeles, California. The charity will promote music education by purchasing and donating musical instruments to public schools. Local cable systems and public school systems joined VH1 in establishing the fund. Celine Dion, Stevie Wonder, James Taylor, Sheryl Crow, Steve Winwood, and the Wallflowers performed live at the show, telecast on April 11, 1997.

Atwood, Brett, *"VH1 Honors" Seeks to Save the Music, Billboard,* April 12, 1997.

Artists and Nonprofit Theatres

Most aspiring artists in New York end up within the national community of not-for-profit theatres—a long road to success which demands that the artist start with nothing and build everything from it.

> Sullivan, John, *You'll Have to Build All That. (How Artists Make a Living)*, *American Theatre*, February, 1997.

§30. HEALTH CARE ORGANIZATIONS

Hospital Lien on Patients' Funds—Attorney Fee

A private nonprofit hospital that enforces its lien on the proceeds of a personal injury settlement must pay its proportionate share of the attorney fees and other costs incurred in the patient's pursuit of his/her claim against a third party. In such cases, the hospital receives direct benefit from the work of the patient's attorney, who should be compensated from the "common fund" he/she helped to create.

> *Martinez v. St. Joseph Healthcare System*, 871 P. 2d 1363 (N.M., 1994). Nebraska held contrary view in *In re Guardianship and Conserv. of Bloomquist*, 514 N.W. 2d 656 (NE App., 1994).

A nonprofit hospital, that seeks to garnish personal injury proceeds, received by a patient, to recover for the costs of medical treatment of the patient for injuries incurred in the accident giving rise to the personal injury action, must present evidence sufficient to support a finding that the treatment was necessary. Necessary evidence might include the use of medical experts.

> *Frankum v. Hensley*, 884 S.W. 2d 688 (MO App. S.D., 1994).

Physician Contracts

A licensed nonprofit or profit hospital may enter into a contract for services with a physician if the contract is consistent with the public health, safety, and welfare.

> *St. Francis Regional Medical Center, Inc. v. Weiss*, 869 P. 2d 606 (KS, 1994).

A health center is not liable to a physician for tortious interference with contract or business expectancy for refusing to allow the physician to sublease his office to another physician, if the health center has authority in the lease to reasonably refuse to allow a sublease, the proposed subleasing physician admits his patients to a competing hospital, and the proposed subleasing physician's credentials do not meet the needs of the health center.

SSM Health Care, Inc. v. Deen, 890 S.W. 2d 343 (MO App. E.D., 1994).

Hospitals' Indigent Patients

Some state statutes for compensating hospitals for services to indigent patients are preempted by ERISA; for example, Connecticut statute.

New England Health Care Employees Union . . . v. Mount Sinai Hospital, 846 F.
    Supp. 190 (D.C. CT, 1994).

In Nevada, a county nonprofit hospital is entitled to reimbursement for medical costs incurred in treating an indigent resident of another county. The county of residence has the burden of proof on the issue of indigency.

Nye County v. Washoe Medical Center, Inc., 877 P. 2d 514 (NV, 1994).

Physician-Assisted Suicide

A mentally competent terminally ill adult has a liberty interest, protected under the Fourteenth Amendment, to choose physician-assisted suicide. A statute that bans physician-assisted suicide, thus, violates the Fourteenth Amendment. Such a statute also violates equal protection where it bans physician-assisted suicide, but allows withdrawal of life-support systems.

Compassion in Dying v. State of WA, 850 F. Supp. 1454 (W.D. WA, 1994).

Nonprofit HMOs

The success of managed care in improving the health status of communities can be directly attributed to the nonprofits. Three of the major nonprofit organizations—Harvard Community Health Plan, Kaiser Permanente, and Group Health Cooperative of Puget Sound—have participated in critical public policy debates of the past 30 years, have conducted and funded emphasis on health, rather than profits, has put these organizations at the forefront of community rating. Nonprofits encourage good relationships between patients and professional caregivers. Nonprofits that deliver superior care are the most effective in controlling costs. And, they have controlled costs while fostering partnerships with organized labor. Now, it is important for nonprofits to communicate their obvious advantages to the general public in order to ensure their survival.

Lawrence, David M., Mattingly, Patrick H., and Ludden, John M., *Trusting in the Future: The Distinct Advantage of Nonprofit HMOs, The Milbank Quarterly*, Spring, 1997.

Will Managed Health Care Endure?

It is hard to predict the future of the U.S. health care system. Since 1959, an economist has made predictions about the health care system, many of which have come true. In 1997, he predicted that managed care will not last long in its current form. However, many changes have taken place in the health care system that no one could have predicted. Among those changes are the growth of for-profit hospital chains by way of mergers and acquisitions, the conversion of nonprofit hospitals to for-profit status, the decline in solo practice, and the changes occurring in medical schools.

See, Kassierer, Jerome P., *Is Managed Care Here to Stay?* (Editorial), *The New England Journal of Medicine*, April 3, 1997.

Profit Versus Quality of Care

Some believe the market competition has brought inflation of health care costs under control. But, many are concerned that for-profit hospitals achieved this cost reduction by sacrificing quality of care. It is well-known that for-profit hospitals provide less charity care and fewer services that typically lose money, such as emergency departments.

Altman, Stuart H., and Schactman, David, *Should We Worry About Hospitals' High Administrative Costs?* (Editorial), *The New England Journal of Medicine*, March 13, 1997. See also, Pear, Robert, *In Separate Studies, Costs of Hospitals are Debated: Nonprofit and For-Profit. The New York Times*, March 13, 1997.

Administrative Costs in Profit Versus Nonprofit Hospitals

Administrative costs in for-profit hospitals have increased faster than in other types of hospitals. Researchers analyzed 1994 Medicare claims to find the administrative costs at 6,227 nonfederal hospitals and the total costs at 5,201 hospitals. Administrative costs accounted for 26 percent of total costs, up 1.2 percent from 1990. For-profit hospitals spent 34 percent more on administrative functions than public hospitals and 23 percent more than private nonprofit hospitals. Also, for-profit hospitals incurred higher costs per patient, with much of the difference associated with administrative costs.

Woolhandler, Steffie, and Himmelstein, David U., *Costs of Care and Administration at For-Profit and Other Hospitals in the United States*. The New England Journal of Medicine, March 13, 1997.

The Capital Structure and Reimbursement of Hospitals

Empirical data has indicated that hospitals are more highly leveraged than other organizations, that their debt/equity ratios are influenced by the extent of cost-based reimbursement, and that investor-owned hospitals have higher leverage than government-owned or nonprofit hospitals. But, this data cannot all be accurately predicted by previous theoretical frameworks. A new model of the reimbursement policy has been developed that demonstrates that the empirical data would be expected ex ante given certain acceptable limitations on the utility functions of nonprofit investors and donors. The new model also shows that the Modigliani-Miller capital structure irrelevance theorem does not hold if reimbursement proceeds according to the indicated pattern.

Ligon, James A., *The Capital Structure of Hospitals and Reimbursement Policy*. *Quarterly Review of Economics and Finance*, Spring, 1997.

Consumers' View of the Health Care Industry

The American Hospital Association used consumer focus groups to determine the public's opinion of the health care industry. The poll revealed sobering results that providers should heed. Most consumers perceived most health care providers as large for-profit enterprises that are more concerned about profits than quality of care. This was the case even when the health care institution in question was a local nonprofit.

Grayson, Mary, *Get the Picture? Consumers Sound Off On Health Care, But You May Not Like What They Tell You, Hospitals & Health Networks*, February 20, 1997.

§31. BENEVOLENT AND FRATERNAL ORDERS, HEALTH, DEATH, AND BURIAL SOCIETIES

Section 501(c)(8) Fraternal Benefit Societies

Permissible Benefits

The IRS, in PLR 9523027, ruled that variable life insurance products serve the exempt purposes of fraternal benefit societies by providing the same type of benefits and protecting against the same type of losses as straight life insurance.

§32. CEMETERY ASSOCIATIONS

New York has a statute, Not-for-Profit Corporation Law Section 1510(m), that provides that no cemetery "shall use construction and demolition debris . . . for the purpose of burying human remains." When a nonprofit public cemetery corporation fought an injunction against burial on property containing construction and demolition debris, the court held that burials on any site that contains construction and demolition debris violate the statute, even where the debris is covered with 10–12 feet of topsoil and there are no hazardous or toxic wastes in excess of regulatory standards on the property.

People v. Cypress Hills Cemetery, 622 N.Y.S. 2d 300 (A.D. 2 Dept., 1995).

The representatives of a proposed class of bereaved survivors sued funeral homes and a crematorium, which the funeral homes recommended to clients, alleging violation of the Racketeer Influenced and Corrupt Organization Act (RICO). The court held that the representatives failed to state a claim against the funeral homes for mail fraud, as a requisite predicate act constituting a pattern of racketeering activity.

In Re Cedar Hill Cemetery Litigation, 853 F. Supp. 706 (S.D. NY, 1994).

§33. RESIDENTS ASSOCIATIONS

Homeless-Housing Organizations

The complex social and legal problems of dealing with housing for the homeless, now a major problem worldwide, is treated in a series of five articles in a Symposium in 23 *Stetson Law Review* 331–496 (1994). Providing "shelters" is not enough.

A nonprofit social service agency may enforce a notice to quit upon a homeless person, who is HIV positive and who resides in a temporary emergency shelter, on the grounds that his license to remain has been revoked and he is no longer in lawful possession of the premises. The court reasoned that the homeless person had no possessory right to be terminated or reinstated and there was no landlord-tenant relationship.

Helping Out People Everywhere, Inc. v. Deich, 615 N.Y.S. 2d 215 (Sup., 1994).

A city ordinance that bans "camping" and storage of personal property in designated public areas does not violate the constitutional rights of homeless persons.

Tobe v. Santa Ana, Calif., CA Sup. Ct. No. S038530, April 24, 1995.

Nonprofit Help for AIDS victims

The nonprofit Housing Works offers housing to homeless AIDS patients in New York City. Housing Works' experiment with this type of housing is to be applauded and, hopefully, duplicated elsewhere.

Iovine, Julie v., *Quality Where It Counts. The New York Times,* April 10, 1997.

Low-Income Housing Associations

See, IRS Proposes Useful New Safe Harbor for Nonprofits that Provide Low-Income Housing. Robert A. Wexler. *The Journal of Taxation,* August, 1995 83 n2 p100(7).

Four nonprofit groups are planning to build 193,800 low-income housing units. The groups are Local Initiatives Support Corp., Habitat for Humanity International, the Enterprise Foundation, and the National Neighborworks Network. These nongovernment groups hope to fill the gap in governmental and social programs by providing more housing for those with low incomes.

Janofsky, Michael, *4 Nonprofit Groups Plan 193,800 Low-Income Housing Units. The New York Times,* March 14, 1997.

Landowners' and Homeowners' Associations

A group of landowners in a subdivision sued their developer, under a declaration of restrictions for their recorded plat, to remove from a boat basin a fence that was a stranding pen for ill or injured marine mammals. The court held that the pen area, which was leased from the heirs of the developer, was a violation of the plat restrictions and was a "structure impeding or obstructing navigation in the waterway, boat basins excepted."

Dolphins Plus, Inc. v. Hobdy, 650 So. 2d 213 (FL App. 3 Dist., 1995).

A subdivision association can acquire rights in a ball field through adverse possession, where the association exercises all rights demonstrative of ownership, the field is used exclusively by the subdivision homeowners for recreation, and the homeowners believe that they have a right to use the property as common ground of the subdivision.

Parkton Association v. Armstrong, 878 S.W. 2d 50 (MO App. E.D., 1994).

A declaration of covenants, conditions, and restrictions for a planned community that contains an unambiguous severability clause that precludes the defense of abandonment of covenants against one restriction based on the alleged failure of a homeowners association to enforce other covenants is enforceable. Equitable defenses available to stop enforcement of restrictive covenants are merger, release, unclean hands, acquiescence, abandonment, laches, estoppel, and changed neighborhood conditions.

> *Mountain Park Homeowners Association, Inc. v. Tydings,* 883 P. 2d 1383 (WA, 1994).

The owners of residential lots in a subdivision sued the corporation which was comprised of all subdivision owners after the corporation drafted new restrictions concerning their land. The court held that, upon interpretation of the articles of incorporation and bylaws, the corporation could adopt new restrictions concerning storage of unused automobiles and the building of residences on docks, even without the consent of all the property owners.

> *Shafer v. Board of Trustees of Sandy Hook Yacht Club Estates, Inc.,* 883 P. 2d 1387
>   (WA App. Div. 1, 1994).

The owners of a parcel in a subdivision are liable for general and special assessments levied on them by the subdivision association, if the parcel owners purchased the property subject to the restriction that "each owner" is required to maintain the property in good order and repair, and the restrictions empower the association to perform any maintenance or repair on the properties and assess the owner for the costs. The restrictions may be enforceable, even where the "owner" fails to formally join the association if "membership" is defined as "ownership."

> *See, Mariner's Village Master Association, Inc. v. Continental Properties,* 639 So. 2d
>   1188 (LA App. 1 Cir., 1994).

§34. COMMUNITY IMPROVEMENT CORPORATIONS (DEVELOPMENT CORPORATIONS)

> *See, IRS Proposes Useful New Safe Harbor for Nonprofits that Provide Low-Income Housing.* Robert A. Wexler. *The Journal of Taxation,* August 1995 83 n2 p100(7); *Nonprofit Organizations in Affordable Housing and Community Development.* (Colorado) J. William Callison. *Colorado Lawyer,* May 1994 23 n5 p1025(8).

Community Revitalization and Governing Nonprofits

Governing nonprofits can provide a platform for restructuring political agendas. They take on roles traditionally reserved for government, and forge coalitions among and across groups, organizations, and sectors. Through this method, governing nonprofits address societal problems. These nonprofit organizations require broad community support, embrace flexible policy agendas, and operate in the public domain. The success of governing nonprofits also lies in their ability to foster positive links with the local leadership, without becoming completely identified with local authorities. (Drawn from work by Schattschneider [1960] and Baumgartner and Jones [1993], and examining nonprofits in three U.S. cities.)

> Hula, Richard C., and Jackson, Cynthia Y., and Orr, Marion, *Urban Politics, Governing Nonprofits, and Community Revitalization. Urban Affairs Review,* March, 1997.

§35. LABOR UNIONS

Section 501(c)(5) Labor Organizations

<u>Nonacquiescence in Morganbesser</u>

The IRS has nonacquiesced in *Morganbesser v. United States,* 984 F. 2d 560 (2d Cir. 1993), calling the decision "wrong as a matter of law," on the grounds that a Section 501(c)(5) labor organization must represent the collective interests of workers in dealings with their employers. Managing the assets of a retirement plan is simply implementing the terms of a contract, even where the contract arose through collective bargaining.

Labor organizations must represent workers in their negotiations with employers. AOD CC-1995-016. The IRS revoked GCM 35862 which the Second Circuit had cited in its *Morganbesser* opinion.

<u>Illustrative Cases</u>

The National Labor Relations Board cannot force a hospital to bargain, pursuant to a 15-year-old union election, where only 20 of the 56 employees currently within the bargaining unit were employed at the time of the 15-year-old election.

> *N.L.R.B. v. Long Island College Hosp.,* 20 F. 3d 76 (2nd Cir., 1994).

A visiting nurse's association, that threatened to deny employment to a contract nurse because she had associated with union employees who were engaging in a "work to rule" protest, committed unfair labor practice, motivated by suspicion of union activity, a violation of the National Labor Relations Act (NLRA).

> *Holyoke Visiting Nurses Association v. N.L.R.B.,* 11 F. 3d 302 (1st Cir., 1993).

A nurses' organization, originally founded as a social or educational body, is not considered to be a "labor organization" covered by the National Labor Relations Act. "Labor organizations" must feature a pattern or practice over time of proposal-and-response exchange between labor and management on working conditions.

NLRB v. Peninsula General Hospital Medical Center, CA 4, No. 94–1202,
      Oct. 18, 1994.

Employee "action committees" that are created, guided, and maintained by management are representational "labor organizations" that are dominated by management and interfere with employee self-organization in violation of the National Labor Relations Act.

Electromation Inc. v. NLRB, CA 7, No. 92–4129, Sep. 15, 1994.

A public sector union must provide prior notice and adequate explanation of the basis of service or agency fees it seeks to collect from nonmembers to ensure that potential objectors will be able to assess the propriety of the fee.

Jibson v. Michigan Education Association-NEA, 30 F. 3d 723 (6th Cir., 1994).

An employer may not deduct money from the wages of employees on federal construction projects to fund union "job targeting programs." Such deductions violate the Davis-Bacon Act, which requires that workers be paid the prevailing wage "without subsequent deduction or rebate."

Building and Construction Trades Department, AFL-CIO v. Reich, CA DC, No.
      93–5129, Dec. 9, 1994.

A union has no right of access to a company's employee bulletin board. An employer's refusal to permit employees to post union material during an organizational campaign does not violate Section 7 of the National Labor Relations Act.

Guardian Industries Corp. v. National Labor Relations Board, CA 7, No. 94–2388,
      Feb. 28, 1995.

Firefighters who prevail in a Section 1983 action against a local union, alleging violation of nonmembers' constitutional rights concerning the collection of services charges or agency fees, are entitled to recover attorney fees under the Civil Rights Attorney's Fees Award Act. Attorney's fees are limited to the percentage of the intended efforts prevailed upon.

Johnson v. Lafayette Fire Fighters' Ass'n, 857 F. Supp. 1292 (N.D. IN, 1994).

An aggrieved party, in Vermont, can appeal an order by the Vermont Labor Relations Board (VLRB), accepting a union election petition, directly to the Vermont Supreme Court, under the authority of the State Employees Labor Relations Act (SELRA).

> *Board of Trustees of Kellogg-Hubbard Library, Inc. v. Labor Relations Board,* 649 A. 2d 784 (VT, 1994).

When members of a union sued their local to obtain documents, the U.S. Court of Appeals for the Seventh Circuit held that Section 201(c) of the Labor-Management Reporting and Disclosure Act requires a plaintiff to obtain a judgment in its favor, not just some level of success before attorneys' fees can be awarded to the plaintiff.

> *Stomper v. Amalgamated Transit Union, Local 241,* CA 7, No. 93-3468, June 22, 1994.

An Illinois appellate judge has qualified immunity from a court staff research attorney's claim that he was fired for conducting union-organizing activity among other researchers. The court reasoned that the judge had a reasonable basis for concluding that the attorney "had an obligation to refrain from taking such an adversarial role to the court."

> *Gregorich v. Lund,* CA 7, No. 94-2505, May 9, 1995.

An employee, who had been appointed a union's environmental officer charged with union opposition to the company's plan to burn hazardous waste as fuel, was fired after he used a company copier to copy an article concerning "sham recycling" of hazardous waste by cement plants. The court held that the employee was engaged in protected concerted activity, under the National Labor Relations Act, when he used the copier, justifying an order for reinstatement and back pay.

> *Blue Circle Cement Co. Inc. v. National Labor Relations Board,* 41 F. 3d 203 (5th Cir., 1994).

An employer's statements, suggesting that plant closure and layoffs might follow a union election victory, are not illegal threats under Section 8(a)(1) of the National Labor Relations Act.

> *Crown Cork & Seal Co. v. National Labor Relations Board,* CA DC, No. 92-1428, Oct. 7, 1994.

A union and male picketers may be liable for sexual harassment, under the New Jersey Law Against Discrimination, if they verbally taunt female workers crossing their picket line with sexually derogatory expletives.

Baliko v. Stecker, NJ SuperCt AppDiv, No. A–1113–93T2F, July 20, 1994, released Aug. 8, 1994.

Serious contempt fines amounting to $52 million imposed against a labor union to coerce compliance with an injunction barring unlawful strike-related activities may be imposed only through criminal proceedings involving the right to jury trial.

United Mine Workers v. Bagwell, 62 LW 4705, June 30, 1994.

A union does not commit a bad faith breach of duty of fair representation by using a union security agreement that requires bargaining unit employees to be "members of the union in good standing."

International Union of Electronic, Electrical, Salaried, Machine and Furniture Workers v. National Labor Relations Board, CA DC, No. 93–1373, Dec. 16, 1994.

An employer that reorganizes for business reasons, without intent to evade bargaining obligations, may be liable under the alter ego doctrine for refusing to continue prior bargaining relationships.

Stardyne Inc. v. National Labor Relations Board, CA 3, No. 94–3054, Dec. 6, 1994.

An employer is protected from unfair labor practice charges if he withdraws from collective bargaining, in response to a decertification petition, if the National Labor Relations Board will not disclose the number of employees supporting the petition.

National Labor Relations Board v. New Associated, CA 3, No. 93–3111, Sep. 16, 1994.

The Labor-Management Reporting and Disclosure Act (LMRDA) is violated by provisions in collective bargaining agreements, requiring the losing party in challenges to a labor arbitration decision to pay the prevailing party's attorneys' fees. Members' LMRDA right to initiate court proceedings are thwarted by such provisions.

Moore v. Local 569, International Brotherhood of Electrical Workers, CA9, No. 93–56717, May 5, 1995.

§37. EDUCATIONAL CORPORATIONS

Enrollment at independent schools continued to increase in 1994–1995. The National Association of Independent Schools in Washington, D.C., which had 840 school members and 832 affiliates worldwide in 1995, reported that, on average, enrollment at preschools increased 4.5 percent, at elementary schools by 3.1 percent, at high schools by 2.9 percent, and at postgraduate or college institutions by 4.7 percent. Minority student enrollment at independent schools was up, comprising 16.6 percent of the total student population, up 5.5 percent from 1984–1985.

Swarden, Carlotta, (article), 9 *NonProfit Times* (10) 5 (October, 1995).

Statutory Regulation

A statute that subjects Oregon schools to regulation by the Office of Education Policy and Planning (OEPP), but exempts certain Oregon schools that are members of certain organizations from certification requirements when all non-Oregon schools must meet the requirements, whether they are members of the organization or not, violates the commerce clause.

City University v. State Office of Educational Policy and Planning, 870 P. 2d 222 (OR, App., 1994).

Although Congress can regulate numerous commercial activities that affect interstate commerce and the educational process, that authority does not include the authority to regulate each and every aspect of local schools. Texas' Gun-Free School Zones Act, which made it a federal offense for any individual to possess a firearm in an area that he/she believes or has reasonable cause to believe is a school zone, exceeded Congress' commerce clause authority.

U.S. v. Lopez, 115 S. Ct. 1624 (U.S. TX, 1995).

A Puerto Rico Statute that gave public school students up to $1,500 to transfer to private schools, violated the commonwealth's constitution. The 1993 education reform measure impermissibly gave private schools substantial assistance and granted them special benefits not available to the public schools.

Asociacion de Maestros de Puerto Rico v. Torres, PR SupCt, No. AC-94-371, Nov. 30, 1994.

The Alabama legislature must provide school children with substantially equitable and adequate educational opportunities, including children with disabilities.

Opinion of the Justices, 624 So. 2d 107 (AL, 1993).

Nonprofit educational organizations may affiliate with local telephone company licenses to provide wireless cable service on the instructional television fixed service spectrum, even though the 1984 Cable Act prohibits local telephone companies from providing video programming in their telephone service areas.

American Scholastic TV Programming Foundation v. Federal Communications Commission, 46 F. 3d 1173 (DC Cir., 1995).

School Immunity

Under the Minnesota Human Rights Act a school being sued by a student is not entitled to "official" or "discretionary" operation immunity.

Engels v. Independent School Dist., No. 91, 846 F. Supp. 760 (D.C. MN, 1994).

Race Discrimination

The University of Maryland's race-based scholarships, established to attract African-American students, were deemed to be unconstitutional in 1994. The program was not narrowly tailored to remedy the present effects of past discrimination.

Podberesky v. Kirwan, CA 4, No. 93–2527, Oct. 27, 1994.

Student Contracts

In Illinois, the analysis of whether a school commits breach of contract with its students depends on breach of promise, made either explicitly or through its academic bulletins or application forms, and whether the school acts arbitrarily, capriciously and in bad faith.

Haynes v. Hinsdale Hospital, 872 F. Supp. 542 (N.D. IL, 1995).

Special Education

A private nonprofit school for special education students is not entitled to reimbursement, under the Pennsylvania Public School Code, for the cost of educating nonexceptional students.

Community Country Day School v. Pennsylvania Department of Education, 641 A. 2d 1282 (PA Cmwlth., 1994).

Campus Security

The Secretary of Education has amended the Student Assistance General Provisions' rules in accordance with various higher education statutes (and 1993 amendments) to require institutions to disclose campus safety policies and procedures, effective July 1, 1994.

HEA Programs, 59 FR 22314.

School Drug Tests

The U.S. Supreme Court held, in 1995, that the Fourth Amendment is not violated by subjecting student athletes to random suspicionless drug testing.

Vernonia School District 47J v. Action, US SupCt, No. 94–590, June 26, 1995.

Nonprofit Scientific Publication on the Internet

Stanford's HighWire Press has brought scientific publishing on-line. The results are that journals may be able to publish articles faster, avoiding periodic publication schedules. Video and sound files may be added to the journals. Associate publisher John R. Sack states that Stanford wants to advance nonprofit scientific publications as publishing moves to the Internet. Librarians are skeptical of on-line publishing, fearing that the material may be difficult to preserve.

Young, Jeffrey R., *Stanford-Based HighWire Press Transforms the Publication of Scientific Journals; Many More Will Be Placed on-line; New Technology May Change the Way Articles Are Presented. The Chronicle of Higher Education,* May 16, 1997.

Information Systems

JSTOR is a nonprofit organization that uses digital technologies to preserve and allow access to important academic journals. JSTOR's pilot group is scanning 10 journals and making them available at test sites in a small group of libraries.

Brunet, Patrick J., *CyberHound's Guide to Associations and Nonprofit Organizations on the Internet, Library Journal,* February 1, 1997.

Investing by Educational Institutions

Stock market investment strategies of universities vary. During the recent bull market, Northwestern's portfolio, whose value on August 31, 1996 was

$1,734 billion, consisted of venture capital, real estate, and foreign investments. Cornell invests mostly in U.S. stocks, with a portfolio value of $1,748 billion on June 30, 1996. Michigan's portfolio, valued at $1,876 billion on June 30, 1996, emphasizes foreign stocks over domestic, an unusual choice for a nonprofit investor.

> Stronsider, Kim, *How 3 Universities Invest Their Funds in the Bull Market, The Chronicles of Higher Education*, January 31, 1997.

Preserving Traditional Technology

See, Bragg, Malara P., *Learning from the Land: Preserving Traditional Technology at Tillers International.* (15-year-old institution near Kalamazoo, MI: includes a schedule of 1997 classes and activities) (Country Skills), *Mother Earth News*, June–July, 1997.

§39. MUTUAL ASSOCIATIONS

If a city purchases liability insurance, it waives liability to the extent of the policy. However, in Mississippi, if the city self-insures itself by participating in a nonprofit municipal risk-sharing pool, participation in the self-insurance pool does not waive sovereign immunity, especially where the bylaws of the mutual self-insurance nonprofit state that participation is not waiver of sovereign immunity.

> *Morgan v. City of Ruleville,* 627 So. 2d 275 (MS, 1993) (drowning death in a city swimming pool).

A government may exclude an insurer as a claimant of a Miscellaneous Guaranty Association where the noncovered classification serves the legitimate governmental interest of protecting individual citizens, rather than insurers, from delayed payment or nonpayment of insurance claims due to an insurer's insolvency.

> *U.S. Fire Insurance Company v. Corporacion Insular de Seguros,* 853 F. Supp. 47 (D. PR, 1994).

Policy holders in a state accident fund brought suit against the state and fund to assert their right to any surplus in the fund over the reserves needed to cover liabilities. During the pendency of the suit, the state passed legislation authorizing the state to sell the fund to a private party, and to retain the proceeds. The court held that vested rights are not created by a statute, unless the legislature covenants not to amend the legislation.

> *In Re Certified Question,* 527 N.W. 2d 468 (MI, 1994).

A nonprofit insurance guaranty association does not stand in the shoes of an insolvent insurer for jurisdictional purposes. A letter sent by such an association to a beneficiary in California regarding his policy is not the "minimum contacts" sufficient for California to exercise jurisdiction over the association if the letter is sent as an indirect result of its interstate liquidating activities. An association must direct its activities toward a California resident or purposely avail itself of the benefits and protection of the state to support jurisdiction in the state.

Pennsylvania Life and Health Insurance Guaranty Association v. Superior Court (Laughlin), 27 CA. Rptr. 2d 507 (CA App. 4 Dist., 1994).

A medical Professional Insurance Association (MMPIA), which is a nonprofit joint underwriting association, is not in the "business of insurance" and therefore is not liable under state statutes prohibiting unfair methods of competition and unfair and deceptive acts and practices in the insurance business. It is also not engaged in "trade or commerce" so as to be subject to suit under the state Consumer Protection Act.

Poznik v. Massachusetts Medical Professional Insurance Association, 628 N.E. 2d 1 (MA, 1994).

Even the state can claim indemnity from the Montana Insurance Guaranty Association (MIGA) for settlement of claims against it where the state was asserting its claim as an insured under its insurance policy with an insolvent insurer.

Howell v. State, 868 P. 2d 568 (MT, 1994).

The Rhode Island Insurer's Insolvency Act excludes payment of subrogation claims due to any "insurer," whether the insurer is a contributor to the fund or not.

Kachanis v. U.S., 844 F. Supp. 877 (D. RI, 1994).

Minnesota has a nonprofit corporation, created by the legislature, that continues the payment of workers' compensation benefits delayed due to the insolvency of a private self-insurer.

See In re Lull Corp., 162 B.R. 234 (Bankr. D. MN, 1993).

The Washington Insurance Guaranty Association (WIGA) assumes the responsibilities of insolvent Washington insurers and provides coverage for the lesser of the policy amount or $300,000. The state workers' compensation fund may recover its lien against the proceeds a worker recovers from the Association.

> *WIGA v. Dept. of Labor and Indus.,* 859 P. 2d 592 (WA, 1993).

§43. FASHIONABLE SPECIAL CORPORATIONS

Nonprofit Aid for Small Business

More than 800 business "incubators" exist across the U.S. to help start-up companies become self-sufficient. Most of these "incubator" services are operated by nonprofit groups seeking to foster the development of small business in a particular community or industry.

> Buss, Dale, *Bringing New Firms Out of Their Shell.* (business incubators; includes tips for evaluating a business incubator), *Nation's Business*, March, 1997.

Child Care Organizations

Child care costs young couples up to one-fourth of their annual income. However, one-fourth of a couple's income does not always produce enough revenue to offer quality care. Child-care educators are often underpaid and undertrained. However, paying higher fees does assure that the industry maintains standards.

> Clark, Jane Bennett, *The Great Day-Care Paradox: How Can This Vital Service Cost Too Much and Too Little at the Same Time,* (includes a related article on nonprofit centers), *Kiplinger's Personal Finance Magazine*, March, 1997.

A study of the geographic variation in levels of formal child care provision in the province of Ontario, Canada, emphasizing the historical development of the decentralized service system and highlighting the emergence of public nonprofit, private nonprofit, and private proprietary service providers was published in May of 1997.

> *See,* Skelto, Ian, *Geographic Variation in Services Under Different Providers: the Case of Formal Child Care in Ontario, The Professional Geographer*, May, 1997.

Nonprofit Organizations for Housing the Elderly

Continuum care apartment facilities for the elderly, that are not used exclusively for the activities of a charitable society, are not exempt from property taxes in Mississippi. Such facilities are used "for profit" if fees substantially cover all operating expenses, the application process is designed to deliver a body of fee-paying residents, and the leases allow eviction.

Hattiesburg Area Senior Services, Inc. v. Lamar County, 633 So. 2d 440 (MS, 1994).

Nursing Homes

The standard of care of a nursing home is "reasonable care" with consideration of a patient's condition. There is no absolute duty to provide the presence of a nurse or attendant at all times. Duty of care is a question of fact.

McCartney v. Columbia Heights Nursing Home, Inc., 634 S. 2d 927 (LA. App., 1994).

See, Bruck, Laura, *Today's Issues in Tax Exemption; Tax Exemption in Non-Profit Long-Term Facilities; Interview with Herman Rosenthal, Joseph Truhe, Jr. and Bill Davidow of Baltimore MD-based Whiteford, Taylor & Preston LLP, Nursing Homes,* Sept. 1996. *See also, Care Management: It's In the Eye of the Beholder, Nursing Homes,* July-August, 1996. *See also, The Ethics of Managed Care, Nursing Homes,* May, 1996.

5

UNINCORPORATED ORGANIZATIONS

§48. NONPROFIT ASSOCIATIONS, IN GENERAL

The Uniform Unincorporated Nonprofit Association Act

The following is a *summary* of the Uniform Unincorporated Nonprofit Association Act. For the complete text *see, Uniform Laws Annotated, 1995 Supplementary Pamphlet,* Volume 6, *The Uniform Unincorporated Nonprofit Association Act,* West Publishing Co., 1995, 614–634.

In 1992, a committee acting for the National Conference of Commissioners on Uniform State Laws prepared the Uniform Unincorporated Nonprofit Association Act. The Act has been adopted in Idaho (1993) and in Wyoming (1993). Portions of the Act have been included in the laws of other states.

The Act changes the common law concerning unincorporated associations in the areas of authority to acquire, hold, and transfer property, including real property; the authority to sue and be sued as an entity; and the contract and tort liability of the officers and members of the association.

At common law, a gift of real property, to an unincorporated association, failed because the association was not considered to be a legal entity. The association was merely an aggregate of individuals. For an association to sue or be sued at common law, all of the members needed to be joined as party plaintiffs or a class action was necessary. Members of unincorporated associations, at common law, were liable for the contracts and torts of the unincorporated association, though the association could not be liable because it was not an "entity." Jointly held property of the members of the association could not be seized to enforce a judgment against the members if fewer than all of the members were found to be liable. The new Uniform Unincorporated Nonprofit Association Act changes the common law in order to deal with the problems above.

The Uniform Unincorporated Nonprofit Association Act applies to all unincorporated associations and is not confined to associations recognized under 501(c)(3), (4), and (6) of the Internal Revenue Code. The Act recognizes unincorporated associations as legal entities "for the purposes it addresses."

Section 1 of the Act defines the terms "Member," "Nonprofit Association," "Person," and "State."

Section 2 states that, "Principles of law and equity supplement this [Act] unless displaced by a particular provision of it." The Act contains no governance rules.

Section 3 states that, "Real and personal property in this State may be acquired, held, encumbered, and transferred by a nonprofit association, whether or not the nonprofit association or a member has any other relationship to this State."

Section 4 (a) states that, "A nonprofit association in its name may acquire, hold, encumber, or transfer an estate or interest in real or personal property." Section 4 (b) further says, "A nonprofit association may be a legatee, devisee, or beneficiary of a trust or contract."

Section 5 provides for a statement of authority to transfer real property and states what the document must set forth. The statement of authority must include the name of the association, the address, name or title of the person authorized to transfer the property, and the action or vote required for authorization. Section 5 also describes the proper manner of execution, treatment of fees, amendments and cancellation of authority, and the method of proving authority through filing or recording of the document.

Section 6 of the Act concerns the liability of the association and its members. The section grants "entity" status to unincorporated associations, and relieves members of liability for association contracts and tortious acts or omissions of the association or other members imposed "merely because the person is a member, is authorized to participate in the management of the affairs of a nonprofit association, or is a person considered to be a member by the nonprofit association." The section also allows members to sue or be sued by the association.

Section 7 of the Act gives unincorporated associations status, in their own name, to institute, defend, intervene, or participate in legal actions. The association may assert a claim on behalf of its members if one or more members have a right to assert the claim, the interests asserted are germane to the association's purpose, and neither the claim or the relief requested require participation of individual members.

Section 8 of the Act states that judgments against the nonprofit are not, by themselves, judgments or orders against a member.

Section 9 concerns the transfer of property of an inactive nonprofit association. The property is to be distributed according to the documents of the organization concerning transfers. If there are no documents, then "to a nonprofit association or nonprofit corporation pursuing broadly similar purposes or to a government, governmental subdivision, agency, or instrumentality."

Section 10 addresses the appointment of an agent to receive service of process. The section describes what the statement must set forth, acknowledgment of the statement, filing, and amendment of the statement.

Section 11 of the Act states that claims against an association are not abated by a change in members or officers of the association.

Section 12, which is optional depending upon the venue rules of the adopting state, assigns resident status to a nonprofit in a "[city or] county in which it has an office."

Section 13, which is also optional, allows service of process on "an agent authorized by appointment to receive service of process, an officer, managing or general agent, or a person authorized to participate in the management of its affairs. If none of them can be served, service may be made on a member."

Section 14 addresses uniformity and construction of the Act.

Section 15 states the name of the Act.

Section 16 states that portions of the Act held to be invalid are severable.

Section 17 is the effective date statement of the Act.

Section 18 provides for repeal of conflicting state laws.

Section 19 deals with transfers of property before the effective date of the Act.

Section 20 is a saving clause denying control of the Act over rights accrued before the effect of the Act or an effect on proceedings then pending.

State Unincorporated Associations Acts

See, The Ramifications of Idaho's New Uniform Unincorporated Nonprofit Associations Act. Kenneth D. Lewis Jr. *Idaho Law Review,* Winter 1994 31 n1 p297–312.

§52. LAWSUITS BY OR AGAINST AN ASSOCIATION

Unincorporated Association Lawsuits

Ohio's statute allows an unincorporated association to "sue or be sued as an entity under the name by which it is commonly known or called."

Ohio Rev. Code §1745.01

Maryland allows such suit if the association has a "group name."

MD Code §6–406(a).

The federal rule is that the association has "standing" to sue when it is representing its members' interests, which are germane to its purposes, and the individual member's participation is not necessary.

Hunt v. Washington Apple Advertising Comn., 97 S. Ct. 2434 (1977); *Restatement of Judgments* 2d §61 (2).

Venue for these lawsuits is in any county in which the association has an office; or if no office *can be found,* in the county in which an officer resides, under some state statutes.

IL Code Civ. Pract. §2–102 (c).

Uniform Unincorporated Nonprofit Association Act

A uniform statute to reform the common law rules that govern unincorporated NPOs has been proposed in almost every state. It has been accepted in Idaho (1993) and in Wyoming (1993). However, only parts of the statute have been accepted in some states, as detailed previously in §48.

§53. ASSOCIATION AGENTS' AND MEMBERS' POWERS AND LIABILITIES

Unincorporated Association Member Injuries

The Texas Supreme Court has ruled that a member of an unincorporated association may sue the association for damages; thus changing the common law rule that had barred such suits in Texas.

Cox v. Thee Evergreen Church, 836 S.W. 2d 167 (TX, 1992).

See §48, The Uniform Unincorporated Nonprofit Association Act.

See, Liability Issues of the Unincorporated Association. . . , casenote on *Cox v. Thee Evergreen Church,* 836 S.W. 2d 167 (TX, 1992), by K.A. Davison, 46 *Baylor L. Rev.* 231–257 (Winter 1994).

7

FOUNDATIONS
(CHARITABLE TRUSTS)

§65. FOUNDATIONS DEFINED

Court Creation of Trusts

If a conservator's petition, for creation of a revocable living trust, does not defeat a ward's estate plan and the intentions set forth in his will, the court may protect the assets through the creation of a trust. This is especially true where the trust sets forth the same goals as the will or where the assets seem to be threatened without the creation of a trust.

Matter of Conservatorship of Sickles, 518 N.W. 2d 673 (ND, 1994).

Foundations and Social Change

In 1997, foundations are becoming much bigger and influential due to the shrinking of government and the rise in the stock market since 1980. Foundations, with their new-found power, are attempting to influence political and social change. An example of such a foundation is the Heritage Foundation, which played a major role during the Reagan-Bush era.

Lemann, Nicholas, *Citizen 501(c)(3): An Increasingly Powerful Agent in American Life Is Also One of the Least Noticed, The Atlantic Monthly,* February, 1997.

§67. STATE SUPERVISION OF FOUNDATIONS

Trustees' Standard of Care

New York's "Prudent Investor Act," which took effect January 1, of 1995 and applies to trusts, requires trustees who invest trust funds to diversify portfolios, weigh the impact of inflation when making financial decisions, and demonstrate "investment skill." Those who fail this standard face civil liability.

9 *NonProfit Times* (2) 8 (February, 1995). *See also* Chapter 29, §305.

§68. COMMON LAW BASES OF FOUNDATIONS

Cy Pres Doctrine

If a testator knows how to create a trust, but does not, a will provision which devises the residue of an estate to a hospital, with income from the fund to be used for hospitalization of members of a fraternal organization, is an outright but restricted gift to the hospital, not a trust. If the charitable bequest becomes "impracticable" under the *cy pres* doctrine, reformation of the will is justified to permit the income to defray costs of other health care services at the hospital, if the testator had the general charitable purpose of underwriting major expenses of serious illness or injury.

Matter of Estate Vallery, 867 P. 2d 210 withdrawn (CO App., 1993).

Charitable trust funds generally revert to the settlor's estate or to heirs at law where one or more specific purposes cannot be fulfilled because of impossibility, even where the trust does not contain a reverter clause or gift-over provision. In a 1994 case, a residuary nonprofit legatee challenged a court's release of a church from a restriction in a trust requiring that the funds of the trust be used exclusively for the construction of a new building. The court held that release of the restriction was improper where a larger church was no longer needed, the church had been declared a historic site, major renovations and repairs had been completed on the existing church, and the congregation expressed no desire for a new church. The funds should have reverted back to the estate.

In Re Estes Estate, 523 N.W. 2d 863 (MI App., 1994).

§69. INTERNAL REVENUE SUPERVISION

See, Private Foundations and Community Foundations: Major Current Developments. J. Edward Shillingburg. New York University Conference on Tax Planning for 501(c)(3) Organizations, Annual 1994 22 p8–1(18).

§73. TESTS OF FOUNDATION VALIDITY

Challenge of a Charitable Trust

A party (the Roman Catholic Diocese) has standing to enforce a trust, even where it is not a beneficiary, if it has an immediate, direct, and substantial interest in the trust. Integral involvement in awarding scholarships from the trust and the prerogative to participate in the establishment of a vocational school under the trust are such interests. Removal of trustees is not proper where there is no waste of the estate and there are no excessive fees or commissions charged any trustee. In Pennsylvania, trustees are entitled to indemnification by the foundation in defending actions brought against them for removal and surcharge.

In re Francis Edward McGillick Foundation, 642 A. 2d 467 (PA, 1994).

A probate and family court may seek a formal accounting of the assets of a testatrix's estate held in charitable corporations rather than in a testamentary trust itself. Resigned trustees must account for their management, since the charitable corporations are the mirror images of the testamentary trust itself.

Matter of Trust Under the Will of Fuller, 636 N.E. 2d 1333 (MA, 1994).

When charitable organizations challenged a probate court order appointing a successor distribution trustee for a charitable trust, the court held that allegations of insufficient evidence to justify modification are "nonjurisdictional error" and cannot be a basis for final collateral attack on a modification order after it becomes a final judgment.

Estate of Buck, 35 Cal. Rptr. 2d 442 (CA App. 1 Dist., 1994).

§75. FORMS FOR FOUNDATIONS

FORM NO. 8S
Articles of Incorporation
(Foundation for Industrial Exchange)

[NOT-FOR-PROFIT CORPORATION]

**Articles of Incorporation
of Foundation for Industrial Exchange, Incorporated**

The undersigned, _____, hereby associate ourselves together for the purpose of organizing a nonprofit corporation under the provisions of chapter 617 of the Florida Statutes and all acts amendatory thereto, and to that end, certify as follows:

Article I

NAME

The name of the corporation is **Foundation for Industrial Exchange, Incorporated.**

Article II

DURATION

The term of existence of the Corporation is perpetual.

Article III

PURPOSES

1.   Permitted Activities.   The purposes for which the Corporation is organized are to receive and maintain real, tangible or intangible property, or all three, and, subject to the restrictions and limitations hereinafter set forth, to use and apply the whole or any part of the income therefrom and the principal thereof exclusively for charitable, religious, scientific, literary, athletic or educational purposes either directly or by contributions to organizations that qualify as exempt organizations under Section 501(c)(3) of the Internal Revenue Code and regulations issued pursuant thereto as they may now exist or as they may hereafter be amended. The Corporation shall have any and all lawful powers provided in Florida Statutes that are not in conflict with these Articles.

2.   Prohibited Activities.   This Corporation is not organized for a pecuniary profit. There shall be no power to issue certificates of stock or declare dividends and no part of the Corporation's earnings, assets or accumulations shall inure to the benefit of any member, director, or individual. Notwithstanding any other provision of these Articles, this Corporation will not carry on any other activities not permitted to be carried on by (a) a corporation exempt from Federal Income Tax under section 501(c)(3) of the Internal Revenue Code of 1986 or any other corresponding provision of any future United States Internal Revenue Law, or (b) a corporation, contributions to which are deductible under Section 170(c)(2) of the Internal Revenue Code of 1986 or any other corresponding provision of any future United States Internal Revenue Law. In particular, the Board of Directors shall not, nor shall it allow members, subscribers, officers or employees of the Corporation to, on behalf of the corporation:

(a)   Allow any part of the net earnings to inure to the benefit of a private individual including any member, director, officer or subscriber of this Corporation.

(b)   To carry on propaganda or to attempt to lobby or influence legislation.

(c)   To intervene in any political campaign or to endorse any candidate for public office.

(d) To do any of the following:

(1) Lend any part of the Corporation's income or corpus without adequate security and a reasonable rate of interest to;

(2) To pay excessive salaries or other compensation over a reasonable allowance to;

(3) To make any part of the corporation's services available on a preferential basis to;

(4) To make substantial purchase of securities or other property for less than adequate consideration from;

(5) Sell any substantial part of the property of the corporation for less than an adequate consideration; or

(6) To engage in any other transaction which results in substantial diversion of the corporation's income, assets or corpus to:

> The subscribers, members, officers or directors of the corporation or to any person who has made a substantial contribution to the corporation, or to any brother or sister, (whether by the half or whole blood), spouse, ancestor or lineal descendant of the foregoing or to any corporation controlled by any of the foregoing either directly or indirectly of 50(FIFTY) percent of the total combined voting power of such corporation.

Article IV

<u>DIRECTORS</u>

There shall be no less than 3(THREE) nor more than 7(SEVEN) members of the initial Board of Directors of the corporation. The number of Directors may be increased by the affirmative vote of the members as provided in the by-laws. The names and addresses of the persons who are to serve as Directors until the first election thereof are as follows:

Name   *Address*

_____   _____

_____   _____

Article V

<u>OFFICERS</u>

The affairs of the corporation are to be managed by a President, Vice-President, Secretary and a Treasurer. The Board of Directors may create other offices. All officers will be appointed by the Board of Directors annually at the regular annual meeting of the

Board of Directors. The names of the persons who are to serve under these Articles of Incorporation and their respective offices are:

Name	*Office*
_____	President
_____	Vice President
_____	Secretary
_____	Treasurer

Article VI

MEMBERS

The corporation shall have members. The different categories or types of membership, the qualifications attendant thereto, together with the rights and duties of the parties composing said categories of membership, financial or otherwise, shall be specified in the by-laws of the corporation.

Article VII

BY-LAWS

The by-laws of the corporation can be modified, altered, or rescinded by the Directors of the Corporation or by the members, pursuant to the By-Laws of the Corporation.

Article VIII

AMENDMENTS TO ARTICLES

The right to amend or repeal any provisions contained in these Articles of Incorporation, or any amendment hereto, is reserved to the Board of Directors and the Members as specified under the laws of Florida.

          (c)   To violate the provision of Florida Statutes, Section 617.0105, Where applicable.

     3.   Dissolution.   In the event of dissolution, the residual assets of the organization will be turned over to one or more organizations which themselves are exempt as organizations described in Section 501(c)(3) and 170(c)(2) of the Internal Revenue Code of 1986 or corresponding sections of any prior or future law, or to the Federal, State or local governments for exclusive public purposes.

Article IX

PRINCIPAL OFFICE AND REGISTERED OFFICE

The principal office of the corporation shall be located at 150 2nd Ave. N., Suite 1600 St. Petersburg, FL 33701, Pinellas County, Florida.

The name and street address of the initial registered agent of the corporation in the State of Florida is: _____ . The Board of Directors may, from time to time, appoint a substitute registered agent and move the registered office or the principal office, or both, to any other address in the State of Florida.

Article X

INCORPORATORS

The names and residence addresses of the subscribers of the Articles of Incorporation are:

Name   *Address*

_____   _____

_____   _____

IN WITNESS WHEREOF, we have subscribed our names this 01 day of February, 1995.

_____ , Incorporator

FORM NO. 8SS
Certificate:
(Place of Business and Agent for Service of Process)
(Foundation for Industrial Exchange)

Certificate Designating Place of Business or

Domicile for the Service Process within This State,

Naming Agent upon Whom Process May Be Served

In pursuance of chapter 48.091, Florida Statutes, the following is submitted, in compliance with said act:

First—That the Foundation for Industrial Exchange, desiring to organize under the laws of the State of Florida, has named _____ _____ as its agent to accept service of process within this state.

ACKNOWLEDGMENT

Having been named to accept service of process for the above stated corporation, at place designated in this certificate, I hereby accept to act in this capacity, and agree to comply with the provision of said Act relative to keeping open said office.

_____
Registered Agent

8

CHARITABLE SUBSCRIPTIONS*

*[*See* Chapter 43: Fund Raising.]

§76. SOLICITATION OF CONTRIBUTIONS

Local Government Supervision of Fund Raising

Supervision of charities by local (county) government offices is often ineffective and expensive. Proposals to cut down such offices, as too expensive, point out that queries from the public are few, or based on inadequate fact records or refusal to file formal complaints. There are few such local offices, and state supervision is said to be sufficient. [See Chapter 43–Fund Raising.]

T.C. Tobin (article), *St. Petersburg Times* (FL), p. S2 (April 18, 1995).

§79. SUBSCRIPTIONS AND CONTRIBUTIONS TO CHARITIES

Enforcement of Pledges

Charitable pledges are enforceable and become binding contracts if they constitute an offer of unilateral contract and are accepted by the charity by incurring liability in reliance thereon. "Disappointed expectations" are insufficient to enforce alleged promises, especially where the donor bequeaths some property to the charity.

Application of Versailles Foundation, Inc. 610 N.Y.S. 2d 2 (NY A.D. 1 Dept., 1994).

For information about the damages for interference with the expectation of an inheritance or gift, *see* 22 ALR 4th 1229, §5[b].

Banks should be careful when analyzing pledges before financing nonprofit projects. They should consider the size and creditworthiness of the pledges and the fundraising history of the institution. State courts vary widely in enforcing pledges, both written and oral. Some specific case histories of enforcement can be found in, McCurdy, Kay W., *Collateral Value of Charitable Pledges, The Journal of Lending & Credit Risk Management,* July, 1996.

> *See,* Seymour, Jim, *The Hands-On Approach to Web Design, PC Magazine,* July, 1996.

Fraudulent Transfers

The Federal District Court in Chicago ordered a Colorado nonprofit to return $120,450 in donations to a receiver because the donor was convicted on securities fraud charges after the donations were made from 1987 to 1989.

> Sinnock, Bonnie, and Nacson, Sharon, (article), 8 *NonProfit Times* (10) 36 (October, 1994).

In Illinois, a fraudulent transfer to a charity or religious organization exists where the evidence establishes that the debtor lacked sufficient funds to pay his debts at the time of the transfer, the indebtedness existed at the time of the transfer, and there is not adequate consideration for the transfer.

> *Scholes v. African Enterprise, Inc.,* 854 F. Supp. 1315 (N.D. IL, 1994).

Under California law, a fraudulent conveyance action, arising out of a judgment debtor's contribution of $500,000 to a political fund-raising committee for a seat at a presidential table during a fund-raising event, requires no proof of intent to defraud if the debtor made the transfer without receiving reasonably equivalent value at the time when the debtor was insolvent or became insolvent as a result of the transfer.

> *1992 Republican Senate-House Dinner Committee v. Carolina's Pride Seafood, Inc.,* 858 F. Supp. 243 (D. DC, 1994).

Religious groups were ordered by a receiver and the Court of Appeals for the seventh Circuit to refund moneys donated to them by corporations and their sole shareholder in violation of the Uniform Fraudulent Transfer Act. Religious organizations are liable under the Act and Illinois' fraudulent transfer statute if the donor obtained the money fraudulently. Neither the defense of lack of knowledge nor the defense of adequate consideration will be available to religious organizations.

> Harmon, Gail, (article) 9 *NonProfit Times* (8) 18, 20, (August, 1995).

Liability for Toxic Waste Sites

After a paint company site, Valspar, was donated to Goodwill of Chicago, Goodwill was notified by the Illinois Environmental Protection Agency that the site was a toxic site and had to be cleaned up. Cleanup costs at that time were reported to be as high as $30 million. Goodwill sued Valspar and the donor, Howard Conant, for the cost of the cleanup. After 12 years and $1.5 million in legal fees, the cleanup costs were transferred to the original owners. Along with approximately $4 million in debts due to poor business management practices, the cost of the cleanup suit forced Goodwill of Chicago into bankruptcy in 1996. This case indicates the absolute necessity of inspecting properties donated to charities for environmental hazards.

Swarden, Carlotta, (article), 10 *NonProfit Times* (7) 37 (July, 1996).

Challenged Donations

If a will unambiguously directs that funds given for research, development, and education be used at a specified university medical school, under the direction of specific doctors or their successors in the medical school, and does not provide any alternative, the funded research, development, and education must occur at the designated medical school.

Wood v. Medical Research Foundation of Oregon, 880 P. 2d 952 (OR App., 1994).

A university, as residual beneficiary of a grantor's estate, was denied enforcement of its possibility of reverter when a jury ruled that land granted to the state, under the proviso that it be used solely and exclusively for state park purposes, was properly being used for state park purposes.

Antioch University v. Department of Natural Resources, 647 So. 2d 915 (FL App. 4 Dist., 1994).

In September of 1996, the Johnson family (as in Johnson & Johnson) fought over a fortune that reaches into the billions. It was a brutal and acrimonious family fight, with allegations of infidelity and illegitimacy and hordes of lawyers. Nothing was settled. A lot of nonprofits are worried that their funding from Johnson & Johnson may evaporate because of the fight.

Clolery, Paul, (article), 10 *NonProfit Times* (12) 25 (December, 1996).

Nonprofits, Accepting Restricted Gifts, Not Bound By Donor's Intent in Connecticut

The Connecticut Supreme Court, in 1997, released a decision that basically says that institutions are free to use a donor's gift in any way the managers choose, regardless of what the donor wants. In the case decided, a foundation made a restricted gift to the University of Bridgeport. When the university was sold, the foundation didn't want its money tossed into the general funds of the university. The court held that institutions that accept restricted gifts are not bound by the donor's intent. The fundamental relationship between donor and institution is threatened by this reasoning. The court also suggested that Treasury regulations provide a donor with a tax-deduction for a gift. However, if the donor restricts the gift usage, then the donor is not entitled to the deduction. Restricted gift deduction will be allowed only if there is a "negligible" change that the restriction would cause the gift to fail.

Melquham, John, (article), 11 *NonProfit Times* (14) 12 (November, 1997).

New Philanthropy Magazine

The American Benefactor is a new philanthropy magazine being marketed to nonprofit organizations. Profit from nonprofits?

Miller, Judith, *New Philanthropy Magazine Seeks Profit from Nonprofits. The New York Times*, March 24, 1997.

Choosing a "Worthy" Charity

A new *NonProfit Times*/Barna Research survey of 1,200 people nationwide in January of 1993 indicated that public giving is closely related to the percent a charity spends on programs. Fifty-four percent of those surveyed said that donation-worthy charities had to spend a certain percent of donations on programs. Only 12 percent said that it is acceptable for a nonprofit organization to spend less than 30 percent on programs. Eleven percent said that a nonprofit must spend 90 percent or more on programs. The median amount the public believes a nonprofit should spend on programs is 75 percent, which reinforces a 1993 Independent Sector study.

Sarver, Patrick (article) 8 *NonProfit Times* (4) 1 (April, 1994).

Information Sources

The *National Charities Information Bureau,* founded in 1918, promotes informed giving to charities and maintains standards for leadership and management of NPOs. Address: 1841 Broadway, New York, NY 10023.

Gift Givers Guide, by Florida Dept. of Agriculture and Consumer Services, published December 1993, lists 1,954 charities registered to show amounts (percent) each one spent on administration and program service as a guide to contributors to charities.

> A. Yoemans, report, Associated Press, *St. Petersburg (FL) Times,* p. 4B (December 21, 1993).

Wise Giving Guide, current issues, issued intermittently by National Charities Information Bureau, Inc., 19 Union Sq. W., New York, NY 10003–3395.

To check on local or state charities call your county Charitable Solicitations Officer; in Florida call the C.S. Section of the Dept. of Agriculture and Consumer Services, (800) 435–7352.

Contributors to charities should not blindly give to unknown ones. Information about a charity can be had, for the asking, from legitimate charities, such as written data on how the money is spent and how much goes to administration and how much to the services offered. For example, in Florida charities must register with the state's Division of Consumer Services at the Department of Agriculture, (800) 435–7352.

To check on national charities, address Philanthropic Advisory Service of the Council of Better Business Bureaus, 4200 Wilson Blvd., Arlington, VA 22303–1804, (703) 276–0100, or the National Charities Information Bureau, 19 Union Sq. W., New York, NY 10003–3395, (212) 929–6300.

Taxpayer Bill of Rights 2

Nonprofit hospitals and other tax-exempt organizations, including health-care industry trade associations, will have to provide greater public access to their books and federal tax returns under the Taxpayer Bill of Rights 2, passed in 1996. The bill also gives taxpayers greater leverage to deal with the IRS for unfair treatment.

> Burda, David, "New Tax Law Opens Books of Not-For-Profits," *Modern Healthcare,* August 5, 1996. *See also,* Jordan, R., and Quynn, Katelyn L., *Planned Giving: Management, Marketing, and Law,* John Wiley & Sons, Inc., New York, NY, 1994 (includes disk); White, Douglas E., *The Art of Planned Giving,* John Wiley & Sons, Inc., New York, NY, 1995.

§84. CONTRIBUTIONS BY CORPORATIONS AND ASSOCIATIONS

See, Chapter 1, §1 for the 1996 Charitable Donation Statistics.

Mandatory Contributions

Mandatory community service, imposed by a school district on students, is not illegal under the Thirteenth Amendment. Parents have no constitutional right that allows their children to opt out of educational curriculum. Where there are a large number of community service options available, involving many "neutral" agencies and organizations, mandatory community service programs do not violate the Fourteenth Amendment.

> *Immediato by Immediato v. Rye Neck School District,* 873 F. Supp. 846 (S.D. NY, 1995).

The portion of an employee's salary, which is voluntarily designated as a donation to their employer, a health care provider, is not costs "actually incurred," as required for reimbursement to participating Medicare providers of "reasonable costs" of medical services where the funds never leave the employer's account and are never paid to the employee.

> *Sta-Home Home Health Agency, Inc. v. Shalala,* 34 F. 3d 305 (5th Cir., 1994).

State Law for Political Contributions

For information about the power of corporations to make political contributions or expenditures under state law, *see* 79 ALR 3d 491, §8[b].

1990s Trends in Corporate Giving

In 1996, there is an increasing trend toward noncash and in-kind gifts by corporations. Those interested should contact local businesses as well as national sources. For information about national donation placement programs, contact:

General Retail, Business, and Industrial Merchandise

National Association for the Exchange of Industrial Resources, 560 McClure St., P.O. Box 8076, Galesburg, IL 61402, Phone (800) 562–0955, Fax (309) 343–3519.

Used Computer Hardware

Non-Profit Computing, 40 Wall St., Suite 2124, New York, NY 10005–1301, Phone (212) 759–2368, Fax (212) 793–5723, e-mail npc@igc.org

Discounted Computer Hardware and Software

Consistent Computer Bargains, 1100 Commerce Drive, Suite 113, Racine, WI 53406, Phone (800) 342–4222, Fax (414) 886–1940.

Software Review Packages, Legal and Surplus Software

CompuMentor, 89 Stilman St., San Francisco, CA 94107, Phone (415) 512–7784, Fax (415) 512–9629, e-mail compumentor@igc.apc.org

Business Donations of Goods and Computers

Gifts in Kind America, 700 North Fairfax St., Suite 300, Alexandria, VA 22314, Phone 703–836–2121, Fax 703–549–1481, e-mail GIKA_donation-@gika.cais.com

Corporations are now looking for investments in charities that help either the company or its employees. Popular in-kind gifts by corporations include equipment, computers, and training. Gifts that accomplish sales and marketing objectives while enhancing the corporate image are favored. Overseas donations by corporations have increased, with 35 percent of polled corporations reporting that they have foreign giving programs in 1995.

See McIlquham, John, (article) 9 *NonProfit Times* (7) 5 (July, 1995).

Corporations in the 1990s are being forced to expand into global markets, trim costs, decentralize, change leadership frequently, and employ total management principles in order to remain competitive. Corporate giving must be related to the company's primary business. Charitable donations are considered to be investments designed to achieve concrete results. Corporate grant-makers are being forced to demonstrate the relevance of their companies' community involvement to the community and to their companies. Thus, companies are focusing on merging societal need with corporate interest and expertise. Most companies want to know and help decide where their money is going. One school of thought believes that companies have a moral obligation to get something back for their stockholders when they donate. Corporate giving often resembles joint venturing. For example, Project Hope's partnership with a major pharmaceutical company on women's health program, in Eastern

Europe, allows Project Hope to get access to a new and potentially lucrative market in exchange for its goodwill. Similarly, AFC, Inc., parent company of Popeye's and Church's Chicken, contributes to Habitat for Humanity in exchange for mention of the restaurant in press material sent out to announce new construction.

Increasingly, public-purpose marketing has allowed companies to invest in issues in order to mesh principles and profits. The results can range from consumer loyalty to enhancement of the company's social image.

> Jepson, Sarah, article, 8 *NonProfit Times* (6) 1, 41 (June, 1994); Mehegan, Sean, article, 8 *NonProfit Times* (6) 1, 36–39 (June, 1994); Steckel, Richard and Lehman, Jennifer, article, 8 *NonProfit Times* (6) (June, 1994).

Gender-Sensitive Giving

A survey by the National Coalition of Girls' Schools indicated in 1994 that alumnae donations are increasing. All 25 schools responding indicated increased giving in the past five years. Both numbers of donations and amounts had increased in 92 percent of the schools. Half the schools received increased annual funds, major gifts, and planned giving. In 1990–1991, gifts to girls' day schools totaled $13.8 million. That figure increased to $16.3 million in 1991–1992.

> 8 *NonProfit Times* (5) 6 (May, 1994).

A study by Molly Mead, of Lincoln Filene Center at Tufts University, indicated that in 1994 only 6 percent of Boston's city foundation dollars were specifically targeted for women and girls, even though women and girls represent more than 76 percent of the city's poor. Though men and boys receive more universal benefit programs, they actually receive only 2 percent of gender-targeted grants.

> 8 *NonProfit Times* (5) 37 (May, 1994).

International Philanthropy

> *See, The Americas: An Expanding Nonprofit Sector.* (international philanthropy) Milton Cerny. *Tax Notes International,* Feb. 20, 1995 10 n8 p650–658, *International Philanthropy; The Pacific Rim—Fertile Ground for the Voluntary Sector.* Milton Cerny. *Tax Notes International,* Dec. 12, 1994 9 n24 p1845–1849.

Charity Complaints

The council of Better Business Bureaus (CBBB) has created an on-line service where consumers can file complaints against businesses and charities on the CBBB's World Wide Web page. The complaints will be forwarded to the non-profit along with a request that appropriate action be taken. The complaint line is located at http://www.bbb.org/bbb/

9

TAX EXEMPTION (FEDERAL)

§85. TAX EXEMPTION, IN GENERAL

Public Opinion of Tax-Exemption

Corrupt practices in associations and other not-for-profit organizations have seriously eroded the public's trust in these institutions. Nonprofits have received negative public attention because of their tax-exempt status, even while they control assets estimated at $1 trillion. Misdeeds by executives have not helped. Some consider nonprofits to be stigmatized "special interest groups." For some measures nonprofits can take to restore the public trust *see,* Waters, Susan B., *Rekindling the Public Trust, Association Management,* June, 1996. *See also,* Herzlinger, Regina E., *Can Public Trust in Nonprofits and Governments Be Restored?, Harvard Business Review,* March–April, 1996.

For additional recent developments in federal tax law, consult the *Non-Profit Legal & Tax Letter,* Organization Management, Inc., 13231 Pleasantview Lane, Fairfax, VA 22033, Phone (703) 968–7039, Fax (703) 818–0259. *See also, Exempt Organizations.* (Important Developments During the Year) *Tax Lawyer,* Summer 1994 47 n4 p1173–1191; *Tax Priorities for Not-For-Profits.* (Brief Article) *Journal of Accountancy,* Sept. 1995 180 n3 p27(1).

Current Developments

Structural Tax Reform

In 1996 there has been discussion of several approaches to structural tax reform, including a flat tax on income or a consumption or sales tax. All of these plans affect tax-exempt organizations and their contributors. All may threaten tax exemption and the charitable contribution deduction, which may be eliminated. Organizations may wish to monitor these developments and participate in the debate. (*See,* H.R. 2060, the Armey flat tax plan, and S. 722, the Nunn-Domenici USA tax.)

IRS Releases

A number of IRS releases have clarified several issues related to qualified retirement plan law changes enacted under the Small Business Job Protection

Act. Notice 96-97 provides guidance on the revised required beginning date for the qualified plan distributions under IRC section 401(a)(9). Revenue Procedures 96-56 and 96-63 identify changes in the private letter ruling process for IRC section 457 nonqualified deferred compensation plans for tax-exempts and state and local government employees.

> Sollee, William L., and Schneider, Paul J., *IRS Guidance Relating to Small Business Act Changes, The Journal of Taxation,* February, 1997.

§86. TYPES OF EXEMPT ORGANIZATIONS

Tax-Exempt Categories

The major categories of tax-exempt NPO purposes and activities are sketched, as to IRC §501(c) types of organizations, pages 276 *et seq.* of the main text of this treatise (6th ed.). That text speaks in general terms as to such organizations that are "charitable," "religious," "educational," "scientific," and so on. Some categories are very specific, such as credit unions. It is emphasized that consultation with IRS agency advisors ought to be sought in specific cases. It is the authors' belief that: It is amazing how much help one can get by just asking.

The IRS can be very specific. For example: *Activity Code Numbers* for very many *specific* (numbered) identification purposes are listed in the *Instructions* for *IRS Form 1024* Application for Recognition of Exemption Under Section 501(a) [main text page 365 of this Treatise]. Applicants choose (and indicate) up to three specific (numbered) activities that apply to their organizations.

General Categories of NPO Exempt Activities

Each category contains a numbered list of more specific descriptive words for various kinds of such activities.

> Religious Activities
> Schools, Colleges, and Related Activities
> Cultural, Historical, or Other Educational Activities
> Other Instruction and Training Activities
> Health Services and Related Activities
> Scientific Research Activities
> Business and Professional Organizations

Farming and Related Activities

Mutual Organizations

Employee or Membership Benefit Organizations

Sports, Athletic, Recreational, and Social Activities

Conservation, Environmental, and Beautification Activities

Housing Activities

Inner City or Community Activities

Civil Rights Activities

Litigation and Legal Aid Activities

Advocacy

Other Activities Directed to Individuals

Other Purposes and Activities

In addition, IRS Form 1024 is more specific as to some kinds of NPOs.

IRS Form 1024, Categories of NPOs for Tax Exemption

IRS Form 1024 [Application for Recognition of Exemption Under Section 501(a) or for Determination Under Section 120 (Rev. Dec. 1989)] lists the following other categories, by IRS Section; specifically on text page 370):

Sec. 501(c)(2)—Title holding corporations.

Sec. 501(c)(4)—Civic leagues, social welfare organizations (including certain war veterans organizations or local associations of employees).

Sec. 501(c)(5)—Labor, agricultural, or horticultural.

Sec. 501(c)(6)—Business leagues, chambers of commerce, and so on.

Sec. 501(c)(7)—Social clubs.

Sec. 501(c)(8)—Fraternal beneficiary societies providing life, sick, accident, or other benefits to members.

Sec. 501(c)(9)—Voluntary employer beneficiary associations.

Sec. 501(c)(10)—Domestic fraternal societies and orders not providing life, sick, accident, or other benefits.

Sec. 501(c)(12)—Benevolent life insurance associations, mutual ditch or irrigation companies, mutual or cooperative telephone companies, or like organizations.

Sec. 501(c)(13)—Cemeteries, crematoria, or like organizations.

Sec. 501(c)(15)—Mutual insurance companies or associations, other than life or marine.

Sec. 501(c)(17)—Trusts providing for payment of supplemental unemployment benefits.

Sec. 501(c)(19)—A post, organization, or auxiliary unit of past or present members of the armed forces of the United States.

Sec. 501(c)(20)—Trust/organization for prepaid group legal services.

Sec. 501(c)(25)—Title holding corporations or trusts.

Sec. 120—Qualified group legal services plan.

Nonprofit Status

For more information about nonprofit purposes and the character that warrants the creation of a nonprofit corporation, *see* 16 ALR 2d 1345.

§88. 501(c)(3) ORGANIZATIONS

The Inurement of Earnings Test

For information about when earnings of a religious, charitable, educational, or similar organization inure to the benefit of private shareholders or individuals within the meaning of 26 USCS §501(c)(3), *see* 92 ALR Fed. 255. *See also, Private Inurement, Private Benefit, and Exempt Purpose: Implications of Airlie Foundation, Inc. v. United States.* Ellen P. Aprill. *Major Tax Planning,* Annual 1994 46 p23–1(28).

Private Inurement

In 1996, Peter Diamandopolous, president of Long Island's Adelphi University and the university's board are being investigated for violation of New York's charities laws. His deferred compensation, living arrangements, and other perks have led to allegations of private inurement. His salary is one of the highest in the nation among small college presidents. Adelphi could have its tax exemption revoked or receive intermediate sanctions for private inurement violations if the allegations are proved.

> Sheppard, Lee A., *Exempt Organizations: A Tale of Guyland Greed, Tax Notes,* August 12, 1996.

Newt Gingrich and Self-Enrichment

Gingrich accepted the copyright to his college course materials from its sponsoring nonprofit group, The Progress & Freedom Foundation. He then lifted many sections of the materials verbatim and put them into a book, earning $471,000 in book sales. Gingrich's personal earnings on the book violated non-profit law tax.

> Chait, Jonathan, *Cooked Book: How Newt Enriched Himself,* (Newt Gingrich's ethics case), *The New Republic,* February 3, 1997.

Intermediate Sanctions

The intermediate sanctions in the Taxpayer Bill of Rights 2, passed by Congress in July, 1996, will act as an alternative penalty for excess benefit transactions and private inurement. The sanctions can result in revocation of an organization's tax-exempt status under existing law. The bill also protects volunteers, honorary directors, and unpaid trustees from the responsible person tax penalty under IRC Section 6672.

> Stokeld, Fred, *Intermediate Sanctions Move Closer to Reality, Tax Notes,* July 22, 1996.

Taxpayers Bill of Rights 2

The Taxpayers Bill of Rights 2, enacted in 1996, establishes penalty excise taxes and higher disclosure standards for transactions between tax-exempt organizations under IRC Sections 501(c)(3) and 501(c)(4) and organizational managers or disqualified persons. Personal liability for the excise taxes attaches for excess benefits accrued in transactions with the organization. While the penalties are considered intermediate sanctions, the IRS may choose to pursue revocation of exempt status as well. Providing contemporaneous documentation will shift the burden of proof on excess benefit transactions to the IRS.

> Griffith, Gerald M., *Impact of the Taxpayer Bill of Rights 2 on Exempt Organizations, Taxes: The Tax Magazine,* August, 1996.

Penalties on Doctors

The IRS can now penalize doctors who profit from financial deals with nonprofit hospitals under legislation signed into law on July 31, 1996. Under the "Taxpayer Bill of Rights 2" the IRS has new legal recourse against individuals who illegally benefit from charitable institutions. Hospital managers, trustees, and directors will also be affected by the legislation.

> Johnson, Julie, *New IRS Tax, Penalties Target Doctors in Deals with Hospitals,*
> *American Medical News,* September 9, 1996.

Compensation Arrangements

In a determination letter issued to *Marietta Health Care Physicians, Inc.,* the IRS has approved incentive compensation where the compensation involves productivity bonuses and not revenue-sharing arrangements not linked to individual productivity.

The payemnt of supplemental compensation to only one university employee by a university foundation will not constitute inurement that jeopardizes the university's exempt status. PLR 9546015.

Reliance on Section 482

In the "National Geographic ruling," the IRS relied on Section 482 to determine whether licensing agreements, rental agreements, and loan agreements between an exempt organization and its taxable subsidiary were negotiated for fair market value. In that case, there were no issues of inurement or private benefit found. PLR 9542045.

§89. RELIGIOUS PURPOSES

Scientology Church

The Scientology Church was ruled by the IRS to be a tax-exempt church, in 30 "determination letters" that it issued in October 1993, ending a fight for exemption that lasted decades.

> Garcia (report), *St. Petersburg (FL) Times,* p. 1 (Oct. 13, 1993).

> *See also,* Rich, Frank, *Who Can Stand Up?, The New York Times,* March 16, 1997.

§90. CHARITABLE PURPOSES

Integrated Delivery Systems

Nonprofit integrated delivery systems (IDSs) are being formed in response to the move toward managed health care systems. IDSs combine hospitals, individual physicians, and other medical service providers. The IRS has exempted such organizations since 1993. However, the IRS balances the community benefits of such organizations with the private interests of those involved. Hospitals must demonstrate "community benefit" "including a medical staff open to all physicians in the area; a board composed of community leaders; a full-time emergency room open to all individuals regardless of their ability to pay; participation in Medicare and similar programs on a nondiscriminatory basis; integration of hospital and physician services to eliminate duplication of tests and procedures and increased efficiency; and the operation of medical research and education programs." The IRS limits, to 20 percent, group representation on the board and will examine whether the medical group and physicians are receiving more than incidental benefit.

> 8 *NonProfit Times* (5) 31 (May, 1994). *See also Integrated Delivery Systems—the "Promised Land" of Health Care: Obtaining a Federal Income Tax Exemption as a Nonprofit Organization Under Section 501(c)(3) of the Internal Revenue Code.* Valerie N. Hosfeld. *University of Dayton Law Review,* Fall, 1994; *Overview of the Tax Treatment of Nonprofit Hospitals and Their For-Profit Subsidiaries: A Short-Sighted View Could Be Very Bad Medicine.* Andrea I. Castro. *Pace Law Review,* Winter, 1995.

Telephone Counseling Services

Telephone counseling services, provided by a nonprofit organization promoting a pro-majority agenda, are not exclusively charitable for the purposes of a federal charitable income tax exemption where the organization is unable to document the amount of calls received per month and shows no evidence as to training of its counselors, advertising of its services, or the scope of its counseling.

> *Nationalist Movement v. Commissioner of Internal Revenue,* 37 F. 3d 216 (5th Cir., 1994).

Section 501(c)(7) Social Clubs

Sale of Land

In *Deer Park Country Club v. Commissioner,* 70 TCM 1445 (1995) the Tax Court held that engagement of a layout designer did not satisfy the direct use test of Section 512(a)(3)(D) and also held that the intent to use the land for the social club's exempt purpose did not satisfy the use test. When the social club sold 11 of 14 homesites, required to be sold by the banks providing the project financing, the IRS determined that the gain on the sales was subject to UBIT under Section 512(a)(3)(D).

§92. EDUCATIONAL PURPOSES

The value of on-campus housing, provided for school staff, may be subject to FICA and income tax withholding. Such housing may be excluded from an employee's gross income if it is furnished on the business premises, furnished for the employer's convenience, the employee accepts the housing as a condition of employment, and the lodging is "necessary to enable the employee to properly perform the duties of his employment."

> Harmon, Gail, & Kingsley, Elizabeth, (article), 8 *NonProfit Times* (10) 38 (October, 1994).

§94. SOCIAL WELFARE ORGANIZATIONS

For more information about federal tax-exempt status as a nonprofit social welfare organization under 26 USCS §501(c)(4), *see* 87 ALR Fed. 708.

Lobbying by Social Welfare Organizations

See, Senate Votes to Ban Federal Grants to 501(c)(4) Groups that Lobby. (Brief Article) John Godfrey. *Tax Notes* July 31, 1995 68 n5 p523–524.

<u>Exempt Purposes</u>

A large homeowner's association for "a large, isolated community that is similar to a town or village" qualified as a Section 501(c)(4) organization. Thus, fee income from the association's recreational facilities will not be taxed as UBI. PLR 9539005.

Under Section 18 of the Lobbying Disclosure Act of 1995, Section 501(c)(4) organizations that lobby, as defined in the Act, would not be permitted to receive federal government grants or enter into contracts with the federal government.

§95. OTHER ORGANIZATIONS EXEMPT UNDER §501(c)

In *Nonprofits' Insurance Alliance of California v. The United States,* the Court of Federal Claims ruled, in 1995, that a mutual self-insurance organization, formed by charities, did not qualify for federal tax-exemption because the organization operated for a substantial nonexempt and commercial purpose. Though mutual benefit corporations are granted an exemption under section 501(c)(15) if premiums are less than $350,000 per year, the organization's premiums rose above the allowable limit. "Competition with commercial firms is strong evidence of predominance of non-exempt commercial purposes."

Harmon, Gail, (article), 9 *NonProfit Times* (3) 42, 46 (March, 1995).

§96. EXEMPT STATUS DERIVED OUTSIDE OF §501(c)

Tax-Exempt Pension Plans

See also, Chapter 32, §336, under Employee 403(b) Tax-Sheltered Annuity Plans and 401(k) Plans.

A hospital, using a pension plan, may be stripped of its tax-exempt status if the IRS audits it and finds lack of compliance with the *complex* rules for retirement plans under Section 403(b). Under this section, "employees may exclude from their gross income, subject to certain limits, premiums paid on a contract that will provide them with an annuity for their retirement. The funding vehicle can be an individual or a group annuity contract. Alternatively, the plan may be funded with mutual fund shares held in a custodial account meeting applicable tax code requirements." This arrangement is termed a "mutual fund custodial account." . . . "Only organizations tax exempt under §501(c)(3), or public school systems, colleges, or universities can offer §403(b) plans to their employees." Many hospitals are exempt under §501(c)(3). The employer pays the premiums. While a hospital may make contributions to a 403(b) plan, this often is done by reducing the employee salaries, by agreement.

Nassau and Marlin, IRS Targets Retirement Programs, *Natl. L.J.,* B8 (Sept. 5, 1994). *See also, Nonprofit Supplemental Pension Plans After 1993.* Michael C. Mann. *The Tax Adviser,* January, 1995.

Taxpayer Voluntary Compliance (TVC) Program

The IRS believes its Taxpayer Voluntary Compliance program, initiated in 1995, has been very successful in examining the tax liability of public schools and tax-exempt charities' annuities. Thus, the IRS will probably extend the program prior to its October 31, 1996 expiration date. Sanctions imposed under the program have been low, averaging 10 percent of the total sanction amount, although few reviews had been conducted by mid-1996. Employers seem afraid of the potentially large sanctions under the program, in which they must correct all identified defects and pay a voluntary correction fee along with any sanctions.

Wright, Caroline, *IRS Touts Annuity Compliance Program; Employers Aren't So Sure, Tax Notes,* August 12, 1996.

Tax Exemption Through Affiliation

A subsidiary health maintenance organization, that is not entitled to exempt status on its own, may only receive exempt status as an integral part of a parent or affiliated entity, qualified as a charitable organization if (1) it is not regularly carrying on a trade or business that is unrelated to the charitable organization's exempt activities, and (2) its relationship to the charitable organization boosts its own exempt character to a point that the subsidiary would be entitled to charitable status.

> *Geisinger Health Plan v. Commissioner of Internal Revenue Service,* 30 F. 3d 494 (3rd Cir., 1994) (exemption denied). *See also, "Year-End" Tax Planning for Partnerships with Tax-Exempt Partners.* Scott St. Clair. *The Tax Adviser,* July, 1995.

College Tuition Trust Funds

A Michigan educational trust fund, established to enable parents to pre-pay tuition at state colleges or universities, does not have to pay tax on its investment income. Such trust funds are "political subdivisions" and "an integral part of the state," according to the U.S. Court of Appeals for the Sixth Circuit.

> *State of Michigan v. United States,* 40 F. 3d 817 (6th Cir., 1994).

§98. SPECIAL RULES FOR 501(c)(3) ORGANIZATIONS

A pro-white advocacy organization, The Nationalist Movement (TNM), was denied 501(c)(3) tax-exempt status by the U.S. Court of Appeals for the Fifth District because a substantial portion of its activities, specifically its litigation activities and its social services programs, did not serve charitable purposes.

> Harmon, Gail, (article), 9 *NonProfit Times* (2) 30 (February, 1995).

The Inurement of Earnings Test

For information about when earnings of a religious, charitable, educational, or similar organization inure to the benefit of private shareholders or individuals within the meaning of 26 USCS §501(c)(3), *see* 92 ALR Fed. 255.

§100. MAINTAINING EXEMPT STATUS

Form 990

1997 Changes to IRS Form 990

An item requiring disclosure of the number of persons employed by an exempt organization was added on March 12, 1997. The data will give the IRS some idea as to the size of the organization as well as aid in employee tax audits.

Bathchilder, Melissa, (article), 11 *NonProfit Times* (14) 4 (November, 1997).

990-T Filers Down, Unrelated Business Tax Up

The IRS, in its quarterly Statistics of Income (SOI) Bulletin stated that the number of Form 990-T filers dropped by 5 percent between 1992 and 1996. However, unrelated business income taxes reportedly jumped 13 percent during the same period.

Sinclair, Matthew, (article), 10 *NonProfit Times* (7) 5 (July, 1996).

Insiders

In 1996, Form 990 began to require more disclosure including requirements for reporting noncash donations, tax-exempt bond liabilities, and member dues allocable to lobbying. Cash and noncash contributions and grants must be reported separately. Program service revenues received, including government fees and contracts must be shown, including the gross amount of program-related sales of inventory. "Key employees" and "family members" are now classified as "insiders." Charities must report major transactions with these "insiders." Deferred compensation to officers, directors, trustees, key employees, and the five highest paid employees must be reported.

8 *NonProfit Times* (5) 17 (May, 1994).

Insider Representation on the Governing Boards of Nonprofit Hospitals

See, Young, Gary J., *Insider Representation On the Governing Boards of Nonprofit Hospitals: Trends and Implications for Charitable Care, Inquiry*, Winter, 1997.

Filing Exemption

Though charities are generally required to file an annual Form 990 with the IRS, churches (and their affiliates) and charities that normally have less than $25,000 in gross receipts each year are exempt from filing Form 990. If required to file a Form 990, a charity must report the names and addresses of all persons who contributed or bequeathed $5,000 or more (cash or property) during the reporting year. However, the names of such donors are not subject to public inspection.

See IRS Form 990 (1996).

Organizations that are affiliated with governmental units are exempt from Form 990 filing requirements.

See, Hanrehan, Barbara, (article), *The Tax Adviser,* March 1995 26 n3 p152(3).

§101. LOSS OF TAX EXEMPTION (PROHIBITED TRANSACTIONS)

Atheists Facing Exemption Revocation

Two well-known atheist organizations, the Charles E. Stevens American Atheist Library and Archives (Library) and the Society of Separationists (Society) are fighting with the Internal Revenue Service (IRS) over the recognition of their exempt status, which was revoked retroactively by the IRS in December of 1996. The organizations are two of the five nonprofit organizations led by the missing renowned atheist Madalyn Murray O'Hair. The IRS determined that the organization provided private benefits to O'Hair and others. The organizations say that any inconsistencies in their records are due to the difficulty the organizations had in obtaining competent accounting assistance because of their unpopular cause. Both organizations have filed petitions for declaratory judgment with the Tax Court to have their exempt status reinstated.

Harmon, Gail, (article), 11 *NonProfit Times* (7) 40 (May, 1997).

Abusive Tax Shelters

An association may be a "partnership," for purposes of filing tax informational returns, even if there is no commonality of interest between members and profits and losses generated by the association. Recently, a barter association's warehouse bank was fined as an "abusive tax shelter" because the bank's advertising material emphasized account holders' privacy and common-law rights of contract. Thus, the Internal Revenue Service (IRS) maintained that the material contained messages that the holders could avoid the IRS. Several members were convicted of tax crimes.

National Commodity and Barter Association/National Commodity Exchange v. US, 843
    F. Supp. 655 (D. CO, 1993).

Hospital-Doctor Recruitment Tax Rules

Health-care NPOs' luring of top-talent specialists, with high-pay benefits, may endanger their tax exemption if *too* plainly profit-intended. Under new 1995 IRS guidelines [IRS Announcement 95–25] the key test of tax-privilege entitlement is whether or not an *incentive* to the M.D. (such as private offices or payment of malpractice insurance premiums) actually helps the hospital to fulfill a community need. A fourfold analysis of this question is: (1) Similar specific incentives of other hospitals in the area; (2) General incentives in the area; (3) Similar incentives in medical schools in the area; (4) Similar operating needs of private practice M.D.s.

Violation of IRS standards may result in heavy tax penalties.

Gary Taylor (article), *Natl. L.J.,* p. B1 (May 8, 1995).

Action and Propaganda Organizations

See, Political Activities of Tax-Exempt Nonprofit Organizations: An Overview. John J. Silver. *Colorado Lawyer,* Sept 1995 24 n9 p2157(4). *See also,* Chapter 39 of the main text and supplement.

The IRS, in 1995, stripped a New York church, the Church at Pierce Creek, of its tax-exempt status after the church bought advertisements denouncing Bill Clinton as a supporter of gay rights, teen sex, and abortion on demand. The advertisement asked, "How then can we vote for Bill Clinton?" Under federal law, 501(c)(3) churches and charities are prohibited from "participating" in or "intervening" in political campaigns, including "the publication or distribution of written . . . or oral statements on behalf or in opposition to . . . a candidate." Jimmy Swaggart Ministries and Jerry Falwell's Old Time Gospel Hour have been, in the past, ordered to pay fines for similar political intervention activity.

Mehegan, Sean, (article) 9 *NonProfit Times* (6) 18 (June, 1995).

In 1995, the IRS denied tax exemption to an organization that conducts seminars and produces newsletters critical of the Israeli government and U.S. Middle East policy. The IRS justified its denial by stating that the organization engages in too much lobbying activity and promotes "anti-Israel propaganda" rather than educational materials. According to the IRS, the organization lobbies by taking positions on legislative issues and encouraging members to contact their Congressional representatives. In order to qualify as an educational institution, organizations must present a "fair and full exposition" of facts in order to provide sufficient information to form their own conclusions. The decision is on appeal and will determine whether the "action organization" standard is constitutional.

Harmon, Gail, 9 *NonProfit Times* (6) 51 (June, 1995).

Standing to Challenge Tax Exemption

A presidential candidate, who was denied the opportunity to participate in a televised election debate, lacked standing and a concrete injury to seek revocation of the tax-exempt status of the bipartisan voter education group that cosponsored the debate.

Fulani v. Bentsen, 35 F. 3d 49 (2nd Cir., 1994).

Disclosure of Financial Information

See also, Herman, Tom, *Tax-Exempt Groups Soon Will Face New Pressure to Disclose Information, (New Legislation Requires Tax-Exempt Organizations to Disclose Financial Information to Public Upon Request), The Wall Street Journal,* August 21, 1996.

Private Foundations

Section 4941 Self-Dealing

When a bank acts as a custodian or investment advisor, but not as a trustee, unbundling banking fees so that fees attributable to investment banking services are separately stated, is not inconsistent with the general banking services exception to the self-dealing rules. PLR 9535043.

A foundation may reimburse members of a council of a family foundation for expenses incurred in connection with training for future service as foundation directors without a finding of self-dealing. PLR 9546020.

A 30-year loan made to a foundation manager as part of his compensation package at the time of his hiring is not an act of continuing self-dealing. Also, a separate act of self-dealing does not occur each year that the principal remains unpaid. PLR 9530032 revoking PLR 9343033.

Section 4942 Mandatory Distributions

A private foundation will not be treated as controlled by one or more disqualified persons unless the disqualified persons have sufficient voting power to determine what distributions are made. PLR 9547035.

A private foundation may recompute its minimum investment return for all open years even if certain years are already closed. PLR 9530033.

A foundation may make contingent set-asides pending the outcome of litigation under Treas. Reg. §53.4942(a)-3(b)(9). PLR 9540045.

§103. UNRELATED BUSINESS INCOME TAX [UBIT]

See, Exempt Organizations and UBIT. (unrelated business income tax) Nicholas Fiore. *Journal of Accountancy,* Sept. 1994 178 n3 p34(1); *Unrelated Business Income Tax: New Developments, Audit Issues and Planning Strategies.* Douglas M. Mancino. New York University Conference on Tax Planning for 501(c)(3) Organizations, Annual 1994 22 p9–1(17).

Trade or Business

The Tax Court, in *Alumni Ass'n. of the University of Oregon, Inc. v. Commissioner,* 71 TCM 2093 (1996) has suggested a potentially significant change in emphasis in the test of whether an activity constitutes a trade or business. The court ruled that "[n] or does a desire to make money standing alone, establish that petitioner is engaged in a trade or business." The Tax Court held that "the primary purpose for engaging in the activity must be for profit." If the primacy of profit motive is found to be consistent with Supreme Court rulings, exempt organizations have a greater scope for avoiding UBIT, even if the activity is regularly carried on and is not substantially related to the organization's exempt purpose. *See also, Commissioner v. Groetzinger,* 480 U.S. 23 (1987).

Regularly Carried On

The IRS looked at the period during which advertising was sold, rather than simply at the time during which the newsletter and newspaper in which it appeared was distributed, to determine whether advertising activity was regularly carried on in TAM 9509002, Issues 4(a) and 6(a).

Substantially Related

In TAM 9550003, the IRS has ruled on whether the sale of various goods and services by a museum are substantially related to the museum's exempt purposes, both in the museum and outside the museum.

This IRS ruling introduced some ambiguity into the substantially related test of Section 513(a) and Treas. Reg. §1.513-1(d), which provide that the activity must bear an important causal relationship to the organization's exempt purpose. TAM 9550003 seems to introduce a primary purpose test, similar to the "principal purpose" test of the now repealed Treas. Reg. §1.513-1(a)(4).

The factors relied on by the IRS to determine primary purpose are, but are not limited to, the degree of connection between the item and the museum's collection, the extent to which the item sold relates to the form and design of the original item, whether "the dominant impression one gains from viewing or using the article relates to the subject matter of the original article." "Reproductions or adaptations" that were "true to the original" were substantially related. However, "interpretations of or that have designs taken from" items in the museum's collection were not substantially related. "Reproductions or adaptations" were generally accompanied by information about the original items; "interpretations" were not. "Interpretations" included furniture, dinnerware, jewelry, place mats, and tote bags. The tax treatment of such items depends on the facts and circumstances of each particular case.

Christmas cards bearing careful reproductions of objects in the museum's collection were substantially related to the museum's exempt purpose. The sale of collectible miniatures was substantially related as "reproductions or adaptations." Souvenirs, such as key rings, steins, and thimbles, carrying the museum's logo or motifs from items in the collection were not substantially related. With respect to "contemporary products," newspapers, magazines, and candy were not substantially related. "Convenience items" such as film, batteries, flashbulbs, ponchos, and umbrellas were substantially related because "they enable visitors to devote a greater portion of their time to viewing the museum," under a convenience rationale.

Off-site sales have again been treated as substantially related to a museum's exempt purpose. Rev. Rel. 73-104, 1973-1 C.B. 263. In that case, Christmas cards were held to be related.

Engraving performed in public was treated as substantially related to the museum's exempt purpose. However, engraving done in private was not substantially related.

Gift-wrapping services were not substantially related.

Sale of Electricity

The IRS has revoked PLR 8732029 in which it ruled that income from a university's sale to the local utility of excess electricity was not unrelated business income. PLR 9540062. The IRS took no position on infrequent sale of excess electricity to the local utility.

Sale of Business Forms

Income from the sale of standard business forms has been held by the IRS to be unrelated business income. PLR 9527001 and PLR 9550001.

Royalties

A Section 501(c)(6) business league, that agreed to provide a credit card company its updated mailing list based on selectivity factors or membership characteristics, and to promote the card among its members, earned UBI which did not satisfy the royalty exception. TAM 9509002, Issue 9.

In *Alumni Ass'n. of the University of Oregon, Inc. v. Commissioner,* 71 TCM 2093 (1996) the Tax Court ruled that an alumni association derived royalty income and not UBI from the provision of services from its licensing agreement with a credit card company that issued an affinity credit card. The association's promotion activities were de minimis, similar to the activities of the Sierra Club's affinity credit card program. The association did not regularly rent its mailing list. Royalties were supported by the absence of a net profits interest and the fact that the alumni association held a gross profits interest.

Trade Show Exception

Selling advertising in a convention newsletter is not a "traditional trade show activity" under the meaning of 513(c) and will be treated as UBI under the fragmentation rule. However, publishing and distributing a convention newsletter is "traditional trade show activity." TAM 9509002, Issue 4(a).

Amounts received from exhibitors who sponsored convention activities, such as the president's reception, a scientific paper presentation, and a party for members of the organization are not UBI where such amounts are received to support traditional trade show activities. TAM 9509002, Issue 8(b).

Section 501(c)(6) organizations that receive contributions for traditional trade show activities could be subject to Section 6113 disclosure of nondeductibility requirements. However, Section 501(c)(6) organizations that do not engage in a clear pattern of coordinated fundraising solicitations are not. TAM 9509002, Issue 8(b).

An organization that runs a trade show at which exhibitors make sales to attendees is not responsible for Section 6041(a) information, if the purchaser, not the sponsoring organization, was the payor within the meaning of Section 6041. (Exhibitors paid the organization a commission on sales, and the purchaser paid the organization, which remitted the sale price minus the commission to the exhibitor).

Bingo

The Tax Court has ruled that instant bingo games do not qualify for the bingo exception of Section 513(f). Instant bingo is a preprinted bingo card covered with pulltabs, which are removed and compared with the winning pattern printed on the back of the card. *Julius M. Israel Lodge of B'nai Brith No. 2113 v. Commissioner,* 70 TCM 673 (1995).

Complex Structures

Control Without Attribution. A Section 501(c)(6) business league may control a taxable subsidiary that operates an electronic plan room available for a fee to members and nonmembers of the parent business league. Neither the dividends distributed to the parent nor the taxable subsidiary's income will be attributed to the parent. PLR 9601047.

Control of Nonstock Corporation. In TAM 9509002, Issue 7, the IRS ruled that control within the meaning of Section 512(b)(13) existed where the board of one organization was elected by that organization's voting members, all of whom were members of the board of another organization, which the IRS ruled was the controlling organization, even though the members were voting in their individual capacities when they elected the members of the controlled organization's board.

Control of Second Tier Subsidiaries. For the purposes of Section 512(b)(13), rental payments from a second-tier subsidiary to the parent of the first-tier subsidiary are not UBI to the parent if the parent does not control the second-tier subsidiary. PLR 9506046.

In PLR 9542045 (the "National Geographic ruling"), the IRS ruled that an exempt parent did not control, within the meaning of Section 512(b)(13), a second-tier taxable subsidiary even though this corporation had been a transitory first-tier subsidiary during the restructuring. Neither the activities of the first- nor second-tier subsidiary would be attributed to the exempt parent.

Debt-Financed Property

Substantially Related Exception. Because the activities of a disabled children's organization were substantially related to the lessor organization's exempt purposes, an organization caring for orphans and other needy children did not earn debt financed property income from its lease of land to an organization that cared for disabled children, even though it had pledged certain securities as collateral for the lessee organization's construction loan. PLR 9521013.

Commercial Type Insurance. Income from the sale of the annuities and interest income on an annuity fund will not be UBI to a college if its tuition plan has qualified as a Section 501(m)(3)(E) charitable gift annuity and has satisfied the Section 514(c)(5) exception to the debt-financed property rules. PLR 9527033.

Payment for Condemned Property. In PLR 9540046, the IRS ruled that Section 512(b)(5) applies to payments received by a Section 501(c)(5) organization in compensation for the condemnation of real property that was neither stock in trade nor property held primarily for sale to customers in the ordinary course of trade or business.

Commensurate in Scope. The IRS considered the activities of volunteers in determining whether an organization's unrelated business activities were commensurate in scope with the organization's exempt activities in TAM 9521004. Volunteers were treated as agents of the organization. The IRS balanced the time they spent on exempt activities against the revenue derived from nonexempt travel tours. The weighing of both time and income is important in understanding how the IRS interprets the commensurate in scope test. The IRS did not address whether it would treat volunteers as agents to determine whether or under what circumstances the IRS might treat volunteers as agents for other purposes such as inurement or the political intervention prohibition.

Mailing List Rental OK, Affinity Card Sales Remanded

In *Sierra Club v. Commissioner,* 9th Cir. June 20, 1996, the U.S. Court of Appeals for the Ninth Circuit found that income received by the Sierra Club, Inc., from the rental of mailing lists is royalty payment, exempt from unrelated business income tax. The collection of fees for rental of mailing lists was not participation in an unrelated business, regardless of whether the fee collection was an active or passive activity. However, the affinity card issue was remanded because the lower court's summary judgment for the taxpayer was premature.

> Wexler, Robert A., *CA-9 Affirms Mailing List Issue, Remands on Affinity Card Participation, The Journal of Taxation,* Sept. 1996.

Royalties of Associate Member Dues

The Ninth Circuit's 1996 *Sierra Club* decision provides exempts with guidance on structuring royalty arrangements, while a 1996 Fifth Circuit case provides similar guidance concerning associate member dues.

> *See* Carson, Marlis L., *Despite Sierra Club, Treatment of Mailing List Rentals Still Uncertain, Tax Notes,* July 15, 1996.

Taxation of Nonprofit Endorsement of Products

The Eighth Circuit's 1996 American Academy decision now clarifies the issues surrounding the tax treatment of nonprofits' product endorsement income. The court ruled that the physician-association involved was not subject to unrelated business income tax for income derived from a group insurance plan sponsorship. Tax liability is tied to the extent of the exempt organization's involvement in such arrangements, similar to the principles expressed in the *Sierra Club* litigation over income derived from the Sierra Club's affinity card program and sales of its mailing lists.

> *American Academy of Family Physicians v. United States* - No. 95-2791WM (8th Cir. Aug., 1996).

Merchandise Sold by College and University Bookstores

The IRS has begun to examine the commerce engaged in by tax-exempt organizations more closely, especially colleges and universities. Merchandise sold by college and university bookstores must be substantially related to the institution's exempt purpose, or offered for the convenience of students and staff, for the income to be exempt from unrelated business income taxation. For example, the sale of multiple computers to the same person in the same year may not be substantially related to the organization's purpose. The convenience test is not met by goods with useful lives exceeding one year. Guidelines, developed by the IRS, identify the limits placed on computer sales and sales to alumni and note how such stores should categorize their revenues.

> Fiore, Nicholas, *College and University Bookstores, Journal of Accountancy,* Sept. 1996 182 n3 p42(1). *See also,* Whitman, Kelcy M., *The IRS Focuses on School, College and University Bookstores, The Tax Adviser,* Sept., 1996.

The IRS issued a private-letter ruling in 1995 stating that the income from a museum's marketing arrangement with a long-distance phone company, involving endorsement of the company in return for a percentage cut of sales, was not related to the museum's exempt purpose and is subject to UBIT. Such income is not "royalties."

> 9 *NonProfit Times* (2) 10 (February, 1995).

The IRS recently clarified its position on income from licensing activities. "Royalties," though generated from unrelated trade or business, are excluded from taxation as unrelated business taxable income (UBIT). Income from licensing agreements with cash/risk management and insurance funds is considered to be "royalties." However, income derived from entities "controlled" by a nonprofit must be included in a nonprofit's UBIT. Exempt royalties must relate only to the use of a valuable right and not to the performance of services. The nonprofit must take a passive and not active role in the production of royalty income. Administrative duties, performed by the nonprofit, are allowed.

> 8 *NonProfit Times* (5) 38 (May, 1994).

If a tax-exempt business league conducts itself in a manner intended to increase profits and not in a manner intended to accomplish its exempt purpose, the income generated is unrelated business taxable income.

> *Independent Insurance Agents of Huntsville, Inc. v. C.I.R.,* 998 F. 2d 898 (11th Cir., 1993) (selling of insurance to public agencies by assigning accounts to its members and retaining 40–60 percent commission).

UBIT and Associate Member Dues

New IRS procedures, in Revenue Procedure 95–21, for monitoring associate member dues will focus on the associate members' motives for joining with an organization creating the class of members. Dues will be subject to UBIT where the "associate member category has been formed or availed of for the principal purpose of producing unrelated business income." The ruling applies only to labor and agricultural organizations under section 501(c)(5), and not to other associations such as trade associations, though trade associations face similar problems.

> *See* Harmon, Gail, (article) 9 *NonProfit Times* (6) 46 (June, 1995). *See also IRS Says Certain Associate Member Dues Could be UBI.* Mark v. Rountree. *The Tax Adviser,* Jan. 1995 26 n1 p32(1); *Membership Dues as Unrelated Business Income.* Brady J. Langford. *The Tax Adviser,* Oct. 1994 25 n10 p608(3).

No UBIT on "Allied" Member Revenue

The Internal Revenue Service (IRS) published a technical advice memorandum which holds that a 501(c)(6) association is not subject to UBIT on dues received for its "allied" members. This ruling might give an indication of the way the IRS will apply the standard to determine the taxability of associate member dues.

> *See,* Harmon, Gail, (article), 11 *NonProfit Times* (14) 16 (November, 1997).

Debt Financed Property

Interest income can be debt-financed.[1] However, the short sale of stock is not debt-financed property for the purposes of the unrelated business income tax.[2]

1. Possin, Jim, (article), *The Tax Adviser,* Feb. 1995 26 n2 p84(1).

2. Wexler, Robert A., (article), *The Journal of Taxation,* May 1995 82 n5 p286(1).

Business Purposes

In a 1995 case, involving the operation of a travel agency by a nonprofit organization that provides remedial reading instruction to school children, the IRS ruled that as long as the conduct of a business by a nonprofit organization is not the organization's primary purpose, determined by the facts and circumstances, the organization will not lose its tax exempt status, especially where the program does not unduly benefit any insider or bestow improper private benefit. Even an unrelated business that is "a substantial part of its total activities" will not result in revocation of exemption. However, the profits received from such a business are taxable as Unrelated Business Income Tax (UBIT).

> *See* Harmon, Gail, (article) 9 *NonProfit Times* (8) 31 (August, 1995); *The Business Activities of Nonprofit Organizations.* Hal Katen. *Los Angeles Lawyer,* Sept. 1995 18 n6 p24(6).

Realty Partnerships

> *See, Final Regulations on UBIT Exception for Realty Partnerships.* Lewis R. Kaster. *The Journal of Taxation,* Aug. 1994 81 n2 p100(2).

Hospitals and For-Profit Subsidiaries

> *See Overview of the Tax Treatment of Nonprofit Hospitals and Their For-Profit Subsidiaries: A Short-Sighted View Could Be Very Bad Medicine.* Andrea I. Castro. *Pace Law Review,* Wntr, 1995 15 n2 p501–538.

"Casino Nights"

In 1995, the U.S. Tax Court imposed unrelated business income tax on the income received by the Executive Network Club, in New York, through "casino nights." Tips received by volunteer waitresses and dealers were not considered to be payments to the club, and were exempted.

> Harmon, Gail, (article), 9 *NonProfit Times* (5) 44 (May, 1995).

Corporate Sponsorship of Universities

The IRS has been relatively liberal toward corporate sponsorships on university campuses, when it considers cases related to the unrelated business income tax (UBIT). For example, scoreboard advertising and advertising income from publications sold at the NCAA's annual "Final Four" men's basketball tournament have been considered to be "not regularly carried on" for purposes of UBIT. Advertising in program brochures for athletic and cultural events has been considered to be "donor acknowledgment" by the IRS, exempt from UBIT.

> 8 *NonProfit Times* (5) 39 (May, 1994); *National Collegiate Athletic Association v. Commissioner,* (Tenth Cir.).

§104. THE IRS "HIT LIST"

Audits

IRS Targets Joint Ventures (Hospitals and Universities

The IRS, as reported in CCH's *Tax Day Report*, will spend 30 percent of IRS audit resources on hospital and university examinations during 1998. Intensive audits of both the nonprofit and for-profit entities of hospital joint venture will be a top priority for the Coordinated Examination Program according to Marcus Owens, director of the IRS Exempt Organizations Division. Tax-exempt bond issuers, and gambling activities such as lotteries or "casino nights" will also be investigated to determine whether funds are being inured to private individuals and if the income constituted unrelated business taxable income. Under a statistical sampling project, examinations for 88 exempt organizations in four categories; travel tours, fraternal associations, low-income housing projects owned by exempt organizations and political organizations will be scrutinized. Political organizations, both federal and state, will be scrutinized to determine whether Forms 1120-POL have been filed reporting investment income.

Bathchilder, Melissa, (article), 11 *NonProfit Times* (14) 4 (November, 1997).

IRS Targeting Conservative Organizations?

The IRS is auditing Gingrich's Abraham Lincoln Opportunity Foundation, the Heritage Foundation, the National Rifle Association (NRA), and Citizens Against Government Waste (CAGW). There is no known cases of similar treatment of well-known liberal groups. There is a rumor that the IRS is simply being used as a tool of the White House against its political opponents, a practice criticized by conservative politicians as an abuse of power. The White House denies any exercise of influence over the IRS, either in favor of some organizations or against others. The IRS has responded to the criticism by issuing publication FS-97-8, which explains, in broad terms, what activities are permissible by certain exempt organizations and forbidden to others; how decisions about the permissibility of activities, or of levels of activity, are approached by the IRS; and what procedural rights and remedies an organization might have if it is suspected of engaging or found to have engaged in prohibited political activities. Copies can be obtained for the IRS's Website at www.irs.ustreas.gov

Harmon, Gail, (article), 11 *NonProfit Times* (7) 41–42 (May, 1997).

Improper IRS Audits of Conservative Nonprofit Organizations?

The U.S. Congress, through the Joint Committee on Taxation, plans to begin investigation into alleged political motivation behind audits of conservative nonprofit organizations by the Internal Revenue Service.

Stevenson, Richard W., *Congress Plans to Investigate Audits of Tax-Exempt Groups. The New York Times*, March 25, 1997.

The Single Audit Act Amendments of 1996

The Single Audit Act Amendments of 1996 expand the program established by the Single Audit Act of 1984, to cover nonprofit organizations that receive federal funds, and raise the threshold that triggers audit requirements. The 1984 Act had covered only state and local governments receiving federal funds. The threshold above which single audits are required has been raised from $100,000 in funding to $300,000. The law will also allow auditors to select the most risky programs and focus their efforts on those programs.

President Signs Single Audit Act of 1996, Journal of Accountancy, Sept., 1996.

In July 1996, President Clinton signed legislation to amend the Single Audit Act of 1984, which governs the auditing process by the federal government of organizations that receive federal money. The final regulations were published in the April 30, 1996 issue of the Federal Register, which is available in most local libraries.

Clolery, Paul, (article), 10 *NonProfit Times* (8) 5 (August, 1996).

Determination Letters

In 1995, IRS Commissioner Margaret Richardson announced that the IRS will create a determination letter clearinghouse in order to more effectively deal with applications by nonprofits for tax-exemption.

Ayayo, Herman P., (article), *Tax Notes,* Feb. 6, 1995 66 n6 p847(1).

Penalties and Sanctions

According to a 1995 report by the General Accounting Office, the IRS levied taxes and penalties against 501(c)(4) social welfare organizations of $484,554,000 in 1994 (up from $138 million in 1990). Taxes and penalties of $20 million were levied against 501(c)(5) labor and agricultural organizations (up from $2.4 million in 1990). Taxes and penalties levied against 501(c)(6) groups were un-changed as compared to 1990. Considering that total government audits of (c)(4)s and (c)(5)s decreased between 1990 and 1994, these figures are alarming and indicate that the IRS is stepping its scrutiny of nonprofits.

9 *NonProfit Times* (5) 5 (May, 1995). *See also Sanctions on Charities for Self-Dealing and Certain Other Activities.* Janet Buehler. *The Tax Adviser,* April, 1994.

Back Taxes

The IRS has levied $544 in back taxes and interest for 1988–92 on the nonprofit Landover Hills Boys & Girls Club Inc. The club opposes the IRS de-cision that it should have withheld federal income and Social Security taxes for volunteers at its fund-raising activities. Landover's President, Lenny Mills, also says that the IRS' demands threaten the future of the club.

Moskal, Jerry, *IRS Targets Nonprofit Kids Club Over Fund-Raisers, Washington Business Journal,* July 26, 1996.

10

FORMS FOR TAX EXEMPTION (FEDERAL)

§109. IRS FORMS FOR APPLICATION FOR RECOGNITION OF EXEMPTION

Form 10S [IRS Form 8718 (1994)]

Form **8718**	**User Fee for Exempt Organization**	For IRS Use Only
(Rev. April 1994)	**Determination Letter Request**	
Department of the Treasury Internal Revenue Service	▶ Attach this form to determination letter application. (Form 8718 is NOT a determination letter application.)	Control number _____ Amount paid _____ User fee screener _____

1 Name of organization

Caution: *Do not attach Form 8718 to an application for a pension plan determination letter. Use Form 8717 instead.*

2   Type of request   **Fee**

a ☐ Initial request for a determination letter for:
- An exempt organization that has had annual gross receipts averaging not more than $10,000 during the preceding 4 years, or
- A new organization that anticipates gross receipts averaging not more than $10,000 during its first 4 years.

$150

Note: *If you checked box 2a, you must complete the Certification below.*

Certification

I certify that the annual gross receipts of ....
name of organization

have averaged (or are expected to average) not more than $10,000 during the preceding 4 (or the first 4) years of operation.

Signature ▶   Title ▶

b ☐ Initial request for a determination letter for:
- An exempt organization that has had annual gross receipts averaging more than $10,000 during the preceding 4 years, or
- A new organization that anticipates gross receipts averaging more than $10,000 during its first 4 years .   . $ 465

c ☐ Group exemption letters .   .   .   . $ 500

Instructions

The law requires payment of a user fee with each application for a determination letter. The user fees are listed on line 2 above. For more information, see Rev. Proc. 94-8, 1994-1 I.R.B. 176.

Check the box on line 2 for the type of application you are submitting. If you check box 2a, you must complete and sign the certification statement that appears under line 2a.

Attach to Form 8718 a check or money order payable to the Internal Revenue Service for the full amount of the user fee. If you do not include the full amount, your application will be returned. Attach Form 8718 to your determination letter application.

To avoid delays, send the determination letter application and

Form 8718 to the applicable IRS address shown below. Use the address below even if a different address appears in another form or publication.

If the organization is in	Send fee and request for determination letter to
Connecticut, Maine, Massachusetts, New Hampshire, New York, Rhode Island, Vermont	Internal Revenue Service EP/EO Division P. O. Box 1680, GPO Brooklyn, NY 11202
Delaware, District of Columbia, Maryland, New Jersey, Pennsylvania, Virginia, any U.S. possession or foreign country	Internal Revenue Service EP/EO Division P. O. Box 17010 Baltimore, MD 21203
Indiana, Kentucky, Michigan, Ohio, West Virginia	Internal Revenue Service EP/EO Division P. O. Box 3159 Cincinnati, OH 45201

Arizona, Colorado, Kansas, Oklahoma, New Mexico, Texas, Utah, Wyoming	Internal Revenue Service EP/EO Division Mail Code 4950 DAL 1100 Commerce Street Dallas, TX 75242
Alabama, Arkansas, Florida, Georgia, Louisiana, Mississippi, North Carolina, South Carolina, Tennessee	Internal Revenue Service EP/EO Division P.O. Box 941 Atlanta, GA 30370
Alaska, California, Hawaii, Idaho, Nevada, Oregon, Washington	Internal Revenue Service EO Application EP/EO Division McCaslin Industrial Park 2 Cupania Circle Monterey Park, CA 91754-7406
Illinois, Iowa, Minnesota, Missouri, Montana, Nebraska, North Dakota, South Dakota, Wisconsin	Internal Revenue Service EP/EO Division 230 S. Dearborn DPN 20-5 Chicago, IL 60604

Attach Check or Money Order Here

Cat. No. 64728Z
♺ Printed on recycled paper

Form **8718** (Rev. 4-94)
*U.S. Government Printing Office: 1994 — 301-62800147

11

TAX DEDUCTIONS FOR CHARITABLE CONTRIBUTIONS*

*[*See also* Chapter 9.]

§110. FEDERAL CHARITABLE DEDUCTIONS, GENERALLY

IRS Publication 526, *Charitable Contributions,* for 1995 filing of 1994 returns, consisted of 18 pages of three column small type; very detailed and complex instructions for claims of deductions for contributions. IRS free forms can be ordered by mail from offices listed on Publication 526; Western U.S.–Rancho Cordova, CA 95743–0001; Central–P.O. Box 8903, Bloomington, IL 61702–8903; Eastern–P.O. Box 85074, Richmond, VA 23261–5074.

The *Omnibus Reconciliation Act* became law on August 11, 1993, eliminating the tax deduction for lobbying expenses. But, local and county level lobbying by chambers of commerce and by associations were exempted. Reporting and penalty requirements were lessened. Chambers spending less than $2,000/yr. were exempted. For IRS information phone (202) 463–5580. *See also* Chapter 39.

> The *Wise Giving Guide,* current issues, issued intermittently by the National Charities Information Bureau, Inc., 19 Union Sq. W., New York, NY 10003–3395.

The Charitable Giving Relief Act

The Charitable Giving Relief Act, passed by Congress and signed by President Clinton, is expected to spur an additional $16.5 billion in charitable contributions between 1998 and 2002. The legislation (HR-2499) gives support to charitable organizations, improves tax fairness and provides equal tax treatment for all charities and those who support them. The act will allow taxpayers who don't itemize on their returns to deduct 50 percent of their annual charitable contributions over $500 each year, in hopes of spurring charitable giving.

> Batchilder, Melissa, (article), 11 *NonProfit Times* (14) 5 (November, 1997).

Unusual Grants by Disqualified Persons

The IRS, in 1997, showed flexibility of application when it issued a ruling that provides further guidance on when gifts to a public charity from a disqualified person are unusual grants that may be disregarded for the public-support test. In the case ruled upon, a charity received a gift from a person disqualified with respect to the charity, due to the fact that she was both a substantial contributor to the trust and the original donor of the charity's land. She donated municipal bonds one day before she died and bequeathed a parcel of land to the charity in her will. The value of the contributions was high enough that if the public-purpose rule were applied, the organization would be tipped into private foundation status. The IRS uses a facts-and-circumstance test to apply the public-support test. The charity must be broadly, publicly supported and thus responsive to the general public, rather than to the private interests of a limited number of donors or other persons. The IRS uses nine criteria as general guidelines to decide when a grant is unusual. The organization met five of the criteria. (1) The organization had in the past attracted a significant amount of public support and would likely continue to do so in the future; (2) The organization had carried on a program of public solicitation and exempt activities; (3) The donor placed no material restrictions or conditions on the use of the donation; (4) Neither the donor nor any related person continued to have influence over the organization and; (5) The organization had a representative governing body as described in regulations.

The grant was, thus, found to be unusual.

Harmon, Gail, (article), 11 *NonProfit Times* (7) 130, 139 (May, 1997).

Property Depreciation Deductions Extended

The IRS has clarified regulations regarding lease terms and like-kind exchanges of tax-exempt properties through a report in Tax Day Report from Chicago-based CCH, Inc. Under the Code Section 168(g), alternative depreciation system, depreciation deductions are determined using the straight-line method over longer recovery periods for tax-exempt properties. Taxable properties are usually depreciated under the general depreciation system. The advanced depreciation system recovery period of tax-exempt property can be no shorter than 125 percent of the lease term.

Sinclair, Matthew, (article), 10 *NonProfit Times* (8) 39 (August, 1996).

Services

The value of personal service rendered free for charity is not deductible.

Reg. §1.170A–1(g); Rev. Rul. 1953–162, 1953–2 CB 127; Rev. Rul. 67–236, 1967–2 CB 103; *Purnell,* T.C. Memo 1993–593.

Volunteer Expenses

Unreimbursed volunteer expenses are deductible, if incurred while rendering services for charity. Deductible expenses include reasonable payment for meals, lodging, and travel expenses, to a ceiling of 50% of the taxpayer's adjusted gross income, with a five-year carry over, if volunteer duties keep the volunteer away from home overnight. However, if there is a significant element of personal pleasure, recreation, or vacation in the travel, the expenses will be disallowed.

Rev. Rul. 55–4, 1955–1 CB 291; *Rockefeller,* 76 TC 178, *aff'd,* 676 F. 2d 35 (CA–2, 1982); Rev. Rul. 84–61, 1984–1 CB 39; IRC §170(k).

Quid Pro Quo Gifts

If the donor receives an economic benefit as a result of a contribution, the donation is not deductible except to the extent that the donor can substantiate that the benefit received was less than the fair market value of the gift.[1] Starting in 1994, when a charity receives a quid pro quo contribution of over $75 it must (1) inform the donor that the deduction is limited to the excess of money or property contributed over the value of the goods or services provided by the charity, and (2) provide the donor with a good faith estimate of the goods or services provided by the charity. If the charity fails to provide such information, a penalty of $10 per contribution will be charged by the IRS, with a cap of $5,000 per fund-raising event or mailing.[2]

1. Rev. Rul. 67–246, 1967–2 C.B. 104. Letter Ruling 9417003.

2. *See,* for guidance in this area, *Internal Revenue News Release* 93–121, Dec. 21, 1993; IRS Publication 1771, *Charitable Contributions-Substantiation and Disclosure Requirements; 1994 IRS Exempt Organizations CPE Technical Instruction Program Textbook:* Chapter J: Substantiation and Disclosure Rules of OBRA '93 (Release date: Oct. 1, 1994); IRS Forms 8282 (Donee Information Return) and 8283 (Noncash Charitable Contributions); Conference Committee's report, T.D. 8544 (May 26, 1994).

Contributors who receive goods or services in return for donations must deduct the value of the goods or services from the contribution amount. However, if the benefit is "insubstantial" the full amount of the contribution is deductible. "Insubstantial" means that (1) the fair market value of the benefit isn't more than 2 percent of the donation or $64, whichever is less, or (2) the donation is $32 or more, and the "low cost articles" have a total value of not more than $6.40. Stickers, mugs, or T-shirts are "low cost articles."

8 *NonProfit Times* (5) 38 (May, 1994).

Substantiation of Gifts

See also IRS Publication No. 1771.

Cash Donations

In 1995 the IRS relaxed its requirement that taxpayers get a receipt for charitable contributions of $250 or more (including a good faith estimate of the value of any goods or services given to the donor in exchange for the gift) before filing their 1994 returns. For 1994 returns, the IRS will accept a canceled check as proof of the contribution as long as the donor made a good-faith effort, by October 16, 1995, to obtain a written acknowledgment from the charity. A letter asking for a receipt is inadequate. The receipt must state that the donor received nothing in return for the contribution. Churches must state that the donor received nothing other than "intangible religious benefits." The substantiation requirement applies only to single donations of $250 or more, not to multiple small donations that add up to $250 or more. Only itemizers need obtain substantiation. Also, starting in 1994, charities that solicit or receive quid pro quo contribution of more than $75 must provide the donor with a written statement estimating the deductible portion of the payment. IRC 170(f)(8).

> *See,* for guidance in this area, *Internal Revenue News Release* 93–121, Dec. 21, 1993; IRS Publication 1771, *Charitable Contributions-Substantiation and Disclosure Requirements; 1994 IRS Exempt Organizations CPE Technical Instruction Program Textbook:* Chapter J: Substantiation and Disclosure Rules of OBRA '93 (Release date: Oct. 1, 1994); IRS Forms 8282 (Donee Information Return) and 8283 (Noncash Charitable Contributions); Conference Committee's report, T.D. 8544 (May 26, 1994). *See also Treasury Official Says Charitable Substantiation Will Soon Be Easier,* Marlis L. Carson. *Tax Notes,* Aug. 14, 1995 68 n7 p788–789.

Noncash Donations

A donor who reports noncash donations of more than $500, but less than $5,000, on a Schedule A, Form 1040, must provide information on Form 8283 in addition to maintaining records telling how the property was acquired and the property's cost or other basis if held less than 12 months before the date of the contribution. For property held 12 months or over before the donation, the donor must keep basis information if available.

Noncash gifts of under $500 must be substantiated by a receipt from the charity and a reliable written record of certain information about the donated property.

Noncash gifts of over $5,000 per item or group of similar items must be accompanied by a qualified appraiser's signature and the signature of an authorized representative of the donee-charity acknowledging receipt of the gift on IRS Form 8283. Subsequent sale by the charity of property valued in excess of $5000 within two years of receipt of the property must be reported to the IRS on Form 8282.

See the following IRS Forms 8282 and 8283.

New Philanthropy Publication

After an eternity of hoopla, the inaugural edition of the *American Benefactor* recently appeared. The magazine is intended for delivery only to the most significant donors to the most amply funded nonprofits. The *American Benefactor* is a sign to the heavy hitters that their gift is welcome, and that they truly stand among our nation's most economically fortunate.

Van Til, John, (article), 11 *NonProfit Times* (7) 22–23 (May, 1997).

FORM NO. 14S
IRS Form 8282 (Donee Information Return)

Form **8282**
(Rev. Nov. 1992)
Department of the Treasury
Internal Revenue Service

Donee Information Return

(Sale, Exchange, or Other Disposition of Donated Property)

▶ See instructions on back.

OMB No. 1545-0908
Expires 11-30-95

Give Copy to Donor

Please Print or Type	Name of charitable organization (donee)	Employer identification number
	Address (number, street, and room or suite no.)	
	City or town, state, and ZIP code	

Note: *If you are the original donee,* **DO NOT** *complete Part II or column (c) of Part III.*

Part I Information on ORIGINAL DONOR and DONEE You Gave the Property to

1a Name(s) of the original donor of the property   1b Identifying number

Note: *Complete lines 2a–2d only if you gave this property to another charitable organization (successor donee).*

2a Name of charitable organization   2b Employer identification number

2c Address (number, street, and room or suite no.)

2d City or town, state, and ZIP code

Part II Information on PREVIOUS DONEES—Complete this part only if you were not the first donee to receive the property. If you were the second donee, leave lines 4a–4d blank. If you were a third or later donee, complete lines 3a–4d. On lines 4a–4d, give information on the preceding donee (the one who gave you the property).

3a Name of original donee   3b Employer identification number

3c Address (number, street, and room or suite no.)

3d City or town, state, and ZIP code

4a Name of preceding donee   4b Employer identification number

4c Address (number, street, and room or suite no.)

4d City or town, state, and ZIP code

Part III Information on DONATED PROPERTY

(a) Description of donated property sold, exchanged, or otherwise disposed of (if you need more space, attach a separate statement)	(b) Date you received the item(s)	(c) Date the first donee received the item(s) (if you weren't the first)	(d) Date item(s) sold, exchanged, or otherwise disposed of	(e) Amount received upon disposition

For Paperwork Reduction Act Notice, see instructions on back.   Cat. No. 62307Y   Form **8282** (Rev. 11-92)

FORM NO. 14SS
IRS Form 8283 (Return for Noncash Charitable Contributions)

Form **8283** (Rev. November 1992) Department of the Treasury Internal Revenue Service	**Noncash Charitable Contributions** ▶ Attach to your tax return if the total deduction claimed for all property contributed exceeds $500. ▶ See separate instructions.	OMB No. 1545-0908 Expires 11-30-95 Attachment Sequence No. **55**
Name(s) shown on your income tax return		Identifying number

Note: *Figure the amount of your contribution deduction before completing this form. See your tax return instructions.*

Section A—Include in this section **only** items (or groups of similar items) for which you claimed a deduction of $5,000 or less per item or group, and certain publicly traded securities (see instructions).

Part I   **Information on Donated Property**—If you need more space, attach a statement.

1	(a) Name and address of the donee organization	(b) Description of donated property
A		
B		
C		
D		
E		

Note: *If the amount you claimed as a deduction for an item is $500 or less, you do not have to complete columns (d), (e), and (f).*

	(c) Date of the contribution	(d) Date acquired by donor (mo., yr.)	(e) How acquired by donor	(f) Donor's cost or adjusted basis	(g) Fair market value	(h) Method used to determine the fair market value
A						
B						
C						
D						
E						

Part II   **Other Information**—If you gave less than an entire interest in property listed in Part I, complete lines 2a–2e. If restrictions were attached to a contribution listed in Part I, complete lines 3a–3c.

2   If less than the entire interest in the property is contributed during the year, complete the following:

a   Enter letter from Part I that identifies the property _____. If Part II applies to more than one property, attach a separate statement.

b   Total amount claimed as a deduction for the property listed in Part I: **(1)** For this tax year _____
(2) For any prior tax years _____.

c   Name and address of each organization to which any such contribution was made in a prior year (complete only if different than the donee organization above). _____

Name of charitable organization (donee)

Address (number, street, and room or suite no.)

City or town, state, and ZIP code

d   For tangible property, enter the place where the property is located or kept _____

e   Name of any person, other than the donee organization, having actual possession of the property _____

3   If conditions were attached to any contribution listed in Part I, answer the following questions and attach the required statement (see instructions):

		Yes	No
a	Is there a restriction, either temporary or permanent, on the donee's right to use or dispose of the donated property?		
b	Did you give to anyone (other than the donee organization or another organization participating with the donee organization in cooperative fundraising) the right to the income from the donated property or to the possession of the property, including the right to vote donated securities, to acquire the property by purchase or otherwise, or to designate the person having such income, possession, or right to acquire?		
c	Is there a restriction limiting the donated property for a particular use?		

For Paperwork Reduction Act Notice, see separate instructions.   Cat No. 62299J   Form **8283** (Rev. 11-92)

FORM NO. 14SS *(Continued)*

Form 8283 (Rev. 11-92)		Page **2**
Name(s) shown on your income tax return		Identifying number

Section B—Appraisal Summary—Include in this section only items (or groups of similar items) for which you claimed a deduction of more than $5,000 per item or group. Report contributions of certain publicly traded securities only in Section A.

If you donated art, you may have to attach the complete appraisal. See the **Note** in Part I below.

Part I	**Information on Donated Property**—To be completed by the taxpayer and/or appraiser.

4   Check type of property:

- ☐ Art* (contribution of $20,000 or more)
- ☐ Art* (contribution of less than $20,000)
- ☐ Real Estate
- ☐ Coin Collections
- ☐ Gems/Jewelry
- ☐ Books
- ☐ Stamp Collections
- ☐ Other

*Art includes paintings, sculptures, watercolors, prints, drawings, ceramics, antique furniture, decorative arts, textiles, carpets, silver, rare manuscripts, historical memorabilia, and other similar objects.

Note: *If your total art contribution deduction was $20,000 or more, you must attach a complete copy of the signed appraisal. See instructions.*

5	(a) Description of donated property (if you need more space, attach a separate statement)	(b) If tangible property was donated, give a brief summary of the overall physical condition at the time of the gift	(c) Appraised fair market value
A			
B			
C			
D			

	(d) Date acquired by donor (mo., yr.)	(e) How acquired by donor	(f) Donor's cost or adjusted basis	(g) For bargain sales, enter amount received	(h) Amount claimed as a deduction	(i) Average trading price of securities
					See Instructions	
A						
B						
C						
D						

Part II	**Taxpayer (Donor) Statement**—List each item included in Part I above that is separately identified in the appraisal as having a value of $500 or less. See instructions.

I declare that the following item(s) included in Part I above has to the best of my knowledge and belief an appraised value of not more than $500 (per item). Enter identifying letter from Part I and describe the specific item: _____

Signature of taxpayer (donor) ▶   Date ▶

Part III	**Certification of Appraiser**

I declare that I am not the donor, the donee, a party to the transaction in which the donor acquired the property, employed by, married to, or related to any of the foregoing persons, or an appraiser regularly used by any of the foregoing persons and who does not perform a majority of appraisals during the taxable year for other persons.

Also, I declare that I hold myself out to the public as an appraiser or perform appraisals on a regular basis; and that because of my qualifications as described in the appraisal, I am qualified to make appraisals of the type of property being valued. I certify that the appraisal fees were not based upon a percentage of the appraised property value. Furthermore, I understand that a false or fraudulent overstatement of the property value as described in the qualified appraisal or this appraisal summary may subject me to the civil penalty under section 6701(a) (aiding and abetting the understatement of tax liability). I affirm that I have not been barred from presenting evidence or testimony by the Director of Practice.

Sign Here

Signature ▶	Title ▶	Date of appraisal ▶
Business address (including room or suite no.)		Identifying number
City or town, state, and ZIP code		

Part IV	**Donee Acknowledgment**—To be completed by the charitable organization.

This charitable organization acknowledges that it is a qualified organization under section 170(c) and that it received the donated property as described in Section B, Part I, above on _____ (Date)

Furthermore, this organization affirms that in the event it sells, exchanges, or otherwise disposes of the property (or any portion thereof) within 2 years after the date of receipt, it will file an information return (**Form 8282**, Donee Information Return) with the IRS and furnish the donor a copy of that return. This acknowledgment does not represent concurrence in the claimed fair market value.

Name of charitable organization (donee)	Employer identification number	
Address (number, street, and room or suite no.)	City or town, state, and ZIP code	
Authorized signature	Title	Date

*U.S. Government Printing Office: 1994 — 387-095/00260

§111. QUALIFIED DONEES

If an organization is facing imminent IRS revocation of its tax exemption, donors who know of the imminent revocation cannot deduct contributions from their taxes, made prior to official revocation.

> See 9 *NonProfit Times* (3) 57 (March, 1995) (the Star Trek Association of Towson, Inc., MD).

To check on local or state charities call your county Charitable Solicitations Officer; in Florida call the C.S. Section of the Dept. of Agriculture and Consumer Services, (800) 435–7352.

§113. INCOME-TAX DEDUCTIONS FOR CHARITABLE CONTRIBUTIONS BY INDIVIDUALS

The 3-percent disallowance rule, which was scheduled to expire after 1995, was made permanent by OBRA '93. In 1995, taxpayers had to reduce their itemized deductions (excluding medical expenses, investment interest, and casualty and theft losses, by the amount that equals 3 percent of their adjusted gross income over $114,700 (over $57,350 if married filing separately). The amount will be adjusted annually for inflation. For example, the 1994 threshold was over $111,800 or over $55,900 if married filing separately.

For more information about the deductibility from a testator's gross estate, under 26 USCS §2055, of bequests for public, charitable, and religious uses, *see* 46 ALR Fed. 246, §§6–9.

§118. INCOME TAX DEDUCTION FOR CONTRIBUTIONS BY CORPORATIONS AND ASSOCIATIONS

Gifts by Corporations

There is a ceiling on the deductibility of corporation gifts equal to 10 percent of the corporation's taxable income with a five-year carry over for any "excess." If the board authorizes a gift and makes payment within 65 days of the close of the tax year, the gift is deductible in the authorization year. Inventory gifts that are donated to the ill, needy, or minors and scientific equipment donated to colleges, universities or tax-exempt scientific research organizations for research, experimentation, or research training, are deductible at the lower of (1) the sum of the property's basis plus half of the appreciation, or (2) twice the property's basis.

>IRC §170(b)(2); IRC §170(d)(2); IRC §170(a)(2); Reg. §1.170A–11; IRC §170(e)(3), (4); Reg. §1.170A–4A.

Gifts by Partnerships

Gifts are deductible by the individual partners, but are not deductible on the partnership return.

>IRC §702(a)(4); Reg. §1.170A–1(h)(7).

§123. OUTRIGHT GIFTS

Cash Donations

Gifts of money are deductible up to 50 percent of the donor's adjusted gross income with a five-year allowed carry over for any "excess."

>IRC §170(b)(1)(A); Reg. §1.107A–8; IRC §170(d)(1); Reg. §1.170A–10(a).

Long-Term Securities and Real Estate

Gifts of securities and real estate held long-term are deductible up to 30 percent of the adjusted gross income of the donor at the full present fair market value, with no tax on the appreciation and a five-year carry over for any excess.[1] The deduction can be increased to 50 percent of the donor's adjusted income if the donor reduces the amount of the deduction, for all long-term property donated during the year, by 100 percent of the appreciation and also similarly reduces the deduction for long-term property gifts carried over from earlier years.[2] The 50 percent election is irrevocable after the tax return's due date.

1. IRC §170(b)(1)(C)(i); Reg. §1.170A–(8)(d)(1); IRC §170(e); IRC §170(b)(1)(C)(ii).

2. IRC §170(b)(1)(C)(iii) & (e)(1)(B); Reg. §1.170A–8(d)(2).

3. 55 TCM 1131 (1988), aff'd 90–1 USTC ¶50,199 (CA–10, Apr. 4, 1990).

Ordinary Income Property

Gifts of ordinary income property, such as inventory, Section 306 stock, collapsible corporation stock, crops, and art works created by the donor, are deductible up to 50 percent of the donor's adjusted gross income with a five-year carry over for any "excess" at the value of the property's cost basis.

IRC §170(b)(1)(A); IRC §170(d)(1); Reg. §1.170A–4(b)(1); IRC §170(e)(1)(A).

Gifts in Kind

Under the Internal Revenue Code, a charitable deduction for a contribution of inventory is generally limited to the donor's basis in the property. However, an increased deduction for such contributions of inventory may be allowed if: (1) The donee's use of the property is related to its exempt purposes and the property is used solely for the care of the ill, needy, or infants; (2) The property is not transferred by the donee in exchange for money, other property, or services; (3) The taxpayer receives from the donee a written statement describing the property and the date of contribution, representing that the use and disposition of the property will be for the care of the ill, needy, or infants, and stating that adequate records of the property's use will be maintained. If the property ultimately is not used for the required purposes, the donee may still take the increased deduction based on a reasonable expectation, at the time of contribution, that the use would meet the requirements of this exception.

Harmon, Gail, (article), 10 *NonProfit Times* (8) 42 (August, 1996).

Short-Term Securities and Real Estate

Gifts of securities, real estate held short-term, and tangible personal property held short-term, are deductible up to 50 percent of the donor's adjusted gross income, at the cost basis, with a five-year carry over for any excess.

IRC §170(b)(1)(A); IRC §170(e)(1)(A); IRC §170(d)(1); Reg. §1.170A–10.

Tangible Personal Property

Donations of tangible personal property, such as antiques, books, and works of art held *long-term* that are *related* to the donee's exempt function (e.g., the gift of a painting to an art gallery or school for its art gallery) are deductible up to 30 percent of the donor's adjusted gross income with a five-year carry over for any "excess."[1] The deduction can be increased to 50 percent of the donors adjusted income if the donor reduces the amount of the deduction for all long-term property donated during the year by 100 percent of the appreciation and also similarly reduces the deduction for long-term property gifts carried over from earlier years.[2] The 50-percent election is irrevocable after the tax return's due date and reduces the deduction to cost basis only.[3]

Unrelated gifts of tangible personal property held *long term* are deductible up to 50 percent of the donor's adjusted gross income for cost basis only.[4]

Gifts of a work of art without the copyright, that are (1) donated to a public charity (501(c)(3)) not a private foundation (IRC §509), and (2) related to the donee's charitable purpose, qualify for a gift and estate tax charitable deduction, but not an income-tax deduction.[5]

1. Reg. §1.170A–4; IRC §170(e)(1)(B)(i); IRC §170(b)(1)(D)(i); IRC §170(d)(1).

2. IRC §170(b)(1)(C)(iii) & (e)(1)(B); Reg. §1.170A–8(d)(2).

3. 55 TCM 1131 (1988), aff'd 90–1 USTC ¶50,199 (CA–10, Apr. 4, 1990).

4. IRC §170(b)(1)(A); IRC §170(e)(1)(B).

5. IRC §2055(e)(4); Reg. §20.2055–2(e)(1)(ii); IRC §2522(c)(3); Reg. §25–2522(c)–3(c)(1)(ii).

Bargain Sales

When a donation is deemed to be a "bargain sale" by the IRS, such as the gift of mortgaged property,[1] the deduction must allow for the difference between the fair market value and the sales price for long-term securities and real estate.[2] The cost basis, for purposes of capital gain, must be allocated between the portion "sold" and the portion "given" to the charity.[3] The appreciation allocable to the gift is not taxable, while the appreciation allocable to the sale is taxable.[4]

1. Reg. §1.1011–2(a)(3); *Guest,* 77 TC 9 (1981).

2. IRC §170(e)(2) and its related cases.

3. IRC §1011(b).

4. *Id.*

§124. TRANSFERS OF PARTIAL INTERESTS

Advantages to Deferred Giving

The charitable deductions, with both pooled income funds and charitable remainder trusts, is immediate for a current gift, or at death by way of a will. Charitable remainder trusts aren't taxed on capital gain income. Thus, these trusts can be used to turn highly appreciated securities, that pay little income, into securities that create significant income for the beneficiaries.

8 *NonProfit Times* (5) 50 (May, 1994).

Planned Giving Professionals

Planned giving professionals have joined to share information through a cyberspace bulletin board. The network can be reached through the Seattle Public Library electronic menu, or directly through telnet by typing "scn.org." For information, contact the offices of Planned Giving Today. Phone: 800–KALL–PGT. E-mail: pgt@scn.org

Nacson, Sharon, (article), 8 *NonProfit Times* (9) (September, 1994).

§125. CHARITABLE REMAINDER ANNUITY TRUSTS

A charitable remainder annuity trust is a deferred giving plan that specifies a fixed dollar amount, of at least 5 percent of the initial net fair market value of transferred property, to be paid annually to an income beneficiary, or recipient, for life. The charity receives the remainder on the death of the beneficiary, or survivor beneficiary if there is more than one.

IRC §664(d)(1).

Gift Annuity Protections

President Clinton signed into law, in 1995, the Charitable Gift Annuity Antitrust Relief Act of 1995 (HR2525) and the Philanthropy Protection Act of 1995 (HR2519) which will protect charitable gift annuities from federal and state antitrust liability by codifying current SEC recognized exemptions for the collective pooling of charitable donations. The laws will allow charities to continue to enter into gift annuity arrangements without paying commercial interest rates. The American Council on Gift Annuities (ACGA) which had been challenged by the heirs to such annuities, had in the past set rates for gift annuities issued by charities. The ACGA will, however, no longer issue recommendations about the rates charities should pay donors.

LaVonne McIver, (article), 10 *NonProfit Times* (1) 4 (January, 1996).

§126. CHARITABLE REMAINDER UNITRUST

A charitable remainder unitrust (CRUT) is a deferred giving plan in which an income beneficiary, or recipient, receives annual payments determined by multiplying a fixed percentage, of not less than 5 percent, by the net fair market value of the trust assets, as determined each year. A charity gets the remainder on the death of the beneficiary, or survivor beneficiary if there is more than one. In a "net income with makeup" (NIMCRUT) unitrust, the trustee can pay only the amount of the trust income, if the actual income is less than the stated percentage, with deficiencies made up in later years if the income starts to exceed the stated percentage. A "net income with no makeup" unitrust requires the trustee to pay only trust income and the actual income is less than the stated percentage, with deficiencies *not* made up in later years.

IRC §664(d)(2); IRC §664(d)(3); Reg. §1.664–3(a)(1)(i)(b).

§126A. GOVERNING INSTRUMENTS FOR UNITRUSTS AND ANNUITY TRUSTS

Specific provisions must be included in instruments creating charitable unitrusts and annuity trusts in order to avoid adverse tax consequences and to make sure that the donor receives a charitable deduction.[1] The IRS has issued model agreements for charitable remainder unitrusts and annuity trusts and will not "ordinarily" issue rulings on the qualification of substantially similar trusts.[2] These forms set out the minimum requirements and should be adapted to the specifics of the donor and the charity.

1. *See* Reg. §1.664–1 through §1.664–3; IRC §508(e); IRC §4847(a)(2); Rev. Rul. 72–395, 1972–2 CB 340; Rev. Rul. 82–128, 1982–2 CB 71; Rev. Rul. 82–165, 1982–2 CB 117; Rev. Rul. 8881, 1988–2 CB 127.

2. *See* Rev. Proc. 90–30, 1990–1 CB 534 ("standard unitrust"); Rev. Proc. 90–31, 1990–1 CB 539 ("net income with makeup" unitrusts); Rev. Proc. 90–32, 1990–1 CB 546 (charitable remainder annuity trusts). To obtain free Revenue Procedures (Rev. Proc.) with unitrust and annuity trust instruments write to: The Internal Revenue Service, Freedom of Information Reading Room, P.O. Box 795, Ben Franklin Station, Washington, D.C. 20044.

§127. POOLED INCOME FUNDS

In a pooled income fund a donor transfers money or securities to a public charity, which must be described in IRC §170(b)(1)(A)(i), (ii), (iii), (iv), (v), or (vi). Some of the qualifying charities include schools, churches, and hospitals. The gift is put by the charity into a separately maintained pooled income fund where it is invested along with other similar gifts. The donor than gets a pro rata share of income fund earnings from the invested fund each year for life, and must pay ordinary income tax on the income. The charity removes the donor's share from the fund, on the donor's death, and uses it for charitable purposes. A donor's gift to a pooled income fund can also be designated to provide life income for a survivor, for example, a spouse.

IRC §642(c)(3), (4), (5); Reg. §§1.642(c)–5 and (c)–6.

A primary characteristic of a pooled income fund is that neither the donors nor any income beneficiaries can serve as trustees. The recipient charity must maintain the trust. The fund cannot invest in securities, exempt from federal income tax. Acceptance of donations of depreciable property is restricted. The recipient charity cannot mingle its assets with the trust.

8 *NonProfit Times* (5) 50 (May, 1994).

Governing Instruments for Pooled Income Funds

Specific provisions must be included in instruments creating a pooled income fund donation in order to assure a charitable deduction and to avoid adverse tax consequences.[1] The IRS has issued a specimen agreement saying that substantially similar agreements will "generally" not cause them to issue a qualification ruling.[2] Of course the suggested form should be adapted to the requirements of the donor and the charity.

1. *See* IRC §642(c)(3), (4), (5); Reg. §1.642(c)–5 and –6; IRC §§508(e) and 4947(a)(2); Rev. Rul. 82–38, 1982–1 CB 96.

2. Rev. Proc. 88–53, 1988–2 CB 712; Rev. Proc. 88–54, 1988–2 CB 715. To obtain free Revenue Procedures (Rev. Proc.) with sample pooled income instruments write to: The Internal Revenue Service, Freedom of Information Reading Room, P.O. Box 795, Ben Franklin Station, Washington, D.C. 20044.

12

STATE TAX EXEMPTIONS

§130. STATE TAXATION, IN GENERAL

"Fee" or "Tax"?

Pennsylvania is attempting to tax nonprofits by imposing some payment from nonprofits to help pay for municipal services used by tax-exempt and tax-paying entities alike. Senate Bill 877 would allow municipalities to assess payments on nonprofits based on the average property taxes paid by commercial establishments in the same district. Nonprofits, led by the United Way of Pennsylvania, were fighting the assessments. The assessments, if approved, were expected to bring $66 million to the Commonwealth.

8 *NonProfit Times* (6) 12 (June, 1994).

In New Jersey, the Commissioner of Health and Essential Health Services Commission may, under a state statute, annually assess hospitals for contribution to a fund to be used to provide financial support to hospitals furnishing the bulk of care to charity patients.

New Jersey Hospital Association v. Fishman, 651 A. 2d 501 (NJ Super. A.D., 1995).

A state may not constitutionally impose impact fees on cars purchased or titled in other states, but subsequently registered in-state by state residents.

Department of Revenue v. Huhnlein, 646 So. 2d 717 (FL, 1994).

New York's $80 registration fee for telemarketers was upheld in 1995 by the U.S. Court of Appeals for the Second Circuit. The court held that, under the First Amendment, a fee may constitutionally include costs of administration as well as costs of enforcement. Similarly, Maryland's fund-raising fees, which are determined on a sliding scale based on agency revenue, have been deemed constitutional.

See 9 *NonProfit Times* (6) 4 (June, 1995); *see also, "Hidden" Taxes in New York State.* Peter Swords. New York University Conference on Tax Planning for 501(c)(3) Organizations, Annual 1994 22 p10–1(32) for a discussion of fees as taxation in New York.

Syracuse Mayor Roy A. Bernardi wants to charge nonprofit tax-exempt institutions a "core service fee" for basic services like road maintenance and police protection.

Glaberson, William, *In Era of Fiscal Damage Control, Cities Fight Idea of "Tax-Exempt," The New York Times,* Feb. 21, 1996.

Foundations are starting to refuse to "take the risk" of dealing with institutions that might have to pay property taxes. For example, because of Washington and Jefferson College's pending court date on its property tax exemption status, the New York-based F.W. Olin Foundation has eliminated Pennsylvania's schools for consideration in its capital projects grant program. Olin's gifts to Pennsylvania schools would have totaled $32.5 million. Dickinson College, Kings College, Lafayette College, and Gettysburg will also be affected. One solution to this problem (used by the Pew Charitable Trust) is for foundations to make grants to educational institutions on a project basis, so the money could not be used by the institution to pay imposed real estate taxes.

Swarden, Carlotta, (article), 10 *NonProfit Times* (8) 1, 11, 12 (August, 1996).

The National Society of Fund Raising Executives (NSFRE) National Government Relations Committee is drafting a study paper on the issue of Payment in Lieu of Taxes (P.I.L.O.T.). The draft will have to be approved by the board to become a formal position paper. The president and chief executive officer of NSFRE, Patricia Lewis, believes that "P.I.L.O.T.s are a major concern in the nonprofit sector. The whole matter has an impact on donor relations."

Swarden, Carlotta, (article), 10 *NonProfit Times* (9) 5 (September, 1996).

Service Tax on Physicians

A society of physicians sued the state after the state imposed a two-percent tax on physicians' services to obtain federal matching money to support Kentucky Medicaid, even though the tax applied to 40 percent of doctors who did not participate in Medicaid programs. The court held that such "classification" is constitutionally permissible if it is neither unreasonable nor arbitrary and it applies equally to all in the class. Unpermissible classification must be proved to be hostile and oppressive against persons and classes.

Com., Revenue Cabinet v. Smith, 875 S.W. 2d 873 (KY, 1994).

Transaction Privilege Tax

In Arizona, a nonprofit fraternal organization that operates a dining facility for members only, on a continuous basis, is considered by the state to be "in the restaurant business," whether it makes a profit or not, and must pay a transaction privilege tax on its gross proceeds.

State ex rel. Arizona Dept. of Revenue v. Phoenix Lodge No. 708, Loyal Order of Moose, Inc., 872 P. 2d 679 (AZ Tax, 1994).

Future of Tax-Exemption

In November, 1996, Colorado voters voted on a proposal that would amend the state constitution to remove the property tax exemption currently extended to religious charitable groups. The ballot initiative was being fought by the Colorado Association of Nonprofit Organizations (CANPO) through its corporation, Citizen Action for Colorado. If the initiative had passed, only nonprofits that own and use property for nonprofit schools, community corrections facilities, orphanages, and housing for low-income elderly, disabled, homeless, or abused persons would have been exempt. However, the proposal was rejected by the people of Colorado by a margin of 5 to 1.

Swarden, Carlotta, (article), 10 *NonProfit Times* (7) 16, 32 (July, 1996). *See also,* Stokeld, Fred, *Colo. Initiative Would Repeal Nonprofits' Property Tax Exemption. Tax Notes,* Sept. 9, 1996. *See also,* Gonzalez, Erika, *Non-Profits Protest Plan to Repeal Colorado Property Tax Exemption, Knight-Ridder/Tribune Business News,* June 1, 1996. *See also,* Stradling, Richard, *Nonprofit Newport News, Va., Hospital Fighting Local Property Tax, Knight-Ridder/Tribune Business News,* April 4, 1996. *See also,* Carricaburu, Lisa, *Nonprofits Group Studies Utah Organizations, Knight-Ridder/Tribune Business News,* Sept. 19, 1996.

State Sales Tax on Internet Sales

Electronic commerce, transacted on the Internet, has proliferated at such an explosive rate, that regulatory authorities cannot keep up. Several states, seeing the potential for revenue, are scrambling to apply sales taxes to such transactions. Bipartisan legislation has been introduced in Washington that would put a moratorium on new state and local taxes on electronic commerce. The concern is that a random assortment of taxes, rather than a unified system, will hurt the economy and stifle growth. Such legislation hopes to prevent "forum shopping," where businesses engaged in commerce over the Internet make location decisions based on the tax structures of various jurisdictions.

McNamara, Don, (article), 11 *NonProfit Times* (7) 4 (May, 1997).

Pennsylvania's HUP Test for Tax Exemption

Since 1985 and the *Hospital Utilization Project v. Commonwealth of Pennsylvania* case, Pennsylvania has used the five criteria of the HUP test to prove whether an organization is exempt from taxation. An exempt organization must prove: (1) It advances a charitable purpose; (2) It donates or renders freely a substantial portion of its services; (3) It benefits a substantial class of persons who are legitimate subjects of charity; (4) It relieves the government of some of its burdens; and (5) It operates entirely free from a private profit motive. In 1994 and 1995, St. Margaret Seneca Place, a nursing home, and Washington and Jefferson College, a liberal arts college, satisfied the HUP test. However, a school district is now challenging the property tax exemption of the Quaker center for study and contemplation, Pendle Hill. Pendle Hill provides adult education programs. The questions are, does the government have an obligation to provide for the religious education of adults, must the children of resident staff and students pay to attend public school in the district, and what value is there in forcing the Quaker community into a defensive litigious, adversarial mode?

Jon Van Til, (article), 10 *NonProfit Times* (8) 16, 18 (August, 1996).

The U.S. Supreme Court will hear, during its 1996–1997 term, cases involving nonprofits' property tax exemptions in Maine.

Tsilas, Vicky, *Punitive Damages, State Issues Head High Court's Calendar, Tax Notes,* Sept. 30, 1996.

§131. SOME COMMON STATE TAXES

Taxpayer "Standing" to Challenge Property Tax Exemption

Taxpayers injuriously affected by a state statute, providing for a nonprofit property tax exemption, have standing to challenge the statute to the extent that the statute is alleged to improperly discriminate, under the State Constitution, against owners of residential property generally. Such statutes neither violate

State Constitution equal protection rights nor destroy uniformity of taxation guarantees if they bear some rational relationship to the conceivable legitimate interest of the government.

Appeal of Barbour, 436 S.E. 2d 169 (NC App., 1993).

§132. STATE EXEMPTIONS

Illustrative Sales and Use Tax Cases

A former minister, who is the director of a incorporated nonprofit musical entertainment group, not affiliated with any church, is not a clergyman and is not exempt from occupation tax in Pennsylvania under the free exercise clause.

Selingsgrove Area School District v. Snyder County, 648 A. 2d 1261 (PA Cmwlth., 1994).

An international bar association, that is not organized and operated exclusively for educational purposes, is not entitled to the sales and use tax exemption, available to educational organizations in New York, especially where the association's organizing documents permit the organization to engage in activities for the professional advancement of its members.

International Bar Association v. Tax Appeals Tribunal of the State of New York, 620 N.Y.S. 2d 582 (A.D. 3 Dept., 1994).

Maine's "snack tax," which taxed Girl Scout cookie sales and Boy Scout popcorn sales, was struck down in 1995. The court ruled that taxing the wholesale price but not "casual" retail sales invited "the risk of arbitrary and capricious interpretation of the law." Hawaii, Kansas, and Georgia charge a surcharge on cookie sales, where the amount of the tax is passed on to consumers.

Sinnock, Bonnie, (article), 9 *NonProfit Times,* (3) 4 (March, 1995).

See 21 ALR 5th 812, §4[a] for the validity of state or local gross receipts tax on gambling.

A city may enact franchise taxes and zoning ordinances authorizing city officials to prohibit and/or remove public pay telephones within city limits without violating the First Amendment free speech of a nonprofit association of pay telephone companies.

Independent Coin Payphone Association, Inc. v. City of Chicago, 863 F. Supp. 744 (N.D. IL, 1994).

In Arizona, the purchase or lease of personal property from a nonprofit organization is exempt from sales tax. Therefore, the sales tax should not be added to the revenue department's estimate of the value of the property.

Waddell ex rel. Arizona Dept. of Revenue v. Mayo Foundation for Medical Education and Research, 859 P. 2d 801 (AZ Tax, 1993).

In Utah, a contractor that is not the final "consumer" of construction materials, purchased directly by a tax-exempt project owner, is not liable for sales tax on such purchases. The tax-exempt project owner is liable for the sales tax if it assumed risks and responsibilities sufficient to establish ownership in connection with the materials in question.

Thorup Bros. Const., Inc. v. Auditing Div. of Utah State Tax Commission, 860 P. 2d 324 (UT, 1993).

Illustrative Property Tax Cases

Colorado

A mansion, used as a community center where the zoning is exclusively commercial, may be classified as a "commercial use" for tax purposes. A commercial enterprise need not be for profit to be classified as commercial for tax purposes.

Mission Viejo Company v. Douglas County Board of Equalization, 881 P. 2d 462 (CO App., 1994).

Georgia

In Georgia, a school board association is not a "purely public charity," for the purposes of a property tax exemption, if its only beneficiaries are member boards and a small class of persons associated with those boards.

Gwinnett County Bd. of Tax Assessors v. Georgia School Bd. Association, 439 S.E. 2d 666 (GA App., 1993).

Illinois

If a charitable organization does not put its property to any use, charitable or otherwise, for 20 years, it is not entitled to a property tax exemption in Illinois.

Comprehensive Training and Development Corp. v. County of Jackson, 633 N.E. 2d 189 (IL App. 5 Dist., 1994).

In Illinois, real property, in which a charitable organization owns a 50-percent undivided beneficial interest, is not subject to property tax if it is used exclusively for charitable purposes and the other owner is not paid for the use. The other owner need not be a charitable organization.

Chicago Patrolmen's Association v. Department of Revenue, 645 N.E. 2d 549 (IL App. 1 Dist., 1994).

Prior to December 5, 1989, the operation of a sanitary landfill on an Illinois forest preserve had to be shown conclusively to be for "public purpose" in order to qualify for a property tax exemption. Now, Illinois' Revenue Act exempts all property belonging to any forest preserve district from property tax.

Forest Preserve District of Du Page County v. Department of Revenue, 639 N.E. 2d 1385 (IL App. 2 Dist., 1994).

Indiana

A taxpayer in Indiana, who was in the business of mailing advertisements, fund-raising requests, and solicitations, challenged the state's assessment against him for non-owned business personal property taxes. Printed material, held as a bailee, is inventory and personal property, just as printed material is inventory and personal property in the hands of the owners, for taxation purposes.

Mid-America Mailers, Inc. v. State Board of Tax Commissioners, 639 N.E. 2d 380 (IN Tax, 1994).

Maine

In Maine, property of a health care institute, incorporated as a charitable organization, and conducted or operated exclusively for benevolent and charitable purposes principally for the benefit of state residents, is exempt from property taxes if it is used to further the organization's charitable purposes.

Town of Poland v. Poland Spring Health Institute, Inc., 649 A. 2d 1098 (ME, 1994); 36 M.R.S.A. Section 652.

Michigan

A property tax exemption, granted to research facilities funded by the state, does not violate the Michigan Uniformity of Taxation Clause if it rationally furthers the goal of encouraging nonprofit entities to do business in the state.

City of Ann Arbor v. National Center for Mfg. Sciences, Inc., 514 N.W. 2d 224 (MI App., 1994).

Missouri

A taxpayer that alleges that part, but not all, of its property is entitled to a charitable exemption from real property taxes must exhaust all administrative remedies with the county board of equalization before taking the case to the circuit court, especially where there is a question of valuation to be assigned to each part of the property by the assessor.

Local Union No. 124, Intern. Broth. of Elec. Workers v. Pendergast, 891 S.W. 2d
    417 (MO banc., 1995).

New Hampshire

A New Hampshire camp school is a "school" for the purposes of a property tax exemption even if the school has the attributes of a summer camp (children lived in tents and participated in recreational activities), where it offers an intensive academic program, standard textbooks are used, and the instructors are qualified teachers. Vacant land not "used and occupied for school purposes" is not exempt.

Wolfeboro Camp School, Inc. v. Town of Wolfeboro, 642 A. 2d 928 (NH, 1994).

New York

Property owned by a nonprofit and used as a nature sanctuary is tax exempt, even where a nonprofit corporation fails to create an overland access to the sanctuary, as long as the property is used consistently with its charitable purpose of maintaining habitat in its natural state and protecting wildlife from undue interference. However, a nonprofit may not deny public access to exempt property entirely or discourage public access while allowing special privileges to the corporation's members.

Adirondack Land Trust Inc. v. Town of Putnam Assessor, 611 N.Y.S. 2d 332 (A.D.
    3 Dept., 1994).

In New York, a nonprofit corporation which is organized for, and conducting, drug and narcotics rehabilitation activities, comes within the "moral or mental improvement of men, women or children" exemption from real property taxes. The "moral or mental improvement" category includes musical and artistic performing arts theatres, land held for environmental and conservation purposes, facilities that inform the public about homosexuality and homophobia and AIDS, and facilities related to the investigation and research of delinquency and narcotics and the care of persons affected by delinquency and narcotics.

Dynamite Youth Center v. Assessor of the Town of Fallsburg, Sullivan County, 620
    N.Y.S. 2d 566 (A.D. 3 Dept., 1994).

North Carolina

A child-care center, that is "reasonable, necessary" to the accomplishment of a hospital's charitable purposes, is exempt from property taxation in North Carolina.

Matter of Moses H. Cone Memorial Hosp., 439 S.E. 2d 63 (FL App. 3 Dist., 1994).

Property used by the Atlantic Coast Conference (ACC) for its administrative offices, owned by individual member educational institutions, and used for activities incident to the operation of an educational institution is exempt from property tax.

Appeal of Atlantic Coast Conference, 434 S.E. 2d 865 (NC App., 1993).

Ohio

In order to qualify for a real property tax exemption, in Ohio, the operators of a nonprofit (nursing home or rest home) must receive a license to operate their facility by the tax lien date of the year for which exemption is sought.

Christian Benevolent Association of Greater Cincinnati, Inc. v. Limbach, 631 N.E. 2d 1034 (OH, 1994).

The property of a church that operates a printing plant, to produce collection envelopes, is not tax exempt. The printing is not charitable even where the users of the envelopes are engaged in charitable purposes. Such "vicarious" use of the envelopes to garner receipts or proceeds does not qualify for tax exemption.

Hubbard Press v. Tracy, 621 N.E. 2d 396 (OH, 1993).

A park owned by a nonprofit association, that is used exclusively for charitable purposes, is exempt from property taxation in Ohio. A homeowners' association is an "institution" within the meaning of the exemption statute.

Highland Park Owners, Inc. v. Tracy, 644 N.E. 2d 284 (OH, 1994); R.C. Section 5709.12.

Oklahoma

In Oklahoma, a nonprofit religious corporation is exempt from *ad valorem* property taxes from the time of its acquisition. If the county treasurer maintains that the property is taxable for the whole year, if purchased after January 1, he/she unconstitutionally abridges the self-executing tax exemption granted by the State Constitution.

Baptist Bldg. Corp. v. Barnes, 874 P. 2d 68 (OK App., 1994).

Oregon

A nonprofit theater company, dedicated to producing plays that expose actors and audiences to scripts, qualifies as a "literary institution," and is exempt from *ad valorem* property taxation in Oregon.

Theatre West of Lincoln City, Ltd. v. Department of Revenue, 873 P. 2d 1083 (OR, 1994).

Depreciation must be deducted from the gross income of the owner of a nonprofit home for the elderly before value may be determined for the property tax purposes, under Oregon's modified income approach to determining real market value.

Gangle v. Department of Revenue, 887 P. 2d 784 (OR, 1995).

Pennsylvania

Property, owned by a college and used as the required residence for the college's vice president, is tax exempt in Pennsylvania if it is actually and regularly used in conformity with the furtherance of the educational purposes of the college. Tax exemption is valid where the house is used to encourage a more personal and informal relationship with college representatives and donors, and used to serve college aims and objectives.

In Re Swarthmore College, 643 A. 2d 1152 (PA Cmwlth., 1994).

College property, occupied by a resident staff employee for the purpose of having personnel available on a 24-hour basis to handle emergencies, is tax exempt in Pennsylvania. Such use is regular and actual use of the property for the purposes of the college and is reasonably necessary for the occupancy and enjoyment of the college.

Swarthmore College v. Wallingford Swarthmore School District, 645 A. 2d 470 (PA Cmwlth., 1994).

In Pennsylvania, a nonprofit organization (nursing home) qualifies as a "purely public charity," entitled to a property tax exemption, if it "advances a charitable purpose, donates or renders gratuitously a substantial portion of its services, benefits a substantial and indefinite class of persons who are legitimate subjects of charity, relieves the government of some of its burden and operates entirely free from a private profit motive."

St. Margaret Seneca Place v. Board of Property Assessment Appeals and Review, County of Allegheny, 640 A. 2d 380 (PA, 1994).

Pennsylvania's Supreme Court recently upheld the property tax exemption of a Pittsburgh nursing home, holding that the existence of a revenue surplus at year's end need not jeopardize an organization's tax-exempt status. The court also held that the nursing home's costs in servicing Medicaid patients should be considered a charitable act. "The test is whether the institution bears a substantial burden that would otherwise fall to the government."

> 8 *NonProfit Times* (6) 4 (June, 1994).

In Pennsylvania, an NPO property tax exemption must be based on five criteria: (1) freedom from private profit motive; (2) advancement of a charitable purpose; (3) rendering or donating of a substantial part of its services gratuitously; (4) benefiting an indefinite but substantial class of persons who are legitimate objects of charity; and (5) relieving government of part of its burden. One criterion is not enough.

> *Washington & Jefferson College* case, Washington Co. (PA) Common Pleas Court (1994), [appeal promised]; *see,* Nocson and Sinnock column, *NonProfit Times,* p. 36 (Oct., 1994).

Rhode Island

The owners of lots in a subdivision are liable for taxes on open-space property conveyed to them by a developer, even though the owner's association to which the developer conveyed the land has not been established legally as a nonprofit corporation.

> *Wallis v. Mainville,* 639 A. 2d 61 (RI, 1994).

Utah

In Utah, the linchpin of a "charity" hospital, for the purposes of a charitable exemption to property taxation, is the notion that a gift is being made to the community on an ongoing basis. Satellite facilities of a hospital may come within the umbrella of a hospital's property tax exemption if the satellite advances the hospital's charitable purposes and is governed by the same charity-care policies that govern the exempt hospital.

> *Howell v. County Board of Cache County ex rel. IHC Hospitals, Inc.,* 881 P. 2d 880 (UT, 1994).

Wyoming

In Wyoming, the city may collect rent from city agencies for office space in the city hall without losing its property tax exempting for the city hall. Such use is "primarily" for express "governmental purpose." The property cannot be apportioned between exempt governmental use and nonexempt use for property tax purposes.

State Board of Equalization v. City of Lander, 882 P. 2d 844 (WY, 1994).

§133. STATE TAX-EXEMPTION STATUTES

In Texas, the state may, under an amendment to the Bingo Enabling Act, constitutionally tax gross receipts of bingo operations.

Aerospace Optimist Club of Fort Worth v. Texas Alcoholic Beverage Commission, 886 S.W. 2d 556 (TX App.–Austin, 1994); Vernon's Ann. Texas Const. Art. 3, Section 47(b); Vernon's Ann. Texas Civ. St. art. 179d, Sections 2A, 3 (repealed).

For more information about the validity and construction of statutes exempting gambling operation carried on by religious, charitable, or other nonprofit organizations from general prohibitions against gambling, *see* 42 ALR 3d 663.

For information about the real property tax exemption of residential facilities maintained by hospitals for patients, staff, or others, *see* 61 ALR 4th 614.

See also, 42 ALR 4th 614 for information about the property tax exemption of theaters or concert halls.

See, 53 ALR 3d 748, §4 for information about the sales and use tax exemption of charitable or educational organizations.

§137. BURDEN OF PROOF CONCERNING EXEMPT STATUS

Several states are beginning to scrutinize nonprofits more fully before granting tax-exempt status. For example, Pennsylvania's five-prong test requires that nonprofits: advance a charitable purpose, donate a substantial portion of services, benefit a substantial number of needy people, relieve government of a burden, and operate free from a private profit motive (the "HUP" test). *See Hospital Utilization Project v. Commonwealth.* Using the HUP test, Pennsylvania is fighting to deny tax-exempt status to St. Margaret Seneca Place Nursing Home. Half the home's patients are Medicaid recipients.

The state argued that the home did not relieve government of a burden. The home also projected a large surplus in 1992, leading the state to believe that there were profit motives involved.

Similarly, Utah denied exemption to Intermountain Health Care, Inc., which owns 19 nonprofit hospitals across the state, based upon a "community benefit" standard for exemption. Utah claimed that Intermountain exaggerated its "charitable activity."

In Oregon, the state denied exemption to a small all-volunteer theater group, Theater West, on the ground that it did not fit the state's definition of a public charity. Oregon demands that "charities" satisfy three standards: having charity as a primary motive, using income directly for charitable purposes, and relieving government of a burden. The Oregon judge, in the case, stated that arts organizations were never specifically declared exempt by the Oregon legislature, angering arts and cultural nonprofits statewide.

8 *NonProfit Times* (5) 1, 20–21 (May, 1994).

Evidence concerning the tax-exempt status of allegedly similar nonprofit facilities is irrelevant in determining the real estate tax exemption of a skilled care facility for the elderly.

Couriers-Susquehanna, Inc. v. County of Dauphin, 645 A. 2d 290 (PA Cmwlth., 1994).

The Anti-Injunction Act (AIA) and Declaratory Judgment Act (DJA) bar taxpayer organization claims for injunctive and declaratory relief from a statute imposing retroactive increase in estate and gift taxes where there are alternative statutory remedies available to many of the members and there is lack of irreparable harm.

National Taxpayers Union, Inc. v. United States, 862 F. Supp. 531 (D. DC, 1994); 28 U.S.C.A. Sections 1346(a)(1), 2201(a); 26 U.S.C.A. Sections 2001, 6212, 6213, 7421(a).

The dormant commerce clause prohibits taxing states from discriminating against foreign enterprises competing with local businesses and commercial activity occurring outside the taxing state.

Oklahoma Tax Com'n v. Jefferson Lines, Inc., 115 S. Ct. 1331 (U.S. MN, 1995).

In Florida, failure to timely challenge a property appraiser's notice of denial of tax exemption removes the issue from circuit court jurisdiction. A taxpayer must timely file for exemption each year unless the appraiser waives or modifies the annual application requirement. The burden of proving entitlement to exemption rests on the taxpayer.

Davis v. Macedonia Housing Authority, 641 So. 2d 131 (FL App. 1 Dist., 1994).

Where an adequate legal remedy exists, Section 1983 of the Civil Rights Act does not call for either federal or state courts to award an injunction and declaratory relief in state tax cases.

National Private Truck Council, Inc. v. Oklahoma Tax Com'n, 115 S. Ct. 2351 (U.S. OK, 1995).

In Texas, if a chief appraiser fails to send a statutory written notice and application form, requiring a nonprofit organization to file a new application to confirm its qualifications for ad valorem tax exemption, the tax exemption is rendered continuous, without the need for refiling. In such cases, the district and county cannot challenge the tax-exempt status of the organization.

Inwood Dad's Club, Inc. v. Aldine Independent School Dist., 882 S.W. 2d 532 (TX App.–Houston [1st Dist.], 1994).

13

LICENSES AND APPROVALS

§138. STATE CONTROL BY AMENDMENT OR REPEAL

General zoning plans can be changed by initiative in California. A Napa county provision that allows land use designations, enacted by initiative, to be changed during the following 30 years by a majority vote of the county electorate is valid.

DeVita v. County of Napa, 889 P. 2d 1019 (CA, 1995).

A nonprofit landowner, that reacquired property in foreclosure, may petition for certiorari to seek review of the board of county commissioners' decision denying a proposed amendment to the county growth plan. Such decisions are quasi-judicial in nature where the amendment pertains specifically to the reacquired property and the landowner is an active participant in the proceedings.

Florida Institute of Technology, Inc. v. Martin County, 641 So. 2d 898 (FL App. 4 Dist., 1994).

In 1996, the governor of Oklahoma vetoed a large portion of the attorney general's budget. In response, the state has stopped processing applications for charitable solicitation licenses due to a backlog of nearly 300 applications. Organizations can't receive a license, and can't solicit without one unless they want to risk loss of tax-exempt status, a $1000 fine, and two years in prison. The Virginia-based Free Speech Coalition Inc., is preparing to develop a plan to deal with this issue, stating, "This is a great opportunity to show the idiocy of it (registration) and how meaningless registration for registration's sake can be."

Holton, Carlotta, (article), 10 *NonProfit Times* (10) 44 (October, 1996).

§139. STATE LICENSING STATUTES

License Statutory Construction

A county was sued by a landfill operator and trash hauler, who both challenged a county ordinance that prohibited transportation of county-generated waste to landfills other than those designated in the ordinances. The court found that such ordinances impose an undue burden on interstate commerce, where the only designated landfills are located in the county.

> *Empire Sanitary Landfill, Inc. v. Commonwealth of Pennsylvania, Dept. of Environmental Resources,* 645 A. 2d 413 (PA Cmwlth., 1994).

A nonprofit association of real estate developers sued a municipality in order to challenge the validity of a residential growth control initiative adopted by voters. The court held that a municipal growth control initiative, imposed by discouraging developers from proposing low-cost housing which qualified for density bonuses, impermissibly conflicted with California state statutes designed to promote construction of low-income housing, and was, thus, void at the time it was passed.

> *Building Industry Association of San Diego, Inc. v. City of Oceanside,* 33 Cal. Rptr. 2d 137 (CA App. 4 Dist., 1994).

By statute, Louisiana exempts organizations that are tax-exempt under the Internal Revenue Code from Licensure requirements of the Louisiana Board of Regents for post-secondary degree-granting institutions. Under the statute, an IRS exempt organization cannot be required to provide paperwork to prove their tax-exempt status.

> *Ieyoub v. World Christian Church,* 649 So. 2d 771 (LA App. 1 Cir., 1994).

If a county's counsel passes, by ordinance, a county-wide planning policy, that action is legislative, not quasi-judicial. Thus, an alliance of a nonprofit organization and individual county residents and property owners could not have the plan reviewed by a statutory writ of certiorari for its compliance with the State Environmental Policy Act (SEPA).

> *Snohomish County Property Rights Alliance v. Snohomish County,* 882 P. 2d 807 (WA App. Div. 1, 1994).

A mayor's agent had no authority, under the District of Columbia's Preservation Act, to order the demolition of an historic landmark based on the "necessary in the public interest" standard or for the health, safety, and welfare of the community. The case was remanded with orders to restore the building to its former appearance, or to refer the case to the condemnation board.

> *District of Columbia Preservation League v. Department of Consumer and Regulatory Affairs,* 646 A. 2d 984 (DC App., 1994).

If a physician is licensed by the statutory endorsement of a Florida nonprofit medical corporation group, he/she may practice at a hospital that is not affiliated with the nonprofit that endorsed him/her, as long as he/she works exclusively for the nonprofit corporation.

Mayo Clinic Jacksonville v. Department of Professional Regulation, Bd. of Medicine, 625 So. 2d 918 (FL App. 1 Dist., 1993) (F.S. 19889, Section 458.313(1)(b).

A nonprofit or for-profit "consumer reporting agency," or credit reporting agency, that investigates civil, criminal, and bankruptcy court records for landlords is exempt from licensing as a private investigation business in Florida. Such an agency is regulated by the Fair Credit Reporting Act (FCRA).

Prospective Tenant Report, Inc. v. Department of State, Div. of Licensing, 629 So. 2d 894 (FL App. 2 Dist., 1993).

Ordinances controlling conditional use permits for controlled income and rent (CIR) housing in Oregon apply comprehensively and exclusively to CIRs as a use, and not only to issues of density in conjunction with that use. Thus, the Land Use Board of Appeals cannot apply planned unit development (PUD) density provisions to CIRs.

Langford v. City of Eugene, 867 P. 2d 535 (OR App., 1994).

Schools Review Courses/Licensing

A school that provides a review course for nurses to take to qualify for state certification must pay a separate annual R.N. fee for each site at which such courses are given.

Review for Nurses, Inc. v. State, 28 CA Rptr. 2d 354 (CA App. 1st Dist., 1994). West's Ann Cal. Educ. Code Sections 94302 (h, r, x), 94331.5(b)(2).

Employment as "License"

Approval of the employment of an adult care facility administrator by the Department of Social Services is a "license" under the state (NY) Administrative Procedure Act, Section 102(4). If fired, the administrator is entitled to a hearing.

Augat v. Dowsing, 613 N.Y.S. 2d 527 (NY Supr. Ct., Albany Co., 1994).

§140. NATURE OF LICENSING LAW

Licensing Constitutionality

The Fair Housing Act

Where a landlord limits occupancy to two persons per unit, such limitations have a disparate impact on families with children, and constitute a prima facie case of familial status discrimination under the Fair Housing Act.

> *Fair Housing Council of Orange County, Inc. v. Ayres,* 855 F. Supp. 315 (C.D. CA, 1994).

A municipality's limit on the number of unrelated persons who can live together in a single-family residential zone is not a maximum occupancy restriction and can be challenged under the Fair Housing Act.

> *Edmonds, Wash. v. Oxford House Inc.,* US SupCt, No. 94–23, May 15, 95 (the lower court must now decide whether a city's exclusion of a group home for recovering substance abusers violated the FHA's ban on disability discrimination).

A neighboring property owner brought suit to enjoin the construction of a proposed community home for the mentally handicapped in his subdivision. The court held that the term "single family residence," in restrictive covenants for the area, referred to the architectural character of the structure, not its use. The neighboring property owner could be sued under the Fair Housing Act for attempting to exclude the handicapped by enforcing the restrictive covenants. In Texas, the state's police power, in protecting the public welfare of its mentally retarded citizens, outweighs impairment of contract rights or deed restrictions.

> *Deep East Texas Regional Mental Health and Mental Retardation Services v. Kinnear,* 877 S.W. 2d 550 (TX App.–Beaumont, 1994).

Discrimination, under the Fair Housing Act (FHA), includes the refusal to make reasonable accommodation in rules, policies, practices or services, if such accommodations may afford handicapped persons equal opportunity to use and enjoy a dwelling. Zoning rules, concerned with the composition of households rather than with the total number of occupants, and which are designed to preserve the family character of a neighborhood, do not fall within the maximum occupancy limit exemption of the FHA.

> *City of Edmonds v. Oxford House, Inc.,* 115 S. Ct. 1776 (U.S. WA, 1995).

A group home for recovering substance abusers sued a village based on the village's failure to make reasonable accommodation under the Fair Housing Act. The court held that the group home's claim was not ripe because the group home had not invoked procedures, such as a request for a special zoning use approval, to afford the village an opportunity to make an accommodation pursuant to its own lawful procedures.

United States v. Village of Palatine, Illinois, 37 F. 3d 1230 (7th Cir., 1994).

Where a city displays discriminatory animus, fails to provide reasonable accommodation for the handicapped under the Fair Housing Act Amendments (FHAA), and refuses to increase the number of occupants allowed in an adult foster home in the city, the city may be required to pay the damages of a foster care homeowner's lost revenue, as well as civil penalties.

United States v. City of Taylor, Michigan, 872 F. Supp. 423 (E.D. MI, 1995).

For information on "standing" to sue under the Fair Housing Act of 1968, *see* 102 ALR Fed. 718.

The Fair Housing Act exempts local occupancy restrictions regarding the maximum number of occupants permitted to occupy a dwelling from its control. However, the exemption applies only to restrictions that apply to *all* occupants. A restriction that excludes group homes of more than five unrelated recovering alcoholics and drug addicts from single-family residential zones is not exempted from the FHAA prohibition against handicap discrimination.

City of Edmonds v. Washington State Bldg. Code Council, 18 F. 3d 802 (9th Cir. [WA], 1994).

A city violates the Fair Housing Act if it refuses to allow the substitution of a side yard for a backyard zoning requirement imposed on a charitable organization's home for disabled residents.

U.S. v. City of Philadelphia, PA, 838 F. Supp. 223 (E.D. PA, 1993).

If developmentally disabled adults choose to remain in their group home, contrary to a restrictive covenant that precludes operation of the home, the threat of their being forced to move confers on them "standing" under the Fair Housing Act. Attempted enforcement of the covenant amounts to "refusal to make reasonable accommodation necessary to afford such adults equal opportunity to use and enjoy a dwelling," a violation of the Fair Housing Act. State attempts to enforce the covenant are not "state action" for the purposes of a Section 1983 claim if the covenant is facially neutral and there is no state court decision on the matter.

> *Martin v. Constance,* 843 F. Supp. 1321 (E.D. MO, 1994).

A nonprofit corporation must prove actionable harm in order to prevail in a claim against the city for violation of the Fair Housing Act.

> *People Helpers Foundation, Inc. v. City of Richmond, VA,* 12 F. 3d 1321 (4th Cir. [VA], 1993).

An eligible African-American applicant for public housing has standing to challenge the lawfulness of the site selection process, under the Fair Housing Act (FHA), of locations for construction of public housing in nonracially impacted areas. Exclusion from nonracially impacted areas and imminent segregation is a sufficient injury. Exclusionary land-use restrictions may be challenged in civil rights suits (Sections 1982 and 1983). Residents of public housing also have "neighborhood" standing under the FHA.

> *Jackson v. Okaloosa County, FL,* 21 F. 3d 1531 (11th Cir. [FL], 1994).

Freedom of Speech

A permanent injunction preventing the application of a county development code's conditional use permit requirements was issued in Minnesota. The code was found to unconstitutionally afford decision makers discretion to deny a permit based on the content of the applicant's speech and lacked procedural safeguards to limit the time within which licensing decisions had to be made.

> *Mga Susu, Inc. v. County of Benton,* 853 F. Supp. 1147 (D. MN, 1994) (suit brought by nude dancing establishment).

The state of Ohio may issue an injunction prohibiting picketing, patrolling, handbilling, soliciting, or engaging in similar activities to demonstrate on private property. However, the state cannot issue injunctions against "communicating" on "any subject."

> *Eastwood Mall, Inc. v. Slanco,* 626 N.E. 2d 59 (OH, 1994).

Equal Protection

A nonprofit owner of a water system can be ordered by the Corporation Commission to provide nondiscriminatory service. The original holders of a "certificate of necessity and convenience" cannot be ordered to transfer their certificate to a homeowner's association currently operating the water system, without an opportunity to be heard before the Commission.

Tonto Creek Estates Homeowners Association v. Arizona Corp.Commission, 864 P. 2d 1081 (AZ App. Div. 1, 1993).

An ordinance prohibiting the operation of a gun shop within one-half mile of a park or school can be blocked by local gun shop owners who have no adequate remedy at law and could suffer irreparable harm without preliminary injunctive relief.

Illinois Sporting Goods Association v. County of Cook, 845 F. Supp 582 (N.D. IL, 1994).

Religious Organizations' Land-Use Plans

See also Chapter 36, Section 367.
A city ordinance that prohibits homeowners from displaying signs with few exceptions, but permits commercial establishments, churches, and nonprofit organizations to erect signs that are not allowed at residences, violates the free speech rights of the homeowners.

City of Ladue v. Gileo, 114 S. Ct. 2038 (U.S. MO, 1994).

A zoning regulation that allows churches to operate day-care centers in a residential neighborhood, but requires a special-use permit for other operators of day-care centers, does not violate equal protection.

Cohen v. City of Des Plaines, 8 F. 3d 484 (7th Cir. [IL], 1993).

§142. SPECIFIC LICENSES AND PERMITS

Gaming

A charity gaming statute may not require "qualified organizations" to be in existence in the state for a period of five years before becoming eligible for a bingo license. Such requirements facially discriminate against interstate commerce and are not a reasonable exercise of the state's police powers.

Department of Revenue v. There to Care, Inc., 638 N.E. 2d 871 (IN App. 5 Dist., 1994).

Under the Indian Commerce Clause, Indian tribes can sue the state to enforce the Indian Gaming Regulatory Act if the state fails to negotiate in good faith, as required by the IGRA, over the terms of a Class III gaming compact.

Spokane Tribe of Indians v. Washington, CA 9, No. 92–35113, July 6, 1994.

Under the Colorado Bingo Act, an administrative fee imposed by the state must be imposed on all of the licensee's games cumulatively. Rent attributed to pull-tab games is a deductible expense in determining the fee.

Catholic Media Groups, Inc. v. Meyer, 879 P. 2d 480 (CO App., 1994).

In South Carolina, nonprofit corporations violate the Bingo Act if they permit "runners" (agents of the corporation) to substitute for bingo players while players are temporarily excused from the floor. Unannounced covert investigations of bingo operations by the Tax Commission for tax purposes are allowed.

Home Health Service, Inc. v. South Carolina Tax Commission, 440 S.E. 2d 375 (SC, 1994).

The state's sovereign immunity, under the Eleventh Amendment, is not absolute. If circumstances indicate consent, congressional abrogation of immunity permits a federal injunction to force a state officer to comply with federal law (*Ex Parte Young* fiction). Congress intended to abrogate the states' sovereign immunity by adopting the Indian Gaming Regulatory Act (IGRA), pursuant to the Indian commerce clause. The Secretary of the Interior may, thus, prescribe regulations governing gaming on tribal lands where the state fails to negotiate in good faith concerning the Act.

Seminole Tribe of Florida v. State of Florida, 11 F. 3d 1016 (11th Cir. [FL], 1994).

In Idaho, the state may not operate a lottery on Indian reservations without a tribal ordinance or resolution and a tribal-state compact authorizing such activity. The state does not have to negotiate with the Indian tribes concerning Class III gaming activities not specifically permitted under Idaho law.

Coeur D'Alene Tribe v. State, 842 F. Supp. 1268 (D. ID, 1994).

Health Permits and Licenses

Asylum Licensing

In granting or denying approval for a community residence facility for developmentally disabled persons, the mayor may consider the needs of the entire county. He is not obliged to base the decision on the needs of only the city or the area.

> *Beech Hill Civic Association, Inc. v. Howe,* 613 N.Y.S. 2d 694 (App. Div., 2d
>   Dept., 1994).

The Department of Social Services (DSS) cannot require adult foster care facilities in Michigan to request and pay for inspections as a condition of licensure.

> *Michigan Residential Care Association v. Department of Social Services,* 526 N.W. 2d
>   9 (MI App., 1994).

Hospitals

Licensing Moratorium: Hospitals

The State Department of Health has the power to impose a *moratorium* on the granting of licenses (certificate of need) for hospitals to add a department of cardiac catheterization, when there are already plenty of such departments in the area.

> *Monmouth Medical Center v. Dept. of Health,* 639 A. 2d 1129 (NJ Super. A.D.,
>   1994).

Challenging Licensing and Zoning Decisions

Standing

Any "person aggrieved" has the right to begin an administrative hearing to resolve a dispute with an agency involving the person's rights, duties, or privileges, according to North Carolina's Administrative Procedure Act (NCAPA). An adjacent landowner can, thus, challenge the issuance of a permit, without an environmental impact statement, for a proposed electric generating plant by the North Carolina Department of Environment, Health and Natural Resources, Division of Environmental Management.

> *Empire Power Company v. N.C. DEHNR,* 447 S.E. 2d 768 (NC, 1994).

In North Carolina, nearby homeowners, who present evidence that they will suffer some special damage (reduction of property value) and raise concerns about health, safety, and traffic congestion, have standing to challenge a decision by a zoning administrator issuing a building permit for a group home to serve patients with full-blown AIDS.

> *Taylor Home of Charlotte, Inc. v. City of Charlotte,* 447 S.E. 2d 438 (NC App.,
>   1994).

Maritime organizations lacked standing to challenge the Cost Guard's granting of fee exemptions to youth-oriented nonprofit charitable organizations involved in teaching maritime skills, where the Coast Guard itself absorbed the costs of the no-fee licenses.

Seafarers International Union of North America v. U.S. Coast Guard, 871 F. Supp. 9
(D. DC, 1994).

Owners of property, that abutted a property specially permitted to be used as a group home for retarded autistic men, did not have standing to challenge the zoning use permit where there was nothing in the record that suggested that the permitted project would diminish or adversely affect their property or legal rights, or would be more adverse than continuation of the present use.

Watros v. Greater Lynn Mental Health, 642 N.E. 2d 599 (MA App. Ct., 1994).

Contract Zoning

An historic preservation foundation executed an easement with landowners preventing them from building a structure encroaching on open space or blocking building view without prior foundation permission. When landowners began to build without permission, the foundation sued. The court held that the unambiguous easement was enforceable, the foundation was not unreasonable in demanding that the addition be demolished before any negotiation could take place, and the foundation was properly awarded attorney fees.

Bagley v. Foundation for the Preservation of Historic Georgetown, 647 A. 2d 1110
(DC App., 1994).

A municipality cannot circumvent substantive powers and procedural safeguards, for the adoption of zoning ordinances, by contracting or settling with the owners of private property. Therefore, a municipal zoning agreement with the owner of a mining company, that was a non conforming use, not discussed at a public meeting and not made available for public inspection was set aside.

Warner Co v. Sutton, 644 A. 2d 656 (NJ Super. A.D., 1994).

Administrative Review

An Oregon land-use decision is final and appealable to the Land-Use Board of Appeals if it is contrary to the requirements of the comprehensive plan and the decision can be carried out, assured by inaction or action, without further decisions by the city.

Central Eastside Indus. Council v. City of Portland, 875 P. 2d 484 (OR App., 1994).

A landowner has a substantive due process action under 42 USC 1983 if a municipal decision, restricting the use of his or her land, is based on arbitrary reasons (i.e., a zoning board official's alleged personal financial interest in the action—unrelated to any legitimate state interest).

DeBlasio v. Zoning Board of Adjustment for the Township of West Amwell, N.J.,
    CA3, No. 93–5301, May 1, 1995.

The Federal Communications Commission (FCC) cannot evaluate applicants seeking to build and operate new broadcasting stations, arbitrarily and capriciously. An "integration" policy preferring stations whose owners promise to participate in management is arbitrary and capricious.

Bechtel v. F.C.C., 10 F. 3d 875 (DC Cir., 1993).

A Circuit Court of Appeal, upon review of a county board of zoning adjustment's imposition of conditions for the construction and operation of a materials recovery facility (MRF) in an agricultural district, cannot consider additional exhibits, not presented at the administrative level regarding the hazards of the proposed MRF. The interpretation of a zoning regulation by the body in charge of its enactment is given great weight.

Greene County Concerned Citizens v. Board of Zoning Adjustment of Greene County,
    873 S.W. 2d 246 (MO App. S.D., 1994).

Adjoining landowners sought review of a board of county commissioners' decision to grant a conditional use permit for construction of a cellular telephone microwave facility in a rural/residential zone. Since the board had denied approval to the same plan for the site, filed less than two months earlier, the court held that the subsequently approved plan was barred from approval by *res judicata.*

Hilltop Terrace Homeowners' Association v. Island County, 863 P. 2d 604 (WA App.
    Div. 1, 1993).

An ordinance, that requires nonprofit owners of nonconforming signs to modify their signs before a future enforcement date, is ripe for review by the court if the owners are presently faced with the choice of modification and will suffer hardship if judicial review is delayed.

Braksator v. Zoning Hearing Bd. of Northampton Tp., 641 A. 2d 44 (PA Commonwealth, 1994).

The Forest Service may close forest trails to off-road vehicles (ORV) if the decision is not arbitrary and capricious and is supported by a reasonable explanation. Such buffer zones for wilderness may be created without the performance of physical monitoring of the actual user conflict in the area.

Northwest Motorcycle Association v. U.S. Dept. of Agriculture, 18 F. 3d 802 (9th Cir. [WA], 1994).

In California, a Land-Use Board of Appeals (LUBA) must consider all arguments raised by interest groups challenging a country land-use ordinance, if the issues remanded to the county by LUBA cannot resolve all the issues raised by the challengers.

Bicycle Transp. Alliance v. Washington County, 873 P. 2d 452 (OR App., 1994).

An association of adjacent landowners has the right to be given notice and the opportunity to contest the issuance of a landfill permit, at the administrative level, as a matter of due process.

DuLaney v. Oklahoma State Dept. of Health, 868 P. 2d 676 (OK, 1993).

Fees to eliminate lake pollution were challenged by a property owners' association suit to enjoin collections of the fees. Held: No injunction granted. No proof of irreparable harm by the fees imposed on issuance of building permits. If there is harm to the property owner, a damages award will be adequate remedy.

Tahoe Keys Property Owners Association v. State Water Resource Control Bd., 28 CA Rptr. 2d 734 (CA App., 1994).

Zoning

In applying for a certificate of occupancy under a zoning regulation, the applicant must indicate a type of activity that is applicable. But, if an organization has several types of activity it is not held to a duty to be perfectly correct in stating a particular purpose on its application.

Kalorama Citizens Association v. Dist. of Columbia Board of Zoning Adjustment, 640 A. 2d 179 (DC App., 1994).

A nudist society may be required to obtain a special exception, to a zoning ordinance governing use of waterfront property, in order to use the property for sun bathing.

New England Naturist Association, Inc. v. George, 648 A. 2d 371 (RI, 1994).

A property owners' association was not successful in challenging a zoning approval for a shopping center expansion. The court held that the decision to allow the expansion was not arbitrary and capricious because the facility met specific zoning requirements.

Indian Trail Property Owner's Association v. City of Spokane, 886 P. 2d 209 (WA
   App. Civ. 3, 1994).

Educational Facilities

A neighborhood association sued to compel a school district and board of education to abandon certification of an environmental impact report for the construction of a planned elementary school in a minority, low-income area. Though the impact report did not include information about other cumulative projects in the school's attendance area or about the low-income housing problem in the larger community, it was held to be sufficient.

Concerned Citizens of South Cent. Los Angeles v. Los Angeles Unified School Dist., 29
   CA Rptr. 2d 492 (CA App. 2 Dist., 1994).

Zoning Changes

A nonprofit association, organized in order to monitor urban growth, challenged a new zoning ordinance that purported to "correct" a prior ordinance in order to issue a permit to a developer. The court held that the purported "correction" was really an "amendment" or "rezone." Thus, the city had to comply with due process and notice requirements before adopting the ordinance.

Responsible Urban Growth Group v. City of Kent, 868 P. 2d 861 (WA, 1994).

In Indiana, the operation of a home day-care business does not violate a residential use covenant if the use is infrequent, or unobtrusive, and is not detrimental to neighbors' property values. Public policy favors day care.

Stewart v. Jackson, 635 N.E. 2d 186 (IN App. 1 Dist., 1994).

A nonprofit corporation and homeowners' association brought an Article 78 proceeding to object to the lease of residential facilities for use by mentally retarded persons. In New York, in order to challenge the site selected, the objecting party must show, by clear, concrete, convincing evidence, that there would be over saturation of similar and other state licensed facilities nearby that would substantially alter the character of the community.

*William Court-White Hill Road Homeowners Association, Inc. v. N.Y. Commissioner of
   Mental Retardation and Developmental Disabilities,* 613 N.Y.S. 2d 322 (Sup.,
   1994).

The state may lease land to a private entity for construction of a fish hatchery, in contravention of a zoning ordinance, and despite the objection of neighbors, if there is a showing of compelling need and the use of the state's land is in furtherance of state purposes or governmental function.

Senders v. Town of Columbia Falls, 647 A. 2d 93 (ME, 1994).

A conditional zoning variance for an automobile racetrack, in an area zoned for agricultural use, may be challenged and revoked if there is sufficient evidence to show that the racetrack would not promote public health, safety, and general welfare, as required by a zoning resolution.

Sheridan Race Car Association v. Rice Ranch, 864 P. 2d 30 (WY, 1993).

In Utah, zoning changes that are administrative are not subject to a referenda by citizens' groups. However, zoning changes that are legislative in nature are subject to referenda (e.g., ordinance allowing a solid waste disposal facility).

Citizens' Awareness Now v. Marakis, 873 P. 2d 1117 (UT, 1994).

Other nonconforming compatible uses in an area do not justify the issuance of a permit for the addition of another nonconforming use in that area.

Jefferson County v. Seattle Yacht Club, 870 P. 2d 987 (WA App. Div. 2, 1994).

Enforcement of a restrictive covenant, limiting construction of more than one single-family dwelling on each lot, may be barred by the special defense of "changed circumstances." If 12 of the original lots have been subdivided or have two residential buildings on them, those conditions are "changed circumstances."

Shippan Point Association Inc. v. McManus, 641 A. 2d 144 (CT App., 1994).

A Korean-American legal advocacy group sued Los Angeles after the city imposed a zoning ordinance making the retail sales of alcoholic beverages, for off-premises consumption, a "conditional use" as a condition for rebuilding businesses after the 1992 Los Angeles riots. Such ordinances are valid in California. Riots are not "acts of God," allowing the licensees to come under the "grandfathering" clause of the Alcoholic Beverage Control Act.

If a conditional-use power to sell liquor is given to an NPO, and revocation of that power (e.g., by zoning) will put that organization out of business, such revocation must be carefully tied to compliance with "due process" law. If a less drastic rule will suffice, it should be used.

> *Korean-American Legal Advocacy Foundation v. City of Los Angeles,* 28 CA Rptr. 2d 530 (CA App., 1st Dist., 1994).

A "fully completed" preliminary plat must be considered only under land-use statutes and ordinances in effect at the time of the application's submission. However, a city council can approve a plat that contains·nonconforming lots, subject to specific conditions.

> *Friends of the Law v. King County,* 869 P. 2d 1056 (WA, 1994).

14

PROMOTERS AND ORGANIZERS

§149. PHASES OF PROMOTION ACTIVITY

Mission Statements

An organization's mission statement is the foundation of the organization's entire planning process. It provides a sense of direction, focus and unity to all organizational members. A good mission statement is clearly articulated, uniquely tailored to the organization, timely, inspiring, and promotes a quest for achievement. A task force usually develops the mission statement, communicates the final statement to the organization and implements the statement.

> Stone, Romuald A., *Mission Statements Revisited, SAM Advanced Management Journal,* Winter, 1996.

Organizational Vision

> *See,* Lipton, Mark, *Demystifying the Development of an Organizational Vision, Sloan Management Review,* Summer, 1996.

Promotion of Seminars and Workshops

> *See,* Shenson, Howard L., *How to Develop and Promote Successful Seminars and Workshops,* John Wiley & Sons, Inc., New York, NY, 1996.

15

PURPOSES AND PURPOSE CLAUSES

§161. CONTRADICTORY PURPOSES

A homeowners' association and country club may pass and implement a resolution allowing the Georgia Department of Natural Resources (DNR) to thin and control a deer herd on its property, over the objections of other local landowners, if the association does not exceed its powers, the local landowners have neither a property interest in the deer nor an interest in hunting the deer, and the thinning does not endanger the health or depreciate the property of the adjacent landowners.

Robinson v. Landings Association, Inc., 440 S.E. 2d 198 (GA, 1994).

§162. ILLEGAL PURPOSES

A nonprofit corporation may guarantee a member's loan and mortgage its property (if to further legitimate corporate business) to secure the guaranty. In one such case, the corporation's Articles stated that its purpose was to assist members in time of need and granted the power to achieve that purpose. However, it is *ultra vires* for a corporation to execute a contract of guaranty not in furtherance of its business, if the Board of Directors does not give its express authority. A statute prohibiting pecuniary remuneration of a member of a nonprofit is not violated by such a guaranty where the member is not recompensed for equivalent service, loss, or expense.

Monsignor Bernard P. Sheridan Counsel No. 6138 Knights of Columbus v. Bargersville State Bank, 620 N.E. 2d 732 (IN App. 1 Dist., 1993).

State Policy v. NPOs Policy (Choice of Officers)

State policy to promote a positive view of homosexuals does not entitle it to compel NPOs to assist this policy contrary to the views of the members of the organization and their First Amendment freedom of choice of its leaders.

Curran v. Mount Diablo Council of Boy Scouts of America, 29 CA Rptr. 2d 580 (CA App., 1994).

16

POWERS AND POWER CLAUSES

§169. STATUTE STATEMENT OF CORPORATE POWERS

Delegated Powers

Delegation of legislative power to a private organization (such as a trade association) (for example, rule-making power) is not valid unless it contains adequate means for preventing abuse of that power, such as the means to prevent pecuniary interest in the exercise of the power.

Independent Contractors of California, Inc. v. Dept. of Indust. Relations, 28 CA Rptr. 2d 550 (CA 1st Dist., 1994).

17

UNAUTHORIZED AND IMPROPER ACTS

§178. UNAUTHORIZED, IMPROPER, TORTIOUS, AND ILLEGAL ACTS MUST BE DISTINGUISHED

Abuse of Charitable Status

Too high self-serving "overhead," salaries, and so on of charities are being attacked by attorneys-general, despite Supreme Court decisions barring interference by government authorities. Use of fraud and deception statutes and use of the media to broadcast warnings are major devices to get around the Supreme Court view.

Bush, (article), *NonProfit Times,* p. 1 (Nov., 1993).

Computer Association Faces Allegations of Mismanagement and High Executive Salaries

The Software Publishers Association has used its anti-piracy skills to cut U.S. software piracy rates in half since the late 1980s through raids by the software police on corporate systems and through threats of lawsuits. Now the SPA finds itself with financial and philosophical difficulties. SPA was $338,000 in debt for 1995, and had a deficit of $137,000 in 1996. Settlements are down 19 percent since 1992. The SPA claims that its deficit is due to increased actions overseas. Many nonprofit managers believe the SPA should sponsor new technologies and licensing procedures to promote prevention, rather than merely seeking out piracy settlements. SBA's rival, Business Software Alliance (BSA) has double the budget of SPA and is backed by Microsoft. SPA President Robert Wasch's salary of $306,000 is much higher than BSA President Robert Holleyman's $137,000 compensation, and the salaries of other nonprofit executives.

Nash, Kim S., *Software Cops Under the Gun. Computerworld,* March 24, 1997.

Embezzlement By Executives

Former executive, Michael Pope, has been charged with embezzlement from the Richard Allen Center on Life foster agency in Harlem, New York City.

Swarns, Rachel, I., *Former Executive is Charged with Bilking Foster Agency,*
The New York Times, May 13, 1997.

Nigerian Scams

In May of 1996, word started getting out about scams running from Nigeria and targeting U.S. nonprofits. Several organizations were contacted about money allegedly left to them. However, a small fee was required to secure the money. Several organizations were almost scammed.

Clolery, Paul, (article), 10 *NonProfit Times* (12) 25 (December, 1996).

Immunity for Inherent Risks

A nonprofit ski resort operator is not liable to a skier for his/her injuries if the resort operator complied with the requirements of the ski statute, and if the injury, which occurs in an ungroomed area, is an inherent risk of skiing. There is no duty in Idaho to mark trails "closed."

Long v. Bogus Basin Recreational Association, Inc., 869 P. 2d 230 (ID, 1994).

Punitive Damages

See, Better to Give Than to Receive: Should Nonprofit Corporations and Charities Pay Punitive Damages? Daniel A. Barfield. *Valparaiso University Law Review,* Summer, 1995 29 n3 p1193–1250.

§179. CHARITABLE IMMUNITY

In July, 1995, New Jersey passed a new law which extends protection to officers, employees, and volunteers of charities against negligence claims filed by the intended recipients of charity. The new law helps to strengthen New Jersey's charitable immunity statute, which formerly protected only the charity, and not individuals. The law is expected to encourage volunteerism, which has been declining in recent years.

9 *NonProfit Times* (10) 5 (October, 1995).

A welfare recipient was injured while working at a community organization and participating in a required workfare program. New Jersey's statutory charitable immunity could not protect the community organization from the workers suit because the worker was not a beneficiary of the work of the organization. Also, when the organization agreed to permit welfare recipients to work at its premises, it was not engaged in charitable objectives, as set forth in its certificate of incorporation.

   Manley v. YMCA of Plainfield, 646 A. 2d 1163 (NJ Super. L., 1994).

A guest at a parish service, who was injured when she fell in the parking lot, sued the parish and the archdiocese. The court held that the guest was a "beneficiary" of the parish. The parish was granted immunity under the New Jersey Charitable Immunity Act, which grants immunity for negligence and gross negligence, to nonprofit corporations organized for religious, charitable, educational, or hospital purposes.

   Monaghan v. Holy Trinity Church, 646 A. 2d 1130 (NJ Super. A.D. 1994);
      N.J.S.A. 2A:53A–7 to 2A:53A–11. *See also George v. First United Presbyterian
      Church of B.,* 639 A. 2d 1128 (NJ App., 1994).

A nonprofit hospital and its agents, under Pennsylvania law, are required to report cases of suspected child abuse, and are immune, absent bad faith, from any liability resulting from child abuse investigations. The parents or relatives of a child must make sufficient allegations of bad faith to overcome the statutory presumption that the hospital and its agents acted in good faith in reporting the suspected child abuse.

   Heinrich v. Conemaugh Valley Memorial Hospital, 648 A. 2d 53 (PA Super.,
      1994); 23 Pa. C.S.A. Section 6318.

Arizona has a statute that provides immunity to lessees or occupants of premises from liability to recreational users.

   A.R.S. Section 33–1551; *Stramka v. Salt River Recreation, Inc.,* 877 P. 2d 1339
      (AZ App. Div. 1, 1994).

The parents of a child brought action against a private nonprofit shelter for refusal to disclose the location of the parents' minor daughter while authorities investigated the daughter's claims of child abuse. In California there is absolute immunity, under the Child Abuse and Neglect Reporting Act, for those, including nonprofits, who report child abuse and for conduct giving rise to the obligation to report the abuse (e.g., collection of data, observation, examination,

treatment performed in a professional capacity, subsequent communications between the reporter and authorities). The immunity is a defense to a Section 1983
Federal Civil Rights action. A nonprofit must have reasonable apprehension that
the child could suffer immediate physical harm, if his or her location were disclosed, in order to gain the privilege of immunity.

> *Robbins v. Hamburger Home for Girls,* 38 Cal. Rptr. 2d 534 (CA App. 2 Dist.,
> 1995).

Oregon has a statute that provides immunity from liability to persons conducting investigation into the possible mental illness of a patient. The statute
provides immunity to the investigator from third parties injured by the allegedly
mentally ill person as well as from liability to the allegedly mentally ill person.
The immunity extends for the acts of investigation as well as for consequences
of negligence in the performance of the investigation.

> *Deming v. Mt. Hood Community Mental Health Center,* 875 P. 2d 484 (OR App.,
> 1994).

Wisconsin's recreational immunity statute exempts "an organization or association not organized or conducted for pecuniary profit" from liability for personal injury, absent willful or malicious failure to guard or to warn against a
dangerous condition. The statute has been held to be constitutional, since it is rationally related to a legitimate government purpose.

> *Szarzynski v. YMCA, Camp Ninikani,* 517 N.W. 2d 135 (WI, 1994).

Waiver/Immunity Clauses

A "waiver of liability," signed by a participant in a ski race, is enforceable
and sufficient to relieve the nonprofit sponsor of the race from liability for the
participant's injuries, if the injuries are of the type intended to fall within the
scope of the clear and unambiguous exculpatory clause.

> *Masciola v. Chicago Metropolitan Ski Council,* 628 N.E. 2d 1067 (IL App. 1 Dist.,
> 1993).

If a written agreement, intended as a release, is signed at the same time as
an agreement binding the parties, there is an obvious conflict in the documents
and parole evidence should be allowed in order to construe the documents.

> *Bianchi's from Roma, Inc. v. Big Five Club, Inc.,* 630 So. 2d 642 (FL App. 3
> Dist., 1994).

Assumption of the Risk

A student who is hurt while participating in practice for cheerleading stunts at a school does not "assume the risks" of doing so where proper supervision by the school is absent.

> *Nova University v. Katz,* 18 FLW D–1880 (FL 4th DCA, 8/25/93); *Kirk v. Washington State Univ.,* 746 P. 2d 285 (WA 1987). Cf: Release form signature: *Deboer v. Florida Offroaders Drivers Association,* 18 FLW D–1805 (FL 5th DCA, Aug. 13, 1993).

§180. GOVERNMENTAL IMMUNITY

The state is not entitled to sovereign immunity from a suit, seeking compensation for the death of one child and for the injuries sustained by another, as a result of the state's delay in investigating child abuse reports. Negligence of state employees in carrying out ministerial tasks can result in liability even where those tasks are part of a function that is strictly and uniquely governmental in nature.

> *Boland v. State,* 615 N.Y.S. 2d 815 (Ct. Cl., 1994).

A child and parent sued a nonprofit community action agency when their child was allegedly molested by a day care worker. The court held that the private nonprofit corporation was not a local agency entitled to government immunity from suit. The county's designation of the corporation as its official community action program did not make the corporation a "governmental unit." Under the Federal Tort Claims Act, a corporation is not an instrumentality or agency of the federal government if its day-to-day operations are not supervised by the federal government. A nonprofit corporation is not vicariously liable for the outrageous actions of an employee that are conducted for personal reasons only.

> *Sanchez by Rivera v. Montanez,* 645 A. 2d 383 (PA Cmwlth., 1994).

A foundation operating a state bar interest on lawyers' trust accounts (IOLTA) program, that was created by the Texas Supreme Court pursuant to its inherent power to regulate the practice of law in the state, is a public agent entitled to state immunity under the Eleventh Amendment.

> *Washington Legal Foundation v. Texas Equal Access to Justice Foundation,* 873 F. Supp. 1 (W.D. TX, 1995).

For information about parties who have standing to seek access to agency information, *see* 82 ALR Fed. 248, §§3, 4, 7, 10.

In Georgia, a city has sovereign immunity from suit by a person injured at a civic center where the city operates the center to provide a facility for community organizations and public recreation, at a reasonable cost, for the benefit of the public, rather than primarily as a source of revenue for the city.

Steinberg v. City of Atlanta, 444 S.E. 2d 873 (GA App., 1994).

The closely involved day-to-day operation of a rayon plant, by the government, during World War II, is enough involvement to waive sovereign immunity and impose liability on the government under the Comprehensive Environmental Response, Compensation and Liability Act (CERCLA).

FMC Corp. v. Department of Commerce, CA 3 (en banc), No. 92–1945, July 5, 1994.

If the government is sufficiently removed from the day-to-day operations, it is not an "operator" or "arranger" of an Agent Orange manufacturing facility. Thus, the government may escape liability for hazardous waste contamination under CERCLA.

U.S. v. Vertac Chemical Corp., CA 8, No. 94–1946, Jan. 31, 1995.

A motorist sued Prison Rehabilitative Industries and Diversified Enterprises (PRIDE), which is a nonprofit corporation providing services to the Florida prison system under lease, after the motorist was injured when she struck a cow owned by PRIDE. The plaintiff's suit was dismissed after the court held that PRIDE is an instrumentality of the state, and statutes concerning waiver of immunity required her to serve the Department of Insurance, which she did not.

Prison Rehabilitative Industries v. Betterson, 648 So. 2d 778 (FL App. 1 Dist., 1994).

A nonprofit corporation, that is responsible for the exclusive control, custody, operation, maintenance, and repair of gas mains in a city, is not a "local government agency" entitled to local government immunity. Thus, a nonprofit corporation was not allowed to avoid liability for a gas explosion, by using a statute in Pennsylvania that prevents subrogation by insurers against local government agencies.

Modern Shoppers World-Mt. Airy Corp. v. Philadelphia Gas Works, 643 A. 2d 136 (PA Cmwlth., 1994).

A corporation is an agency of government when the state specifically creates the corporation to further governmental objectives and controls the operation of the corporation through its appointees. The national Railroad Passenger Corporation (Amtrak) is such a corporation.

Lebron v. National R.R. Passenger Corp., 115 S. Ct. 961 (U.S. CA, 1995).

An Indian treaty, guaranteeing an Indian tribe that the state shall not have the right to pass laws for the tribe's government, imparts sovereign immunity, but does not confer super sovereign authority to interfere with another jurisdiction's sovereign right to tax the income of residents in the jurisdiction.

Oklahoma Tax Com'n v. Chickasaw Nation, 115 S. Ct. 2214 (U.S. OK, 1995).

A nonprofit corporation, organized to provide education and health services to Indians, has tribal sovereignty, which bars suits against it if sovereignty is not unequivocally waived in the corporation's articles of incorporation. Waiver of sovereign immunity cannot be implied, but must be expressed unequivocally.

Ransom v. St. Regis Mohowk Educ. and Community Fund Inc., 611 N.Y.S. 2d 935
   (N.Y.A.D. 3 Dept., 1994).

The Red Cross has a sufficient relationship with the federal government to be protected from trial by jury by the federal government's sovereign immunity, because it performs governmental purposes and obligations resulting from the Geneva treaties. The federal charter of the Red Cross confers federal jurisdiction on suits by and against the Red Cross.

Berman v. American Nat. Red Cross, 834 F. Supp. 286 (N.D. IN, 1993) (injury
   sustained while giving blood).

An interstate agency (bistate) created by an interstate compact has Eleventh Amendment immunity (governmental).

Hess v. Port Authority Trans.–Hudson Corp., 114 S. Ct. 1292 (1994).

School Immunity

Under the Minnesota Human Rights Act, a school being sued by a student is not entitled to "official" or "discretionary" operation immunity.

Engels v. Independent School Dist., No. 91, 846 F. Supp. 760 (D.C. MN, 1994).

§181. TORT LIABILITY

Copyright Infringement

A commercial copying service, that prepared and sold unauthorized anthologies to university students without paying royalties or permission fees, is not entitled to the fair use defense of copyrighted works where the copying was purely for profit. Such acts, if blatant and willful, are penalized by increased statutory damages.

Princeton University Press v. Michigan Document Services, Inc., 855 F. Supp. 905
(E.D. MI, 1994).

To prevail on a claim for trademark infringement, a claimant must show that it has a valid interest in the mark and that the defendant's use of the valid mark is likely to cause confusion.

Comedy Hall of Fame, Inc. v. George Schlatter Productions, Inc., 874 F. Supp. 378
(M.D. FL, 1994).

Liability for infringement of copyright in musical composition is established by proof of (1) originality and authorship of the compositions involved; (2) compliance with all formalities required to secure the copyright; (3) status as proprietors of the copyrights of compositions; (4) defendant's public performance of compositions; and (5) lack or permission from any plaintiffs or their representatives.

Major Bob Music v. Stubbs, 851 F. Supp. 475 (S.D. GA, 1994); 17 U.S.C.A.
Section 101 et seq.

See 82 ALR Fed. 9, §§3[c], 4[a, c] for a discussion of designs on recreational objects as valid trademarks.

A research scientist cannot photocopy articles in a scientific journal for predominantly archival, rather than research purposes, under the fair use doctrine of Section 107 of the Copyright Act. Such use harms the publisher's photocopy licensing market.

American Geophysical Union v. Texaco Inc., 37 F. 3d 881 (2nd Cir., 1994).

A nonprofit trade association may violate copyright law if it copies a daily trade newsletter for distribution to its staff. Such use is not "fair use" under the "fair use" defense. Independently created work is "original" to the author and qualifies for copyright protection.

Television Digest, Inc. v. U.S. Telephone Association, 841 F. Supp. 5 (D. DC, 1993).

Parody trading cards infringe on the rights of publicity, under Oklahoma law, given to the Major League Baseball Players Association, an unincorporated association with exclusive collective bargaining agency rights for all major league baseball players.

Cardtoons, L.C. v. Major League Baseball Players Association, 838 F. Supp. 1501
   (N.D. OK, 1993).

Under the copyright statutes, a handgun control organization may photo-copy and send to its members a list of state legislators which a gun ownership organization included in a letter to its membership urging opposition to gun control measures pending before the state legislature. Such use is "fair use" of the list and not copyright infringement.

National Rifle Association of America v. Handgun Control Federation of Ohio, 15 F. 3d
   559 (6th Cir. [Ohio], 1994).

The National Football League, which is an unincorporated association, sued to enforce its copyright on games "blacked out" in Ohio. The court held that bars and restaurants that installed special antennas to receive distant city stations violated the NFL's copyright. The exemption of "home systems" from copyright liability does not apply to bars and restaurants.

National Football League v. Rondor, Inc., 840 Supp. 1160 (N.D. OH, 1993).

Fair Use Guidelines for Educational Multimedia

The Copyright Law of 1976 outlines the concept of fair use, which permits copyrighted materials to be used without royalties for nonprofit educational purposes. What material schools are able to use, however, is subject to interpretation. Specific guidelines were laid out only for print and music. In multimedia, fair use analysis is relatively new. The Creative Incentive Coalition has developed a set of guidelines, which reiterate some of the major points of fair use. Educational institutions can use parts of copyrighted works for educational purposes. The Creative Coalition guidelines specify acceptable quantities, including three minutes of a motion media work, 1,000 words of a text, or 30 seconds of a musical work. If a student or teacher wants to exceed these limits, permission from the holder of a copyright must be obtained.

Milone, Michael N., *Fair Use Guidelines for Educational Multimedia, Technology &
   Learning,* February, 1997.

Members' Personal Implied Liability

If an NPO has a written or generally recognized policy or custom that causes injury to other persons, the individual members (as well as the corporation) may be held liable. For example, if a college club has a custom of excessive consumption of alcohol in its initiation or welcoming parties, and a newcomer drinks to such excess as to die, his/her parent is held to have a cause of action for wrongful death damages against the individual members who participated in (and thus encouraged) the excessive drinking.

> *Haben v. Anderson*, 597 N.E. 2d 655 (IL, App., 1992): (even though Illinois
> Rev. Stat. *forbade* such initiation and hazing).

If a member of an NPO (a political candidate's election committee) authorizes or ratifies a contract (purchase order) of that unincorporated NPO, he/she may be held personally liable if the organization fails to pay for goods or services ordered and accepted.

> *Victory Committee v. Genesis Convention Center,* 597 N.E. 2d 361 (IN App., 1992)
> (catering contract).

Organization Liability

A sailing association that reasonably relied upon a "load line exemption certificate" (the equivalent of a license to carry passengers), issued by the Department of Transport of the United Kingdom, did not breach its duty to trainees to exercise due and reasonable care in choosing and approving vessels for sail training, under the Death on the High Seas Act (DOHSA), when trainees died on the ship.

> *McAleer v. Smith,* 860 F. Supp. 924 (D. RI, 1994).

See 88 ALR 3d 1197, §3[b] for information regarding the liability of a nonprofit swimming facility operator for injury to or death of a trespassing child.

A writing that is sufficient to satisfy the statute of frauds is necessary in order to make a contract between a construction company and a nonprofit corporation enforceable.

> *Durante Brothers Construction Corp. v. College Point Sports Association, Inc.,* 615
> N.Y.S. 2d 455 (A.D. 2 Dept., 1994); McKinney's General Obligations
> Law Section 5–701, subd. a, par. 1.

A nonprofit plumbing association was held to be liable for physical harm caused when it failed to exercise reasonable care in inspecting pipe manufacturers before it listed their plastic pipe as conforming with standards in its uniform plumbing code (UPC) and by failing to "delist" pipe that did not conform. Consumers were harmed by reliance of the local building inspectors upon the association's listings.

FNS Mortg. Service Corp. v. Pacific General Group, Inc., 29 CA Rptr. 2d 916 (CA App. 3 Dist., 1994).

In Pennsylvania, a campus police officer, not appointed by court order, is not a "police officer" as defined by the Vehicle Code. Thus, such a campus officer has no authority to arrest a motorist for driving while intoxicated. The motorist's license, in such cases, cannot be suspended for refusing to submit to chemical testing.

Snyder v. Com., 640 A. 2d 490 (PA Commonwealth, 1994).

The "apparent authority" of an association of hotels, over a hotel which was sued by a guest for personal injury, derives from what the principal manifests to a third party and what the third party reasonably believes. Where the association exercises considerable control over the individual hotels, there may be liability of the association under the theory of "apparent authority."

Giamo v. Congress Motor Inn, Corp., 847 F. Supp. 4 (D. RI, 1994).

An adoption agency may bring a declaratory action against a mother, mother's husband, and a mother's boyfriend to determine the validity of a surrender of parental rights and an adoption process. The bringing of declaratory action is not reckless or extreme conduct that will subject the agency to a claim against it for intentional infliction of emotional duress.

Families First v. Gooden, 439 S.E. 2d 34 (GA App., 1993).

Prospective parents who pay an adoption fee for a child, and then return the child, are entitled to restitution in equity and return of the fee where the agency subsequently collects a second fee for the placement of the child.

Friends of Children, Inc. v. Marcus, 876 S.W. 2d 603 (AK App., 1994).

Although the traditional common-law causes of action for fraud and negligence apply to the adoption setting, a court held in a recent case that the agencies allegedly involved in nondisclosure of an adopted child's significant history of physical and sexual abuse, have no common-law or statutory duty to investigate a child's mental and physical health in Pennsylvania.

Gibbs v. Ernst, 647 A. 2d 882 (PA, 1994).

Hospital Liability

A patient has a cause of action for negligence against a nonprofit hospital where she slipped and fell, allegedly due to a crack in the sidewalk at the clinic entrance, where the crack had existed for several years and where the clinic employees knew of the crack but took no steps to fix it.

McKenzie v. City of Miami, 648 So. 2d 291 (FL App. 3 Dist., 1995).

A patient of a nonprofit hospital can bring action, under the Emergency Medical Treatment and Active Labor Act (EMTALA), for inappropriate medical screening and transfer while in an unstable condition. Proof of bad motive or nonmedical reason is not required to establish a disparate treatment claim under EMTALA. Hospitals must prove that screening procedures are uniformly applied. In Virginia the state's limitation of liability of charitable and tax-exempt hospitals, for negligence or other tort, applies to patient dumping claims.

Power v. Arlington Hospital Association, 42 F. 3d 851 (4th Cir., 1994); Social Security Act, Section 1867, as amended, 42 U.S.C.A. Section 1395dd.

In a malpractice action against a nonprofit hospital, for brain damage to a child as a result of an independent contractor physician's failure to diagnose spinal meningitis, the court found that the alleged justifiable reliance of the minor's father was sufficient to state a cause of action against the hospital based on apparent or ostensible agency theory.

Chicago Title & Trust Company v. Sisters of St. Mary, 637 N.E. 2d 543 (IL App. 2 Dist., 1994).

In a malpractice action brought by parents of a disabled child against a nonprofit hospital, the court held that spoliation of nursing records raised a rebuttable presumption that medical negligence was the legal cause of the injuries. However, the spoliation of records did not give rise to a separate tort theory of recovery.

Sweet v. Sisters of Providence in Washington, 881 P. 2d 304 (AK, 1994).

An obstetrician's failure to perform a Caesarean section delivery in time, causing brain damage to a baby, does not preclude liability of the hospital. However, the court's refusal to strike the hospital defense of sole proximate cause, with erroneous law instructions, placed undue emphasis on its claim of sole liability of the physician.

Reusch v. Richland Memorial Hospital, 632 N.E. 2d 658 (IL App., 1994).

In a medical malpractice action against a nonprofit hospital involving the brain damage of a child during delivery, the court held that the judge may not instruct the jury that nurses are obligated to carry out the orders of their doctors, so long as there is no incompetence or negligence. Such jury instructions are not harmless error.

Bremner By and Through Bremner v. Charles, 859 P. 2d 1148 (OR App., 1993).

A hospital may be held accountable through the theory of agency by estoppel, even for the negligence of independent medical practitioners operating in the hospital if (1) the hospital holds itself out to the public as a provider of medical services and (2) the patient looks to the hospital, in the absence of notice or knowledge to the contrary, as opposed to the individual practitioner, to provide competent medical care.

Clark v. Southview Hosp. and Family Health Ctr., 828 N.E. 2d 46 (OH, 1994).

A trial court cannot admit evidence of a settlement between a malpractice plaintiff (infant injured during birth) and a nonprofit hospital in the plaintiff's case against a codefendant (physician). The admission of such evidence is prejudicial to the plaintiff.

Pounds By and Through Pounds v. Holy Rosary Medical Center, 872 P. 2d 437 (OR App., 1994).

A nonprofit hospital may be liable for negligence and breach of contract if its sterilization procedure, a tubal ligation, is not done, resulting in the birth of a child. Damages, a question for the jury, may include the expenses of raising the child and providing for the child's college education.

Zehr v. Haugen, 871 P. 2d 1006 (OR, 1994).

A private nonprofit mental hospital is not liable under Section 1983 or the Racketeer Influenced and Corrupt Organizations Act (RICO) for the suicide death of an involuntarily committed patient. Respondeat superior and vicarious liability do not apply to Section 1983 actions. The hospital's action is not the "state action" required for Section 1983 liability simply because the state designates the hospital to be an emergency receiving and treatment facility. Neither the hospital nor the physician acted "under color of law."

Trimble v. Androscoggin Valley Hosp., Inc., 847 F. Supp. 226 (D. NH, 1994).

Defamation

If statements about a charity in a series of newspaper articles, raising questions about the founder's financial competency as chief executive officer and about whether she misled the public about the charity's achievements, are "substantially true" as a matter of law, such statements will not support a claim of libel against the newspaper.

Rogers v. Dallas Morning News, Inc., 889 S.W. 2d 467 (TX App.–Dallas, 1994).

Allegedly defamatory statements made by an adjoining landowner at a hearing before a Zoning Board of Appeals are absolutely privileged if relevant. Such hearings are quasi-judicial in nature and statements made enjoy immunity and privilege, even where the speaker is not a party to the proceedings and speaks voluntarily.

Allan and Allan Arts Ltd. v. Rosenblum, 615 N.Y.S. 2d 410 (A.D. 2 Dept., 1994).

A different standard for summary judgment is employed in defamation cases in order to protect free speech. The chairman of a nonprofit organization did not survive a motion for summary judgment in his suit for defamation against a radio station caller, radio station, and station employees where the caller merely complained of the chairman's general leadership, alleged that the chairman alone was "running the show," and referred to a tax problem actually facing the board.

Bell v. Roddy, 646 So. 2d 967 (LA App. 1 Cir., 1994).

A diocese, relief society, and mental health care group have a conditional privilege in defamation actions, based on a common professional interest in mental health care, to communicate about a relief society care group, concerning the quality of care provided to mentally ill patients in group homes. The privilege may be forfeited by abuse, if there is coherent argument with references to the record to support the assertion of abuse.

Shannon v. Alliance for the Mentally Ill of Greater Milwaukee, 525 N.W. 2d 299
   (WI App., 1994).

A correction officer sued a nonprofit corporation, representing prisoners, for defamation when the corporation circulated a letter and printout which referred to the officer's alleged excessive use of force. Actual malice must be shown in order for the jury to find defamation in such cases. The officer was awarded $35,000 in the case.

Sweeney v. Prisoners' Legal Services of New York Inc., 610 N.Y.S. 2d 628 (NY
   A.D. 3 Dept., 1994).

A nonprofit organization has an absolute privilege against liability for making allegedly damaging and false statements, about applicants for the office of associate judge, in letters sent to the judges of the circuit court in which the applicants are seeking office. Public interest and policy requires disclosure of any information that relates to the applicant's performance in office.

Muck v. Van Bibber, 621 N.E. 2d 1043 (IL App. 4 Dist., 1993).

Statements made by a chancellor of the Roman Catholic diocese about a priest, indicating that the priest had made "wild charges" and "threatens to continue his untrue and disruptive public statements" are not defamation per se. Such statements do not indicate that the priest is unable to discharge his duties.

May v. Myers, 626 N.E. 2d 725 (IL App. 3 Dist., 1993).

An animal trainer brought suit against animal rights organizations for defamation and invasion of privacy when the organizations showed and distributed videotape of the trainer as he prepared his animals for show. The court held that such a showing of videotape is not false or defamatory. Public comment that the videotape depicted abuse of animals is an opinion. No tort occurred.

People for the Ethical Treatment of Animals v. Bobby Berosini, Ltd., 867 P. 2d 1121 (NV, 1994).

Slander of an accrediting officer (inspector) by a religious college (falsely calling him incompetent and a homosexual) is actionable tort; a program evaluator for the Missouri Dept. of Education.

Nazeri v. Missouri Valley College, # 75201 (MO Supr. Crt., Aug. 17, 1993).

Insurance for Torts and Crimes

Lawsuits are very expensive and can damage the image of a nonprofit organization. Thus, management should be fully aware of employment laws and their nuances and should seek coverage from pertinent insurance companies to avoid liability.

McMillan, Mary, *Controlling the Risks of Lawsuits, Association Management,* August, 1996.

An insurer has a duty to defend a nonprofit organization, that treated a priest for pedophilia for alleged molestation occurring before the inception date of the policies, in a case where victims alleged they were unable to perceive the existence of their psychological injuries until years after the abuse while the policies were in effect.

Servants of the Paraclete, Inc. v. Great American Insurance Company, 857 F. Supp.
     822 (D. NM, 1994).

A nonprofit organization, that treated priests for pedophilia, brought action against its insurer for breach of duty to defend and indemnify concerning actions against the organization for alleged sexual abuse by a priest. The court held that an insurer lacks a duty to defend when there are material fact issues existing regarding whether the insurer ever issued a policy alleged to provide coverage.

Servants of the Paraclete, Inc. v. Great American Insurance Co., 866 F. Supp. 1560
     (D. NM, 1994).

For the purposes of insurance policies, a sexual molestation victim's exposure to a negligently supervised priest, in each of four different policy periods, constitute separate occurrences where the policies state that multiple exposures can constitute a single occurrence but only if multiple exposures occurring during the same period of insurance.

Interstate Fire & Casualty Co. v. Archdiocese of Portland in Oregon, 35 F. 3d 1325
     (9th Cir., 1994).

When a joint underwriting association sued its liability insurer for failure to defend and settlement costs, the court held that an assault and battery endorsement in the insurer's special multiperil policy did not exclude coverage for a claim alleging negligent failure to provide security.

Liquor Liability Joint Underwriting Association of Massachusetts v. Hermitage Insurance Company, 644 N.E. 2d 964 (MA, 1995).

A nurse's liability insurer has no duty to defend or indemnify the nurse in a patient's tort suit alleging sexual abuse, where the insurer's policy barred coverage for intentional injury. A complaint and tort judgment is sufficient basis to infer intent to injure. The hospital was not liable because its policy coverage included only "rendering of or failure to render professional services."

American Casualty Company v. Corum, 885 P. 2d 726 (OR App., 1994).

A "dependent" child's residence is with the parents for the purposes of insurance coverage, not at the private nonprofit hospital where the child is being treated.

Cardinal Glennon Children's Hospital v. St. Louis Labor Health Institute, 891 S.W.
     2d 560 (MO App. E.D., 1995).

The organizers of a nonprofit boat festival are not liable under an indemnification clause to the owners of a boat for damages sustained during a voyage to the festival where the boat owner breached an implied warranty of seaworthiness in his contract with the festival.

Missouri Dry Dock v. M/V Ste. Genevieve, 867 F. Supp. 879 (E.D. MO, 1994).

A nonprofit insured must disclose, in response to questions in its insurance application, any fact, circumstance, or situation which the insured has reason to believe might afford valid grounds for any future claim against it, especially where the application disclaims coverage if such information is known, but not disclosed.

International Surplus Lines Ins. Co. v. University of Wyoming Research Corp., 850 F. Supp. 1509 (D. WY, 1994).

The court will examine the activities of a nonprofit organization to determine whether it is engaged "in the business of selling and serving alcoholic beverages," for purposes of an insurance policy exclusion for such activity, rather than the corporate structure or status. A nonprofit that operated a tavern was, thus, excluded from coverage under its property and liability policy for selling alcohol to an underage person, despite its nonprofit nature, where its corporate structure empowered it to engage in business activities and its bylaws envisioned a bar business.

Sprangers v. Greatway Ins. Co., 514 N.W. 2d 1 (WI, 1994).

§182. CRIMES COMMITTED BY CORPORATIONS

RICO Actions

Union members, who bring action against their union and employer based on allegations that the union negotiators had agreed to concessions, in a collective bargaining agreement, in exchange for pension payments to which they were not entitled, have both a cause of action under RICO and for breach of contract.

Cox v. Administrator U.S. Steel & Carnegie, 17 F. 3d 1386 (11th Cir. [AL], 1994).

When trustees threaten to withhold trust assets from a beneficiary, if the beneficiary refuses to release fraud claims against the trustees, the threats are sufficient to allege a violation of the Hobbs Act, as a predicate racketeering act under the Racketeer Influenced and Corrupt Organization Act (RICO). Use of interstate mails and wire communications to fraudulently obtain settlement of a lawsuit by the beneficiary are also sufficient predicate acts in a RICO action. RICO actions are governed by a four-year statute of limitations which begins when the plaintiff discovered or should have discovered the injury.

Turkish v. Kasenetz, 27 F. 3d 23 (2nd Cir., 1994).

A nonprofit organization's threat to sue a real estate company for housing discrimination, if the company did not agree to settlement, is not a predicate act for Racketeer Influenced and Corrupt Organization Act (RICO) purposes and is not extortion under the Ohio Corrupt Activities Act.

Heights Community Congress v. Smythe, Cramer Co., 862 F. Supp. 204 (N.D. OH, 1994).

State courts have concurrent jurisdiction over claims under the Racketeer Influenced and Corrupt Organizations Act (RICO).

Gervase v. Superior Court (Prudential Securities, Inc.), 37 Cal. Rptr. 2d 875 (CA App. 3 Dist., 1995).

Illegal Gambling

"Casino Nights" have been deemed by the Oklahoma Attorney General to be illegal. According to the Attorney General, any gambling that involves "money, checks, credits, or any representative of value" is illegal, even where participants do not walk away with cash. Lotteries are prohibited under Oklahoma's Charity Games Act. Prizes awarded at public events such as rodeos, animal shows, fair and athletic events, some bingo games, and "breakopen" ticket games are exempt.

See, Mehegan, Sean, (article), 9 *NonProfit Times* (5) 23 (May, 1995).

Penalties for Crimes

Excess Benefits to Insiders

The Clinton administration proposed, in 1994, and passed in 1996, a set of sanctions designed to help the IRS monitor charities. The sanctions include (1) a 25-percent tax on "excess benefits" received by an "insider," including excess compensation and "nonfair market value transfers," (2) a tax imposed on nonprofit executives who authorize the "excess benefits" of 10 percent on the amount, (3) a requirement that nonprofits mail 990s to anyone requesting them for a reasonable mailing and copying fee, (4) new penalties for late filing of 990s ($100 a day fine, up to $50,000 for NPOs with more than $1 million in annual gross receipts), and

(5) a requirement that NPOs report all excise taxes paid on their 990s, and state in their fundraising literature that 990s are available on request.

> 8 *NonProfit Times,* (4) 1, 15 (April, 1994). *See, Sanctions on Charities for Self-Dealing and Certain Other Activities.* Janet Buehler. *The Tax Adviser,* April, 1994.

Crimes by Partners

For information about embezzlement, larceny, false pretenses, or allied criminal fraud by a partner, *see* 82 ALR 3d 822, §6[c].

Illegal Sale of Liquor

For information on what constitutes the sale of liquor in violation of statutes or ordinances, *see* 89 ALR 3d 551, §22[a].

§184. CIVIL RIGHTS LIABILITY

Free Speech and Constitutional Law

The private nonprofit organizer of a municipal festival is not a "state actor" who can be held accountable for a civil rights violation under Section 1983 for denying booth space to a union that wants to distribute literature on its "Buy American" campaign. A permit to use public streets and sidewalks did not transform the organization into a "state actor."

> *United Auto Workers, Local #5285 v. Gaston Festivals, Inc.,* 43 F. 3d 902 (4th Cir., 1995).

Free speech, picketing, demonstrations, and so on of NPOs or members are not unlimited. Thus, abortion-opponent views that are carried to the point of substantial amounts of harassment and name calling against patrons of abortion clinics may be enjoined by courts, or restricted by court order.

> *Operation Rescue v. Women's Health Center, Inc.,* 18 FLW S–559 (FL, Oct. 28, 1993); 16 A Am. Jur. 2d Constitutional Law §519 (1993 pocket supp., p. 109).

Demonstrators who seek to conspire to hinder state law enforcement officers from securing the constitutional right to abortion by women face action under the hindrance clause of the Ku Klux Klan Act, 42 U.S.C.A. Section 1985(3).

> *National Abortions Federation v. Operation Rescue,* 8 F. 3d 680 (9th Cir. [OR], 1993).

A nonprofit corporation, established to promote downtown revitalization through the holding of a yearly festival, can deny booths to organizations whose goals are "controversial" or it deems incompatible with the festival's goals of "fun and entertainment." The Kentucky Supreme Court has deemed such restrictions to be "content neutral," and thus, not violations of free speech. The festival corporation denied booths in 1990 to the Capital Area Right to Life, Inc. (CARTL), after CARTL distributed plastic models of fetuses in baskets at the 1989 festival. The festival corporation also denied booths to Kentucky NOW and the Kentucky Religious Coalition for Abortion Rights, associations with a message opposed to that of CARTL.

See, Capital Area Right to Life, Inc. v. Downtown Frankfort, Inc., 114 S. Ct. 2153
    (U.S. KY, 1994) (dissent by Justice O'Connor).

A nonprofit family planning clinic can obtain an injunction against antiabortion protesters that effectively bars them from the public sidewalk in front of the clinic. The injunction may require that all picketing, demonstrating, or counseling take place on the public sidewalk across the street, without a violation of the First Amendment. Such restrictions are "content neutral, serve a substantial government interest in protecting patients' physical and emotional health and safety, are narrowly tailored to effectuate a substantial state interest and permit ample alternative channels of communication."

Planned Parenthood Shasta-Diablo, Inc. v. Williams, 873 P. 2d 1224 (CA, 1994).

A court of equity may issue an injunction against antiabortion protesters at a family planning clinic if the injunction reasonably imposes restrictions on peaceful expressive activities, is content neutral, and serves a significant government interest. First Amendment scrutiny applies. The injunction must be narrowly drawn and necessary to serve a significant compelling state interest. Reasonable time, place, and manner restrictions in a traditional public forum are valid. Accessibility of medical services including abortion, maintenance of medical standards, preservation of health, and protection of private property constitute significant government interests. Manner restrictions should focus on the noise that protesters produce, rather than the content of their speech. Place restrictions may prohibit invading or trespassing on property and intentional interference with the flow of traffic into and out of a clinic.

Horizon Health Center v. Felicissimo, 638 A. 2d 1260 (NJ, 1994).

State statutes requiring "demonstrators" to stay over 36 feet away from abortion clinics do not unduly restrict the demonstrators' freedom of speech, the

Supreme Court ruled (6 to 3) in June 1994. This decision upheld a Florida judge's order imposing a "buffer zone."

Activist organizations (or their members) do not have the right to express or impose their views by conduct that amounts to trespass or assault or intimidation.

Aware Woman Center for Choice v. Operation Rescue National, U.S. Supr. Ct.; Rehnquist opinion (June 30, 1994), Scalia dissent opinion.

Right to Privacy

In California, both the state's Privacy Initiative of the Constitution and the common law of right to privacy apply to intercollegiate athletic organizations. An intercollegiate athletic association's drug testing policy, involving the monitoring of urination, testing of urine samples, and inquiry concerning medication does not violate the right to privacy.

Hill v. National Collegiate Athletic Association, 865 P. 2d 633 (CA, 1994).

Discrimination

A nonprofit alcohol rehabilitation center is not a state actor, for purposes of a Section 1983 civil rights action brought against the center based on the fact that the patient is a Native American, even where the city used the center which received most of its funding from the state, if there is no evidence that the state controlled treatment. Supervisory liability for civil rights violations exists only where the supervisor (1) had notice of a continuing, widespread, persistent pattern of unconstitutional acts being committed by employees under their supervision and control, (2) demonstrated deliberate indifference or tacit authorization of the acts after notice, (3) failed to take sufficient remedial action that reasonable persons would have taken, and (4) caused the plaintiff's injuries by failure to act.

Scout v. City of Gordon, 849 F. Supp. 687 (D. NE, 1994).

For information about the standing of a housing association or organization to sue in its own right under the Fair Housing Act of 1968, as amended (42 USCS §3604), *see* 102 ALR Fed. 718.

A nonprofit organization brought action against an owner of property for discriminatory conduct in violation of the Fair Housing Act (FHA) when the property owner allegedly reneged on an oral agreement to rent (with an option to buy) two houses to the organization, after the property owner found out the houses would be used as a group home for persons infected with Human Immunodeficiency Virus (HIV). The court held that the proposed rental house was a "single family house" within the meaning of the FHA exemption from the Act.

> *Hogar Agua Y Vida En El Desierto, Inc. v. Suarez-Medina,* 36 F. 3d 177 (1st Cir., 1994).

A city charter amendment that prohibited the city from enacting or enforcing a rule or policy that would provide gays, lesbians, and bisexuals with any protection or preferential treatment based on their sexual orientation, status, conduct or relationship, was declared unconstitutional in Ohio. The court held that such provisions violate the First Amendment by deterring political speech and association and also run afoul of the equal protection clause. Gays, lesbians, and bisexuals fall into a quasi-suspect status, requiring that laws concerning them be substantially tailored to sufficiently important governmental interest.

> *Equality Foundation of Cincinnati v. City of Cincinnati,* 860 F. Supp. 417 (S.D. OH, 1994).

Equal Protection

The state of Hawaii may charge mooring fees to boaters who anchor and navigate in ocean waters surrounding the Hawaiian islands without violating the commerce clause, equal protection clause, or the privileges and immunities clause.

> *Barber v. State of Hawaii,* 42 F. 3d 1185 (9th Cir., 1994).

A class of tenants in public housing sued to enjoin and get declaratory relief from a determination by the Department of Housing and Urban Development (HUD) that Washington's state court eviction procedures for tenant eviction satisfied the basic elements of due process. The promulgation of a substantive rule by HUD without notice to the tenants and an opportunity to be heard, in violation of HUD's own regulations, rendered the rule invalid.

> *Yesler Terrace Community Council v. Cisneros,* 37 F. 3d 442 (9th Cir., 1994).

Civil Rights: Hospitals

A visitor to a nonprofit hospital was arrested and subsequently brought a Section 1983 action against the hospital and city, among others. The court held that there was no agreement between the private nonprofit hospital and police (hospital and agents were not state actors) to deprive the visitor of her constitutional rights, as required to support the visitor's Section 1983 action.

Velaire v. City of Schenectady, New York, 862 F. Supp. 774 (N.D. NY, 1994).

Under a provision of the Civil Rights of Institutionalized Persons Act, the Attorney General may institute civil action against state institutions (for example, for the mentally retarded) if he or she is satisfied that the case is serious enough to warrant federal involvement based on reasonable cause to believe that a "pattern or practice" of state government is leading to "egregious or flagrant conditions" causing "grievous harm."

United States v. Pennsylvania, 863 F. Supp. 217 (E.D. PA, 1994).

A plaintiff, who claims that the staff of a state mental health facility was deliberately indifferent to the suicidal tendencies of a voluntarily committed patient who subsequently committed suicide, has a claim under Section 1983 for which relief can be granted.

Estate of Cassara by Cassara v. State of Illinois, 853 F. Supp 273 (N.D. IL, 1994).

Civil Rights: Schools

A school that dismissed a pupil for hysterical conduct when she had cut herself is liable for a civil rights violation if it does not make reasonable provision for her condition of a bad autoimmune blood system disorder.

Thomas By and Through Thomas v. Davidson Academy, 846 F. Supp. 611 (D.C.
TN, 1994).

A nonprofit religious school does not commit discrimination if it implements a school policy that classroom doors remain open, for a legitimate reason, and a parent voluntarily withdraws his/her child from the school after the child repeatedly runs out of a nursery school classroom.

Posner v. Central Synagogue, 609 N.Y.S. 2d 195 (N.Y.A.D. 1 Dept., 1994).

Employee Association's Civil Rights Action

A firefighters' association' of black city employees was successful in challenging the city's policy of "skip promotions" in a consent decree. Such promotions violate the equal protection clause of the Constitution.

Black Fire Fighters Association of Dallas v. City of Dallas, 19 F. 3rd 992 (5th Cir.
    TX, 1994).

Corporate Categorization/Civil Rights

An employee (African-American) cannot sue for racial harassment damages under the Civil Rights Act merely because the president of her employer corporation said, in her presence, that the corporation was a white supremacist organization.

Lewis v. American Foreign Service Association, 846 F. Supp. 71 (D.C. DC, 1994);
    and 846 F. Supp. 77.

"State Action" Test of NPO

When rules of an unincorporated national athletic association are the main factor in the suspension of a state university's basketball team coach by the university, that suspension is not "state action" for the purposes of the Fourteenth Amendment (in a 42 U.S. Code §1983 lawsuit).

Nat'l. Collegiate Athletic Assn. v. Tarkanian, 488 U.S. 179, 109 S. Ct. 454 (1988),
    102 L. Ed. 2d 469.

§185. CONTEMPT OF COURT

Abortion protesters, found in civil contempt for willfully violating a temporary restraining order, can be assessed attorney fees and costs. Their financial circumstances and ability to pay are irrelevant. Fees are calculated according to the prevailing market rate.

Pro-Choice Network of Western New York v. Project Rescue Western New York 848 F.
    Supp. 400 (W.D. NY, 1994).

18

CORPORATE NAME, SEAL, AND OFFICE

§192. DECEPTIVE NAMES

Incorporation Name/Assumed Name

Filing of a certificate of an assumed name is not enough to be binding on a vendor of goods, as notice that a partnership has changed to corporation status (business corporation; but the same rule presumably applies to an NPC).

> *Horizon Hobby Distributors v. Gurriero,* 613 N.Y.S. 2d 550 (Supr. Ct. Suffolk Co., 1994).

§200. REMEDIES FOR INVASION OF RIGHTS IN A NAME

Names: Trade Regulation

A Texas golf club may enjoin an Arkansas club's use of the word "Champions" as a service word for its golf club services.

> *Champions Golf Club, Inc. v. Sunrise Land Corp.,* 846 F. Supp. 742 (D.C. [AK], 1994).

The Society of Financial Examiners sued the National Association of Certified Fraud Examiners, Inc. over the use of the letters CFE to designate "certified financial examiner" or "certified fraud examiner" respectively. The court held that summary judgment was precluded because there was a genuine issue of material fact as to whether CFE was a generic mark or whether the use by two organizations was likely to cause confusion.

> *Society of Financial Examiners v. National Ass'n of Certified Fraud Examiners,* 41 F. 3d 223 (5th Cir., 1995).

The United Way of Southeastern New England (UWSNE) was enjoined from using the name, without permission, of a local Rhode Island organization, the Fund for Community Progress (FCP) in its United Way fund-raising literature, which was based on the solicitation of donations through *donor options*. The FCP argued that the use of the name competes with its own fund-raising campaigns, leads donors to believe that the funds are received by FCP, and has caused a decrease in the amount of donations and numbers of donors to the FCP.

McIver, La Vonne, (article), 9 *NonProfit Times* (7) 4, (July, 1995).

19

INCORPORATION: ARTICLES AND PROCEDURES

§205. PREPARATION OF ARTICLES (CERTIFICATE) OF INCORPORATION

Constitution Drafting (Articles of Incorporation)

Professor Albert P. Blaustein, who wrote more national constitutions for more nation-states than has any other person in this century, summed up the learning that his vast experience gave, in an essay. Speaking in terms of nation states, his advice is equally applicable to private (or public) nonprofit societies/organizations.

In brief, he said that "a constitution is the queen of legal documents . . . It is not just a supreme law . . . (It) must express national (the organization's) purpose, . . . spirit, and aspirations . . . (It must avoid) 'deplorable' writing . . . and 'dangerous' provisions . . . designed to achieve specific political ends, (and) unduly complex language (and) wordiness . . . (It should try to compose) grand, inspiring provisions. . . ." He gave many illustrations of these concepts, from constitutions all around the world. They will help "drafters" everywhere.

A.P. Blaustein, *Constitution Drafting: The Good, The Bad, and The Beautiful,* 2
 SCRIBES Journal of Legal Writing 49–61 (1991; issued June, 1993).

Membership Corporate Outfits, including membership certificates, printed minutes and bylaws, corporate record books, seals, and so forth can be obtained through Excelsior-Legal, Inc., 62 White Street, New York, NY 10013, phone (800) 221–2972, FAX (212) 431–5111.

Binding Effect of Articles of Incorporation

The stock of a mutual irrigation corporation, that was established to allocate water to shareholders who already own the right to use that water, represents a real property interest and is not a certificated security. Thus, the corporation's articles of incorporation, if valid, govern any stock transactions.

The Uniform Commercial Code (UCC) provisions do not apply to stock transactions by corporations not organized to make a profit for shareholders.

> *Salt Lake City Corp. v. Cahoon and Maxfield Irrigation Co.,* 879 P. 2d 248 (UT, 1994).

A national osteopathic association, as a third-party beneficiary to the local board's charter, has standing to enforce its approval rights over a local board's directors, articles, and bylaws where those rights are granted by the local board's charter. Neither the local board's merger with another local board nor a restatement of its articles of incorporation can serve to eliminate the national association's approval rights.

> *National Board of Examiners for Osteopathic Physicians and Surgeons, Inc. v. American Osteopathic Association,* 645 N.E. 2d 608 (IN App. 4 Dist., 1994).

In Minnesota, articles of association, that create a broad grant of indemnity for members who are sued on the basis of their membership, indemnify the members against an antitrust action filed against the association and particular members, even though the articles fail to expressly include antitrust liability.

> *Firemen's Fund Insurance Company v. Western National Mutual Group,* 851 F. Supp. 1361 (D. MN, 1994).

Incorporation in Delaware

A recent study of Delaware's corporation law and its effect on the people of Delaware strongly argues that incorporation in that state is good for some big-money banks and other corporations, but not for the poor people in that state. Incorporation of *business* there is still very popular. However, incorporation of NPCs there has been relatively rare, and continues to be so. Thus the view of Delaware as "the home of corporations" is *not* applicable to NPOs.

> R. Hornstein and D. Atkins, *Piercing the Corporate Veil; A Different Delaware Beyond the Boardrooms,* 41 Clev. St. L. Rev. (2) 297 (1993).

§208. FILING FEES

NPO Records Fees

Statutory fees charged by a public agency for costs of copying documents for an NPO cover only that service, and should not include fees for ancillary tasks involved in the retrieval and handling of the file that contained those documents.

> *North County Parents Organization for Children With Special Needs v. CA Dept. of Educ.,* 28 CA Rptr. 2d 359 (CA App. 4th Dist., 1994).

§210. CORPORATION SERVICE-COMPANIES

A "corporation agent" for filing documents and providing other administrative services to NPOs, that the authors recommend, which has had some name changes in recent years, is *CSC Networks Prentice Hall Legal and Financial Services,* with offices at 375 Hudson Street, New York, NY 10014; (212) 463–2700 or (800) 221–0770, formerly named Prentice Hall Corporation Service.

20

ORGANIZATION MEETINGS*

*[*See Successful Meetings* (magazine) concerning worldwide current hotel and other meeting facilities, supplies, and services, 355 Park Ave., So., New York, NY 10010, (212) 592–6403 (editorial office).]

[*See also* Chapters 21 and 24.]

Conferences

Many nonprofits in 1997/98 are having conferences. A study by the American Society of Association Executives (ASAE) shows a marked increase in the number of gatherings, and projects a 39% increase for 1997. The most popular conference cities are Baltimore, Charlotte, Chicago, Cleveland, Colorado Springs, Denver, Detroit, Las Vegas, Miami Beach, Minneapolis, Nashville, New Orleans, New York, Orlando, Philadelphia, Phoenix, San Francisco, Seattle, St. Louis and Washington, D.C.

> Swarden, Carlotta, (article), 10 *NonProfit Times* (9) 1, 30–31 (September, 1996). *See also,* Shenson, Howard L., *How to Develop and Promote Successful Seminars and Workshops,* John Wiley & Sons, Inc., New York, NY, 1996.

21

MINUTES OF MEETINGS

§222. THE MINUTE BOOK

Membership Corporate Outfits, including minute books, can be obtained through Excelsior-Legal, Inc., 62 White Street, New York, NY 10013, Phone (800) 221–2972, Fax (212) 431–5111.

§227. INSPECTION OF MINUTES AND RECORDS

For more information concerning what constitutes an agency subject to the application of state freedom of information acts, *see* 27 ALR 4th 742 §§5, 6.

An animal rights group brought action against the University of Washington to get access to an unfunded grant proposal under the Public Records Act. The court held that the personal information exemption did not apply to the grant proposal. "Valuable formulae," "deliberative process" and "research data" were protected as intellectual property. However, the rest of the proposal had to be disclosed. Once the proposal is funded, "deliberative process" becomes "implemented" and therefore disclosable.

> *Progressive Animal Welfare Society v. University of Washington,* 884 P. 2d 592 (WA, 1994).

A team selected by a private association of school administrators, to investigate the problems at a public school, is not a "public body" within the meaning of an inspection of public records law. Only when the report is submitted to the board can the report affect matters of public concern. Then, the report would be accessible as a public record of the school board.

> *Marks v. McKenzie High School Fact-Finding Team,* 878 P. 2d 417 (OR, 1994).

A newspaper publisher and its employees may get access, under the public records law, to a "memorandum of understanding" reciting the settlement terms of a former district superintendent's breach of contract and defamation action against the school board, even if the memorandum was drafted largely by the board's law firm.

> *Journal/Sentinel v. School Board of the School District of Shorewood,* 521 N.W. 2d 165 (WI App., 1994).

Sealed proxy votes, that are exercisable only at an election which has not occurred and are revocable at any time prior to the election, are not "official records" of the association. Therefore, such proxies are not subject to examination, under Florida law, by the members of the association, prior to the election.

> *Islander Beach Club Condominium Association of Volusia County, Inc. v. Johnston,* 623 So. 2d 628 (FL App. 5 Dist., 1993) (member engaged in proxy fight wanted inspection).

Under Georgia law, the Commissioner of the Department of Community Affairs (DCA) has statutory authority to conduct performance audits of all nonprofit corporations created by regional development centers. The statute authorizes access to all of the defendants' preenactment books and records.

> *Coastal Georgia Regional Development Center v. Higdon,* 439 S.E. 2d 902 (GA, 1994).

California's Public Records Act allows a public agency to recover the "direct costs," from a nonprofit organization, of copying documents that the organization wants to review, such as those documents involving all local school district action relating to a special education service. The agency cannot recover the costs of ancillary tasks, such as retrieval and handling. The agency may, however, waive the fee.

> *North County Parents Organization for Children With Special Needs v. CA Dept. of Educ.,* 28 CA Rptr. 2d 359 (CA App. 4 Dist., 1994).

A nonprofit local corporation, formed to encourage the growth of small businesses and to reduce employment, and which was administering government loan programs, is an "agency" subject to the Freedom of Information Law (FOIL). A newspaper was, thus, allowed access to its records.

> *Buffalo News v. Buffalo Enterprise Development Corporation,* 644 N.E. 2d 277 (NY, 1994).

For information about the right of a member of a nonprofit association or corporation to possession, inspection, or use of membership lists, *see* 37 ALR 4th 1206.

22

BYLAWS

§232. BYLAWS AND CONTRACTS

Hospital/Physician Contracts

Nonprofit hospital bylaws constitute a contract between a physician and a hospital. A hospital must comply with all bylaws before it can terminate a physician's staff privileges.

Bass v. Ambrosius, 520 N.W. 2d 625 (WI App., 1994).

A nonprofit hospital must "substantially comply," rather than "strictly comply," with its bylaws in terminating a doctor's medical staff privileges. However, the hospital's obligation to follow medical staff bylaws is paramount. The hospital must provide its medical staff with all of the process and protections encompassed by its bylaws.

Owens v. New Britain General Hospital, 643 A. 2d 233 (CT, 1994).

A private nonprofit hospital improperly exercised its authority when it removed a physician as chief of staff without the three-fourths vote required under the hospital bylaws.

Keane v. St. Francis Hospital, 522 N.W. 2d 517 (WI App., 1994).

A plaintiff, who is a member of an organization, and who seeks judicial relief, must first invoke and exhaust all remedies provided by the organization that are relevant to his grievance. A physician was precluded from suit, under this principle, because he failed to exhaust his intraorganizational remedies at a nonprofit hospital that restricted his staff privileges, and failed to thereafter file a petition for writ of mandate pursuant to the medical staff bylaws.

Devaughn Peace, M.D., Inc. v. St. Francis Medical Center, 33 Cal. Rptr. 2d 459 (CA App. 2 Dist., 1994).

§233. AMENDMENT OF BYLAWS

A state bar association may protect the privacy and tranquillity of personal injury victims against intrusive unsolicited contact by lawyers through rules banning targeted direct-mail solicitations to victims and their relatives for 30 days following an accident or disaster, and by banning the acceptance of referrals in violation of that prohibition.

> *Florida Bar v. Went For It, Inc.,* 115 S. Ct. 2371 (U.S. FL, 1995).

§234. BINDING EFFECT OF BYLAWS ON MEMBERS AND OTHERS

The members of an unincorporated association of residential lot owners are not entitled to vote for the trustees of a real estate developer's property owners association, if the developer's association's bylaws authorize lot owners to vote for trustees only after all building sites in the development are sold, and the sites are still held by the developer.

> *Club Corp of America v. Concerned Property Owners for April Sound,* 881 S.W. 2d 620 (TX App.–Beaumont, 1994).

Disciplinary Action

The United States Figure Skating Association violated its bylaws by scheduling a disciplinary hearing for Tonya Harding just three days after her reply to the charges was due and by not giving the skater a reasonable time to prepare her defense. Injunction was issued against the hearing. However, the action became moot when the skater resigned from the association and pleaded guilty to criminal charges against her. The injunction was vacated and the action dismissed.

> *Harding v. United States Figure Skating Association,* 851 F. Supp. 1476 (D. OR, 1994).

Bylaws and Statutes

The bylaws of a state university, providing that no member appointed to the board may serve unless approved for a specific term by the Senate, do not effect the eligibility of persons "grandfathered" in their position by the statute.

> *Dunn v. Alabama State University Bd. of Trustees,* 628 So. 2d 519 (AL, 1993).

24

MEETINGS AND CONVENTIONS OF MEMBERS*

*[*See Successful Meetings* (magazine) as to worldwide, current hotel and other meeting facilities, supplies, and services, 355 Park Ave., So., New York, NY 10010, (212) 592–6403 (editorial office).] *See also,* Shenson, Howard L., *How to Develop and Promote Successful Seminars and Workshops,* John Wiley & Sons, Inc., New York, NY, 1996.

§240. MEETINGS, IN GENERAL

Meetings Industry

Travel, tourism, and meetings (conventions) are a major industry in the United States, perhaps the number two employer and number three retail industry. Thus, NPO officers should be acquainted with such sources of assistance as *Meeting Planners International* (MPI), the *Professional Convention Management Association* (PCMA), and the *International Association for Exposition Management* (IAEM). Very helpful in this area of NPO (and business) activity is the elaborate and resource presentation monthly magazine *Successful Meetings,* which also publishes a *Successful Meetings Sourcebook.* Address: Bill Communications, Inc., 355 Park Ave, So., New York, NY 10010, (212) 592–6403, FAX (212) 592–6409.

Meetings Locations and Expenses

American Express has issued a *Group Travel Index* that gives comparative costs (per day figures) at 20 U.S. cities, year by year, for air, hotel, and food and beverage costs, beginning with 1993, quarterly.

Benchmarking (note), *Successful Meetings,* (magazine), p. 11 (July, 1994).

Definition of Meeting

The definition of "meeting" or "committee" may be very specific in some kinds of NPOs. For example, in a condominium association unit owners' meeting, the Florida statute [c. 718.103] defines a committee to mean an appointed group of board members and/or unit owners to make recommendations or take action on behalf of the board. It is an official entity and must give notice, report its actions, and be open to observation.

Jack Holeman, Condo Line, *St. Petersburg (FL) Times,* p. 1D (June 25, 1994).

§241. MEETINGS OF MEMBERS

Business Travel Kits for Meetings

Both U.S. and foreign travel promotion offices will provide helpful meetings and conventions program assistance. For example, the British Tourist Authority in the United States will assist in this manner. Address their Incentives and Corporate Meetings Office, 551 Fifth Avenue, New York, NY 10176–0799, (212) 986–2200, FAX (212) 986–1188.

Meetings Promotional Material; England

All kinds of promotional materials may be had for the asking. Thus a query to the *British Tourist Authority* in 1994 resulted in the receipt of big packages of books (*Who's Who and What's What, 1994, 5th edition*) and various other informational material, maps, and so on. The U.S. address is 551 Fifth Avenue, 7th Floor, New York, NY 10176, (212) 986–1188.

§247. CONVENTIONS AND ASSEMBLIES

Meetings: Site Selection and Inspection

Successful Meetings magazine offers a service to meetings/conventions planners to save time and money. Tell the *SM* officer (800–326–7211) the locales you are considering for meetings and that person will handle all arrangements for a site inspection for you, including details such as accommodations, meals, transfers, and sightseeing.

Announcement (p. 45), *Successful Meetings,* (July, 1994).

Trade Show Meetings

Annual trade shows for meetings managers are available (for example, *Affordable Meetings Exposition and Conference*) in major cities, with free admission, presented by, for example, HSMAI (*Hospitality Sales and Marketing Association International*), (800) 272–7462.

Incentive Travel Programs

Incentive Travel Programs are now used by some organizations to reward valuable officers and members and also to achieve various other purposes. One leader in this kind of programming is the Society of Incentive Travel Executives (SITE) based in New York City.

> Shannon Nee (ed.), Incentive Travel Strategy Guide, *Successful Meetings,* 221
> (22 pp.) (July, 1994).

Meetings/Conventions "Partnering"/MPI/PCMA/ASAE

An important recent development in successful planning/conducting collaboration of various entities, for conventions, is called "partnering." This is defined by Ed Rigsbee in *The Art of Partnering* (Kendall/Hunt Publ. Co., 1993) as ". . . the process of two or more entities coming together for the purpose of developing synergistic solutions to their challenges." Thus, managers involve employees, tourism officials involve chambers of commerce, rival hotels involve each other, and so forth.

> Michael Adams, Working in Sync, *Successful Meetings,* (magazine), 38 (Aug.,
> 1994).

This same issue of *S.M.* has a number of other useful articles on "sponsors" for meetings of associations, also about *Meeting Planners International* (now named *Meeting Professionals International*). MPI address is: 1950 Stemmons Freeway, Dallas, TX 75207, (214) 712–7700.

> Other such associations are PCMA (*Professional Convention Management Association*) and ASAE (*American Society of Association Executives*). *See S.M.* same
> issue, Donoho article, p. 52.

§248. AGENDA FOR MEETINGS OF MEMBERS

Making Meetings Productive

To be sure that a meeting is not a waste of time and effort: (1) Plan carefully as to purpose(s), schedule(s), and methods; (2) Remember that each person wants a "What's in it for me?" answer, and allow plenty of cross exchanges; (3) Sum up (and report) the benefits of what actually was done during the meeting.

> T. McDonald, "A New Paradigm," *Successful Meetings,* p. 38 (June, 1994);
>   also R. Solmo (ed.), "Playing the Perfect Host," *Guidelines,* p. 75.

Speaker Sources

There are many local and national sources for speakers at meetings. An example is the Resource Center of the Florida Humanities Council's Speakers Bureau, which provides a list of available speakers and presented more than 350 programs in 200 communities in 1994. The Speaker's Bureau can be contacted through the Florida Humanities Council, 1514½ East Eighth Avenue, Tampa, Florida 33605–3708, (813) 272–3473.

25

VOTING AND ELECTIONS

§254. VOTING BY PROXY, IN GENERAL

Sealed proxy votes, that are exercisable only at an election which has not occurred and are revocable at any time prior to the election, are not "official records" of the association. Therefore, such proxies are not subject to examination, under Florida law, by members of the association, prior to the election.

> *Islander Beach Club Condominium Association of Volusia County, Inc. v. Johnston,* 623 So. 2d 628 (FL App. 5 Dist., 1993) (member engaged in a proxy fight wanted inspection).

§256. ELECTIONS AND ISSUES, IN GENERAL

Voting in Elections Write-Ins

State voting laws, for *general elections,* usually specifically allow a voter to vote for a *"write-in"* candidate "by writing the name of such person in the blank space provided."

FL Stat. Section 101.011 *Voting by paper ballot.*

But a person "seeking to qualify for election to office as a write-in candidate shall file his/her qualification papers with the respective qualifying officer" during the time set for such filings. This refers to disclosures of financial interests.

FL Stat. Section 99.061 *Method of qualifying . . . .*

In view of the common law's generally neutral attitude towards write-in voting (*see* main text, 6th edition, p. 839), Florida's law suggests that write-in voting is valid in organizations unless an express contrary provision is made in the articles, bylaws, or statutes.

Ordinarily, at common law, a person may be elected to corporation office by "write-in" of his/her name on a ballot. He/she need not have been nominated.

> *Commonwealth ex. rel. Laughlin v. Green,* 351 PA 170, 49 A. 2d 492 (1945);
> *Moon v. Moon Motor Car Co.,* 17 DE Ch. 176, 151 A. 298 (1930).

There seems to be little expressly provided to deal with the matter of write-in disputes.

§258. CHALLENGED ELECTIONS

Court-Ordered Seating of Directors

In 1995, a judge in Los Angeles ordered the American Lung Association of Los Angeles County (ALALAC) to seat 27 new directors after its 40-member board refused to seat them due to an internal power struggle. The court held that the sitting board had ignored a vote of the membership in a legitimate and binding election and admonished the defendants for postponing a board meeting without 30 days notice, in a move to keep the new board members from voting.

See, 9 *NonProfit Times* (5) 4 (May, 1995).

26

PROXIES

§261. MEMBERS' PROXIES

Inspection of Proxies

Sealed proxy votes, that are exercisable only at an election which has not occurred and are revocable at any time prior to the election, are not "official records" of the association. Therefore, such proxies are not subject to examination, under Florida law, by the members of the association, prior to the election.

Islander Beach Club Condominium Association of Volusia County, Inc. v. Johnston, 623 So. 2d 628 (FL App. 5 Dist., 1993) (member engaged in a proxy fight wanted inspection).

27

DIRECTORS AND TRUSTEES: SELECTION, STATUS, AND REMOVAL

§273. FIDUCIARY STATUS OF DIRECTORS

Directors' Fiduciary Liability

(*See also* Section 284; *Personal Liability*)
(*Raymond L. Potts* contributed research for the cases cited here.)

Directors who sold their NPO hospital for $5 million below fair market price, to a buyer who also bought several other businesses owned mainly by those directors, were guilty of "self-dealing" and "waste" of corporate assets.

> *Mary v. Lupin Foundation,* 609 S. 2d 184 (LA, 1992); (threatened similar conduct enjoined); *Butterworth v. Anclote Manor Hospital, Inc.,* 566 S. 2d 296 (FL App., 1990).

If a director of an unincorporated foundation manipulated the foundation stock in other corporations in order to get himself and his wife on the board, but did not injure the foundation in so doing, and the net result is fair to the foundation, he is not guilty of breach of *fiduciary* duty.

> *Oberly v. Kriby,* 1990 WL 183884 (DE Supr., 1990); *Kirtley v. McClelland,* 562 N.E. 2d 27 (IN App., 1991).

Articles of incorporation or bylaws and so on may create specific fiduciary duties, as in the requirement of careful maintenance of insurance coverage. In one such case, failure to set up a subsidiary's board to so assure insurance coverage made the parent board members liable.

> *Munder v. Circle One Condominium, Inc.,* 596 S. 2d 144 (FL App., 1992); *Brenner v. Powers,* 584 N.E. 2d 569 (IN App., 1992).

A labor union officer's use of power to enrich himself made him liable for breach of his union's international or local officer fiduciary duty, as a matter of contract duty.

> *Shea v. McCarthy,* 953 F. 2d 29 (2d Cir., 1992) (unincorporated associations' documents).

If a director's conduct is blatantly bad, courts may find personal liability even where statutory protection is generally available to directors. For example, where a director contracted with a plumbing contractor, but did not disclose his organization's real protected legal status, he was held liable as an *agent*.

> *Benjamin Plumbing, Inc. v. Barnes,* 470 N.W. 2d 888 (WI, 1991).

Church Officers

In 1994 a group of 49 ministers and lay workers of the Evangelical Lutheran Church in America sued their church hierarchy and Board of Pensions for breach of fiduciary duty in making investments mainly on the basis of the social/political philosophy of the corporation, rather than on anticipated income yield. Retired pensioners, thus, suffered depleted pension income, and sued for lump-sum release of their funds, for more profitable investments. But churches are exempt from ERISA.

> *Basich v. Board of Pensions E.L.C. . . .,* MN 4th Jud. Dist. Ct., Ct 93–016711; Dickson (note), *Natl. L.J.,* p. A19 (July 18, 1994).

Directors' Duties

Members of a board of directors are duty bound to continually remain informed about corporate matters and obligations.

> *Ameritrust Co. Natl. Association v. Hicks Dev. Corp.,* 632 N.E. 2d 939 (OH App., 1993). *See also,* Overton, George W., ed., *Guidebook for Directors of Nonprofit Corporations.* Chicago: American Bar Association, Section of Business Law, 1993; *Privatization and the Delivery of Personal Social Services: Is the Voluntary Board of Directors Up to the Task?* (Canada) Bowlby McMahon, Bradshaw, and Murray, *The Philanthropist,* Spring 1994 12 n1 p21–43.

Health Care Organization Boards

Nonprofit health care organization boards have distinct and necessary responsibilities. Their chief responsibility is a commitment to ensuring board accountability. Board members should actively discuss board duties and performance. They should take time to assess actual or potential board duties and performance. They should take time to assess actual or potential failings or concerns. It is crucial that boards remain cohesive units. Board members must allow all members to air grievances and make suggestions. Nonprofit health care boards must never allow their essential visions to become compromised by the covert actions of disgruntled members.

> Holland, Thomas P., Rivito, Roger A., and Kovner, Anthony R., *Better Boards and Beyond.* (excerpt from *"Improving Board Effectiveness: Practical Lessons for Nonprofit Health Care,"* (includes related article on board leader habits), *Hospitals & Health Networks*, April 5, 1997.

Insider Representation on the Governing Boards of Nonprofit Hospitals

See, Young, Gary J., *Insider Representation on the Governing Boards of Nonprofit Hospitals: Trends and Implications for Charitable Care, Inquiry*, Winter 1997.

§275. NUMBER OF DIRECTORS

IRS Raises Number of Physicians That Can Be on the Board

After nonprofit hospitals argued that the 20 percent cap on physician representation, on the board of directors, hinders the networks' ability to create integrated health systems, and tax-exempt or nonprofit physician networks, the IRS changed its 20 percent cap. The IRS recently granted tax-exempt status to a physician network, whose board of directors is staffed almost entirely by physicians.

> Burda, David, *IRS Opening Boards to More Docs, Ruling Shows, Modern Healthcare,* August 5, 1996.

Physician Boards

The IRS has introduced its 1996 Continuing Professional Education manual, for agency auditors, which redefines the nonprofit hospital's governing board. The board should have 51 percent of its members as "independent community members." The remaining 49 percent can be physicians and key hospital employees. Previously, physicians could only control 20 percent of the board.

Burda, David, *IRS Mulls Rules to Open Boards to More Docs, Modern Healthcare,* July 8, 1996. *See also,* Carson, Marlis L., *IRS Eases Stance on Physician Board Representation, Tax Notes,* July 15, 1996 (change in policy due to increased acceptance of integrated health care delivery arrangements).

Japanese Bureaucrats and the Nonprofit Sector

As of September, 1996, Japanese nonprofit corporations must limit the number of retired government officials on its board to less than one-third of the total board members. The new rules were passed to address foreign criticism of the Japanese practice of offering retired bureaucrats positions in the nonprofit public interest corporations which they used to regulate.

Kubota, Coco, *Japan Battles Bureaucratic Conflicts, Journal of Commerce and Commercial,* August 20, 1996.

§279. ELECTION OF DIRECTORS

Court-Ordered Seating of Directors

In 1995, a judge in Los Angeles ordered the American Lung Association of Los Angeles County (ALALAC) to seat 27 new directors after its 40 member board refused to seat them due to an internal power struggle. The court held that the sitting board had ignored a vote of the membership in a legitimate and binding election, and admonished the defendants for postponing a board meeting without 30 days' notice in a move to keep the new board members from voting.

See, 9 *NonProfit Times* (5) 4 (May, 1995).

See also, Ward, Ralph, *21st Century Corporate Board,* John Wiley & Sons, Inc., New York, NY, 1996.

§282. SUSPENSION OR REMOVAL OF DIRECTORS

Wrongful Removal

When former board members sued their federal credit union for wrongful removal and defamation, the court held that there is no common law cause of action for wrongful removal. Neither federal regulation nor removal by the supervisory committee is "governmental action" for purposes of constitutional restrictions. The supervisory committee is privileged to inform members about allegations against the credit union's directors as long as the statements are not published with "malice." "Actual malice" is knowledge of the falsity of a statement or reckless disregard for the truth.

Jessinger v. Nevada Federal Credit Union, 24 F. 3d 1127 (9th Cir. [NV], 1994).

Removal by the Court

In Washington, a court, without express statutory authority, cannot remove a director, who was sued by the membership of a nonprofit road maintenance corporation, after the director allegedly made contracts between the corporation and a construction company owned by the president of the board. Washington's Nonprofit Corporation Act provides for removal of directors only by vote of the members. The court may, however, rescind the contract and award attorney fees to the members under the "common fund/common benefit" theory.

Lyzanchuk v. Yakima Ranches Owners Association, Phase II, Inc., 866 P. 2d 695
    (WA App. Div. 3, 1994).

28

DIRECTORS AND TRUSTEES: POWERS, DUTIES, AND LIABILITIES

§283. DIRECTORS' AND TRUSTEES' POWERS, IN GENERAL

Apparent Authority

The majority of the board of a nonprofit corporation has the apparent authority to consent to a search, by the police, of the office containing corporate records of a board member, who is charged with fraud, grand theft, and forgery, if the board members have the ability to inspect the documents whenever they wish, they vote, at the time, to consent to the search, and they believe they have authority to consent to the search. Consent must, however, be given voluntarily.

> *State v. Justice,* 624 So. 2d 402 (FL App. 5 Dist., 1993). *See also,* Adams, Denby, and Zipser, *A Nonprofit Director's Roadmap for Survival, Trusts & Estates,* March, 1996; Duca, Diane J., *Nonprofit Boards: Roles, Responsibilities & Performance,* John Wiley & Sons, Inc., New York, NY, 1996.

Directors as Fund Raisers

Many directors don't realize that their functions include Management, Policy-Making, and *Fund Raising.* When directors fail to make available their fund raising sources to the organization, a phenomenon known as the "Resources Unused are Resources Abused" Syndrome appears. Organizations plagued by this syndrome must try to instill a greater awareness of the importance of fund raising in board members, and take action against directors who refuse to fund raise.

> Borenstein, Henry P., *"Resources Unused are Resources Abused" Syndrome, Fund Raising Management,* (August, 1996).

§284. DIRECTORS' STANDARD OF DILIGENCE AND CARE (PERSONAL LIABILITY)

[*See also* Chapter 27 §273.]

Legal Responsibilities of Nonprofit Directors

Directors of nonprofit organizations owe a legal duty of care and loyalty to the organization they serve. Though the duty of care varies from state to state, it is essentially the same as that of for-profit corporations. Pennsylvania's standard is typical and provides that the director's duties are to act "in good faith, in a manner he reasonably believes to be in the best interests of the corporation and with such care, including reasonable inquiry, skill, and diligence, as a person of ordinary prudence would use under similar circumstances." However, in Pennsylvania, directors of charities that receive funds "in trust" for charitable purposes are held to the same high fiduciary standard as any other trustee.

The duty of loyalty is mostly found in state case law and provides that directors exercise their power free from any material self-interest or interest of another entity.

Many states shield directors from liability by allowing the bylaws or articles of incorporation to protect directors from liability except in cases of action that constitutes self-dealing, willful misconduct, or recklessness. Many states also extend protection from liability to unpaid volunteers. However, this protection may be limited to specific volunteers, such as athletic coaches.

The director's duty can be enforced by the members of a corporation or the corporation itself. In many states the attorney general oversees the activity of directors. The IRS and the Securities and Exchange Commission also have jurisdiction over nonprofits. Even donors, employees, and other third parties can force a director to perform his duties.

Most potential problems arise out of conflicts of interest, bogus or risky investment schemes, intentional wrongdoing by an officer or employee entrusted with the institution's funds, and lack of overseeing and involvement by the board.

The organization's accountant and attorney should establish an investment policy with specific permitted investments that they believe, with the input of the Board, will allow for an appropriate amount of risk for the institution. Bylaws should be reviewed often and include all of the liability-limiting provisions allowed by law with the broadest indemnification allowable. The Board should seek advice by relying on experts, especially in making complex legal, accounting, or financial decisions. Directors should purchase directors' and officers' liability insurance without exclusions, if possible. Directors must always exercise informed sound judgment using the most information available.

> Scott, Kevin B., (article), 10 *NonProfit Times* (10) 48–49 (October, 1996).

In an action by members of a rural electric membership corporation (REMC) against its board of directors for economic damages, allegations of negligence, *ultra vires* acts, and material misrepresentation were unfounded where members had no right to attend the board meetings or access board minutes and records, and there were no allegations that the board members knew they were giving out incorrect information in newsletters to the members or that the board did not intend to benefit the corporation.

> *Absher v. Clark County Rural Elec. Membership Corp.,* 629 N.E. 2d 870 (IN App. 4 Dist., 1994).

Bylaws Indemnification

If corporate bylaws indemnify officers and directors for liability incurred "by reason of" such status, the federal CERCLA personal liability of corporate officers and directors does not nullify that indemnification.

> *U.S. v. Lowe,* CA 5, No. 93–2634, Aug. 15, 1994.

Sources of Guidance for Directors

> *Not-for-Profit Organizations: The Challenge of Governance in an Era of Retrenchment,* April 9–10, 1992, Santa Monica, CA: ALI-ABA course of study materials, ALI-ABA, 4025 Chestnut St., Philadelphia, PA, 1992.

> Overton, George W., ed., *Guidebook for Directors of Nonprofit Corporations.* Chicago: American Bar Association, Section of Business Law, 1993.

> Ward, S.L., *Tort Liability of Nonprofit Governing Boards,* Garland Pub., New York, 1993.

> Zick, Kenneth A., *A Selected Bibliography of Study and Reading Materials: Officers Powers and Duties in Non-Profit Organizations,* ALI-ABA Course of Study, November 14–15, (1975), Wake Forest University, School of Law, Winston-Salem, NC.

> *See also,* Chapter 2, §16, Bibliography.

Directors and Officers Liability Insurance for Sexual Harassment

In 1995, over 76 percent of the estimated one million nonprofit organizations in the U.S. did not carry Directors and Officer's Liability Insurance, even though the average premium for a standard policy was about $4,000 a year for $1 million coverage. The number of insurance companies offering D & O insurance rose from 8 to 27 between 1992 and 1995. Customers must often ask in order to have D & O insurance broadened to include sexual harassment claims. The filing of sexual harassment suits increased from 6,892 in 1991 to 12,537 in 1993, according to the Equal Employment Opportunity Commission (EEOC). Under the Civil Rights Act of 1991, an organization may be liable for as much as $300,000 in punitive damages as well as compensatory damages for emotional distress.

> Gurevitz, Susan, (article) 9 *NonProfit Times* (2) 1, 12, (February, 1995). *See also, Corporate Affairs: Nepotism, Office Romance, & Sexual Harassment,* Bureau of National Affairs, Washington, D.C., c1988.

Quo Warranto Actions by the State

Quo warranto action can be brought against the directors of nonprofit corporations under a statute in Tennessee providing that an action lies against directors of a corporation to bring them to account for management of property entrusted to their care, to remove such officers or trustees on proof of misconduct, and to compel faithful performance of duty. A statute which grants immunity to directors and officers of nonprofit corporations, except when their conduct amounts to willful, wanton conduct or gross negligence, does not preclude a quo warranto action by the state.

> *State by Pierotti Ex Rel. Boone v. Sundquist,* 884 S.W. 2d 438 (TN, 1994); T.C.A. Sections 29–35–102, 48–58–601.

Breach of Fiduciary Duty

The Board of Internal Medicine does not breach its fiduciary duty to its members by requiring that members be recertified every 10 years through retesting.

> *DeGregorio v. American Bd. of Internal Medicine,* 844 F. Supp. 186 (D. NJ, 1994).

The officer of a condominium developer, who is also a director of the condominium association, cannot be held individually liable for corporate acts of the developer, solely on the basis of his/her status as a director of the association. To impose individual liability on such an officer, for breach of fiduciary duty, the association must prove that the officer willfully breached his/her duty, and that his/her conduct rose to the level of actual wrongdoing such as fraud, self-dealing, or unjust enrichment. That proof must be presented as a jury question.

Taylor v. Wellington Station Condominium Association, Inc., 633 So. 2d 43 (FL App. 5 Dist., 1994).

If the trustee of an irrevocable charitable religious trust breaches his/her fiduciary duty to the trust by allowing funds from the trust to be used by a Chapter 7 debtor investment group, the trustee is personally liable. The trustee is an "insider" and cannot be a "creditor" in such situations of wrongdoing.

In re Square Real Estate, Inc., 163 B.R. 108 (Bankr. W.D. MI, 1994).

Ethics and Volunteer Directors

See, Ethical Dilemmas of the Volunteer Lawyer/Nonprofit Director. Peter B. Nagel. *Colorado Lawyer,* Dec. 1994 23 n12 p2735(4).

Directors' and Officers' Insurance

Competition in the market is driving the cost of Directors' and Officers' insurance downward. To receive information contact:

The Chubb Group of Insurance Companies, David Lapin, 82 Hopmeadow St., Simsbury, Conn. 06070, (203) 244-8900.

NonProfit's Mutual Risk Retention Group, Sandra Whitty, 300 S. Wacker Drive, #2100, Chicago, Il. 60707, (312) 922-6100.

CNA Insurance Co., Todd Webber, P.O. Box 66943, Chicago, Il. 60666, (708) 330-6773.

Coregis, Louis Lubruno, 70 Pine Street, New York, N.Y. 10270, (212) 770-7000.

Philadelphia Indemnity Insurance Co., William Cole, 94 SE, Pace Ferry Rd., Suite 1890, Atlanta, Georgia 30326, (404) 231-2366.

Carlotta Swarden, (article), 10 *NonProfit Times* (1) 21–24 (January, 1996).

§287. COMPENSATION OF DIRECTORS OR OFFICERS

Executive Salaries (The Intermediate Sanctions Law)

In 1996, President Clinton signed the Taxpayers Bill of Rights 2. The law subjects executives who receive what the IRS determines to be excessive salaries or benefits to stiff penalties: (1) Intermediate sanctions may be imposed on those who knowingly approve of excessive benefit transactions, retroactive to September 14, 1995; (2) The person benefitting from an excess benefit is subject to a penalty equal to 25 percent of the excess benefit. Managers involved in the transaction are subject to a 10-percent penalty; (3) If there is no correction of the excess benefit, a penalty of 200 percent of the excess benefit may be imposed on the disqualified person; (4) There is a three-year statute of limitations, except in case of fraud; (5) 501(c)3 and (c)4 organizations must report such penalties and any for illegal lobbying or political activities on their Form 990; (6) 501(c)3 and (c)4 organizations must provide copies of their three most recent tax returns to anyone who requests them in person or in writing; (7) Anyone requesting a Form 990 copy in person gets one "immediately." Those who mail a request must be sent the form within 30 days. The only costs are for copying and mailing; (8) There is a $20 per day fine for failure to file a Form 990, up from $10, to a maximum of $10,000 or 5 percent of gross receipts; (9) Organizations that raise more than $1 million that fail to file a Form 990 are assessed a $100 per day fine, to a maximum of $50,000; (10) The penalty for willful failure to allow public inspection of returns is increased from $1,000 to $5,000; (11) Disqualified person is defined as "any individual who is in a position to exercise substantial authority over an organization's affairs, regardless of the individual's official title. Certain family members and 35-percent controlled entities of disqualified persons are also treated as disqualified persons."; (12) Excess benefit transaction is defined as "any transaction in which an economic benefit is provided by an applicable tax-exempt organization directly or indirectly to or for the use of any disqualified person if the value of the economic benefit provided exceeds the value of the consideration (including the performance of services) received for providing such benefit."

Sinclair, Matthew, (article), 10 *NonProfit Times* (9) 6 (September, 1996).

§290. ADVISORY BOARDS OR COUNCILS

An Efficient Board

Often the Board of Directors fails to achieve its purpose of being a strategic planning arm, especially where the CEO does not heed the board's suggestions. Board members need to identify their goals. Management and trustees must work together to decide direction and articulate issues of importance. Often, experts should be contacted.

Taylor, Chair, and Holland, *The New Work of the Nonprofit Board: Is Your Board Adding Value or Simply Wasting its Members' Time?*, Harvard Business Review, Sept.–Oct., 1996.

29

OFFICERS AND MANAGERS

§293. RESTRICTIONS ON OFFICERS (COMPENSATION, MISCONDUCT, AND INTERESTS IN CONTRACTS)

Compensation Statistics

According to a study by the American Research Co. in Great Falls, VA, almost a quarter of 1,677 nonprofit chief executives polled did not receive a raise in 1995. CEOs are being hired at salary levels that are 17.2 percent less than their peers at similar associations. Pay scales were up only 2.7 percent, .3 percent less than the nation's three-percent inflation rate. Males earn 27 percent more than females, up from 24 percent in 1994. Trade association executives earned an average of $140,145. Individual membership organizations paid their executives an average of $95,134 in 1995.

Clolery, Paul, (article), 9 *NonProfit Times* (10) 5 (October, 1995).

Interference with Officer Contracts

Under Pennsylvania law, the chairman of a board of directors of a nonprofit organization has an action for intentional interference with existing contractual relations where his complaint alleges that a management company made disparaging remarks to the nonprofit corporation about the chairman, attempted to coerce and intimidate the board into ignoring the management company's poor management and into discharging the chairman, and if the alleged interference caused monetary, consequential, emotional, and reputational damages to the chairman.

Total Care Systems, Inc. v. Coons, 860 F. Supp. 236 (E.D. PA, 1994).

§297. OFFICERS' LIABILITIES

Building and Loan Associations Officers

Officers of B & L Association imputed liability for knowledge of fraud in a failed savings and loan (S & L) is tested by state (California) rather than by federal law.

O'Melveny & Myers & F.D.J.C., 114 S. Ct. 2048 (1994). *See,* as to procedure: 2974 Properties, Inc. v. R.T.C., 28 CA Rptr. 2d 667 (CA App., 1994).

§301. POWERS AND DUTIES OF THE SECRETARY

See, Serving as Secretary. (to a nonprofit charity) (Canada) Fred Burnard. *The Philanthropist,* Summer, 1994.

§302. POWERS AND DUTIES OF THE TREASURER

Treasurer; Condominium Financial Operations

In a *Community Association* the *Treasurer* is usually the person in charge of finances and budget, keeps its financial records, is responsible for deposit of monies in depositories designated by the board, sees to an annual audit by a CPA, and receives no compensation for such duties. He/she should understand the basics of financial statements (balance sheets, equation of assets, liabilities, and members' equity).

> Becker and Polikoff, *93 Community Update* (May, 1994) (Fort Lauderdale, FL). (This issue contains a useful summary of accounting methods and basic law.)

§305. INVESTMENT MANAGERS

See also, Chapter 42, Management Techniques in Nonprofit Organizations.

Duties and Liabilities

A fiduciary's duties must be discharged under The Prudent Expert Rule, "with the care, skill, prudence and diligence under the circumstances then prevailing that a prudent man acting in a like capacity and familiar with such matters would use in the conduct of an enterprise of a like character and with like aims."

Investments should be examined according to the following four criteria: (1) Is the investment appropriate in terms of liquidity, return versus risk, fit to portfolio, diversification, fit to the funding and cash requirements, relevant economic factors? (2) Does the asset meet the prevailing rate of return in the market consistent with the stated desired level of risk for that asset class? (3) Relative to other investment choices, is the return appropriate to the desired risk level? (4) What objective standards have been put in place to measure the prudence of that investment judged solely in the context of the total plan portfolio? Decisions should be based on a written Objective and Investment Policy Statement containing the considerations in the following Form 135S outline.

> Marvin Anderson, Smith Barney, Continuing Education Seminar on Client Financial Needs and Investments, October 17, 1995, Clearwater, FL.

> *See also, Nonprofit Directors and Officers—Duties and Liabilities for Investment Decisions*. Harvey P. Dale. New York University Conference on Tax Planning for 501(c)(3) Organizations, Annual 1994.

Less Optimism in Investing and Managing Organization Money

According to a *NonProfit Times* poll of 510 senior officials at nonprofits of all sizes and missions, in 1996, 30.4 percent said that primary investment decisions were made by the chief executive and the treasurer. That has declined from 33 percent in 1995. The use of outside investment counsel has also declined, from 22 percent in 1995 to just 17 percent in 1996; 40.2 percent of organizations are putting the investment decisions on the board of directors and trustees in 1996, compared to 37 percent a year ago. Also, 8.5 percent of the organizations indicated that investment decisions are now more of a collaborative process in 1996.

> Clolery, Paul, (article), 10 *NonProfit Times* (7) 23–25 (July, 1996). Landskroner, Ronald A., *The Nonprofit Manager's Resource Directory,* John Wiley & Sons, Inc., New York, NY, 1996; Blazek, Jody, *Financial Planning for Nonprofit Organizations,* John Wiley & Sons, Inc., New York, NY, 1996.

Investing by Educational Institutions

Stock market investment strategies of universities vary. During the recent bull market, Northwestern's portfolio, whose value on August 31, 1996 was $1,734 billion, consists of venture capital, real estate, and foreign investments. Cornell mostly invests in U.S. stocks, with a portfolio value of $1,748 billion on June 30, 1996. Michigan's portfolio, valued at $1,876 billion on June 30, 1996, emphasizes foreign stocks over domestic, an unusual choice for a nonprofit investor.

> Strosnider, Kim, *How 3 Universities Invest Their Funds in the Bull Market, The Chronicle of Higher Education,* January 31, 1997.

FORM NO. 135S
Outline for Objective and Investment Policy Statement
for Investment Managers

Objective and Investment Policy Statement

I. **Purpose**

A. Secure benefits for the beneficiaries of the trust

B. A plan of action

C. Guidance for investments of trust

II. **Liquidity and Cash Flow Requirements**

A. Income needed and when

B. Time Frame

C. Emergency needs

III. **Investment Objectives**

A. Absolute rate of return

B. Real rate above inflations

C. Relative to market indexes

D. Time frames to meet objectives

IV. **Constraints**

A. Asset allocation

B. Guidelines on equity investments

C. Guidelines on income investments

V. **Reviews and Monitoring**

A. Guidelines for selection, monitoring and evaluating investment manager and investments

B. Guidelines for monitoring and evaluating the trustee operation

VI. **Periodic Review**

On-line Services

CompuServe offers the NonProfit Forum, including articles and discussion topics on news and trends, professional and association news, leadership, management, volunteers, philanthropy, planned giving, fundraising and career strategies. For information, call (800) 524-3388, e-mail 75162.3366@compuserve.com

See also, Zeff, Robbin, *The Nonprofit Guide to the Internet,* John Wiley & Sons, Inc., New York, NY, 1996.

32

AGENTS AND EMPLOYEES

§330. AGENTS, EMPLOYEES, AND VOLUNTEERS

Education and Work in the Nonprofit Sector

In the Information Age, where an increasing number of jobs in the marketplace and in the government are being automated, the nation's nonprofit sector will be largely relied upon for work. Educators and the American school system must face the task of preparing graduates for potential work in both the marketplace and in the Third Sector. Schools and colleges, hospitals, social services, youth groups, and other similar institutions are serving more and more neighborhoods in the U.S. With the amount of jobs offered by the Third Sector, a rethinking of the mission of public education and American education as a whole should be considered.

> Rifkin, Jeremy, *Preparing Students for "The End of Work." (Rethinking American Education), Educational Leadership*, February, 1997.

Women's Power-Lack in NPO's

Women long have had a predominant role in American NPO's; two-thirds of the nearly 8 million employees and over half of the nearly 90 million volunteers. But statistics show that they seem to encounter the "glass ceiling" in power/authority positions.

A valuable new book on this subject is:

> T. Odendahl and M. O'Neill (eds.), *Women and Power in the Nonprofit Sector* (Jossey Bass, Publ., 1994), 350 Sansome St., San Francisco, CA 94014, (415) 433–1740 or Fax (415) 433–0499.

In a 1994 survey conducted by the National Center for Nonprofit Boards (NCNB) involving 600 national, regional, and local nonprofits, respondents reported that about 40 percent of their board members were women. This statistic probably reflects an increase in the overall size and nature of nonprofit boards, rather than a desire to diversify boards. In 1992, women comprised 28.7 percent of the responding boards while men represented 71.3 percent.

> Gurevitz, Susan, (article), 8 *NonProfit Times* (9) 1, 17–19 (September, 1994).

Executive Pay for Women in California

According to the 15th annual nonprofit wage and benefit survey, conducted by the Management Center in San Francisco, women hold a majority of nonprofit jobs in California, but they are in the minority at the top levels of management. Women are also being paid just 97 cents on the dollar compared to their male counterparts. The organization polled 345 nonprofit employers in 27 northern California counties with a total of 15,061 employees. Job functions related to child care, elder care, food services, independent living, personal/residential care, preschool education and recreation pay below jobs relating to computer operations, financial management, grant making, legal, medical, and writing positions.

> Swarden, Carlotta, (article), 10 *NonProfit Times* (7) 4 (July, 1996). *See also,* Drury, Tracey Rosenthal, *It's a Man's World at Nonprofits, Business First of Buffalo,* July 15, 1996.

African-American Nonprofit Professionals

According to a 1994 study by the Nonprofit Management Program of the New York-based New School for Social Research, African-Americans hold only 7.9 percent of nonprofit managerial positions and 5.6 percent of the professional jobs. African-Americans constitute about 11.1 percent of the working adult population.

> 8 *NonProfit Times* (12) 23 (December, 1994). *See also,* Guttenberg, John P., Jr., *Nonprofits: You Can Make a Career, and a Difference, Washington Business Journal,* May 17, 1996.

Employees of European and Japanese Nonprofits

The nonprofit sector in Europe accounts for 3 to 5 percent of total employment, which is similar to the U.S. figure. In fact, several German nonprofits employ more people than the business giants Volkswagen and Mercedes. European nonprofits are more involved in sports than are U.S. nonprofits.

In Japan, nonprofits employ about 3 percent of the work force.

> 8 *NonProfit Times* (4) 6 (April, 1994).

Employee Contracts

"Express employee contracts" are ones where the parties declare the terms in writing or orally at the time the contract is formed. "Implied in fact contracts for employment" arise from acts or conduct of the parties. Employee handbooks or policies are "implied in fact contracts." Promises of "permanent" employment do not alter the at-will presumption without additional consideration by the employee or explicit language stating that termination may only be for cause. A special relationship of trust and reliance must be shown in order for an employer to violate an implied covenant of fair dealing. Damages for intentional or reckless infliction of emotional distress may be had only upon a showing of "outrageous conduct," conduct which goes beyond all possible bounds of decency, with resulting emotional feelings including shame, humiliation, embarrassment, and extreme worry. Intentional interference with prospective contractual relations must be improper; truthful statements are not actionable when the actor acts in good faith to protect economic interests.

Wilder v. Cody County Chamber of Commerce, 868 P. 2d 211 (WY, 1994).

A court has no authority to order the reinstatement of a terminated teacher at a private school, based on the teacher's allegation that the school breached its contract by terminating her contrary to the prohibitions of the corporation's code of practice. The teacher was employed by contract. There is a common-law prohibition against specific performance as a remedy for such a contractual breach.

Chady v. Solomon Schechter Day Schools, 645 N.E. 2d 983 (IL App. 1 Dist., 1995).

To establish tortious interference with a contract relationship, a teacher, who brought action against a nonprofit provider of educational services to children with physical and emotional limitations, had to prove (1) that a contract actually existed or was being negotiated, (2) that the defendants knew about the contract or negotiations, (3) that the defendants interfered with the contract or negotiation, (4) that the defendants acted maliciously and without legal justification, and (5) that the teacher was damaged by the defendant's actions.

Hoicowitz v. Positive Education Program, 645 N.E. 2d 89 (OH App. 8 Dist., 1994).

A Colorado nonprofit association of state employees, and others, sued the state Department of Administration after the department contracted out to community programs serving developmentally disabled persons for custodial services previously performed by classified state employees. In such a suit, the plaintiff association did not need to exhaust administrative remedies before the state personnel board, because that board was not authorized to determine the constitutional issues raised by the employees. In contracting out the services, the Department violated the Civil Service Amendment to the State Constitution because no statute or rule set forth the standards for contracting for the services at issue.

Horrell v. Department of Admin., 861 P. 2d 1194 (CO, 1993).

A county awarded a contract to a nonprofit bidder for jail food supply, even though the nonprofit bidder was not the lowest bidder. When the contract was challenged by an unsuccessful bidder, the court held that the county reasonably concluded that the nonprofit bidder's employment of mentally handicapped persons made it more suitable to the county's requirements.

Court Street Steak House, Inc. v. County of Tazewell, 643 N.E. 2d 781 (IL, 1994).

A nonprofit corporation, which operates a private school, is entitled to reduce its payment of back wages owed to teachers by the amount of unemployment benefits that have already been paid.

Powell v. Dougherty Christian Academy, Inc., 451 S.E. 2d 465 (GA App., 1994).

A joint employee of a public university and of a private nonprofit educational corporation sued for tortious interference with his university contractual relationship and defamation, after an allegedly defamatory memorandum was distributed to the board of the nonprofit, suggesting his dismissal as executive director. The court held there was no tortious interference or defamation involved.

Hylton v. American Association for Vocational Instructional Materials, Inc., 448 S.E. 2d 741 (GA App., 1994).

Employee Liability

See also Chapter 17, Unauthorized and Improper Acts.

A volunteer firefighter was sued, by the city fire chief, after the volunteer was involved in an automobile accident while proceeding to a fire in response to a call from a volunteer fire department. The plaintiff failed to give proper notice under Maine's Tort Claims Act. Therefore, the claim did not survive motion for summary judgment for the defendant.

Smith v. Voisine, 650 A. 2d 1350 (ME, 1994).

In 1994, an Oklahoma relief group affiliated with Feed the Children sued three former employees alleging that the employees stole a proprietary information donor list "for their own profit."

8 *NonProfit Times* (9) 8 (September, 1994).

§331. VOLUNTEERS

1997 Summit on Volunteerism

The 1997 Summit for America's Future in Philadelphia, PA created a sense of optimism about volunteerism in America. However, unless employers allow paid time off for volunteer work, the summit's goals cannot be met. The nation's corporate leaders will have to show a firm commitment to ensure the success of the summit.

Alter, Jonathan, *Down to Business, Newsweek,* May 12, 1997.

At the President's Summit for America's Future, about 230 U.S. corporations and nonprofit groups pledged new volunteer and charitable programs at the volunteerism summit held in April of 1997. Many of the volunteer programs are old ones that are being expanded or programs that were planned before the Summit. Some of the announced pledges are described.

Barnes, Julian E., *"New" Volunteering, or Just Newly Packaged: Hyping Corporate Do-Gooding at the Summit, U.S. News & World Report,* May 12, 1997.

Suspension of Volunteers

A volunteer, with a volunteer fire department, sued the department under Title VII and Section 1983, when she was placed on suspension after she filed a sexual assault complaint against a fellow volunteer. Firefighting must be a public function in order to render the company's action "state action" under Section 1983. Volunteers must receive sufficient compensation to be "employees" under Title VII. "State action" by a private actor exists where there is a symbiotic relationship between the state and the action of a regulated entity; where there is extensive governmental regulation of a private entity and the state exercises coercive power or has provided significant encouragement; or where a private entity has exercised powers that are traditionally or exclusively the prerogative of the state.

Haavistola v. Community Fire Co. of Rising Sun, Inc., 6 F. 3d 211 (4th Cir. [MD], 1993).

Mandatory Volunteerism

The legal profession today is an outstanding example of *volunteer* work that is *ordered* (mandatory) by bar associations, courts, and other authorities. In some states the attorney (bar or court-ordered) obligation is to do so many hours of *Pro Bono* legal work or to contribute so many dollars to provide for free legal services to indigent people. Law students are often required to contribute voluntary work used for such purposes by practicing attorneys in clinical law training.

> See Sol M. Linowitz (with Martin Mayer), *The Betrayed Profession,* cc. 9 (3) (Scribner's, NY, 1994).

Mandatory community service, imposed by a school district on students, is not illegal under the Thirteenth Amendment. Parents have no constitutional right that allows their children to opt out of educational curriculum. Where there are a large number of community service options available, involving many "neutral" agencies and organizations, mandatory community service programs do not violate the Fourteenth Amendment.

> *Immediato by Immediato v. Rye Neck School District,* 873 F. Supp. 846 (S.D. NY, 1995).

Volunteer Associations

President Clinton, in 1993, signed into law the creation of Americorp, an association through which more than 300 nonprofits receive grants from federal and state authorities to pay volunteers for housing rehabilitation, care for the elderly, and literacy programs. The volunteers receive, in return, stipends to pay back student loans and health benefits. There is a move, in 1995, to end Americorp's existence, supported by Newt Gingrich and others who believe that the program and its bureaucrats symbolize Washington waste. Habitat for Humanity and the National Multiple Sclerosis Society use their Americorp funded volunteers primarily to train and supervise other volunteers.

> Mehegan, Sean, 9 *NonProfit Times* (3) 1, 10, 12, (March, 1995).

Certified Volunteer Administrators

The Association for Volunteer Administration (AVA) has developed a certification program for volunteer administrators. The designation "CVA" is awarded to applicants who meet the AVA professional standards and certification criteria. For information, contact: AVA, P.O. Box 4584, Boulder, Colorado 80306, (303) 541–0238.

Insurance for Volunteer Liability

Insurance for volunteer liability and injuries to volunteers is a *must* today. For information regarding insurance policies, *see* Tremper and Lally, article, 8

NonProfit Times, (4) 27, 28 (April, 1994); contact Nonprofit Risk Management Center, Washington, D.C.

Volunteer Immunity

The introduction of volunteer-protection legislation in the U.S. House of Representatives would protect individuals from legal liability in the course of their activities as volunteers. Many states have such protection in their statutes. However, the statutes are limited in their scope and offer no uniform type of protection. The American Society of Association Executives (ASAE) believes that a lack of protection will cause individuals to shy away from volunteer activity because of fear of being sued for something that happens while they are trying to do good. Though volunteer-protection measures have been introduced, without success, every year since 1986, this year looks more promising. House Speaker Newt Gingrich supports the bill. Senate Majority Leader Trent Lott has listed volunteer protection as one of 14 priorities he would like to see pursued.

McNamara, Don, (article), 11 *NonProfit Times* (7) 4 (May, 1997).

Getting More Volunteers

Many programs that seek to alleviate pressing social problems, such as youth crime and delinquency, teen parenting, and school performance have a hard time attracting volunteers. Often the volunteers have to work at night and during weekends in unsafe neighborhoods. One proposal to increase volunteers involves the establishment of a "volunteer reimbursement account" for people who want to volunteer but lack the disposable income to pay for volunteer work-related expenses.

Pearson, Glenice B., *Is It Time for a Paradigm Shift on Volunteers?, Fund Raising Management,* August, 1996.

Discipline and Dismissal of Volunteers

In 1996, Linda Graff of Graff and Associates, Ontario, Canada gave a two-hour seminar at the Points of Light Foundation's recent 15th annual Community Service Conference in San Francisco on how to discipline or dismiss volunteers. The consequences of volunteer mistakes may be potentially grave-death, property damage or stolen property, and loss of credibility for the organization. Graff emphasized four criteria for her disciplinary strategy: (1) Discipline should be progressive; (2) Discipline should increase in severity with either the volunteer's failure to improve or the severity of the transgression; (3) Allow the opportunity to improve before moving to later, more severe steps; (4) You can skip steps and accelerate toward dismissal quickly if the transgression warrants. Discipline should be thought of as feedback or a constructive criticism. Make sure that policies are known and understood. A volunteer may do better if redirected to another position within the organization. If sexual harassment is grounds for dismissal, it must be defined.

Makenta, Nefretiti, (article), 10 *NonProfit Times* (8) 49 (August, 1996).

Volunteers (Literature)

Books on recruitment of volunteers, and training and utilization of them by NPOs (and others), many by Susan J. Ellis (some with collaborator-authors), and texts on workshops, by and for volunteers, are available from *Energize, Inc.,* of 5450 Wissahickon Ave., Philadelphia, PA 19144, 1–(800)–395–9800.

Volunteer Suits Against Nonprofits

In March of 1997, the New Jersey State Supreme Court ruled that a volunteer who is injured while doing volunteer work for a charitable organization can sue that organization. The ruling came from a case in which a man doing volunteer work for Habitat for Humanity was injured when he fell from a ladder. New Jersey has a charitable immunity law. However, since the injured man was found not to be a beneficiary of Habitat's activities, even though Habitat's certificate of incorporation said that its purposes were to aid people "by providing them with opportunities to volunteer their time and efforts," the court ruled that the state's immunity law did not apply to the volunteer suing the organization.

McNamara, Don, (article), 11 *NonProfit Times* (7) 4 (May, 1997).

FORM NO. 151S
Volunteer Application (for Museum)

Volunteer Application

[Please Print. Items marked with an asterisk (*) are necessary for security clearance.]

*Full Name

Last _____ First _____ M.I. _____

Mailing Address _____ Apt. No. _____

City _____ State _____ Zip Code _____

Home Phone _____ Best Time to Call _____

Work Phone _____ Best Time to Call _____

* Birthdate: Month _____ Day _____ Year _____ *Sex: Male _____ Female _____

*Social Security No. _____ - ___ - _____

In case of emergency, notify:

Name _____ Phone _____

Volunteer Shift Position Preferences: Indicate 1st, 2nd, and 3rd choices. (See list above.)

    1. _____

    2. _____

    3. _____

☐ I'd like to volunteer for the Museum Speakers Bureau/Educational Outreach Program

☐ I'd like to volunteer for special events

Shift Preferences: Please check the times you would be available to volunteer and indicate your order of preference.

Shift Times	8:30 a.m.-Noon	11:45 a.m.-3:15 p.m.	3 p.m.-6:30 p.m.	6:15-9:45 p.m.
Monday				
Tuesday				
Wednesday				
Thursday				
Friday				
Saturday				
Sunday				

Each volunteer will be assigned a minimum of one $3^1/_2$-hour shift per week. A minimum of 16 shifts is required to be eligible for a special gift. Please list dates you are available.

Please share your Volunteer Skills and Interests with us: (Check all that apply.)

☐ Public Speaking   ☐ Computer experience

☐ Leadership/management skills   ☐ WordPerfect

☐ Enjoy working with children   ☐ Lotus

☐ Calligraphy skills   ☐ dBase

☐ Foreign language(s) (list) _____   ☐ Other (list) _____

☐ Office skills (list) _____   Other interests or skills: _____

     ☐ Available before January 199___

Holidays: The Exhibition will be open on holidays. Please indicate which ones you would be willing to work. Holiday shifts count double for hours. (Each holiday shift equals seven hours.)

☐ M.L. King Jr. Birthday Celebration (Jan. 16)   ☐ Easter (April 16)

☐ Mother's Day (May 14)   ☐ Memorial Day (May 29)

Are you representing an organization? (Name) _____

Comments: _____

FORM NO. 152S
Volunteer Application

FAMILY AND MENTAL HEALTH SERVICES, INC.
SERVING WEST AND SOUTHWEST

CORPORATE OFFICE: Boulevard,   34620 – (813)555-5555

DIRECTOR INTERGENERATIONAL PROGRAMMING   **PRESIDENT, CEO**

LIFETIMES
VOLUNTEER MENTOR APPLICATION FORM
(*Time Factor*: 4 hours per week; minimum 1 year)

PERSONAL DATA:

Name _____
        Last   First   Middle   Maiden

Current Address _____
                    Street   City/State   Zip

Length of Residence _____Previous Address _____
                                                        Street

_____Length of Previous Address _____Religion _____
City/State   Zip

Home Phone _____Business Phone _____SS# _____

Birth Date _____Birth place _____Age _____

Education—Highest grade completed _____College Attended _____

Degree(s) received _____Major _____

How did you hear about Lifetimes? _____

MARITAL STATUS/FAMILY:

Check as appropriate: Single _____Married _____Widowed _____Divorced _____

Your spouse's name _____Age _____Occupation _____

How does your spouse feel about your being a professional volunteer? _____

Contact in case of emergency: _____Phone _____

_____

Ages of children:

                    In home: Female:_____   Male:_____
                    Out of home: Female:_____   Male:_____
        Ages of grandchildren: Female:_____   Male:_____

Other persons living in your home: _____

REFERENCES: (Excluding Relatives)   Full Address   Phone   Length of Acquaintance

1. _____

2. _____

3. _____

GENERAL INFORMATION:

Do you have a car? _____Insurance? _____Home/Apt. Insurance? _____

Are you prepared to transport a child? _____

Have you ever been arrested? _____When? _____Where? _____

Were you convicted? _____When? _____Explain _____

_____

General Health _____Physical limitations _____

Do you currently take medication or use any drugs which might in any way interfere with or hinder your driving or visits with a "mentee" (indicate name of drugs, if applicable) _____ Have you ever been treated for a mental or emotional problem? _____When? _____Why? _____ _____ Still receiving treatment? _____ Is there a relative or person who will have regular contact with your child who has ever been arrested or treated for a mental or emotional problem? _____If so, name _____Relationship to you: _____

Please check the problems you are uncomfortable with: Shoplifting _____ Truancy _____ Low Income _____ Drugs _____ Physical _____ Family Illness _____ Learning Disabilities _____ Other: _____

Please describe any experience you have had with children (include child rearing, teaching, day care, babysitting) _____

FORM NO. 152S
Volunteer Application (continued)

Have you had any previous volunteer experience? If YES, please tell us about it: _____
_____

If you have been employed, what kind(s) of jobs have you had mostly? _____

Do you have any skills or hobbies? (For example, crafts, sports, sewing, cooking, woodworking, gardening) If YES, please describe: _____
_____

Do you belong to any clubs or organizations, such as women's or men's clubs, senior centers, church or synagogue groups? If YES, please describe: _____
_____

What types of activities would you most enjoy doing with a youth? _____
_____

Please tell us why you are interested in becoming a Lifetimes mentor. _____
_____

Lifetimes mentors must spend at least four (4) hours per week with their youth, and a Lifetimes mentor promises to work with a youth for one year. Are you willing to make this time commitment?
_____YES   _____NO

VOLUNTEER POLICY PROFILE

The Lifetimes Program is a social service program designed to help children who have shown a need for a strong relationship with an interested adult. While the program is an interfaith and interracial one, the desires of the child's parent or guardian are respected in the selection of the appropriate adult for each child.

In determining whether an applicant may be considered for a match and what information shall be communicated to each party involved in any prospective match regarding the others, due consideration must be given to those past and present factors in the health, personality and behavior of each individual and/or family constellation which professional Agency personnel deem, under the circumstances, may have a significant effect upon the relationship, and which, if revealed at a later date, might affect it adversely. Relevant information shall be provided, however, the name or names of the parties described shall be held confidential before a match is made. Any party has the right to refuse to enter into the match based upon the information so communicated.

An assignment interview is designed to establish a profile of each mentor and their interests. This profile will be used by the Agency to best match the mentor with a child. Except for the prescreened children being considered for a match, all elements of your profile will be kept in the strictest confidence. Of course, prior to any assignment of a child a similar profile of the child and family will be discussed with you to ensure that your desires will be respected.

AUTHORIZATION STATEMENT

I authorize Lifetimes Program to secure such information as may become necessary as part of the routine evaluation of this application to become a participant in Lifetimes. It is my understanding that this information will be held in the strictest confidence. I further understand that this is essential in keeping the image of Lifetimes on the highest level and that I have completed this questionnaire truthfully, to the best of my knowledge and belief.

Signature of Applicant: _____
This _____ **day of** _____, 19 _____

FAMILY AND MENTAL HEALTH SERVICE, INC.
WAIVER FORM

Employee/Volunteer:	last	first	middle

Maiden Name _____ Alias _____
D.O.B. _____ Race _____ Male _____ Female _____ SS# _____
of _____
    Street address

City _____ State _____ Zip _____
hereby agrees to waive any privacy privilege I might have, only regarding the background investigation, and allow Family and Mental Health Services, Inc. to check my name with Sheriff's Department and the Department of Law Enforcement files and to allow them to notify: Family and Mental Health Services, Inc., Boulevard, Fl 34620 as to any entries therein and deliver such report in confidence to the President/CEO for processing as outlined in the Agency personnel code.

                                      Employee Volunteer Signature
                                      (ONLY SIGN IN FRONT OF NOTARY)
Sworn to and subscribed before me this _____ day of _____, 19 _____ .

                                      Notary Public
                                      In and for the County of _____
                                      State of _____
                                      My Commission expires: _____
                                      Job Site/Project _____

FORM NO. 152SS
Volunteer Background Check

Volunteer Background Check
Department of Health and Rehabilitative Services
(STATE) PROTECTIVE SERVICES SYSTEM BACKGROUND CHECK

☐ Original

☐ Annual

I. To be Completed by APPLICANT: PLEASE PRINT LEGIBLY. ALL information must be completed or form will be returned. I (we) hereby give consent for the Department of Health and Rehabilitative Services to conduct a check of reports of abuse, neglect, or exploitation on record concerning me. I (we) also consent to a check of acts of delinquency for background checks requiring same.

Applicant's Signature	Date	Current Phone Number	Applicant's Signature	Date

	LAST NAME	FIRST NAME	FULL MIDDLE NAME	MAIDEN/PRIOR LAST NAMES	RACE SEX	DATE OF BIRTH	SOCIAL SECURITY NUMBER
Applicant(s)							
Spouse							
Children and							
household members.							
DO NOT LIST							
Foster Care Clients.							

List all residences within the State from 1978 until present. In the event of multiple occupancy within one county, list address of longest occupancy.

1. Applicant's Present Address	Street	City	Zip Code	County	Dates of Residence
1. Applicant's Previous Address	Street	City	Zip Code	County	Dates of Residence
1. Applicant's Previous Address	Street	City	Zip Code	County	Dates of Residence

II. To Be Completed by EMPLOYER, HRS REPRESENTATIVE of FACILITY Requesting Background Check
Please Mark Block Which Best Describes Applicant Whose Record Is To Be Checked:

SUMMER CAMP:
☐ Employee
☐ Program Director
☐ Volunteer

DAY CARE:
☐ Employee
☐ Owner/Operator
☐ Owner/Operator (Facility located in
      or adjacent to owner/operator's home)

HRS:
☐ Employee
☐ Other Volunteer (non-85-54)
☐ Volunteer (85-54)

FAMILY DAY CARE HOME:
☐ Household Member
☐ Owner/Operator
☐ Sitter/Relief

SHELTER CARE:
☐ Household Member
☐ Owner/Operator
☐ Sitter/Relief

☐ Household Member
☐ Owner/Operator
☐ Sitter/Relief

GROUP HOME:
☐ Household Member
☐ Owner/Operator
☐ Sitter/Relief

NURSING HOME:
☐ Certified Nursing Assistant
☐ Owner/Operator
☐ Staff

HOME HEALTH CARE:
☐ Owner/Operator
☐ Staff

ACLF:
☐ Owner/Operator
☐ Staff

HOME STUDY:
☐ Divorce/Custody/Adoptions/
      OTI/IPIC

ICF/MR:
☐ Program Director
☐ Staff

CONTRACTED DELINQUENCY PROGRAMS
☐ Employee
☐ Program Director

ALCOHOL/DRUG ABUSE/MENTAL HEALTH
☐ Employee
☐ Program Director

VOLUNTEER
☐ _____
      Program Facility

OTHER:
☐ Adult Foster Care
☐ Adult Sitter
☐ Home Care for the Elderly
☐ Private Babysitter
☐ RN/LPN
☐ Other _____

I (we) agree to keep confidential all information received as a result of background checks conducted, as required by State Statutes. I (we) understand that release of this information to unauthorized persons is prohibited by law.

	Signature of Requesting Party	Date
Requestor's Name	Telephone No.	County in Which Located
Requestor's Street Address City	Zip Code	Applicant's Date of Employment

FORM NO. 152SS
Volunteer Background Check (continued)

III. To Be Completed by HRS DISTRICT

District _____   Attn: District Screening Coordinator

Name		Telephone No.	SunCom Number	
Mailing Address	Street or P.O. Box	City		Zip Code

IV. To Be Completed by HRS Employee Performing Record Check

ABUSE/NEGLECT RECORD CHECKS: This information is confidential and shall not be disclosed except as specifically authorized by Chapter 415, State Statutes

Abuse/Neglect Record Found: ☐ No: No further follow-up necessary.

☐ YES Local records must be reviewed to determine if a substantial report exists.

Report Number(s)	Date of Report (mo/da/yr)	County of Report	FPSS	ARIS
Report Number(s)	Date of Report (mo/da/yr)	County of Report	FPSS	ARIS
Report Number(s)	Date of Report (mo/da/yr)	County of Report	FPSS	ARIS
Report Number(s)	Date of Report (mo/da/yr)	County of Report	FPSS	ARIS
Report Number(s)	Date of Report (mo/da/yr)	County of Report	FPSS	ARIS
Report Number(s)	Date of Report (mo/da/yr)	County of Report	FPSS	ARIS

DELINQUENCY RECORD CHECKS: This information is confidential and shall not be disclosed except as specifically authorized by Chapter 39 and 959, State Statutes

Delinquency Record Found in   ☐ No: No further follow-up necessary.
Client Information System (CIS):   ☐ YES Local records must be reviewed to determine if delinquency charges disqualify applicant(s).

Offender's Name		Offender's DOB (mo/da/yr)
Offender's CIS ID	Date of Report (mo/da/yr)	County of Report

Other significant information: _____

_____

_____

_____

Date FPSS Clearance Completed	Signature of Employee Completing Record Check	SunCom

§332. STATUTORY AGENTS

Registered Agents; Duties

Great elaboration of the statutes regarding *Registered Agents* of NPCs has been notable in recent years; as in Florida, for example, (FL Stat. Section 617.0503, as amended by Laws 1993, c. 93–281, Section 54, eff. May 15, 1993). The rules to be followed now are stated in page after page of this section of the statute. (*See also:* Registered office and agent of *foreign corporation,* FL Stat. Sections 17.1507–09, also amended in 1993.)

§333. APPOINTMENT AND DISCHARGE OF AGENTS

Generally, a hospital that wants to terminate a doctor must follow common-law requirements of procedural due process, showing adequate cause for termination. A due process hearing is not required where the termination is incidental to a hospital's reorganization and is the result of administrative decisions, rather than adjudicatory decisions about a particular doctor. However, a physician may waive rights to a due process hearing upon termination of staff privileges.

> *Abrams v. Saint John's Hospital and Health Center,* 30 CA Rptr. 2d 603 (CA
>   App. 2 Dist., 1994).

A hospital, found by a jury to have wrongfully discharged an employee, may be retried on the issue of damages and fined for failing to disclose information relevant to the employee's wrongful discharge claim as a sanction for discovery abuses, where the former employee does not discover the new evidence until after the jury verdict is rendered.

> *Sullivan v. Sisters of Charity of Providence of Montana,* 885 P. 2d 488 (MT, 1994).

A nonprofit dental health plan must give participating dentists their common-law right to fair procedure, even where a dispute over usual, customary, and reasonable fees is not subject to arbitration. The plan's internal review committee decision, regarding fees, is subject to judicial review by way of administrative mandamus, especially where there is an issue of alleged bias with respect to internal review procedures.

> *Delta Dental Plan of California v. Banasky,* 33 Cal. Rptr. 2d 381 (CA App. 2
>   Dist., 1994).

Under Florida's statute of frauds, an employee who has a verbal contract with a charitable organization, that cannot be completed within one year, is an at-will employee and has no action for breach of contract or promissory estoppel upon his/her discharge. An employee suffers no invasion of privacy, if an employer releases a report concerning the employee to the national media, where the employee becomes an actor in a newsworthy event and fails to make clear what private facts were publicly disclosed.

Merlo v. United Way of America, 43 F. 3d 96 (4th Cir., 1994).

Racial Discrimination

The employer (hospital) and not coemployees may be held liable under Title VII for discriminatory discharge of a black employee.

Smith v. St. Bernard's Regional Medical Center, 19 F. 3d 1254 (8th Cir., AR, 1994).

A black former employee brought suit against a nonprofit corporation alleging that he was terminated due to race discrimination. The court held that the nonprofit properly pleaded a counterclaim against the employee for defamation by asserting that the employee intended only to prevent his termination by maliciously publishing a memorandum to parties beyond those necessary to protect a recognized public interest, thus possibly waiving his absolute privilege from defamation.

Johnson v. Resources for Human Development, Inc., 860 F. Supp. 218 (E.D. PA, 1994).

Employee Free Speech

The U.S. Court of Appeals for the Second District held, in 1995, that a university's reasonable expectation that a controversial speech made by a professor, on racial matters, would disrupt university operations was sufficient justification for ending his term as a department chairman. The court ruled that speech-based discipline of public employees is permissible under the First Amendment if the employer's prediction of disruption is reasonable, the potential disruptiveness outweighs the value of the speech, and the disciplinary action is based on the likely disruption, not retaliation for the speech.

Jeffries v. Harleston, CA 2, No. 93–7876, Apr. 4, 1995.

Hospital employee (nurse) inappropriate derogatory remarks that discouraged other nurses is unprotected and may be the basis of discharge from employment.

Waters v. Churchill, 114 S. Ct. 1878 (1994).

A discharged employee could not establish that he was deprived of his rights of free speech, free association, and access to the courts through termination of his employment, even though he contended that his discharge resulted from his protected association with a not-for-profit corporation founded to advance the causes of the hospital.

Zaretsky v. New York City Health and Hospitals Corporation, 638 N.E. 2d 986 (NY, 1994).

Statements made by an employee, subsequently discharged by a hospital, challenging the hospital's president's proposed spending of money raised by a tax levy and claiming that new work rules might lead to "patient endangerment," do not touch upon matters of public concern so as to be protected by the First Amendment, where the employee contacted the media, the public was aware of the facts, and the press release was characterized as an employee grievance concerning internal office policy.

Rahn v. Drake Center, Inc., 31 F. 3d 407 (6th Cir., 1994).

Employee Loyalty

Doctors employed by a medical school violated their duty of loyalty by taking part in negotiations to provide radiation oncology services to that school's hospital while so employed. They were properly dismissed.

Higgins v. Medical College of Hampton Roads, 849 F. Supp. 1113 (D.C. VA, 1994).

The WARN Act

Under the Worker Adjustment and Retraining Notification (WARN) Act, employees must be given 60 days' advance notice of the closing of a nonprofit employer. However, a nonprofit hospital and its management foundation were not liable under the Act where there were "unforeseeable business circumstances" that "caused" the hospital to close (an exception to the Act).

Jurcev v. Central Community Hospital, 7 F. 3d 618 (7th Dir. [IL], 1993).

Suits under the Worker Adjustment and Retraining Notification Act (WARN) must borrow analogous state statutes of limitations because WARN is silent on a limitations period.

North Star Steel Co. v. Thomas, US SupCt, No. 94–834, May 30, 1995.

The Fair Labor Standards Act

A society that is an amusement or recreational establishment, and whose average receipts for any six months of the year are not more than one-third of its average receipts for the other six months of the year, is exempt from the Fair Labor Standards Act. Thus an employee, who brought an action for overtime compensation against an agricultural society that held an annual county fair, was denied relief, even though he performed nonexempt labor. Rental of facilities to a nonexempt entity does not disqualify the exempt entity from its exemption.

Chaney v. Clark Cty. Agricultural Soc., Inc., 629 N.E. 2d 513 (OH App. 2 Dist., 1993).

Age Discrimination

A chef sued a monastery and a university after he was allegedly fired due to age discrimination. In Pennsylvania, the test for proving the employment relationship is the common law test for distinguishing between employee and independent contractor. The university was absolved of liability because it was not involved in a parent/subsidiary relationship with the monastery and did not act jointly with the monastery in firing the chef. The monastery was not an extension of the university.

Stouch v. Brothers of Order of Hermits of St. Augustine, 836 F. Supp. 1134 (E.D. PA, 1993).

In order for a terminated employee to establish a prima facie case under the Age Discrimination in Employment Act (ADEA), an employee must show that he or she suffered materially adverse employment action. An employee who refuses an employer's offer of lateral transfer, which would not have changed his salary and benefits and which involved comparable responsibilities with a greater growth potential, cannot show that he or she suffered materially employment action.

Flaherty v. Gas Research Institute, 31 F. 3d 451 (7th Cir., 1994).

A pay scheme linking salary to work experience does not violate the Age Discrimination in Employment Act, even where there is a disparate impact on older job applicants when coupled with a salary cap for hirees.

> *Equal Employment Opportunity Commission v. Francis W. Parker School,* CA 7, No. 93–3395, Oct. 21, 1994.

The ADEA, Age Discrimination in Employment Act, was enacted by Congress in an ongoing effort to eradicate discrimination and invidious bias in employment decisions in the workplace. Private litigants can seek redress for their injuries through the ADEA, which has both a deterrence and a compensation objective.

> *McKennon v. Nashville Banner Pub. Co.,* 115 S. Ct. 879 (U.W. TN, 1995); 29 U.S.C.A. Section 621 *et seq.*

There is no fundamental right to be free of age discrimination, by an employer of less than five people, under California's Fair Employment and Housing Act (FEHA).

> *Jennings v. Marralle,* 876 P. 2d 1074 (CA, 1994); West's Ann. Cal. Gov. Code, Section 12926(d).

Under the Age Discrimination in Employment Act (ADEA), a nurse challenged a hospital's decision not to retain her in its obstetrics/gynecology unit and requiring her to undergo a skills assessment. The court held that bald assertions that the hospital had a "phase-out policy," without evidence that their decisions were motivated by age discrimination, were not sufficient to demonstrate age discrimination.

> *Brown v. Saint Anthony Hospitals,* 858 F. Supp. 146 (D. CO, 1994).

A terminated teacher at a Catholic high school was denied the use of the Age Discrimination in Employment Act (ADEA) to judicially challenge her termination. Application of the ADEA would violate the free exercise and establishment clauses of the First Amendment in cases where the teacher was employed by the archdiocese solely as a Roman Catholic theology teacher at a Catholic high school, whether there was a "religious reason" for the termination or not.

> *Powell v. Stafford,* 859 F. Supp. 1343 (D. CO, 1994).

A former employee of a nonprofit Rhode Island social service agency showed a prima facie case of age discrimination by proving (1) she was over 40 years of age, (2) she suffered adverse job action, (3) her job responsibilities were assumed by another person, (4) her employer continued to need her skills, (5) she was qualified for the position she held, and (6) she was performing well enough to rule out the possibility that adverse job action was for inadequate job performance.

Keisling v. Ser-Jobs for Progress, Inc., 19 F. 3d 755 (1st Cir. [RI], 1994).

Retaliatory Discharge

To establish a Title VII retaliatory discharge claim against an employer, a discharged employee has to show that (1) he or she engaged in a protected activity as an employee, (2) was subsequently discharged from employment, and (3) there was a causal connection between the protected activity and the discharge.

Hoeppner v. Crotched Mountain Rehabilitation Center, Inc., 31 F. 3d 9 (1st Cir., 1994).

A college's requirement that a former employee, who complained of job discrimination, obtain permission before coming onto campus did not violate the anti-retaliation provision of Title VII of the 1964 Civil Rights Act.

Nelson v. Upsala College, CA 3, No. 94–5453, Mar. 24, 1995.

Criminal Background Checks

The National Child Protection Act (NCPA) of 1993 and Violent Crime Control and Law Enforcement Act (VCCLEA) of 1994 require states to adopt measures to require criminal background checks, including fingerprinting and filling out of forms listing convictions, on volunteers and employees nationwide. The VCCLEA caps the cost per volunteer at $36 ($18 each for the state and the FBI). Nonprofits, therefore, will face increased costs as a result. For example, local organizations sponsoring scout troops will face as much as $42 million in order to investigate scouting's million-plus volunteers. Thirty-one states now have laws regarding background checks. In 1995, Tennessee was the only state that passed legislation in response to the new law.

Sarver, Patrick, (article), 9 *NonProfit Times* (1) 1, 16–18 (January, 1995).

For information about access under the Freedom of Information Act (5 USCS §552) to presentence, probation, and parole reports and recommendations, *see* 81 ALR Fed. 801, §§7[b], 9[b].

Disabled Employees

Individuals cannot be held liable under the Americans with Disabilities Act unless they are an "employer" under the Act. An "employer" is defined in the Act to be "a person engaged in an industry affecting commerce who has 15 or more employees . . . and any agent of such person."

EEOC v. AIC Security Investigations, CA 7, No. 93–3839, May 22, 1995.

"Private clubs," with meaningful conditions of "limited membership," are exempt from employment discrimination suits under the Americans with Disabilities Act (ADA). Informing members of applicants, voting on members, and requiring sponsorship members to confirm that an applicant met qualifications for membership is "limited membership."

Kelsey v. University Club of Orlando, Inc., 845 F. Supp. 1526 (M.D. FL, 1994).

A handicapped employee of a nonprofit organization may sue under the Illinois Human Rights Act if forced to resign her employment because the organization fails to have a wheelchair ramp installed at his/her place of employment.

Muraoka v. Human Rights Com'n., 625 N.E. 2d 251 (IL App. 1 Dist., 1993).

Employers must make reasonable accommodation for handicapped persons who apply for jobs. Under the Rehabilitation Act, an employee must prove that (1) he/she is "handicapped," (2) is "otherwise qualified" for the position at issue, and (3) was excluded or discharged from a position solely because of that handicap. Then the burden shifts to the employer to show that the justifications offered for its refusal to "accommodate" her/him are "job related" and that to make the necessary accommodation would impose "undue hardship" on its operations (firefighter with asthma).

Huber v. Howard County, MD, 849 F. Supp. 407 (D. MD, 1994).

For information about the application of the National Labor Relations Act (29 USCS §§141 et seq.) to handicapped persons and charity-sponsored work programs for the handicapped, *see* 68 ALR Fed 905.

Promotion

A "long-term goal," in a city consent decree, for achieving an overall work force containing 9.5 percent black police officers and for appointing to promotional positions proportions of groups represented in the classes of employees eligible for promotion, does not require 9.5 percent black representation be achieved in each of the ranks of police officers.

> *Brotherhood of Midwest Guardians, Inc. v. City of Omaha,* 9 F. 3d 677 (8th Cir. [NB], 1993).

A female college employee filed a sex-discrimination claim against a non-profit college, alleging that the college refused to promote her and changed the job qualifications for a position in order to exclude her from consideration. The court held that the employee did not, as required under the "opposition" and retaliation clause of Title VII, prove a statutorily protected expression, adverse employment action, and a causal link between the protected expression and the adverse action. The elements of proof are the same under a Section 1981 employment discrimination claim.

> *Aldridge v. Tougaloo College,* 847 F. Supp. 480 (S.D. MS, 1994).

A decree, applicable to a city fire department, that enjoined it from discriminating against employees or potential employees based on race, color, sex, or national origin, may be terminated if the effects of past discrimination have been eliminated, even though women and minorities remain underrepresented in promotional ranks. Unanticipated circumstances may also warrant modification of a consent decree (i.e., difficulty of recruiting certain groups into the fire department).

> *U.S. v. City of Miami,* 2 F. 3d 1497 (11th Cir. [FL], 1993); *See also Brotherhood of Midwest Guardians, Inc. v. City of Omaha,* 9 F. 3d 677 (8th Cir. [NB], 1993).

State Action Requirement for Civil Rights Suits

In an employment dispute, involving termination, a nonprofit corporation must act "under color of law" for liability under Section 1983 (wrongful discharge and defamation) to apply. Title VII employment discrimination actions must be filed within 90 days of delivery of notice, by the Postal Service, that the employee can pick up his/her Equal Employment Opportunity Commission's (EEOC) right-to-sue letter.

> *Watts-Means v. Prince George's Family Crisis Center,* 7 F. 3d 40 (4th Cir. [MD], 1993).

Employee Manual Effects

See, Chapter 22, §232 for the effect of bylaws on hospital/physician contracts.

An employee handbook that describes some conduct that could subject an employee to discipline and lists disciplinary actions that could be taken is not a promise (or contract) to follow that course of progressive discipline prior to termination. This is especially true where the handbook provided for a nonprofit hospital's complete discretion in the implementation of discipline.

> *Frank v. South Suburban Hosp. Foundation,* 628 N.E. 2d 953 (IL App. 1 Dist., 1993).

A college handbook is not part of an employment contract where the college president's introductory letter says that it is not an employment contract but an introduction to the institution.

> *Raines v. Haverford College,* 849 F. Supp. 1009 (D.C. PA, 1994).

When an employee manual provision is inconsistent with employment at will, the question of whether an employee can only be discharged for cause is a question for the jury. Where an employee is fired after being placed under suspension while under investigation for trying to buy drugs, and the employee refuses to meet to discuss the terms of the suspension, the termination is not outrageous, even if the employee is fired after filing compensation and sexual harassment complaints.

> *Baldwin v. Upper Valley Services, Inc.,* 644 A. 2d 316 (VT, 1994).

Where there is no indication that a nonprofit corporation violated its manual procedures, the mere existence of a policy manual or internal grievance procedure is not sufficient to limit a nonprofit employer's right to terminate an at-will employee. An article 78 proceeding is the proper vehicle for a terminated employee to challenge his termination, based on allegations that the nonprofit violated employee manual rules.

> *De Petris v. Union Settlement Association, Inc.,* 618 N.Y.S. 2d 276 (A.D. 1 Dept., 1994).

Religious NPO Employees

A church may not be sued for firing an employee after excommunicating him/her for failing to work in harmony with other employees.

> *Carol Geraci v. Eckankar Church;* New Hope, MN (MN Ct: Appls., Jan. 17, 1995); *Natl. L.J.,* p. A10 (Jan. 30, 1995). *See also,* Chapter 36, §364.

§334. STATUS OF AN AGENT OR EMPLOYEE

Worker Classification and Withholding Obligations

In an attempt to simplify and clarify application of the common law factors used in worker classification as employees or independent contractors, the IRS has issued *Employee or Independent Contractor,* a draft training manual. The draft manual also addresses relief available under Section 530 of the Revenue Act of 1978 (available at 96 TNT 73-23).

For use in the new Classification Settlement Program, the IRS has released three standard closing agreements (available at 96 TNT 91-10).

If a state-affiliated educational institution retains the right to supervise an instructor's work and to require that she perform her duties in a manner consistent with the state policy manual and the institution's faculty handbook, the instructor will be classified as an employee, even where the institution did not train the instructor (PLR 9615006). For similar rulings with respect to educational organization workers, *see* PLR 9615022 and PLR 9617012.

Employee Status

A physician with staff privileges at several hospitals is not a hospital "employee" within the meaning of the Arizona Civil Rights Act. The Arizona Civil Rights Division does, thus, not have the jurisdiction to investigate such a physician's employment discrimination charge against a hospital or to subpoena the hospital's peer review materials.

St. Luke's v. State Dept. of Law, 884 P. 2d 259 (AZ App. Div. 1, 1994).

A driver, who was assigned work by the county as part of a sentence for a speeding ticket, is an "employee" of the state and county, and must look to the exclusive remedies of the Workers' Compensation Act for compensation for injuries sustained when she was overcome by the toxic fumes of a solvent she used to clean a ventilation duct. A person who performs work under a court order is not a "volunteer." Credit against an imposed fine is "remuneration" for purposes of the Act.

Arriaga v. County of Alameda, 29 CA Rptr. 2d 212 (CA App. 1 Dist., 1994).

A terminated oil refinery worker sued his employer refinery and the non-profit firm that administered a safety test for discrimination after he failed the safety test, due to a learning disability, and was terminated. The court held that the nonprofit safety organization was not an "employer" of the worker and, thus, was not responsible for the alleged discrimination.

   Daniels v. Allied Elec. Contractors, Inc., 847 F. Supp. 514 (E.D. TX, 1994).

A participant in the "work therapy" rehabilitation program of a charitable organization is not an "employee" entitled to minimum wages under the Fair Labor Standards Act (FLSA). The guiding principles applicable to employment status under FLSA are contemplation of the parties, economic realities, totality of the circumstances, and the basic relationship between the parties.

   Williams v. Strickland, 837 F. Supp. 1049 (N.D. CA, 1993).

A prison inmate, who participates in community service for a village and church, is not "hired" by the village, state, or church and is not an "agent" or "employee" of the village, state, or church, so as to invoke the protections of Labor Law.

   D'Argenio v. Village of Homer, 609 N.Y.S. 2d 943 (NY A.D. Dept., 1994).

A person who participates in a "workfare" program in return for a public assistance grant is not an "employee" for the purposes of unemployment compensation benefits. Such programs are "unemployment work-relief or work-training programs" that make no contributions to the unemployment compensation fund.

   Costello v. Board of Review, Dept. of Labor, 642 A. 2d 1034 (NJ Super. A.D.,
      1994).

The former members of communal religious colonies were not "employees" under ERISA because they were voluntary members, not hired as employees, received no wages and did not participate in any program affecting their employment relationship (social security, federal withholding, unemployment insurance, workers' compensation). Also, church organizations are exempt from participation in ERISA. Further, the First Amendment forbids civil courts from interfering in decisions of hierarchical polity made by church tribunals if extensive inquiry into religious law and polity is necessary. Thus, the former members were denied their alleged property interests in the colony assets.

   Wollman v. Poinsett Hutterian Brethren, Inc., 844 F. Supp. 539 (D. SD, 1994).

The determination of whether an employee of a nonprofit organization, who is injured while performing duties for the organization, is entitled to workers' compensation benefits, is made by analyzing whether the activity is operated for the purpose of pecuniary gain, not whether the organization is set up as a nonprofit. To be conducted "for pecuniary gain," the purpose of a business must be profit.

Ponca City Welfare Association v. Ludwigsen, 882 P. 2d 1062 (OK, 1994).

§336. EMPLOYEE COMPENSATION

Nonprofit Salaries (Executives)

A survey by Abbott Langer & Associates indicated that, on average in 1994, CEOs at organizations with operating budgets less than $250,000 were paid $29,000 a year while CEOs at organizations with operating budgets over $25 million were paid $140,000. Data from Towers Perrin indicated salaries of $71,000 for executives at organizations with less than $1 million in revenue and salaries of $240,000 at organizations with more than $50 million in revenue. A *NonProfit Times* survey indicated that the median salaries of nonprofit executives rose to $55,000 per year, an increase of 5.45 percent over 1993, continuing a yearly small rise since 1992.

Weeks, David A., (article), 9 *NonProfit Times* (1) 21–24 (January, 1995).

According to an Ernst & Young LLP Not-for-Profit Business Services survey of 200 nonprofits in New York, top nonprofit executives in New York earn an average of $118,000 per year. That figure is more than twice the national average and represents an increase in executive salaries in New York of 4.9 percent in 1994.

McNamara, Don, (article) 9 *NonProfit Times* (7) 13 (July, 1995).

Incentive Compensation

Nonprofits are facing stiff competition from the for-profit sector in the hiring of top executives and employees. Nonprofit executive salaries are 20 percent behind their for-profit counterparts according to a study by Ernst & Young. Many nonprofits have turned to "incentive compensation" in order to compete. However, a growing number of nonprofits feel that cash incentives and bonuses lead to loss of the charitable mission's message. Notably the National Wildlife Federation (NWF) believes that bonuses and cash incentives do not use donations in the most effective way in carrying out their mission. The American Society of Association Executives (ASAE), based in Washington, D.C., cautions against incentive programs that defeat the overall goals of the association and may place federal grants at risk.

> McIver, La Vonne, (article), 9 *NonProfit Times* (8) 1, 6 (August, 1995); *See also,* Bailey and Risher, *"If the Shoe Fits": Not-For-Profits Try Out New Compensation Plans, Compensation and Benefits Review,* May–June, 1996.

Unemployment Compensation Benefits

See 90 ALR 3d 987, §§12[a], 13[b] for information about repayment of unemployment compensation benefits erroneously paid.

Employee 403(b) Tax-Sheltered Annuity Plans

The IRS has developed a voluntary correction program, in effect through October 31, 1996, to allow nonprofit employers to correct defects in their 403(b) tax-sheltered annuity plans in order to avoid audits and possible suspension from the program. The Tax-Sheltered Annuity Voluntary Correction Program (TVC) will allow the IRS to accept a fee and a negotiated sanction in return for written assurance against any further sanctions due to the defects. Once an audit begins, nonprofits cannot get into the voluntary program. The 403(b) plan allows nonprofit employees to save for retirement on a tax-advantaged basis while employers contribute either on a matching or discretionary basis.

> *See, IRS Promises Fair Treatment Under Tax-Sheltered Annuity Voluntary Compliance Program.* Rod Garcia. *Tax Notes,* August 14, 1995 68 n7 p853–854; *IRS Issues Voluntary Compliance Program for S. 403(b) Plans and Proposed Audit Guidelines for Use by Field Staff. Tax Management Compensation Planning Journal,* June 2, 1995 23 n6 p152–154; *The Service Seeks Increased Enforcement of Tax-Sheltered Annuities.* Hoffman and Lerner. *Journal of Taxation of Investments,* Spring 1995 12 n3 p238–243.

Compensation Techniques

> *See, Compensation Techniques for Non-Profits.* Barbara Bromberg, New York University Conference on Tax Planning for 501(c)(3) Organizations, Annual 1994 22 p3–1(33).

Minimum Wage Regulations

Neither Oregon's "multiunit accommodations" exception, nor the "companionship services" exemption contained in the federal minimum wage regulation, apply to deny a former resident manager of an adult foster care home his recovery for minimum wages, overtime compensation, and damages for discrimination in a suit against his former employer.

Baxter v. M.J.B. Investors, 876 P. 2d 3331 (OR App., 1994).

Day care centers must comply with federal minimum wage and maximum hour standards whether they offer preschool education, purely custodial care, or some of each.

Reich v. Miss Paula's Day Care Center, Inc., CA 6, No, 93–3706, Oct. 19, 1994.

Pension Plans

After a 10-year battle to reinstate 401(k) plans for nonprofits (such plans were wiped out during the Tax Reform Act of 1986) nonprofits can once again offer 401(k) retirement plans to their employees, beginning January 1, 1997, under a provision tacked to the minimum wage law signed by President Clinton in 1996. The inability to establish 401(k) plans had put nonprofits at a disadvantage in attracting and retaining qualified employees. Contributions will be made through salary reductions, before federal income tax is calculated, and may be matched by the employer. Trade associations and welfare organizations, which didn't have the ability to have a 401(k) or 403(b) plan, can now establish 401(k) plans.

Sinclair, Matthew, (article), 10 *NonProfit Times* (9) 1, 12, 14 (September, 1996).

The Small Business Job Protection Act

The Small Business Job Protection Act, passed in May, 1996, by the House, will benefit nonprofits. Charitable risk pools for insurance would be exempt under the legislation. Agricultural membership dues up to $100 would be excluded from unrelated business income tax. The bill also clarifies EO deferred compensation issues concerning section 457, 401(k), and 403(b) plans, particularly focusing on Indian tribes' plans. Other provisions govern political expenditures, first-time farm buyers' exempt bonds, and other EO tax issues.

Stokeld, Fred, *Small-Business Tax Relief Bill Has Plenty for EOs, Tax Notes,* June 17, 1996.

A number of IRS releases have clarified several issues related to qualified retirement plan law changes enacted under the Small Business Job Protection Act. Notice 96-67 provides guidance on the revised required beginning date for qualified plan distributions under IRC section 401(a)(9). Revenue Procedures 96-56 and 96-63 identify changes in the private letter ruling process for IRC section 457 nonqualified deferred compensation plans for tax-exempts and state and local government employers.

> Sollee, William L., and Schneider, Paul J., *IRS Guidance Relating to Small Business Act Changes, The Journal of Taxation*, February, 1997.

Bankers expect to benefit from several retirement-plan provisions of the federal minimum-wage law. The savings incentive match plan for employees (Simple) mandates employer matching for up to 3 percent of compensation, allows only $6,000 annual contributions from workers, and is easier for bankers to administer.

> *See also,* Hensley, Scott, *Good News for Banks: Wage Law Expands on 401(k), IRA Plans, American Banker,* August 23, 1996. *See also,* Stokeld, Fred, *New Section 401(k) Provisions Good for Non-Profits, Attorney Says, Tax Notes,* Sept. 23, 1996.

Withheld Payroll Taxes

Internal Revenue Code S6672 provides guidelines on how payroll tax, withheld from employees, that was not paid to the government by a corporation or other entity, can be assessed. IRC S6672 also applies to unpaid tax of the board of directors of nonprofit organizations. The IRS may impose a penalty against the board of directors of the organization if it finds that the key elements of "responsibility" and "willfulness" are present. Directors should insist that the nonprofit pay for "Plan B" liability insurance to make sure that they do not have to pay the withholding liabilities.

> Switzer, Osterhout, and Gallagher, *Personal Liability of Directors of Not-For-Profit Corporations, The National Public Accountant,* Feb., 1996.

Cash-or-Deferred Arrangements

Tax-exempt organizations may now offer their employees the same cash-or-deferred arrangements available to workers at for-profit entities. The new SIMPLE plans also can be used by exempt employers. The SIMPLE options are in addition to the still-available Section 403(b) and Section 457 plans. Special rules may apply for exempt employers. Employers should carefully analyze all the choices before adopting any benefit plan.

> Baum, Stanley D., *Renewed Availability of Section 401(k) Plans Gives Tax-Exempt Employers Greater Options. Journal of Taxation*, April, 1997.

Intermediate Sanctions

Since executive compensation must be considered reasonable to avoid the sanctions, retroactively applicable to September, 1995 transactions, organizations may wish to consult compensation experts for assistance. Unreported taxable benefits to disqualified persons, such as reimbursements, may also result in penalties, regardless of the compensation involved.

> Schoenfeld and Repass, *"Intermediate Sanctions"–Issues, Pitfalls, and Protective Measures, Tax Notes,* August 19, 1996.

UBIT and Employee Retirement Plans

Attorney Louis Mazawey, speaking at the September, 1996 ABA/ALI conference said that UBIT (Unrelated Business Income Tax) may be applicable to the employee retirement plans of tax-exempt organizations. He pointed out the possibility of UBIT being applied to various trusts and IRAs, particularly focusing on welfare benefit funds and real estate investment trusts.

> Stokeld, Fred, *Employee Plans Can Be Hit with UBIT, Attorney Warns, Tax Notes,* Sept. 16, 1996.

NPO Salaries in Delaware

In a study of 103 nonprofit organizations compiled by the Delaware Association of Nonprofit Agencies, the average female executive of a nonprofit in Delaware takes home 18 percent less than her male peer. In a national study by Abbott, Langer & Associates, the average salary of an executive director nationally was $56,000 while in Delaware it was $48,235. This trend continues in other positions.

> Swarden, Carlotta, (article), 10 *NonProfit Times* (8) 5 (August, 1996).

Fringe Benefits

The IRS is seeking back taxes from the former basketball coach at the University of Nevada-Las Vegas. The coach received 223 free tickets per game, valued at $40,140 per year in 1987–1991 as a fringe benefit. The IRS guidelines deem personal transportation expenses, awards or prizes, and free or specially discounted tickets to be income to college employees.

> *See* Harmon, Gail, (article), 9 *NonProfit Times* (2) 30 (February, 1995). *See also, Administration Takes Aim at Compensation and Benefit Practices of Tax-Exempt Employers.* Sieller, Hall, and Shultz. *Employee Relations Law Journal,* Winter, 1994; *Thrasher: IRS Will Examine Exempt Organizations' Deferred Compensation, Fringe Benefit Programs.* (Michael Thrasher) Meegan M. Reilly. *Tax Notes,* Sept. 12, 1994.

Employee Health Plans

The federal court has exclusive jurisdiction, under the Employee Retirement Income Security Act (ERISA), over disputes concerning county health plans in which nongovernmental employees and employers participate.

> *Nord Community Mental Health Center v. County of Lorain,* 638 N.E. 2d 623 (OH App. 9 Dist., 1994).

§337. PERSONNEL POLICIES (REGULATIONS)

Religious Society Officers

See also Chapter 36 §364.

Clergy employed by a religious society may lawfully be subjected to employment decisions where the decisions involved would be arbitrary and subject to civil court review in other kinds of organizations.

> *Young v. Northern Illinois Conference of United Methodist Church,* 21 F. 3rd 184 (7th Cir. [IL], 1994).

Governmental Regulation of Employees

An Arizona law that prohibited state and local employees from using any language other than English while performing their official duties violated free speech rights and was unconstitutionally overbroad.

> *Yniguez v. Arizonans for Official English,* CA 9, No. 92–17087, Dec. 7, 1994.

A federal law, Section 501(b) of the 1978 Ethics in Government Act, banning federal employees from accepting honoraria for speeches or articles violates the First Amendment as applied to the executive branch employees below grade GS–16.

U.S. v. National Treasury Employees Union, US SupCt, No. 93–1170, Feb. 22, 1995.

The federal government cannot prohibit government employees from accepting travel reimbursement from private sources for unofficial work-related speeches or articles, but permit such reimbursement for officially approved speeches. Such prohibitions violate the First Amendment.

Sanjour v. Environmental Protection Agency, CA DC (en banc), No. 92–5123, May 30, 1995.

A private group home, providing residential services for disabled adults and a union representing its employees, has standing to challenge changes by the Department of Mental Health in the state's standard contract with such associations, where the contract directly affects the terms and conditions of the employees' employment and the changes are designed to thwart attempts to unionize employees. Such contract changes are subject to formal rule-making procedures under the Administrative Procedures Act.

American Federation of State, County and Municipal Employees v. Department of Mental Health, 522 N.W. 2d 657 (MI App., 1994).

A nonprofit organization of city police officers has standing to challenge a city ordinance requiring new city employees to reside within the city. The organization was held to have a real and substantial interest in future employees and in the pool of applicants. A state statute providing that no residency requirement could be applied to disqualify persons from holding a position as a peace officer was upheld.

City of Ashland v. Ashland F.O.P. #3, Inc., 888 S.W. 2d 667 (KY, 1994).

Municipalities may mandate a residency requirement for municipal employees. Direct public employment is not a fundamental right protected by the Privileges and Immunities Clause.

Salem Blue Collar Workers Association v. Salem, N.J., CA 3, No. 93–5622, Aug. 26, 1994.

§338. ORGANIZATION LIABILITY FOR EMPLOYEES AND AGENTS

See also Chapter 17.

Criminal Liability

The legal liability of a church for a priest's crimes (child abuse) seems to be recognized if church authorities' failure to properly supervise can be shown. In addition, the rules as to who shall pay (insurers, church, and so on) are now being thrashed out. Insurer liability was found in *Society of Roman Catholic Church of D. of L. etc. v. Interstate Fire and Casualty Co.,* #93–4068 (5th Cir. [U.S.], May 27, 1994) (declaratory judgment to be appealed).

> R. Samborn, *Who Will Pay Victims of Pedophile Priests?, Natl. L.J.,* p. A21 (July 4, 1994).

A female former employee brought suit for sex discrimination in violation of Title VII, assault, intentional infliction of emotional distress, negligent retention, negligent supervision, and negligent entrustment against her nonprofit employer after she was allegedly raped by a coemployee. The court held that the former employee has a sex discrimination claim, under Title VII, based on the employer's failure to remedy a work environment it knew was hostile to women and that resulted in the alleged rape and the female employee's subsequent constructive discharge. The other claims fell under the exclusive remedy of the Workers' Compensation Statute.

> *Al-Dabbagh v. Greenpeace, Inc.,* 873 F. Supp. 1105 (N.D. IL, 1994).

Hospital Liability

An employee must have been acting in a corporate or an employment capacity when the conduct occurs for an employer to be liable for punitive damages in connection with the employee's conduct. For an organization to be liable for punitive damages for performing, ratifying, or approving an agent's malicious conduct, the agent must be acting as the organization's representative, not in some other capacity. Fault by the employer itself is required for punitive damages to be assessed (i.e., a pure respondeat superior basis is not sufficient).

> *College Hospital, Inc. v. Superior Court,* 882 P. 2d 894 (CA, 1994) (off-premises consensual sexual affair between hospital's psychiatric patient and hospital employee).

A hospital may be negligent for the acts of independent medical practitioners ("independent contractors") operating in its hospital if: (1) the hospital holds itself out as a medical services provider to the community, and (2) the patient looks to the hospital, rather than the individual practitioner, in absence of notice or knowledge to the contrary, to provide competent medical care.

Clark v. Southview Hosp. and Family Health Ctr., 628 N.E. 2d 46 (OH, 1994).

Volunteers' Background Checks

New federal statutes push states to require criminal background checks of volunteers, especially those caring for the elderly and children. These will be expensive and may discourage many volunteers. States have until the end of 1996 to adopt laws required by the federal statutes.

P. Sarver, (article), *NonProfit Times,* p. 1 (Jan., 1995).

Negligence Suits Brought by Employees

A member of a nonprofit corporation, who was injured after he volunteered to install an air-conditioning unit in the corporation's attic, brought suit against the nonprofit claiming that the corporation was negligent and violated Illinois' Structural Work Act (SWA). The court held that although the SWA mandates that adequate supports be installed for workers, the plank that collapsed under the worker was being used as a pathway by the worker and was not a "support" under the Act.

Baldwin v. Twin Rivers Club, 636 N.E. 2d 1024 (IL App. 3 Dist., 1994).

A suit by a volunteer, against a nonprofit thrift shop corporation, is barred by the exclusive remedy of Workers' Compensation Law, where the plaintiff is a volunteer employee of the corporation and the corporation has elected, prior to the plaintiff's accident, to bring its employees under the coverage of Workers' Compensation Law.

Kligman v. Call Again Thrift Shop, Inc., 618 N.Y.S. 2d 288 (A.D. 1 Dept., 1994).

33

FREEDOM TO ASSOCIATE

§339. RIGHT OF FREE CHOICE OF ASSOCIATES

Right to Association: Privacy

The First Amendment's "right to association" carries with it, according to the [Supreme] Court, the right to keep those associations private. In *NAACP v. Alabama,* the Court denied the state of Alabama its request to force the NAACP to *disclose* its *membership lists.* The Court recognized that the inability to keep one's affiliations private would have a chilling effect on the fundamental right of association. [*NAACP v. Alabama,* 357 U.S. 449, at 462 (1958) (that disclosure can be mandated only upon a showing of a rational and compelling state interest).] Subsequent cases similarly affirmed a constitutional right to privacy in one's affiliations [*See, Katz v. U.S.,* 389 U.S. 347 (1967); *DeGregory v. New Hampshire,* 383 U.S. 825 (1966); *Griswold v. Connecticut,* 381 U.S. 479, 483 (1965) (that membership is a (protected) form of expression of opinion . . .)].

> Jana Nestlerode, Re-"Righting" the Right to Privacy: . . ., 41 *Clev. St. L. Rev.*
> (1) 59, 62 (1993).

The Texas Supreme Court followed the *NAACP v. Alabama* rule in 1994, in *Texas Human Rights Commission v. Texas Knights of the KKK (Griffin, atty.)*; *See* Nat Hentoff, column, *St. Petersburg (FL) Times,* p. 20A (June 25, 1994).

§340. CONSTITUTIONAL FREEDOM OF ASSOCIATION

Freedom of Speech and Freedom to Associate

Massachusetts' public accommodation law, that required private organizers of a St. Patrick's day parade to permit gay, lesbian, and bisexual descendants of Irish immigrants to participate, violated the organizers' First Amendment free speech rights. Such statutes require the organizers to alter the expressive content of the parade and have the effect of declaring the organizers' speech itself to be public accommodation.

Hurley v. Irish-American Gay, Lesbian and Bisexual Group of Boston, 115 S. Ct.
   2338 (U.S. MA, 1995).

A nonprofit association, which had received a permit to stage an artistic
and cultural festival can, consistent with the First Amendment, prohibit a "street
preacher," who planned to give speeches on political, religious, and ideological
or social causes, from having a booth at the festival, and can also prevent the
preacher from speaking on the grounds.

Brandon v. Springspree, Inc., 888 P. 2d 357 (CO App., 1994).

Though the message of the Ku Klux Klan, in applying to participate in an
adopt-a-highway program in or near the city, was an attempt to intimidate minority residents and to disrupt any desegregation of a housing complex, such
speech is expressive conduct subject to First Amendment protection. However,
the KKK does not have a First Amendment right to participate in an adopt-a-
highway program where the state's compelling interest, in better facilitating the
government's program of desegregating city housing to comply with federal prohibitions of discrimination, outweighs the KKK's First Amendment right.

State of Texas v. Knights of the Ku Klux Klan, 853 F. Supp. 958 (E.D. TX, 1994).

A cross erected by the KKK in the square about the Ohio State House in
Columbus, Ohio, is entitled to constitutional protection and does not violate the
Establishment of Religion clause. So held the U.S. Sixth Circuit Court of Ap-
peals. The cross was vandalized after one day in December 1993.

Pinette v. Capitol Square Review and Advisory Board, #93–4367. Reported in
   Nat'l. L.J., p. A8 (Aug. 8, 1994).

§341. ASSERTION OF RIGHT TO ASSOCIATION

Student Athletes' Associational Rights

A student who is not participating in a formal written individualized education program (IEP), established under the Individuals with Disabilities Education Act (IDEA), has no federally protected right to participate in interscholastic
sports in contravention of eight-semester and four-season eligibility rules.

J.M., JR. v. Montana High School Association, 875 P. 2d 1026 (MT, 1994).

The actions of a state High School Activities Association are "state actions," for the purpose of constitutional analysis, if the power to regulate athletic programs is conferred by the state legislature on the local school board, and the school board delegates the authority to the Association. A high school student has an expectation, and not an entitlement, to participate in athletics. A school rule, precluding for one year participation in interscholastic athletic competitions after transfer to a school outside the district of residence, is constitutional. Such rules encourage and promote fair competition among schools and deter odious recruitment tactics, both legitimate state purposes.

Mississippi High School Activities Association, Inc. v. Coleman By and on Behalf of Laymon, 631 So. 2d 768 (MS, 1994).

Student athletes have no constitutional right to participate in any particular sport in their college or to participate in intercollegiate or high school athletics. Accordingly, male wrestlers, who sued a private nonprofit university to force re-instatement of an intercollegiate wrestling program, failed to obtain a preliminary injunction.

Gonyo v. Drake University, 837 F. Supp. 989 (S.D. IA, 1993).

A state high school athletic association may not enforce its age participation limit against students who were held back in school due to learning disabilities. Injunction against such action can be secured under the Americans with Disabilities Act and Section 504 of the Rehabilitation Act.

Sandison v. Michigan High School Athletic Association Inc., DC EMich, No. 94–CV–73231, Sept. 13, 1994.

In Missouri, a learning disabled high school athlete obtained a preliminary injunction, under Section 504 of the Rehabilitation Act and the Americans with Disabilities Act, allowing him to play high school baseball despite a Missouri rule barring students over age 19 from interscholastic competition. However, the U.S. Court of Appeals for the Eighth Circuit, on Nov. 16, 1994 reversed the preliminary injunction.

Pottgen v. Missouri State High School Activities Association, CA 8, No. 94–2324, Nov. 16, 1994.

Membership Requirements

The Virginia Board of Bar Examiners violated the Americans with Disabilities Act by broadly wording a bar application question about mental health history. The question asked whether the applicant has been "treated or counseled for any mental, emotional or nervous disorders" within the past five years. The court held that the question is ineffective, contributes to the stigmatizing of disabled individuals, and deters them from seeking beneficial counseling and treatment.

> *Clark v. Virginia Board of Bar Examiners,* DC EVa, No. 94–221–A, Feb. 23, 1995.

The Department of Transportation cannot require preemployment alcohol testing for all commercial truck drivers. *See* 47 USC App. 2717(a).

> *American Trucking Association Inc. v. Federal Highway Administration,* CA 4, No. 94–1209, Apr. 4, 1995.

IRS Regulation and Inspection of Records

A organization of tax protesters brought action (a *Bivens* claim) against the Internal Revenue Service (IRS) for chilling of associational rights through seizure by IRS agents of the organizations' membership lists, records and personal property. The case was remanded to determine whether the IRS agents were entitled to qualified immunity. IRS agents must find that an organization is engaging in pervasive fraudulent operations in order to defend the execution of allegedly defective search warrants.

> *National Commodity and Barter Ass'n v. Archer,* 31 F. 3d 1521 (10th Cir., 1994).

State Action Requirement

A private nonprofit corporation that holds annual festivals on public property is not a state actor that must grant access to festival booths under the First Amendment. Such a nonprofit neither engages in a function that is traditionally the exclusive prerogative of the state nor assumes complete governmental power over the property in question.

> *United Auto Workers Local 5285 v. Gaston Festivals Inc.,* CA 4, No. 94–1387, Jan. 10, 1995.

Tenure

A college can deny tenure to an instructor who lacks collegiality or does not work with colleagues in a collaborative manner. In a 1994 case, a dance teacher was denied tenure in such a situation because the court held that cooperation and collegiality are essential to a department that may have to work with other departments.

> *Bresnick v. Manhattanville College,* 93 CIV. 7305 (VLB) (July 19, 1994).

Professional Status

An insurance examiner has no vested franchise or property right in the expectancy of being granted certified status by a professional society of financial examiners that fails to certify him.

> *State ex rel. Scanlon v. National Association of Ins. Commissioners (NAIC),* 875 P. 2d 340 (MT, 1994).

A chiropractor has no procedural right to due process if a nonprofit hospital maintains its bylaw policy of excluding chiropractors, as a class, from membership on the hospital staff. The chiropractor is, however, entitled to have his claim reviewed under a special deferential standard developed in case law for review of administrative decisions excluding certain classes of physicians. For antitrust purposes, a hospital is incapable of "conspiring" with its staff to deny staff privileges.

> *Petrocco v. Dover General Hosp. and Medical Center,* 642 A. 2d 1016 (NJ Super. A.D., 1994).

Right to Volunteer

A retired driver, whose license is suspended for refusal to submit to a chemical test, cannot receive an exception to revocation for driving to and from his place of employment in order to attend volunteer meetings.

> *Fauss v. Department of Public Safety,* 889 P. 2d 1288 (OK App., 1995).

§342. *DELECTUS PERSONAE* AND FREEDOM TO ASSOCIATE

Public v. "Private" Clubs

Freedom of association for social and friendship purposes often collides with considerations of public interest in problems of discrimination by race, religion, sex, etc. More and more states now are requiring public accountability of NPOs concerning what used to be deemed purely private accommodations. New

York City's ordinance, for example, defines a *social* club as *public* in nature if it has over 400 members, provides regular meal service, and gets funds from nonmembers for trade or business purposes. This was upheld as constitutional in *New York State Club Association v. City of NY,* 108 S. Ct. 2225 (1988). Kansas and Florida cases upheld this kind of law in 1994, in Attorney General rulings. Ending of discriminatory practices by private clubs is being pushed in California, Kentucky, Michigan, Ohio, and so forth. In Louisiana in 1994, a race discrimination claim in a club was denied to a black businessman on the finding that the club was not for business purposes and was small and social in purpose; appeal to the Fifth Circuit Court of Appeals was taken, a Supreme Court ruling (test-standards evaluation statement) is expected.

Marcia Chambers, *Sua Sponte, National Law J.,* p. A21 (June 13, 1994).

Clubs that are social in nature, as opposed to having a business purpose, are entitled to the fullest protection of their associational rights under the First Amendment. In 1995, a New Orleans municipal statute, that prohibited discrimination in "public accommodations" and provided a mechanism for investigation and administrative adjudication of discrimination claims, was struck down. The court held that the statute was not the least intrusive means to accomplish the state's objective of eradicating discrimination and impermissibly impinged upon the privacy rights of the members.

Louisiana Debating and Literary Association v. City of New Orleans, 42 F. 3d 1483
(5th Cir., 1995).

Public Accommodations

A nonprofit organization, that provided information to the public concerning cults and provided support to cult members, is not a "public accommodation," subject to Title II prohibitions against discrimination. Thus, an African-American member of the Church of Scientology failed in his suit against the organization based on race and religious discrimination, after he was denied membership.

Clegg v. Cult Awareness Network, 18 F. 3d 752 (9th Cir. [CA], 1994).

A Boy Scout council is not a "business establishment," so as to be liable under California's Unruh Civil Rights Act for refusing to approve a homosexual adult leader. Scout activities are "expressive association" and "intimate association" protected by the First Amendment. The court should look to the viewpoints and beliefs as expressed by the organization, not the individual council members. The state's interest in stopping discrimination is not compelling outside the commercial context and should not reach voluntary activities.

> *Curran v. Mount Diablo Council of Boy Scouts of America,* 29 CA Rptr. 2d 580 (CA App. 2 Dist., 1994). *But see* the case below held *contra (Randall).*

The county council of the Boy Scouts of America cannot exclude members from the scouts on the basis of their religious beliefs, in California. The county council of the Boy Scouts is a "business" within the meaning of the Unruh Civil Rights Act there. However, packs and dens, not included as parties in the suit, may not be enjoined against the exclusion.

> *Randall v. Orange County Council, Boy Scouts of America,* 28 CA Rptr. 2d 53 (CA App. 4 Dist., 1994). *But see Curran* case above. *See also, Bid to Exempt Scouts from Bias Laws Stalls.* (Boy Scouts of America) (California) Hallye Jordan. *The Los Angeles Daily Journal,* May 3, 1995.

In Kansas, the Boy Scouts' organization is not a "public accommodation" under state law. Thus, the Scouts' policy of permitting only those willing who show a strong reverence to God to be adult leaders does not subject them to liability under the Kansas Act Against Discrimination. The organization has been challenged by an atheist who was rejected as a scout leader.

> *Seabourn v. Coronado Area Council, Boy Scouts of America,* Kan SupCt, No. 70,772, Mar. 10, 1995.

Gender Discrimination

"The ruling in the Virginia Military Institute (VMI) case could endanger private single-sex schools' tax exemptions, if the U.S. Supreme Court decides publicly funded VMI must accept women applicants to pass scrutiny under the Equal Protection Clause. Such a ruling could establish public policy prohibitions on single-sex admissions practices in all schools, including private ones. Private schools could lose both their tax-exempt status as charitable educational organizations as well as their ability to solicit charitable contributions if public single-sex education is declared unconstitutional."

> Alexander, Donald C., *Validity of Tax Exemptions & Deductible Contributions for Private Single-Sex Schools, Tax Notes,* Jan. 8, 1996.

A nonprofit *social* golf association or corporation is exempt from liability for gender discrimination under the Kansas Act Against Discrimination. K.S.A. 44–1001 et seq.

> *Kansas Human Rights Commission v. Topeka Golf Association,* 869 P. 2d 631 (KS, 1994).

A state university can cancel a men's athletic team while saving the women's counterpart without violating Title IX of the 1972 Education Amendments or the Equal Protection Clause where there is a proportional under-representation of women in intercollegiate athletics at the school.

> *Kelley v. Board of Trustees, University of Illinois,* CA 7, No. 93–3205, Sept. 1, 1994.

Michigan's Elliott-Larsen Civil Rights Act (MELCRA), which was amended to eliminate exclusionary and restrictive practices of private clubs including club rules restricting the times when spouses and children of members can use certain club facilities, has been found to be constitutional.

> *Benevolent and Protective Order of Elks of the U.S. v. Reynolds,* 863 F. Supp. 529 (W.D. MI, 1994).

Mandatory Membership

State university students sued to enjoin as unconstitutional an allocation to a public interest research group of a portion of their mandatory student activity fee. The court held that a district court may not unduly narrow and interfere with the fulfillment of a university's educational opportunities by imposing an on-campus geographic limitation on the use of student activity fees. Court-directed use for any activities that "benefit" or "involve" university students is overbroad. The public research group was properly ordered to redefine its membership to include only those students who consented to becoming members, as opposed to all students who paid mandatory student activity fees. The research group "may provide for written notification of a desire to join."

> *Carroll v. Blinken,* 42 F. 3d 122 (2nd Cir., 1994).

§344. "HATE" ORGANIZATIONS

New Jersey's hate-crime statutes were declared to be unconstitutional in 1994. Some other states have held otherwise, if the statute is not too vague.

> *State v. Vawter,* 642 A. 2d 349 (NJ, 1994).

§345. SUBVERSIVE (SEDITIOUS) ORGANIZATIONS

Domestic Terrorism

In response to the bombing of the Alfred Murrah Federal Building in Oklahoma City in 1995, there has been a rush in Congress to pass anti-terrorism legislation. The bill also allows increased deportation of terrorist-linked aliens without disclosing the reason. Certain target groups may find it hard to file for nonprofit tax status, even though groups can appeal the President's terrorist designation through the Justice Department.

The anti-terrorism bill passed in 1996 without the limitations on fund raising that civil libertarians had feared.

Reisner, Hiram, (article) 9 *NonProfit Times* (6) 1, 6 (June, 1995).

Nonprofit Response to Terrorism

In Oklahoma City, nonprofits were, in April of 1996, operating at full speed one year after the bombing of the Alfred Murrah Federal Building. In the year after the bombing, more than $33 million was spent or committed to nonprofit operations in Oklahoma City.

Clolery, Paul, (article), 10 *NonProfit Times* (12) 25 (December, 1996).

Subversive Organizations' Employees

[*Correction* of main text item on page 1061.]

New York's *Feinberg Law* (of 1949) permitted NPOs to dismiss employees who were members of subversive organizations (e.g., advocating violent overthrow of the government). The statute and administrative agency rules for its enforcement were held to be unconstitutionally vague and in violation of the First Amendment, in 1967.

Keyishian v. Board of Regents, 385 US 589, 87 S. Ct. 675, 17 L. Ed. 2d 629 (1967).

34

DISCIPLINARY AND ASSOCIATIONAL RIGHTS*

*[*See* constitutional law cases in Chapter 33.]

§346. WHAT ARE ASSOCIATIONAL RIGHTS? INTERESTS?

Transferability of Memberships

An unincorporated association brought a declaratory judgment action to challenge the transferability of memberships under a membership plan operated by LandFall Club, Inc. The court held that the unincorporated association lacked representational standing to sue because one of the unincorporated association's members did not belong to the club operated by LandFall Club, Inc. All members of representational organizations must have standing to sue in their own right.

LandFall Group v. LandFall Club, Inc., 450 S.E. 2e 513 (NC App., 1994).

Liability Through Association

A manufacturer of asbestos products cannot be held solely liable for wrongful conduct (alleged conspiracy and concert of action to continue selling asbestos without warnings and to conceal their knowledge of the dangers of asbestos from the public) permitted by an asbestos trade association or its members unless the manufacturer takes actions in relation to the trade association that are specifically intended to further such wrongful conduct. Such imposed liability could chill the exercise of freedom of association by those who want to contribute to, attend meetings of, and associate with, trade groups and other organizations involved in public advocacy and debate.

In Re Asbestos School Litigation, 46 F. 3d 1284 (3rd Cir., 1994).

Mandatory Associations Regulation

Condominium associations now are quite thoroughly regulated by law in most states. But state laws have been less adequate as to associations of single-family houses. Yet there now are many such residential associations, which often are mandatory in nature. Developers form them in many cases, and turn them over to buyers, often with important deed restrictions. Many times the buyers are hardly aware of these restrictive agreements.

Even where local (or state) law is fairly express about such "mandatory" associations, there may be no governmental agency created for enforcement of such law. Since the 1995 political increase of tendency to reduce government control of business, politicians tend to evade this problem, while developers (exploiters!) tend to favor the *absence* of regulation. Lawsuits, and arbitration if there is any provided for by the law, are the remedies now often employed. There are some associations of associations (e.g., such as the Homeowners Rights Alliance of Florida) that try to counter the tendency of homeowner association boards to do anything they please, without real regulation. Deed-restricted communities are now so numerous that more elaborate law and regulation are deemed desirable. This is because the real estate industry finds it very profitable to get more people on less land, thus providing higher density with something resembling home ownership. Then the associations may become dictatorial, charging fees upon fees and imposing overly strict rules. But more and more people like the orderly developments that deed-restricted association provide.

P. Wallsten (article), *St. Petersburg Times* (FL), p. S3 (Apr. 17, 1995).

Associates: Secrets Privilege

Therapeutic associations (for example, Alcoholics Anonymous) have believed that members' exchanges of information about themselves have secrecy protection like a penitent's confession to a priest. But that secrecy may be breached if social utility so requires: for instance, waiver by putting one's mental state into issue in a lawsuit; or prospective crime revelation; or some spousal issues. New Jersey recently allowed spiritual advisors to reveal confidences in some cases [*Natl. L.J.,* June 13, 1994].

Editorial, *Keeping Confidences, Natl. L.J.,* p. A20 (June 27, 1994).

§350. FINES, SUSPENSION, AND EXPULSION OF MEMBERS: GENERAL RULES

Volunteer Fireman Expulsion

The secretary of a volunteer fire company, who is entitled to written notice before being removed only if removal is for incompetency or misconduct, is not entitled to a hearing if the removal is for violating the fire department's bylaws.

Armstrong v. Centerville Fire Co., 1994 WL 262243 (June 16, 1994) NY.

Employee Free Speech Limits

A hospital was justified in removing its president from the staff because of allegations of financial improprieties.

Matter of Herbert Zaretsky v. NY City Health and Hosp. Corp., 1994 WL 31470 (June 5, 1994).

License Revocation

A cat fancier association member sued the association after her license as an "all breed" cat judge was revoked by the association. Under the New Jersey Law Against Discrimination (LAD), the association was a "place of public accommodation" (anyone 18 or older interested in cats could join), even though the organization considered itself to be "private." The removed judge's position was a "privilege" under LAD. There is a cause for action for wrongful discipline by a private organization in New Jersey. The court must balance the organization's interest in autonomy and its reason from straying from its rules, the magnitude of the interference with a member's interest, and the likelihood that established procedures would safeguard that interest. An action for tortious interference with prospective contractual relations may lie where "malice" is shown.

Brounstein v. American Cat Fanciers Association, 839 F. Supp. 1100 (D. NJ, 1993).

Discipline of Students

If a college states, in a student handbook, that due process would be afforded "insofar as the procedures of the College permit," and that a student's due process rights could not "be coextensive with or identical to the rights supported in a civil or criminal legal proceeding," it is not contractually bound to provide students, subject to disciplinary proceedings, with procedural protections equivalent to those required under the federal and state Constitutions. The college could breach its obligations only by deviating from its procedures to issue fundamentally unfair, arbitrary, or capricious disciplinary action.

Fellheimer v. Middlebury College, 869 F. Supp. 238 (D. VT, 1994) (student charged with rape by the college).

A male college student has a cause of action under Title IX of the 1972 Education Amendments where he alleges that he was found guilty of false charges of sexual harassment by the school's disciplinary board because of his gender.

Yusuf v. Vassar College, CA 2, No. 93–7519, Sept. 15, 1994.

It is a violation of the First Amendment for a state statute [N.C. Gen. St. §74A] to allow the attorney general to delegate to a religious university the police power of the state; e.g., authorizing campus police to arrest a motorist for drunk driving (at Campbell University, N.C.).

State v. Pendleton, #478A93; N.C. Supr. Ct. (Dec. 30, 1994); *Natl. L.J.,*
    p. B22 (Jan. 23, 1995).

Peer Review and Disciplinary Immunity

The Health Care Quality Improvement Act (HCQIA) provides hospital immunity from liability for monetary damages pursuant to actions brought against them arising out of peer review and disciplinary decisions. Thus, a hospital was given immunity after a physician brought action against a nonprofit hospital that terminated his staff privileges.

Bryan v. James E. Holmes Regional Medical Center, 33 F. 3d 1318 (11th Cir.,
    1994).

Bylaws and Disciplinary Action

The United States Figure Skating Association violated its bylaws by scheduling a disciplinary hearing for Tonya Harding just three days after her reply to the charges was due and by not giving the skater a reasonable time to prepare her defense. Injunction was issued against the hearing. However, the action became moot when the skater resigned from the association and pled guilty to criminal charges against her. The injunction was vacated and the action dismissed.

Harding v. United States Figure Skating Association, 851 F. Supp. 1476 (D. OR,
    1994).

35

ACCOUNTING FOR NPOs

§355. STANDARDS AND SOURCES

Accounting for NPOs: Standards

For fiscal years beginning on or after December 15, 1994, the *Financial Accounting Standards Board* (FASB) has provided two rules for accounting for *special monies:* SFAS 116 "Accounting for Contributions Received and Contributions Made," and SFAS 117 "Financial Statements of Not-For-Profit Organizations." NPOs with less than $5 million total assets and less than $1 million in annual expenses were given an additional year to comply.

> *See, Implementing FASB 116 and 117,* (Financial Accounting Standards Board Statements) (includes related article on accounting by the American Heart Association) Benson, Glazer, Jaenicke, Williams, and Friedman, *Journal of Accountancy,* Sept., 1995. *See also, FASB Proposes Statement on Not-For-Profits' Investments, Journal of Accountancy,* July, 1995. *See also,* Garner, William C., *Accounting and Budgeting in Public and Nonprofit Organizations: A Manager's Guide.* San Francisco, Jossey-Bass, 1991.

Many nonprofit organizations and their accountants find compliance with Statement of Financial Accounting Standard (SFAS) Nos. 116 and 117 a cumbersome process. For an article explaining the easiest way to comply, s*ee* Anthony, Robert N., *Coping with Nonprofit Accounting Rules, The CPA Journal,* August, 1996. *See also,* Reynolds, Brian M., *SFAS 117: Financial Statements of Not-For-Profits, The National Public Accountant,* June, 1996.

Accounting Standards

The FASB's Statement of Financial Accounting Standards (SFAS) No. 124, "Accounting for Certain Investments by Not-for-Profit Organizations," provides guidelines on how nonprofit organizations should account and report certain investments in securities. However, aside from these standards, nonprofits must also comply with generally accepted accounting principles embodied in SFAS No. 105 "Disclosure of Information About Financial Instruments with Off-Balance Sheet Risk and Financial Instruments with Concentrations of Credit

Risk," SFAS No. 107 "Disclosure About Fair Value of Financial Instruments," and SFAS No. 119, "Disclosures About Derivative Financial Instruments and Fair Value of Financial Instruments." SFAS No. 124 takes effect for fiscal years starting after December 15, 1995 and interim periods within these years. Earlier compliance is recommended.

> Thompson, James H., *Accounting for Certain Investments Held by Not-For-Profit Organizations, The CPA Journal,* Sept., 1996.

Multi-Year Contributions and the New Accounting Rules

The new accounting rules require nonprofits to count the full amount of multi-year pledges as gifts received. The rules create problems, considering that 7 percent of all contributions are either gifts to foundations or are otherwise unallocated in the present year. This rule also causes problems when some contributions are designated for capital purposes.

> Clolery, Paul, (article), 11 *NonProfit Times* (8) 47 (June, 1997).

Accounting for Multipurpose Appeals Involving Advocacy and Education

The Council of Better Bureaus' Philanthropic Advisory Service is concerned over joint cost allocation accounting procedures and has issued a new set of guidelines. The guidelines, which take effect in September of 1994, suggest that nonprofits (1) include a clear statement in multipurpose solicitations that explains whether the charity is carrying out its public education or advocacy activities in conjunction with fund-raising appeals and (2) include the advocacy and public education disclosure in a prominent position in the same (or larger) type size as the main body of the multipurpose appeal. "Prominent position" means either on the first page of the appeal or in a postscript on the same page as the signature line. For example, the council suggests the following phrase, "Some of the cost of this appeal is regarded . . . as a public education program rather than as a fund-raising expense."

> 8 *NonProfit Times* (4) 4 (April, 1994).

Accounting for Pledges

> *See, Accrual Method Required for Pledges to Tax-Exempt Organizations.* (brief article) Gladstone and Luchs. *The Tax Adviser,* May 1995 26 n5 p281(1).

Accounting for "Gifts in Kind"

Five national charities have been fined more than $200,000 in civil penalties and grants to settle suits filed against them, by the Connecticut Attorney General, for "creative accounting" related to gifts-in-kind. The organizations allegedly conspired to donate goods to each other at inflated prices. Then, the transactions were recorded as program expenses in their tax returns and annual reports. The settlement requires that the charities adhere to the following accounting procedures in the future: (1) Report gifts as program expenses only if they benefit the charity's target audience. Goods passed to another organization must benefit the original target audience. (2) Report gifts as revenue only if they are consistent with the agency's mission, received from the original donor, and are not required to be passed on to another agency. (3) Organizations exchanging goods must not share any board members or facilities. (4) Donated material must be assessed at fair market value. (5) IRS forms or certificates of valuation must be presented to the state, from the original donor, revealing the fair market value of any gift of $5,000 or more.

8 *NonProfit Times* (7) 4 (July, 1994).

Health Care Companies and Determination of Shareholder Value

Health Care companies are beginning to look at economic value added (EVA) in order to value a company for shareholders. EVA has traditionally not been used with nonprofit organizations. However, hospitals and for-profit health care firms, such as drug manufacturers, are becoming to realize that EVA is less limited than more traditional ways of measuring a company, like market share and net profit.

Appleby, Chuck, *The New Lingood Added Value, Hospitals & Health Networks*, February 5, 1997.

Accountant Liability

An accountant, hired to investigate a nonprofit manager's performance, must intentionally and improperly submit a false report or a report that exceeded his/her duties, in order for the accountant's conduct to rise to the level of intentional interference with the manager's contractual relations. A manager cannot maintain a professional negligence action against the investigating accountant unless the report submitted was prepared for the manager's benefit and guidance. False information is not "improperly submitted" unless the accountant knew or believed that the report contained inaccuracies.

Demetracopoulos v. Wilson, 640 A. 2d 279 (NH, 1994).

§356. TREASURER'S DUTIES

Treasurer; Condominium Financial Operations

In a *Community Association* the *Treasurer* is usually the person in charge of finances and budget, keeps its financial records, is responsible for deposit of monies in depositories designated by the board, sees to an annual audit by a CPA, and receives no compensation for such duties. He/she should understand the basics of financial statements (balance sheets equal equation of assets, liabilities, and members' equity).

Becker and Polikoff, *93 Community Update* (May, 1994) (Fort Lauderdale,
   FL). (This issue contains a useful summary of accounting methods and
   basic law.)

§357. STATE ACCOUNTING REQUIREMENTS

Statewide accounting workshops, explaining new accounting rules for non-profit organizations, are being held in many states. One such workshop was offered by FANO, the Florida Association of Nonprofit Organizations, Inc., in 1995 in Miami. For information contact FANO, 7480 Fairway Drive, Suite 206, Miami Lakes, FL 33014, (800) 362–FANO, Fax (305) 821–5228.

§358. BOOKKEEPING

Software for Fund Accounting

Advanced Data Systems, P.O. Box 2130, Bangor, ME 04402–2130,
   (800) 779–4494.

American Fundware, Inc., 1358 South Colorado Blvd., Suite 400, Denver,
   CO 80222, (800) 551–4458.

Blackbaud, Inc., 4401 Belle Oaks Dr., Charleston, SC 29405,
   (800) 443–9441.

Consultech-Synergy Systems, 300 Henry Pl., Spartanburg, SC, (800) 849–0348.

DacEasy, Inc., 17950 Preston Road, Dallas, Texas 75252, (800) DAC-EASY.

Donor II / Systems Support Services, 8848-B Red Oak Blvd., Charlotte, NC 28217, (800) 548-6708.

Echo Management Group, P.O. Box 540, Center Conway, NH 03813, (800) 635-8209.

Fund E-Z Development Corporation, 106 Corporate Park Drive, White Plains, NY 10604, (914) 696–0900.

Manzanita Software Systems, 2130 Professional Drive, Suite 230, Rosedale, CA 95661–3751, (800) 447–5700.

Microgap Integrated Accounting, Target 1 Fundraiser, 27 Millett Dr., Auburn, ME 04210, (800) 888–0111.

Micro Information Products, Inc., 505 East Huntland Dr., Suite 340, Austin, TX 78752, (800) 647-3863.

MIP Fund Accounting, 505 E. Huntland Dr., Suite 340, Austin, TX 78752, (800) 647–3863.

NEBS Computer Forms & Software, 500 Main Street, Groton, MA 01471, (800) 255–9550.

Samuelson Computer Services Co., 350 S. Schmale Rd., Carol Stream, IL 60188, (708) 668–1598.

9 *NonProfit Times* (6) 32 (July, 1995); *The Not-For-Profits Toolbox.* (accounting software) Sam W. Stearman. *Journal of Accountancy,* Sept. 1995 180 n3 p50(11).

See also, Chapter 42, §423 for nonprofit management software; Chapter 43, §438 for fund-raising software.

Accounting Software

Accountants who evaluate the software needs of nonprofits must examine the organization itself to determine what it needs, matching these needs with the software available in the market and checking the references of software vendors.

Wolosky, Howard W., *Evaluating a Nonprofit's Accounting Software Needs, The Practical Accountant,* July, 1996.

Switching Accounting Methods

Organizations that adopt the accounting methods specified in the Statement of Financial Accounting Standards (SFAS) No. 116 will not be required to file form 3115 "Application for Change in Accounting Method," with the IRS. If a 501(c) organization chooses to switch to the revised methods of SFAS No. 116, it may simply reflect the effect of the change on the Form 990 information return it files for the year of the change of accounting methods.

Clolery, Paul, (article), 10 *NonProfit Times* (8) 4 (August, 1996).

36

RELIGIOUS ORGANIZATIONS*

*[*See also* specific subject references, in the Index, such as Officers, Agents.]

§359. RELIGIOUS ORGANIZATIONS, IN GENERAL

[A church minister is two "persons:" (1) a religious leader, and (2) a corporate-group leader. As to role (2), he/she should have some training in nonprofit organizations law and practice, and should have/use this volume in becoming skilled in voluntary association work.]

Revitalizing Communities Through Faith-Based Community Organization

In Washington, D.C., a plan to convert Buchanan School into a community center which will function as home to D.C. Christian and nonprofit groups, will be managed by the Hope Center and financed by a suburban church. Nationwide, Christian community development efforts have begun to improve social conditions in inner cities by emphasizing renewed faith.

Rosenberger, Ron, *Spiritual Capital for the Capital City, Policy Review,*
March–April, 1997.

Religious Societies' Torts

Parents of children allegedly injured by asbestos in church preschool and kindergarten are not entitled to bring lawsuit under the general statute allowing suit by any person injured by violation of a statute. The parents were not personally injured by the violation, within the purpose of that statute.

Michols v. Wm. T. Watkins Memorial United Methodist Church, 873 S.W. 2d 216
(KY, App., 1994).

§360. CONSTITUTIONAL BASES OF U.S. "CHURCH AND STATE" LAW

Church-State Clashes [NPO v. NPO]

In late 1994, the pressures of fundamentalist right-wing religious groups, on public schools, for example, to obey *their* biblical views, had become so strident that the fundamentalists had caused the creation of strongly constitution-minded citizens groups. Volcanic religious and cultural disputes raged in, for example, Colorado Springs, CO, so that secular humanists and would-be religious fundamentalist chiefs were confronting each other about what the schools should teach children. The same occurred in many other places.

> M. Shanahan, Out of Control, (Religious News Service), *St. Petersburg (FL) Times,* p. 10 of *City Times* Section (Sept. 3, 1994).

For latest developments inquire of Americans United for Separation of Church and State, 1816 Jefferson Pl., N.W., Washington, D.C. 20036.

The 1993 Religious Freedom Restoration Act

The U.S. District Court for the Western District of Texas has declared the 1993 Religious Freedom Restoration Act to be unconstitutional and certified its decision for interlocutory appeal. The court declared the Act to be void under the separation of powers doctrine. The court believes that Congress, through the Act, is encroaching upon the judiciary by directing the interpretation of the First Amendment's Free Exercise Clause.

> *Flores v. Boerne, Texas,* DC WTexas, No. SA–94–CA–0421, Mar. 13, 1995.

Freedom of Association and Religious Organizations

The state cannot address, under the "ecclesiastical abstention doctrine," a Catholic newspaper publisher's claims against a diocese and various diocesan officials, claiming wrongful excommunication due to views he expressed in his newspaper. Resolution of the claims would require resolution of controversies over church doctrine, law, administration, or polity. Secular law cannot determine criminal penal ecclesiastical violations; schism; whether church law is violated by establishing a separate church; whether one has misrepresented Roman Catholic faith; whether, in matters of church dogma, one is fanatic or has neolithic frame of mind; whether one is duping the faithful; whether one causes others to lose their souls; whether one is disloyal to the Pope; or whether one must be excommunicated to save other souls.

> *O'Connor v. Diocese of Honolulu,* 885 P. 2d 361 (HI, 1994); U.S.C.A. Const. Amends. 1, 14; Const. Art. 1, Section 4.

Church-Owned Hospitals

In California, the relatively high efficiency of church-owned hospitals suggests that allowing such hospitals to retain their tax-exempt status would be a wise economic policy. Research has revealed that church-owned hospitals are more efficient than other nonprofit hospitals, when hospital location, size, system membership, and kind of church affiliation are taken into account.

> White and Ozcan, *Church Ownership and Hospital Efficiency, Hospital & Health Services Administration,* Fall, 1996.

Catholic Hospitals in 1996

Catholic hospitals face formidable challenges in the health care market because of their nonprofit nature. In response, Denver's Mercy Hospital converted from an acute care hospital to an outpatient clinic in 1995. Also, Catholic Health Initiatives is forming a large health care system in 21 states with projected revenues of over $4 billion.

> MacPherson, Peter, *Church and Fate, Hospitals & Health Networks,* March 20, 1996.

§363. RELIGIOUS TAX EXEMPTION

See also Chapter 9, §89.

The IRS ruled that the Church of Scientology is a tax-exempt church, in 30 "determination letters" that it issued in October 1993, ending a fight for exemption that lasted decades.

> Garcia, report, *St. Petersburg (FL) Times,* p. 1 (Oct. 13, 1993).

Church "Peculiarity" Tax Exemption

Church storage of weapons and business activities led to an IRS withdrawal of the tax exemption of the apocalyptic sect, Church Universal and Triumphant in Montana. An *agreement* by the church to stop stockpiling weapons, and also to form separate taxable corporations to handle its business operations, caused the IRS to restore its tax exemption, except for a past two-year period. However, individual members may keep (at home) weapons, under the general laws. U.S. District Court approval of the agreement was expected.

Note, 47 *Church and State* (7) 3 (147), July/August 1994.

Property Tax

Subjective intent and not actual use of church property may decide whether church property is used primarily for religious purposes.

First Baptist Church v. Bexas County Appraisal Rev. Bd., 833 S.W. 2d 108 (TX, 1992); Note, 34 *So. Tex. L. Rev.* 579–598 (1993).

§364. RELIGIOUS ORGANIZATION OFFICERS AND AGENTS

Employment Disputes

Whether to employ a person as a parochial school teacher is an ecclesiastical issue. Courts may not inquire into contractual matters of church employment if enforcement would require a searching, and therefore impermissible, inquiry into church doctrine. Interference with ecclesiastical hierarchies, church administration, and appointment of clergy is precluded by the First Amendment.

Gabriel v. Immanuel Evangelical Lutheran Church, Inc., 640 N.E. 2d 681 (IL App. 4 Dist., 1994). *See also, Yaggie v. Indiana-Kentucky Synod Evangelical Lutheran Church in America,* 860 F. Supp. 1194 (W.D. KY, 1994).

A jury may decide whether a nonprofit corporation breached its contract with a pastor and wrongfully terminated him without good cause. Such matters are not an improper decision of an ecclesiastical question where the issues involve an employment contract and its alleged breach. The jury may decide whether the termination was proper under the church's own bylaws as a nonprofit corporation.

Fellowship Tabernacle, Inc. v. Baker, 869 P. 2d 578 (ID App., 1994).

Age Discrimination

Religious employers can be sued under the Age Discrimination in Employment Act without infringing on the First Amendment.

Weissman v. Congregation Shaare Emeth, CA 8, No. 94–1464, Oct. 28, 1994; 66 Fair Employment Practice Cases 113.

Gender Discrimination

A female former employee of a church brought suit alleging gender discrimination, defamation, and promissory estoppel. The court held that the church had a legitimate business reason for giving a male employee more responsibility and more pay than the female employee, where the male had more experience. A two-year commitment, requested by an employer from an employee does not imply a reciprocal promise that the employer will employ a worker for at least two years. Neither Minnesota's constitutional Freedom of Conscience Clause, nor the federal Establishment Clause bars judicial review of discharge based claims against religious organizations.

Geraci v. Eckankar, 526 N.W. 2d 391 (MN App., 1995).

Religious Discrimination

Summary judgment is improper, where the question is whether religious discrimination was the reason for firing a Jewish Vice-President of Student Life, by a Catholic university. The Human Rights Law permits religious institutions to prefer to employ persons of the same religion.

Scheiber v. St. John's University, 1994 WL 270421 (June 21, 1994); NY.

Black Churches Burning

The National Bankers Assn., a coalition of minority-owned banks plans to create a $5 loan fund to finance the rebuilding of Afro-American churches destroyed by arson fires in the South. Affected churches need to contact the National Bankers Association to be referred to a nearby member bank to evaluate their loan. Other associations are helping, including Habitat for Humanity, the Department of Housing and Urban Development, and the National Council of Black Churches.

Yavorskyk, Sarah, *Minority Bankers Creating Fund to Rebuild Churches, American Banker,* Oct. 3, 1996.

Unemployment Compensation

An incorporated nonprofit association of churches, that owns and operates a cemetery, is not exempt from employer contributions to unemployment compensation in Illinois. The church did not qualify for statutory exemption as a church or church association because it was separately incorporated and distinct from the churches which formed it. The association primarily performed the secular function of burying the dead and could not qualify for exemption as a church, operated primarily for religious purposes.

> *Bethania Association v. Jackson,* 635 N.E. 2d 671 (IL App. 1 Dist., 1994).

Liability for Agents and Officers

See also Chapter 17, Unauthorized and Improper Acts.

For the purpose of an exclusion of insurance policy coverage, a jury's finding that the action of a priest was willful, deliberate, and reckless conduct did not preclude churches from contending that they did not expect the abuse of a boy which occurred for over eight years.

> *Diocese of Winona v. Interstate Fire & Casualty Company,* 858 F. Supp. 1407 (D. MN, 1994).

The legal liability of a church for a priest's crimes (child abuse) seems to be recognized if church authorities' failure to properly supervise can be shown. In addition, the rules as to who shall pay (insurers, church) are now being thrashed out. Insurer liability was found in *Society of the Roman Catholic Church of C. of L. etc. v. Interstate Fire and Casualty Co.,* #93–4068 (5th Cir. [U.S.] May 27, 1994; declaratory judgment; to be appealed).

> R. Samborn, *Who Will Pay Victims of Pedophile Priests?, Natl. L.J.,* p. A21 (July 4, 1994).

Damages claims against churches for sexual abuses done by ministers were daily news items in 1994, and heavy damages settlements were common. Church insurance companies were trying to educate their customers, by seminars, to prevent abuses and how to handle problems. *Church Law and Tax Report* newsletter carried articles to keep churches informed on current legal issues. Many churches adopted plans for dealing with the problem. It is unwise to try to hide such cases; that increases the probability of lawsuit. So does hiring a person with a history of abuses, even if supposedly reformed.

> V. Culver, article, *Religious News Service* (Oct. 8, 1994).

§365. CHURCH-STATE CONFLICTS

> *See* (Symposium) *Religion and the Public Schools after Lee v. Weisman* (112 S. Ct. 2649, 1992), 44 *Case W. Res. L. Rev.* 699–1020 (1993).

Special School Districts for Religious Enclaves

A city may not create a special school district, following the lines of an incorporated village containing a religious enclave (Satmar Hasidim, Judaism), to exclude all but its practitioners. Such action is a violation of the establishment clause of the First Amendment, if there is no assurance that similarly situated groups would receive such special districts. The government cannot prefer one religion to another, or religion to irreligion. Bilingual and bicultural special education can be provided to the enclave in public schools, if administered according to neutral principles, without special treatment to particular religious groups.

> *Board of Educ. of Kiryas Joel Village School Dist. v. Grumet,* 114 S. Ct. 2481
> (U.S., NY, 1994); R. Boston, Forbidden Fusion, 47 *Church and State* (7) 4
> (148), July/August 1994.

But see the case below, *Grumet.*

The First Amendment infirmities of the New York statute, that created a separate school district out of a village populated by the members of a single religious group, were resolved when the legislation was converted into general legislation, allowing the establishment of a separate school district by any state municipality that satisfied the statutory eligibility criteria.

> *Grumet v. Cuomo,* 617 N.Y.S. 2d 620 (Sup. Aug. 9, 1994); McKinney's Education Law Section 1504, subd. 3, par. a; U.S.C.A. Const. Amend. 1.

Public Funding of Religious Organizations

The U.S. Department of Commerce may deny a university's application for funding of certain broadcast facilities, under the public telecommunications facilities program (PTFP), if the university uses federally funded broadcast equipment for essentially sectarian purposes. Denial of eligibility and regulations prohibiting sectarian purpose are consistent with the Establishment Clause. Such regulation does not excessively entangle government with religion.

> *Fordham University v. Brown,* 856 F. Supp. 684 (D. DC, 1994).

If a university program is neutral toward religion when it makes funds available for a student publication with a religious editorial viewpoint, the funding provided does not violate the Establishment Clause.

> *Rosenberger v. Rector and Visitors of University of Virginia,* 115 S. Ct. 2510 (U.S.
> VA, 1995).

A county office supervisor can be ordered by the county not to use government resources to support an employee religious group, and can be ordered to remove religious objects, including a Bible, from his office without violating Free Speech or the Free Exercise of Religion.

Brown v. Polk County, Iowa, CA 8, No. 93–3313 SI, Oct. 6, 1994.

See Keever, D.A., (Comment), *Public Funds and the Historical Preservation of Churches,* 21 *FL St. L. Rev.* 13271343 (1994).

Use of Public Facilities by Religious Organizations

A school board may condition the use of public school facilities on a Bible club's waiver of its rule requiring officers to be Christians.

Roslyn Union Free School District No. 3, DC ENY, No. CV–94–0659, Feb. 21,1995.

A school district, its board members, and employees may allow the Boy Scouts of America to distribute its literature during school hours and to hang its posters on school grounds and use the school facilities, without violating the Establishment Clause (a blanket regulation that applied to religious and nonreligious groups alike). The fact that the Boy Scouts require its members to believe in God cannot be attributed to the school district, which is, thus, not liable for an alleged equal protection violation. The Boy Scouts are not a "state actor" for purposes of Fourteenth Amendment liability of the school district.

Sherman v. Community Consol. School Dist. 21 of Wheeling Tp., 8 F. 3d 1160 (7th Cir. [IL], 1993).

A city may lease airport space to the Catholic Diocese for operation of an airport chapel without violating the Establishment Clause of the First Amendment, if the chapel serves the secular purpose of accommodating religious needs of travelers, a reasonable observer would not conclude that the city endorsed religion, and there is no excessive government entanglement with religion.

Hawley v. City of Cleveland, 24 F. 3d 814 (6th Cir. [OH], 1994).

Public Display of Religious Symbols

The state does not violate the Establishment Clause by allowing a private organization to display an unattended cross on the grounds of the state capitol, if the state does not sponsor the expression, the government property is open to the public for speech, and permission is granted through the same application process and on the same terms as for other private groups.

Capitol Square Review and Advisory Bd. v. Pinette, 115 S. Ct. 2440 (U.S. OH, 1995).

A rabbi sought injunctive and declaratory relief to compel a city to allow him to display a menorah in the lobby of the city-county building during Chanukah after the city erected a Christmas tree in the lobby. The court held that "the holiday season" was too broad and amorphous a subject to be considered to be a subject matter for speech that would have required the city to allow the rabbi to place the menorah. The Establishment Clause does not prohibit the city from allowing private groups to display religious symbols in a nonpublic forum after it puts up secular Christmas decorations in that forum.

Grossbaum v. Indianapolis-Marion County Building Authority, 870 F. Supp. 1450 (S.D. IN, 1994).

A monument depicting the Ten Commandments, which is positioned in a public park across the street from the state capitol, does not violate the First Amendment's Establishment Clause or Colorado's constitutional counterpart, especially where the monument is embellished with various secular symbols and is positioned in a park with several other secular monuments.

Colorado v. Freedom from Religion Foundation Inc., Colo SupCt, No. 93SC554, June 12, 1995.

A public secondary school cannot display a painting of Jesus Christ in a hallway without violating the Establishment Clause and all three prongs of *Lemon v. Kurtzman,* 403 U.S. 602 (1971), the seminal case for the identification of Establishment Clause violations.

Washegesic v. Bloomingdale Public Schools, No. 93–1248, Sept. 6, 1994.

A city council resolution, barring fixed outdoor displays of religious or political symbols in parks, is an unconstitutional content-based regulation of speech in traditional public fora. The equal access policy permits religious displays in parks without violation of the Establishment Clause.

Flamer v. City of White Plains, NY, 841 F. Supp. (S.D. NY, 1993).

A state does not violate the Establishment Clause of the First Amendment by permitting the display of a menorah on a public plaza during Chanukah, under the neutral open-access policy. Under the strict scrutiny test, the state's total exclusion of the menorah must be narrowly tailored to serve a compelling state interest. In this case, the state could have avoided endorsing religion by closing the forum, posting signs to explain the nature of public forum, or enacting time, place, and manner restrictions to govern the form of the presentations.

Chabad-Lubavitch of Georgia v. Miller, 5 F. 3d 1383 (11th Cir. [GA], 1993).

Prayer Restrictions

In public schools, student-led prayers are not violations of the separation of church and state (in Texas, Louisiana, and Mississippi) under the 1993 Fifth Circuit ruling in *Jones v. Clear Creek Independent School District.* Bills to allow this type of prayer have been passed in many states. The Supreme Court will be the final arbiter, because many cases on this issue are being appealed to it.

R. Boston, The School Prayer Mess, 47 *Church and State* (5) 7 (127), June, 1994.

The federal District Court does not have supplemental jurisdiction to hear a declaratory judgment action, brought against a nonprofit organization by a high school principal, to determine whether the First Amendment prohibits prayer at a high school graduation ceremony, if the Court cannot determine whether the nonprofit would file suit to prohibit prayer or who the parties would be in the threatened suit.

Oldham v. American Civil Liberties Union Foundation of Tennessee, Inc., 849 F. Supp. 611 (M.D. TN, 1994).

A city council in Utah may permit prayer during a portion of the city council meeting set aside for opening remarks. Such a practice does not violate provisions of the Utah Constitution prohibiting expenditure of public money to support religious exercise, the union of church and state, or domination of government by any church.

Society of Separationists, Inc. v. Whitehead, 870 P. 2d 916 (UT, 1993).

The U.S. Court of Appeals for the Ninth Circuit has held that student-initiated prayers at public high school graduations violate the Establishment Clause. The school district cannot shirk its constitutional responsibilities by delegating them.

Harris v. Joint School District No. 241, CA 9, No. 93–35839, Nov. 18, 1994.

Students, parents, and a civil liberties organization brought suit against state authorities to challenge a Mississippi statute that permitted public-school students to initiate nonsectarian, non proselytizing prayer at various compulsory and noncompulsory school events alleging that such activities violate the Establishment Clause. The court held that the statute involved sufficient "state action" to satisfy Section 1983. The likelihood of success on the merits justified the court's injunction against such activities, except for a provision allowing such prayer at high school commencement ceremonies.

Ingebretsen v. Jackson Public School District, 864 F. Supp. 1473 (S.D. MS, 1994).

The U.S. District Court for the Southern District of Indiana has ruled that Indiana University may include an invocation and benediction in its commencement ceremonies without offending the First Amendment's Establishment Clause. The court reasoned that college students don't need as much protection from the coercion that bars such prayers at the elementary and secondary school level.

Tanford v. Brand, DC SInd, No. IP 95–492 C B/S, May 4, 1995.

Government Discrimination Against Religion

A borough may erect and lock a gate, between a public park and property which was to be used for a religious tent revival meeting by a minister and his nonprofit incorporated ministry, without violating either the Establishment Clause or Free Exercise Clause, if the ministry does not receive different treatment from other similarly situated individuals or groups.

Brown v. Borough of Mahaffey, PA, 35 F. 3d 846 (3rd Cir., 1994).

It is a violation of both the Free Speech and Free Exercise Clause (discrimination and interference with, or a burden to the church's right to speak and practice religion), for a school board to impose higher rents for churches to rent school facilities than those imposed on other nonprofit organizations. The board is required to return such illegally collected rent.

Fairfax Covenant Church v. Fairfax County School Bd., 17 F. 3d 703 (4th Cir. [VA], 1994).

Other Church-State Conflicts

A state may issue a child support order, as the least restrictive means for the state to have parents recognize the obligation to provide support for children, even where the obligated parent claims that his First Amendment freedom of religion is violated by his spouse's choice to leave him without just cause in the eyes of the church, and that he could not, consistent with his faith, work outside his religious community and earn money to meet the support obligation. However, a contempt order and incarceration are not the means, to enforce the support order, least restrictive with the father's Free Exercise rights.

   Hunt v. Hunt, 648 A. 2d 843 (VT, 1994).

A church must get a second approval by the court, if it modifies a court approved contract to sell real estate, under New York's Religious Corporations Law. New York's requirement that religious corporations notify the Attorney General of the sale of real estate does not violate the Establishment Clause. The Law has the secular purpose of insuring that the sale is in the best interest of the corporation and its members.

   Greek Orthodox Archdiocese of North and South America v. Abrams, 618 N.Y.S. 2d
      504 (Sup., 1994).

The state may require a person convicted of drunk driving to attend a self-help program, even where the principal program available has religious overtones, without violating the Establishment Clause.

   O'Connor v. State of California, 855 F. Supp. 303 (C.D. CA, 1994).

Inspection of Church Records

In Florida, the U.S. District Court for the Middle District held that Florida's corporate code, which requires that churches provide members with the right to inspect all organizational books and account records (including their donation information) controlled a case where the First Baptist Church Markham Woods of Orlando fought disclosure of amounts donated by individuals. A state court-ordered $500-per-day fine, for withholding the information from the public, was upheld.

   Sinnock, Bonnie, (article), 9 *NonProfit Times* (2) (February, 1995); *Hochberg v.
      Howlett,* 50 F. 3d 3 (CA 2 1995) *(rev. denied,* 64 L.W. 3232 (10–3–95)).

Church Privileges: Drug Use

Native American Church members may lawfully use *peyote* (a hallucinogenic drug) in prayer sessions. A statute passed by the House and Senate (awaiting presidential signature) in October 1994 exempts the church from a 1990 Supreme Court decision barring use of drugs. Twenty-eight states had permitted use of peyote by 1994 while 22 states did not.

> Religion Digest (section), *St. Petersburg (FL) Times,* (Oct. 8, 1994). [*See also,* Religious Freedoms Restoration Act.]

A 1990 Supreme Court decision (*Oregon v. Smith*) in a case of a religious organization's use of the drug *peyote,* abandoned the principle that the government must show *"compelling state interest"* before restricting religious freedom. In November 1993 that test was restored by enactment of the *Religious Freedom Restoration Act of 1993.*

> *See* Kilpatrick column, *St. Petersburg (FL) Times* (op. ed.), Nov. 26, 1993. [See *Church Privileges: Drug Use* on page 135.]

§366. RELIGIOUS SCHOOL ACTIVITIES

Delegation of State Powers to Religious Schools

It is a violation of the First Amendment for the state attorney general to delegate to a religious university the police power of the state. For example, the state may not authorize campus police to arrest a motorist for drunk driving (at Campbell University, NC).

> *State v. Pendleton,* #178A93, N.C. Supr. Ct. (Dec. 30, 1994); *Natl. L.J.,* p. B22 (Jan. 23, 1995); N.C. Gen. St. §74A.

Public Aid to Religious Schools

> See, Pavlischeck, Keith J., *When Sacred and Secular Mix: Religious Nonprofit Organizations and Public Money.* (book reviews), *First Things: A Monthly Journal of Religion and Public Life,* April 1997.

A state law, allowing the leasing of public school buses to other organizations, including religious organizations, does not violate the state or federal constitutional requirement of separation of church and state, if the students are being transported to "educational" programs within the statutory definition. To refuse to rent the buses to religious organizations, based on their religious viewpoint, would be discrimination.

> *St. James Church v. Board of Education of Cazenovia Central School District,* 621 N.Y.S. 2d 486 (Sup., 1994).

The Ninth Circuit, in 1995, clarified the issue of public aid to parochial schools by fashioning a two-part test which requires government neutrality toward religion and the avoidance of "symbolic union." A school district may provide remedial educational services to students attending sectarian schools through the shared use of mobile classrooms parked in close proximity to parochial schools, through administrative cooperation between personnel, and through loaning of instructional materials and equipment to parochial schools. Such cooperation has a valid secular purpose and neither advances nor inhibits religion.

> *Walker v. San Francisco Unified School District,* 46 F. 3d 1449 (9th Cir., 1995); *see also Zobrest v. Catalina Foothills School District,* 61 LW 4641 (US SupCt, 1993).

A law approving public taxpayer money use to fund "vouchers" that parents can use in *any* school they wish (public or private) was held to be in violation of the U.S. First Amendment in Puerto Rico in 1994, by the Superior Court, despite great pressure from religious school supporters. The law violates Article II, Section 5 of the Puerto Rico Constitution as well as the U.S. First Amendment. Appeal to the U.S. Supreme Court was certain. The Roman Catholic hierarchy is trying to water-down language governing church-state relations.

> J.L. Conn, Caribbean Controversy, 47 *Church and State* (5) 4 (124), June, 1994.

Louisiana's special education statute, which allowed state-paid special education teachers to teach on the premises of pervasively sectarian institutions, violated the Establishment Clause as applied. Reimbursement of nonpublic schools for required costs incurred in maintaining records and providing administrative services required by state or local law, rule, or regulation, also violated the Establishment Clause as applied. Parish transportation of separate public and nonpublic school children and appropriation of additional funds for the additional cost of providing Chapter 1 services to private schools did not violate the Establishment Clause.

> *Helms v. Cody,* 856 F. Supp. 1102 (E.D. LA, 1994).

A county fiscal court cannot direct payments of county tax revenues to private schools for school transportation subsidies. Such payments violate the Kentucky Constitution which requires that taxes can be levied and collected for public purposes only, and violate state statutes providing that county funds may be used only "for lawful purposes." By statute in Kentucky, the county may provide transportation by utilizing existing governmentally operated transportation systems or governmentally contracting for service, but cannot provide transportation through direct payments to private institutions. The county's award of

99% of its transportation subsidy to private educational institutions that promote religious teachings, coupled with its denial of equivalent funds to public schools for optional education programs, is a violation of the Kentucky Constitution prohibiting preference to any religious sect, society, or denomination.

>*Fiscal Court of Jefferson County v. Brady,* 885 S.W. 2d 681 (KY, 1994); Const. Section 171; KRS 67.080(1); KRS 158.115(2); Const. Section 5.

Congress cannot, under the Commerce Clause, prohibit the mere possession of a firearm in or near a school. Possession does not, by itself, "substantially affect" interstate commerce.

>*U.S. v. Lopez,* US SupCt, No. 92–1260, Apr. 26, 1995.

§367. CHURCH ZONING

Zoning laws must accommodate religious exercise. If they make exercise of religion inaccessible to practitioners, they violate First Amendment rights. However, zoning codes may require a proposed church to show that its use is compatible with the neighborhood and will not be detrimental to health, safety, and the general welfare of residents and that the use is in keeping with the master plan. Such requirements do not necessarily restrict the practice of religion, which may be carried on in other locations.

>*U.S. v. Village of Airmont,* 839 F. Supp. 1054 (S.D. NY, 1993).

The constitutional protections of the free exercise of religion do not prohibit a city from designating a church building as a landmark under the city's landmarks preservation ordinance. However, free exercise of religion prohibits the landmarks board from restricting the modification of the building in any way until the building ceases to be used primarily for religious purposes.

>*First United Methodist Church of Seattle v. Hearing Examiner for the Seattle Landmarks Preservation Board,* 887 P. 2d 473 (WA App. Div. 1, 1995).

Local zoning laws cannot be applied to thwart a church's practice of feeding the homeless. Feeding the homeless in its building is a religious tenet protected by the Free Exercise Clause of the First Amendment and the 1993 Religious Freedom Restoration Act.

A Board of Zoning Adjustment may not prohibit a church from feeding homeless persons on its premises, through enforcement of zoning regulations, where the feeding program is religious conduct and zoning regulations would substantially burden the free exercise of religion. The church argued that feeding programs are acts of charity, an essential part of religious worship, and a central tenet of all major religions, motivated by sincere religious beliefs.

Western Presbyterian Church v. Board of Zoning Adjustment of the District of Columbia,
  862 F. Supp. 538 (D. DC, 1994).

A county that denies a special zoning permit to allow a church to operate a religious school in a residential neighborhood, not zoned for schools, violates the church's First Amendment right to free exercise of religion, where religious education is an integral part of the religious beliefs of the church's membership and the school is to be held in a church building that is legitimately located in a residential neighborhood.

Alpine Christian Fellowship v. Pitkin County, 870 F. Supp. 991 (D. CO, 1994).

§368. CHURCH POLITICKING

A physician and nonprofit family-planning organizations cannot intervene in a state health department's appeal to challenge the granting of a religious group's Freedom of Information Act (FOIA) request for statistical information about the termination of pregnancies, where there was no motion to intervene in the trial court, before the trial court lost jurisdiction to the Supreme Court, and where there are no compelling or unusual circumstances.

Arkansas Department of Health v. Westark Christian Action Council, 890 S.W. 582
  (AR, 1995).

§370. NONPROFIT (CHURCH) ORGANIZATION

For information related to Social Security and other information for members of the clergy and religious workers, see IRS Publication 517.

37

CONDOMINIUMS AND COOPERATIVES

§371. CONDOMINIUMS AND COOPERATIVES, IN GENERAL

Condo Sales

In 1994, condo unit sales in the United States numbered about 436,000 per year (annual rate), which was about 18 percent higher than in 1993, according to a report released by the National Association of Realtors. The national median price was $87,000 (up 5.3 percent over the 1993 price). In the southern states about 148,000 units were sold (up 19.4 percent over 1993 total), with a median price of $70,800 (up 1.9 percent over 1993 price). In 1993 the average increase over the year before was 15 percent. This may only mean that that increase was the rate of inflation of the real estate dollar.

E. Patterson, Condo Corner, *Sunset Gazette* (FL), p. 9 (Sept. 1, 1994).

Community Association Manager Licensing

Licensing of full-time managers of community associations is required in most states. Unit owners now are seldom allowed to serve as such managers without licensing (even though that was allowed in Florida until 1994). Finger-printing of license applicants now is required in Florida so as to aid background investigation. The Florida office of coops/condos may order a manager who improperly takes any assets to return them. Management of time-share associations must include at least one licensed manager.

1994 Legislation . . ., 93 *Community Update,* (July 1994; Becker and Poliakoff newsletter, Fort Lauderdale, FL).

Condo Governing Statutes

Statutory state regulations of *homeowners' associations* are sketchy and inadequate in general. Thus, Florida's over 21,000 such associations still (1994) lacked statutes that compare with those available for condos or coops. The Florida Statute (ch. 617), that covers NPCs generally, contains few specifics as to homeowners' associations. A 1994 study commission appointed by Governor Chiles at the request of the House Judiciary Committee may make recommendations to the state legislature by 1995. Meanwhile the Community Associations Institute (providing education and information to managers of residential associations) is a good source for inquiries; address c/o Exec. Dir. Jess McBride at (813) 521–3054 in the Tampa Bay Area.

Jack Holeman (column), *St. Petersburg (FL) Times,* p. 7D (July 23, 1994).

Definition of Condominium

In Colorado, a townhome complex is not a "condominium" for the purposes of liability for a townhome resident who was injured in a common area of the townhome complex. The operative documents creating the townhome complex and the association-prescribed duties of the association to the owners control in determining the duty owed by the association, to the extent that those documents are consistent with public policy. The documents can create duty giving rise to tort obligations as well as contractual obligations. General negligence principles also apply.

Trailside Townhome Association, Inc. v. Acierno, 880 P. 2d 1197 (CO, 1994).

Condominium Contracts

A condominium association is entitled to reformation of the legal descriptions of its property if it can show, by clear and convincing evidence, that there has been a meeting of the minds and an agreement, reduced to writing and executed, and that an agreed-upon provision was omitted or a provision inserted was not agreed upon due to a mutual mistake of the parties.

LaSalle Nat. Bank v. 850 DeWitt Place Condominium Association, 629 N.E. 2d 704
(IL App. 1 Dist., 1994).

The Financial Institutions Reform, Recovery, and Enforcement Act (FIRREA) preempts a condominium association's contractual right of first refusal upon sale of condominium units by the Resolution Trust Corporation (RTC), as receiver and successor in interest to the holder of promissory notes for the purchase of the condominiums. Thus, the RTC can transfer the units without the association's consent.

Resolution Trust Corporation v. Charles House Condominium Association, Inc., 853 F.
Supp. 226 (E.D. LA, 1994).

Associations' Fiduciary Duty

After a condominium was damaged by fire, the owner's condominium association secured a restoration contractor who performed unsatisfactory work and mistreated the owner's personal belongings, among other matters of concern. The association repeatedly refused to get another contractor, to require the contractor to adequately perform repairs, and to allow the owner to engage a satisfactory contractor. Upon suit, the court held that the association breached its fiduciary duty to the owner as the owner's agent. Damages assessed against the association included the reasonable cost to the owner of replacing her condominium in the condition it was in before the fire, plus consequential damages for the time spent by the owner to correct the repair problems.

> *Sassen v. Tanglegrove Townhouse Condominium Association,* 877 S.W. 2d 489 (TX App.–Texarkana, 1994).

§377. OPERATIONAL ASPECTS OF CONDOS

Condo Rentals, Complaints, Votes

Unit owners may have to waive their rights to use of common areas when they rent out their units. Statutes in some states are detailed as to this, such as the new Florida law which now provides for confusing mixtures of tenant-owner leasing documents. That state in 1994 also enacted ever more detailed statutes as to unit owner complaint handling by the condo board, votes on funding of statutory reserve funds, outside building changes (for example, hurricane shutters), and so forth.

> *FL Stat.* §§718.106 (4), 718.111 (13), 718.112 (2) (f), discussed in 93 *Community Update,* p. 4 (July 1994), (Becker and Poliakoff of Fort Lauderdale, FL newsletter).

Condo Insurance Caps

Condo insurance premium rates were capped by Florida's State Insurance Commissioner Bill Nelson in early 1995 because of "an unconscionable gouging of condominium residents" by insurance companies; some cases hitting 1600 percent rate increases in two years, plus multimillion-dollar deductibles that made coverage useless. This temporary solution was to be followed by proposals for legislative action, he said, as to the statutory requirements of insurance.

> *St. Petersburg Times,* p. 5B (Jan. 21, 1995).

Condominium Association Legal Actions

Condo unit owners may sue, in Florida, over defects in common areas, but must represent the interests of other unit owners, and need not depend solely on corporate action.

> Assoc. Press item, *St Petersburg (FL) Times* report of FL Supr. Ct. decision, Nov. 11, 1993.

Attorney fees that apply to the condo act or the declaration of incorporation document suits do not apply to a condo unit owner's lawsuit against another member for intentional infliction of mental suffering.

> *Kamhi v. Pine Island Ridge Condo F. Association, Inc.,* 634 S. 2d 730 (FL App., 1994).

A law firm may defend a successor condominium developer and management company for a condominium association against a suit brought by the association, even though the firm represented the association before its turnover to the unit owners, where the matters in litigation are not the same or substantially similar to the matters in which the firm represented the association before the turnover.

> *Daily Management, Inc. v. Thomas,* 635 So. 2d 1049 (FL App. 4 Dist., 1994).

The board of directors of a condominium association sued a principal and surety for breach of performance and maintenance bonds, bad faith, and unfair and deceptive practices. The court found that although a surety owes a duty of good faith and fair dealing to both the principal and obligee under a bond, the surety is not liable in tort to the obligee of any bond if there is no contractual obligation under the bond.

> *Board of Directors of the Association of Apartment Owners of the Discovery Bay Condominium v. United Pacific Insurance Company,* 884 P. 2d 1134 (HI, 1994).

A condominium association has standing to bring action against the builder of the complex for fraudulent misrepresentation related to substantial compliance with condominium plans, and assurances that the buildings were constructed in a good and workmanlike manner, free from defects. However, displays and models of the condo units do not constitute representations of workmanlike construction to the purchasers of the units, and cannot give rise to an action for fraud.

> *Sandy Creek Condominium Association v. Stolt and Egner, Inc.,* 642 N.E. 2d 171 (IL App. 2 Dist., 1994).

Liability Releases

A condominium association may include, in its declaration of covenants, conditions, and restrictions (CC&Rs), an exculpatory clause to relieve a non-negligent association of any contractual liability for property damage to an owner's floors caused by a leak in the common plumbing system. Such a clause is not against public policy. However, the association may not be relieved of its statutory duty to maintain and repair common areas by such a clause. Also, an equitable servitude action against the association may be enforced in such cases.

> *Franklin v. Marie Antoinette Condominium Owners Association, Inc.,* 23 CA Rptr. 2d
>   744 (CA App. 2 Dist., 1993).

Condo Agents and Employees

An agent of a condominium has a duty to protect residents from criminal acts of third parties if the agent had supervision or control over the premises where the acts were committed, the criminal conduct is forseeable, and is the result of the agent's negligence (realty company with control over a parking garage).

> *Siegler v. Centeq Realty, Inc.,* 874 S.W. 2d 304 (TX App. –Hous. [14 Dist.],
>   1994).

Treasurer; Condominium Financial Operations

In a *Community Association* the *Treasurer* is usually the person in charge of finances and budget, keeps its financial records, is responsible for deposit of monies in depositaries designated by the board, sees to an annual audit by a CPA, and receives no compensation for such duties. He/she should understand the basics of financial statements (balance sheets equal equation of assets, liabilities, and members' equity).

> Becker and Poliakoff, *93 Community Update* (May, 1994) (Fort Lauderdale,
>   FL). (This issue contains a useful summary of accounting methods and
>   basic law.)

Liability of Officers to Trustees

The officer of a condominium developer, who is also a director of the condominium association, cannot be held individually liable for corporate acts of the developer, solely on the basis of his/her status as a director of the association. To impose individual liability on such an officer, for breach of fiduciary duty, the association must prove that the officer willfully breached his/her duty, and that his/her conduct rose to the level of actual wrongdoing such as fraud, self-dealing, or unjust enrichment. That proof must be presented as a jury question.

> *Taylor v. Wellington Station Condominium Association, Inc.,* 633 So. 2d 43 (FL App. 5 Dist., 1994).

Condominium Questions/Answers

Questions put to condo boards of directors must be answered in writing if posed in writing by certified mail; answer must be substantive and sent within 30 days. It may say that a legal opinion or state officer answer has been requested. Otherwise the board may not recover attorney fees in subsequent litigation.

> FL Stat. §718.112 (2) (a) 2; *see* Holeman, Condo Line, *St. Petersburg (FL) Times,* D, (Oct. 8, 1994).

Association Rules

Homeowners are not allowed to post "For Sale" signs in coops or condos if the rules so provide. The association rules are *contractual* in nature. Recently the U.S. Supreme Court held that such rules violate the First Amendment if they bar *political* protest signs. Florida has enacted a law that prohibits owners of mobile home parks from enforcing a rule that prevents a home or lot owner from posting a "For Sale" sign.

> L.J. Raybourn, (column), *St. Petersburg (FL) Times,* p. D1 (Aug. 20, 1994).

In late 1994 the federal Department of Housing and Urban Development (HUD) was considering a change in the Fair Housing Act (amended in 1989) that forbids discrimination against families with children, and allows "adults only" communities, if 80 percent or more of the units are occupied by a person over 55 years old, and housing for older people is the plan. HUD is trying to make its rules more specific on this subject.

> *St. Petersburg (FL) Times,* p. D6 (Aug. 20, 1994).

Some people argue that the whole concept of real property controllers is a bad concept, and that developers' powers to place legal restriction on NPOs that *they* control or build should be limited. Many of the over 150,000 homeowners' associations in the U.S. have rules barring children, pets, signs, TV antennas, pickup trucks, and so on. In effect rules have taken away the power of elected government to control (police) communities while government is still obliged to provide police and sanitation and other services. NPOs collect "taxes" and act as "governments." It is estimated that by the year 2000 over 25 percent of Americans will live in such private-government communities. Constitutional protections that apply to "state action" do not apply to "private associations." Thus, some people say, private residential developments should be *treated* as new *forms* of "government," and be subject to the constitutional protections of *"individual"* rights.

> E. McKenzie (column, *NY Times*), in *St. Petersburg (FL) Times,* p. D8 (Aug. 21, 1994).

In condos, for instance, a bull-headed individual often can and does "bulldoze" the other residents, simply because no other person *(or director)* is willing to enter into a "brawl" in order to stop dictatorial bullying. We *elect* officers to govern under *systems of law,* and empower and *pay* them, so as to *protect* us by restraining the brute in our society. NPOs should *not* become a system for sterilizing the *public* law.

Condo Accessory Style Control

A condo board has the right to control style (appearance) of storm shutters. In 1994, Florida amended its statute [c. 718.113 (5) and 718.115 (1) (c)] to allow the purchase of shutters as a common expense if the purchase gets majority approval of the unit owners. Unit owners may not be deprived of the right to protect their units.

> Jack Holeman, Condo Line, *St. Petersburg (FL) Times,* p. 1D (June 25, 1994).

Pet Restrictions

A condominium unit owner may be enjoined from bringing a pet onto the premises of the condominium, even though his/her physician testifies that he/she would benefit medically from being allowed to keep a pet.

> *Pillsbury v. Bayshore Condominium Association,* 637 So. 2d 51 (FL App. 1 Dist., 1994).

A condominium use restriction that prohibits most pets is considered to be reasonable in California, even where the unit owner's cats never make noise or leave the unit.

> *Nahrstedt v. Lakeside Village Condominium Association,* Calif SupCt, No. S029132, Sept. 2, 1994.

For a form to amend a condominium declaration and rules to exclude pets, *see,* Form No. 163S in §384.

Community Associations Rules Exceptions

Community association rules apparently may be bent by individual unit owners in order to enable them to have fair reasonable use of their premises. Thus a disabled (wheelchair) veteran was allowed to install a glass door and a door chime without getting a two-thirds-owners' consent which the condo rules required. Under the Federal Fair Housing Amendments Act of 1988 and state law the association may not discriminate against disabled persons. So, too, a handicapped owner was allowed to install an elevator in a two-story condo, without the required two-thirds-owners' consent, under HUD rules (U.S. Dept. of Housing and Urban Development). It seems that associations will have to make *reasonable accommodations* in their rules and practices so as to afford handicapped unit owners full enjoyment of their units. No hard and fast law seems to be available as to what is "reasonable."

Laura J. Rayburn, *Community Commentary, St. Petersburg, (FL) Times,* p. 3D (Aug. 6, 1994).

Condo Rules Limitations/Disputes

Individual condo unit owners' rights, as to dominion and control, are often limited by the condo association's rules and regulations as well as by the declaration, articles of association, and bylaws. Very little statutory procedural law has yet been enacted as to disputes about control limitation. Maryland has such a statute as to promulgation of rules. Nevada's statute says that rules must be "reasonable." Florida applies constitutional law (Due Process, Equal Protection) in testing condo rules. The "reasonableness" and constitutional tests of validity of restrictive condo rules now seem to be the generally followed standards. Florida and some county statutes in some states now so provide expressly. [FL Stat. §718.1255 (1993); Montgomery County, MD Code c. 10 b (1991).]

L.A. Schiller, *Limitations on Enforceability of Condominium Rules,* 22 Stetson L. Rev. (3) 1133–1168 (1993).

A condominium association might be estopped from enjoining condominium owners from installing address numbers next to their front doors if it approves the installation of storm doors that obliterate address numbers resulting in endangerment of the owners' health and safety. However, an association declaration of condominium, prohibiting the unit owners from changing the exterior without association approval, but without a specific provision regarding the placement of apartment numbers, gives the association discretion in the matter.

> *See Korandovitch v. Vista Plantation Condominium Association, Inc.,* 634 So. 2d 273
>   (FL App. 4 Dist., 1994).

Tender of Fees

Homeowners may not offset their own liability for assessments imposed by their homeowners' association with alleged defects in the capital improvements for which the homeowners' association has contracted. Any action against the contractor's breach can be asserted only by the association against the contractor, and not by the individual members against the association's assessments.

> *Panther Lake Homeowner's v. Juergensen,* 887 P. 2d 465 (WA App. Div. 1, 1995).

If contract purchasers of a condominium have a vested undivided interest in the common areas, they have to pay assessments for the common area's repair and maintenance, even where building of all of the individual condominium units has not been completed. In Arizona, a reduction in the owner's obligation to pay assessments, if construction on their unit is not substantially complete, is allowed only where the condo declaration so provides.

> *Mountain View Condominiums Homeowners Association, Inc. v. Scott,* 883 P. 2d 453
>   (AZ App. Div. 2, 1994).

The membership of a homeowners' association may be assessed as a whole for maintenance of a fence on the homeowners' property, even where association documents do not authorize assessment of the membership as a whole, if association document provisions do allow the association to enter and repair homeowners' lots when the homeowners fail to maintain them.

> *Demaio v. Coco Wood Lakes Association, Inc.,* 637 So. 2d 369 (FL App. 4 Dist.,
>   1994).

§378. HISTORY OF COOPERATIVES

Lawyer Coops

Prepaid legal service plans of various kinds have been offered in the 1990s, operated by *lawyer coops* and also by unions or employer groups. Today, these plans are said to cover as many as 70 million people in some of their activities.

Natl. Resource Center for Consumers of Legal Services, *Legal Plan Newsletter* (Aug. 30, 1991 issue), ABA *Legal Educ. and Professional Development,* p. 68 (1992).

§380. OPERATIONAL ASPECTS OF COOPS

Statutory Control

If a mutual water company alone is empowered with the right to manage and control the affairs of the company, through its articles of incorporation, a shareholder of the corporation has no right to file an application to change a point of diversion, in its own name, without the consent of the corporation. Directors, rather than shareholders, control a nonprofit corporation in Utah under the Utah Nonprofit Corporation and Cooperative Association Act.

East Jordan Irrigation Co. v. Morgan, 860 P. 2d 310 (UT, 1993).

A North Carolina Utilities Commission may not reassign lucrative customers from a nonprofit electric membership corporation (EMC) in order to "punish" the corporation for service customer complaints. The Commission must provide a delay period in order to provide EMC with the opportunity to improve its service by providing improvement orders, progress reports, and further public hearings.

Dennis v. Duke Power Co., 442 S.E. 2d 104 (NC App., 1994).

A statute (provision of the Agricultural Marketing Agreement Act [AMAA]) that requires the Secretary of Agriculture to consider the vote of a producer-cooperative association to be representative of the votes of all of the association's member-producers is not a violation of free speech and equal protection. Such a statute is "rationally related to the congressional goals of encouraging cooperative membership and establishing an efficient marketing system."

Cecilia Packing Corp. v. U.S. Dept. of Agriculture/Agricultural Marketing Service, 10 F. 3d 616 (9th Cir. [CA], 1993).

In Virginia, the Public Service Commission (PSC) may use customer preference to resolve a territorial dispute between a nonprofit privately owned electric cooperative and a public electric utility. The PSC's decision cannot be disturbed unless its finding is contrary to evidence, without evidence to support it, or is arbitrary, or results from misapplication of legal principles.

Harrison Rural Electrification Association, Inc. v. Public Service Commission of West Virginia, 438 S.E. 2d 782 (WV, 1993).

The Pennsylvania Public Utility Commission (PUC) has jurisdiction to prohibit the furnishing of rural electric service by a cooperative if the cooperative cannot lawfully provide service there. Only a "central station service" can provide service in rural areas, as set forth in the cooperative's law.

Somerset Rural Elec. Coop., Inc. v. Pennsylvania Public Utility Commission, 641 A. 2d 1249 (PA Commonwealth, 1994).

When a nonprofit apartment association sued to invalidate rent control regulations, the court held that such regulations must provide rent adjustment mechanisms. A rent control regulation may be invalid on its face if, by its terms, those who administer it cannot avoid confiscatory results in its application to complaining parties.

Apartment Association of Greater Los Angeles v. Santa Monica Rent Control Bd., 30 CA Rptr. 2d 228 (CA App. 2 Dist., 1994).

Coop Tax Rules

A nonprofit corporation distribution center, organized in Delaware without capital stock, which buys and sells food and supplies for its franchisee members, is not entitled to an exemption from corporate excise taxes as an agricultural cooperative where the distribution center is not engaged in farming activity or operating for agricultural purposes.

Dunkin' Donuts Northeast Distribution Center, Inc. v. Commissioner of Revenue, 645 N.E. 2d 67 (MA App. Ct., 1995).

A nonprofit housing cooperative cannot keep real estate tax assessments low by self-imposed restrictions on income and transferability of the ownership of its real estate, if those restrictions are amendable in its bylaws and articles of incorporation. If the actual consideration paid for establishing membership rights in the cooperative bears no relation to the price a willing buyer would pay a willing seller, and fails to reflect all uses to which the property might be applied, the consideration is not germane to fair market value.

Pennypack Woods Home Ownership Association v. Board of Revision of Taxes, 639 A. 2d 1302 (PA Commonwealth, 1994).

Coop Financial Reserves Report

The requirement of year-end financial reports to state authorities has ended in Florida. Board formalities in handling members' complaints have been reduced. Maintenance of statutory reserves may be waived by a majority vote.

> *FL Stat.* §§719.104 (a), 719.106(1)(a)(2), 719.106(1)(f). And *see* §377 item
>   Becker and P., *Community Update*.

Coop Alterations

Some statutes (for example, Florida's) now provide that alteration of sub-stantial parts of coop property may be made when 75 percent or more of the total votes so agree, unless the bylaws or corporation articles provide for a smaller number or bar such changes entirely.

> *FL Stat.* §719.1055 (1994 amend.).

Coop Legal Actions

A bank, which brings an interpleader action to determine a debtor coop housing association's claims to deposited funds, may recover attorney's fees for the interpleader action.

> *In re Mandalay Shores Coop Housing Association, Inc.,* 21 F. 3d 380 (11th Cir.
>   [FL], 1994).

An action by a city-operated electric system, brought in state court against a rural electric cooperative and others to condemn certain facilities and electric customers of the cooperative in the city, was federally preempted under the su-premacy clause of the federal Constitution by virtue of conflict preemption. Such actions frustrate the federal purpose in the Rural Electrification Act (REAct) of providing low-cost reliable electricity to rural areas.

> *City of Stilwell, Oklahoma v. Ozarks Rural Electric Cooperative Corp.,* 870 F. Supp.
>   1025 (E.D. OK, 1994). *See also Morgan City v. South Louisiana Electric Coop-
>   erative Association,* 31 F. 3d 319 (5th Cir., 1994).

A water users' association was sued by residential property owners to gain permanent and temporary access to the water system. The court held that al-though the association's bylaws provided that any new service or hookup could only be added with 100% vote of the association's members, this bylaw provi-sion did not authorize the association to require a 100% vote for transfer of an unused water hook-up from another water system user to the aggrieved association members.

Roe v. Corbin Water Users' Ass'n, 885 P. 2d 419 (MT, 1994).

For information about recovery of anticipated lost profits of a new business, *see* 55 ALR 4th 507 §§3, 10[d], 11[b].

Liability of Cooperative

A nonprofit rural electric cooperative owes a roofer an ordinary degree of care in placing its wires, but ordinary care is a high degree of care when dealing with electricity's inherently dangerous nature. The roofer need not notify the utility before working near low voltage power lines where a statutory required notice is mandated only for working near high voltage lines.

Wyrulec Co. v. Schutt, 866 P. 2d 756 (WY, 1993).

In a cooperative members' breach of contract and fraud action against the cooperative, if sale and production agreements between a nonprofit agricultural cooperative and its members/producers are internally ambiguous, and ambiguous when read in conjunction with the membership agreement and cooperative's bylaws, the resulting material issues of fact must be heard by the court.

Gold Kist, Inc. v. Wilson, 444 S.E. 2d 338 (GA App., 1994).

For information about the duty of nonprofit cooperatives to furnish utilities, *see* 56 ALR 2d 413.

§384. CONDOMINIUM FORMS

FORM NO. 163S
Minutes of Board (Condo) Meeting on Insurance Purchase

_____ **YACHT CLUB CONDOMINIUM, BUILDING B, INC.**

_____ _____, FLORIDA _____

Minutes of a Special Meeting of the Board of Directors
August 22, 1994 — Captain's Quarters

Board Members Present: Bruce _____, Martha _____, Chuck
_____, Jack _____, Bill _____,

Representing _____ **Management Company:** Bill _____

Representing _____ **Associates Insurance:** Carol _____

The meeting was called to order at 10:00 A.M. by President Martha _____.
Proof of meeting was established, and it was determined that a quorum was present.

Bill _____ advised us that he had sent out five letters to _____ insurance agents asking them to submit proposals for our insurance. The results were:

3 declined to submit proposals
1 did not reply
1 proposal submitted

The proposal was submitted by _____ & Associates. The proposal was for
$18,096, broken down as follows:

Amount	Coverage	Carrier	
$15,380	Multiperil	_____	Assurance*
716	Fidelity Bond	Ian _____	
750	Directors – Officers Liability	_____	
1,250	Umbrella Liability	_____	Assurance*
$18,096			

*Reinsured by _____

The annual premium paid for the current year was approximately $6,000.

A discussion followed in which it was indicated that only _____ Assurance and
_____ were taking on new customers. Some companies like _____, our current carrier, were discontinuing their business, and others like _____ and
were continuing coverage on current customers with only modest increases in yearly
premiums.

FORM NO. 163S
Minutes of Board (Condo) Meeting on Insurance Purchase
(continued)

The multiperil policy covers fire, wind, glass breakage, sprinkler leakage, smoke, volcano, earthquake, internal water damage, theft, collapse, car, airplane crashes into building, and so on. There was a $100,000 deductible on wind-caused damage. We were advised that glass breakage insurance could be obtained from _____ Insurance for an annual charge of $25 per unit plus the cost of the common areas for a total annual premium estimated to be approximately $2,000.

Ms. _____ believed that the premium on the _____ Bond might be reduced by three or four hundred dollars. In addition she indicated that she could arrange financing the premium. The terms would be 30 percent down, the balance at the end of five months with interest of 6.8 percent.

The following motions were made by Mr. _____, seconded by Mr. and unanimously approved by the Board.

Authorize the purchase of multiperil insurance, the _____ Bond, Directors and Officers Insurance and a $3,000,000 Umbrella Liability coverage for an annual premium not to exceed $18,096.

Authorize the purchase of glass breakage replacement insurance with no deductible for an annual premium approximating $2,000.

Authorize entering into a premium financing arrangement for the multiperil insurance calling for 30 percent downpayment and the balance to be paid five months after the inception with interest not to exceed a rate of 7 percent per annum.

In a general discussion it was noted that insurance now constituted more than 10 percent of our yearly assessment and the amount was likely to increase in the future with the property manager and the Board of Directors not being able to do much about it. It was suggested that this matter be thoroughly discussed with the owners at this year's budget meeting. There was unanimous agreement.

The next Board meeting is scheduled for Monday, September 12, 1994, at 10:00 A.M. in the Captain's Quarters.

The meeting was adjourned at 11:10 A.M.

Bruce _____

Secretary

38

TRADE ASSOCIATIONS

§387. GENERAL TAX LAW ASPECTS OF TRADE ASSOCIATIONS

For information about what constitutes a business league entitled to federal tax exemption under §501(c)(6) of the Internal Revenue Code of 1954 (26 USCS §501(c)(6)), *see* 48 ALR Fed. 187.

§395. LITIGATION BY TRADE ASSOCIATIONS

In California, the state may constitutionally prohibit manufacturers or distributors of consumer goods from representing that their products are "ozone friendly," "biodegradable," "photodegradable," "recyclable," or "recycled," unless the goods meet the statute's definition of those terms. Such statutes regulate commercial speech and are subject to intermediate scrutiny for the purposes of First Amendment analysis.

Association of National Advertisers, Inc. v. Lungren, 44 F. 3d 726 (9th Cir., 1994).

Telephone companies, affiliates, and a trade association of local telephone companies brought suit to challenge the constitutionality of the Cable Communications Act, which prohibits telephone companies and their affiliates from providing video programming to subscribers within their service areas. The statute was held to violate the First Amendment in that it burdens substantially more speech than is necessary to effectuate its goals in promoting competition and providing diversity of video programming. The statute directly abridged the telephone companies' right to express themselves.

US West, Inc. v. United States, 855 F. Supp. 1184 (W.D. WA, 1994).

A Western coal-related trade association brought suit to challenge the Illinois Coal Act, which required Illinois generating plants to install scrubbers in their Clean Air Act compliance plans so that they would be able to continue using Illinois coal. The court held that the association had standing based on an "injury in fact" in the invasion of their legally protected interest. The Act violated the commerce clause as an attempt to eliminate western coal use by Illinois electric generating plants as a means of complying with the Clean Air Act.

Alliance for Clean Coal v. Miller, 44 F. 3d 591 (7th Cir., 1995).

A Chicago anti-graffiti ordinance, banning the sale of spray paint and jumbo indelible markers within the city limits, was found to be constitutional under due process and commerce clause analysis.

National Paint & Coatings Association v. Chicago, CA 7, No. 93–3969, Jan. 24, 1995.

An association of soft drink manufacturers and distributors sued to challenge the constitutionality of a Michigan state statute, that imposed duties on them to report collected bottle deposits collected, and refunds paid, and to pay unrefunded deposits to the state. The court held that the association had standing to sue, even though it would not suffer direct economic injury. The state's statute was declared not to be an unconstitutional taking.

Michigan Soft Drink Association v. Department of Treasury, 522 N.W. 2d 643 (MI App., 1994).

A class of manufactured home owners and a manufactured housing association brought suit to have a county public utility district's resolution, which charged a $2,000 new facility charge for hookup of dwellings not meeting energy efficiency standards of the district's energy efficiency program, ruled invalid. The court held that the resolution was valid and did not violate the constitutional commerce clause and was not preempted by the National Manufactured Housing Construction and Safety Standards Act.

Washington Manufactured Housing Association v. Public Utility District No. 3 of Mason County, 878 P. 2d 1213 (WA, 1994).

A Colorado Water Conservancy District and its Ground Water Management Subdistrict may, under the federal and state Constitutions, require sand and gravel pit owners and operators, who expose tributary ground water to evaporation during their mining activities, to file augmentation plans with the state.

Central Colorado Water Conservancy District v. Simpson, 877 P. 2d 335 (CO, 1994).

Anti-blockbusting regulations that prohibit real estate agents from soliciting in certain geographic areas of the state restrict commercial speech in violation of the First Amendment.

New York State Association of Realtors, Inc. v. Shaffer, CA 2, No. 93–9160, June
   23, 1994.

An association of thoroughbred racehorse owners and trainers brought suit
against a racetrack owner and out-of-state entities that received simulcast trans-
mission of races and accepted wagers. The court held that, under the Interstate
Horseracing Act, the racetrack had to negotiate with the horsemen's trade association in order to obtain consent for off-track wagering.

*Kentucky Div., Horsemen's Benev., and Protective Association, Inc. v. Turfway Park
   Racing Association, Inc.,* 20 F. 3d 1406 (6th Cir. [KY], 1994).

Amendments to the rules regulating pharmacy technicians do not require a
public hearing before adoption by the California Office of Administrative Law.
The rules must be consistent with their enabling legislation and must be reasonable, consistent, and clear.

Californians for Safe Prescriptions v. California State Bd. of Pharmacy, 23 CA Rptr.
   2d 755 (CA App. 2 Dist., 1993).

§396. LOBBYING BY TRADE ASSOCIATIONS

See, Lobbying Expenditures of Trade Associations, Harold Tailsman, *The Tax Adviser,* Sept., 1995.

The First Amendment bars civil conspiracy and concert of action claims
against an asbestos manufacturer, brought simply because of the manufacturer's participation in a trade association's lobbying and public relations
activities, especially where there was no evidence that the manufacturer's actions
were specifically intended to further the alleged concealment of asbestos dangers.

In re Asbestos School Litigation (Pfizer Inc. v. Giles), CA 3, No. 94–1494, Dec. 28,
   1994.

§398. ILLEGAL ACTIVITIES

In North Carolina, a nonprofit association of distributors, suppliers, operators, and manufacturers of amusement machines, among others, sued to get a
declaration that video poker games are not illegal slot machines. The court held
that the games are prohibited slot machines.

*Collins Coin Music Co. of N.C., Inc. v. North Carolina Alcoholic Beverage Control
Commission,* 451 S.E. 2d 306 (NC App., 1994).

An association of insurance underwriters sued the New York State Banking Department after the Department allowed commercial banks to sell and purchase annuities. The court held that annuities are not "insurance" which banks are not authorized to sell.

*New York State Association of Life Underwriters, Inc. v. New York State Banking
Dept.,* 632 N.E. 2d 876 (NY, 1994).

§399A. PROFESSIONAL ASSOCIATIONS

When a professional corporation of anesthesiologists brought suit against a nonprofit hospital for breach of contract to provide anesthesia services, the court held that the compensation that would have been paid to the professional association's shareholders, had the contract been performed, was the professional association's corporate expense, avoided by breach, not income to be used in calculating lost profits.

Anesthesiologists Associates of Ogden v. St. Benedict's Hospital, 884 P. 2d 1236 (UT,
1994).

The Supreme Court ruled, in 1995, that the Florida Bar rule prohibiting lawyers from targeted mail solicitation of accident and disaster victims within 30 days of the incident does not violate the Free Speech Clause.

Florida Bar v. Went For It Inc., US SupCt, No. 94–226, June 21, 1995.

For information about the restrictions on the right of legal services corporations or public interest law firms to practice, *see* 26 ALR 4th 614.

See 5 ALR 4th 866, §3[b] for the modern status of the law regarding solicitation of business by or for an attorney.

Professional Sports

See, Rulings in Search of a Rationale. (tax-exempt charitable purpose and the Kansas City Royals) Paul Streckfus. *Tax Notes,* August 14, 1995 68 N7 p891–893.

Civic Baseball

The IRS ruled that operating a major league baseball franchise is a Section 501(c)(3) exempt activity that relieves the burdens of government. One controversial aspect of this ruling is that a community foundation, as an accommodation party for the eventual sale of the franchise, could eventually sell the franchise to a taxable entity after three years. The taxable purchaser would not be required to keep the franchise in Kansas City. PLRS 9530024, 9530025, 9530026.

Diplomatic Golf and Tennis

An organization, that seeks to promote international understanding through golf and tennis tours of foreign countries, does not qualify for exempt status as a Section 501(c)(3) organization, if the tours are arranged by two taxable travel agencies owned in part by a member of the organization's board of directors; especially where the organization fails to maintain adequate records of its expenses and "allows the travel agencies unrestricted use of the funds without accountability." PLR 9540002.

Continuing Medical Education

An organization, that provides continuing medical education, qualifies for exemption under Section 501(c)(3) if the organization benefits both the physicians who attended and the general public who received health care from physicians with knowledge of current medical developments. The ruling did not address the organization's potential qualification as a school under Section 170(b)(1)(A). PLR 9539013.

Family Church

An organization, seeking exemption as a local branch of the Religious Society of Friends, was denied exempt status where eight members of the organization were members of the same family. The organization has filed a declaratory judgment action.

Relieving the Poor and Distressed

The IRS found charitable purpose in an organization's provision of employees or retirees of a corporation and its subsidiaries certain disaster assistance and hardship grants where the recipients constituted a charitable class based on the size of the class and its open-endedness and where the program would be administered by a committee of employees independently of the employer. PLR 9516047.

Low-Income Housing

In Announcement 95-37, 1995-20 IRB 18, the IRS set forth a safe harbor and circumstances test for determining whether organizations providing low-income housing qualify for Section 501(c)(3) status as organizations that relieve the poor and distressed. Under the safe harbor, at least 75 percent of the units must be occupied by low-income persons and at least 20 percent of the residents must meet the very low-income limit for the area. Or, alternatively, at least 40 percent of the units must be occupied by residents who do not exceed 120 percent of the area's very low-income limit. Organizations outside the safe harbor must demonstrate that they relieve the poor and distressed by satisfying a facts and circumstances test. Compliance with the requirements under Section 142(d)(1)(A) or (B) does not in itself establish relief of the poor and distressed.

Procedure 96-32 and other IRS guidelines have established standards to ensure that tax-exempt status is maintained when a housing development qualifies as having the charitable purpose of providing housing to low-income and very-low-income people. The IRS has also established a facts and circumstances test to determine whether an organization that does not qualify for the safe harbor is still considered tax-exempt.

See, Kaster, Lewis R., S*afe Harbor for Low-Income Housing Exempt Organizations Finalized, The Journal of Taxation,* June, 1996.

African American Professional Associations

An African American architect has founded the Studio for Afri-Culturalism in Architecture and Design in Harlem, New York, NY. The association promotes black culture in relation to architectural practice.

Travis, Jack, *Speak Out: Mentoring in Harlem: "Try to Give Them the Truth of My Experience," Architectural Record,* February, 1997.

Nonprofit Publishing

Sharon L. Taylor began publishing *The Barricade* in 1992 in order to provide esoterica about the musical *Les Miserables* to its fans around the world. With cooperation from the producers, Taylor operates the newsletter on a nonprofit basis and depends on unpaid correspondents for copy.

McDougal, Dennis, *"Miz" Magazine a Hit. Variety,* March 10, 1997.

Visual Effects Society

The Visual Effects Society (VES) is a trade association that informs, educates and recognizes special-effects artists. The VES' initial plans do not include collective bargaining.

Stalter, Katherine, *Org's Cause Is Effects: F/x Pros Conjuring Trade Group to Promote Industry. Variety,* February 10, 1997.

39

LOBBYING AND POLITICAL ACTION

§401. LOBBYING, IN GENERAL

The lobby tax, which applies to noncharitable businesses that have annual lobbying and political expenses of $2,000 or more, has been challenged by the American Society of Association Executives and 10 coplaintiffs. The suit was filed in response to provisions expanding the definition of lobbying, and seeks to have the tax declared unconstitutional.

> 8 *NonProfit Times* (6) 6 (June, 1994); *Non-Profits Mobilize Against Lobbying Bill,* Marianne Lavelle, *The National Law Journal,* Sept. 4, 1995.

The IRS has provided regulations for non-501(c)(3) agencies containing guidelines to the new laws prohibiting business deductions for lobbying. Only activities whose specific purpose is to create or support lobbying communication are treated as lobbying by the regulations.

> *See* 8 *NonProfit Times* (7) 30 (July, 1994).

The new lobbying law, that prohibits business deductions for lobbying, also applies to nonprofits. Under the new law, "specific legislation" includes legislation introduced in a legislative body and specific proposals supported or opposed by taxpayers. "Lobbying communications" are defined as those that are made to government officials, refer to specific legislation, and reflect a view on it. The communication must clarify, amplify, modify, or support views in prior communications relating to the legislation. "Attempt to influence legislation" includes both the lobbying communication and any related research or preparation. "Lobbying" includes activities whose specific purpose is to create or support lobbying communication.

Activities that take place two or more years before the communication are presumed to be for nonlobbying purposes. "Monitoring activities," such as complying with a law's requirements, reading general publications and viewing or listening to mass media, have no lobbying purpose. Determining the status of legislation or hearings, or preparing brief summaries of legislation are not lobbying if there has been no prior "evidenced purpose" to influence legislation.

The costs of multiple-purpose activities must be allocated reasonably between lobbying and nonlobbying purposes. "Paid volunteers" include the use of services or facilities of another taxpayer without full compensation. In such paid volunteer cases, the purposes of the first taxpayer are imputed to the second. The IRS regulations include an "antiavoidance" rule that allow the IRS to "achieve reasonable results" when taxpayers "purposely structure[e] [their] attempts to influence legislation to achieve results that are unreasonable in light of the [new law's] purpose."

Coping with the Lobbying Deduction Disallowance, Repass. Levey, and Carlisle, *Journal of Accountancy,* May, 1994; *Tax Aspects of Lobbying by Public Charities,* Matoney, Higgins, and Beausejour, *The Tax Adviser,* Jan., 1994.

The IRS has released draft regulations, interpreting the Revenue Act of 1987 which taxes political expenditures made by charities. "Political expenditures" are defined as "amounts paid or incurred to participate or intervene in the political campaign of a candidate for public office." The new regulations also include political expenditures made by "certain organizations formed primarily for the purpose of promoting a person's candidacy, or used primarily for that purpose and effectively controlled by the candidate." The tax equals 10 percent of the expenditure (or 100 percent of the amount if the organization fails to "correct" the expenditure).

Harmon, Gail, (article), 9 *NonProfit Times* (3) 44, 46 (March, 1995). *See also, Calculating "In-House" Lobbying Expenses Under IRS Safe Harbors,* Repass and Levey, *The Tax Adviser,* July, 1994.

Associations of Associations

American Society of Association Executives' Associations Advance America is a project that has been created to lobby Congress on issues that are of interest to associations and other nonprofit organizations. Such programs show that the nonprofit sector can be responsible members of society as promoters of social and community welfare as well as supporters of governmental and national programs.

At Home and on the Hill: Associations Advance America, Association Management, August, 1996.

Advantages to the 501(h) Election to Lobby

Section 501(h) allows (c)(3) charities to lobby within certain limits and provides definitions to determine what constitutes lobbying. The specific regulations and definitions allow charities to avoid the imprecise "substantiality test" and the associated general rules that define lobbying. Marcus Owens, director of the IRS's Exempt Organization Division, recently suggested that 501(h) electors are less likely to be audited because they are working within a clearly defined framework.

Clolery, Paul, (article), 10 *NonProfit Times* (8) 4 (August, 1996).

§402. FEDERAL LOBBYING LAW

Lobbying Tax Exemption

Under OBRA's new lobbying regulations, 501(c)(4) or (c)(5) organizations will receive automatic lobbying exemptions only if 10 percent or less of their annual dues comes from payment of more than $50 or if at least 90 percent of their members are 501(c)(3)s. Noncharitable organizations not meeting the test must apply for a private letter ruling waiver.

Harmon, Gail, & Kingsley, Elizabeth, (article), 8 *NonProfit Times* (10) 37 (October, 1994).

The Omnibus Reconciliation Act

The Omnibus Reconciliation Act became law on August 11, 1993, eliminating the tax deduction for lobbying expenses. But local and county level lobbying by chambers of commerce and associations were exempted. Reporting and penalty requirements were lessened. Chambers spending less than $2,000/yr. were exempted. For IRS information, phone (202) 463–5580.

Lobbying by Trade Associations

See, *Lobbying Expenditures of Trade Associations,* Harold Talisman, *The Tax Adviser,* Sept., 1995.

Lobbying by Social Welfare Organizations

See, *Senate Votes to Ban Federal Grants to 501(c)(4) Groups That Lobby,* (brief article), John Godfrey, *Tax Notes,* July 31, 1995.

Lobbying Disclosure Act of 1995

Lobbyists are required to register if they devote at least 20 percent of their time to lobbying activities and if they make at least two lobbying contacts in a six-month period.

The Section 501(h) definition of lobbying will apply to organizations making the Section 501(h) election, not the definition in the Lobbying Disclosure Act of 1995. The definition in the Act includes self-defense lobbying at the federal level as well as contacts with senior executive branch officials, but excludes state and local government lobbying.

Registration statements must be filed with the Clerk of the House of Representatives and the Secretary of the Senate.

Section 18 of the Act makes Section 501(c)(4) organizations that engage in "lobbying activities" ineligible for federal grants or contracts. Under the Act, lobbying includes contact with both legislators and with certain higher level executive branch officials. "Lobbying activities" do not include activities at the state or local government level, grassroots lobbying, or the activities of volunteers.

Final Regulations on Lobbying Activities for Purposes of Section 162(e)

The final regulations are generally consistent with the proposed regulations. The most significant change is to provide an illustrative but not inclusive list of relevant facts and circumstances that indicate that an activity is undertaken for a lobbying purpose. Treas. Reg. §1.162-29.

If an organization performs preparatory activities but does not make any lobbying communication, the tax adjustment is made in the year when there is no longer a reasonable expectation that there will be a lobbying communication. Thus, the organization will not have to file an amended return. Any amount of the adjustment in excess of the amount required to reduce the Section 162(e) amount to zero may be carried forward without limit of time. Treas. Reg. §1.162-29(c)(1).

The final regulations also contain a general anti-abuse provision. Treas. Reg. §1.162-29(f).

Final Regulations on Allocating Costs to Section 162(e) Lobbying Activities

The final regulations require that the taxpayer use a "reasonable method" to allocate lobbying costs. Methods must be applied consistently and must be consistent with the rules provided in the regulations in order to be "reasonable." Treas. Reg. §1.162-28(b)(1).

The ratio method, the gross up method and the method derived from the uniform capitalization rules of Section 236A, are the three "reasonable" methods enumerated in the regulations. Treas. Reg. §1.162-28(b)(1).

Complying with the Section 6033(e) Notice Requirement

Guidance for Section 501(c)(6) business leagues, Section 501(c)(4) social welfare organizations, and organizations that rely on the membership dues exception of Section 6033(3)(3) is provided in Rev. Proc. 95-35, 1995-40 IRB 1.

An organization that receives more than 90 percent of its annual dues from qualifying sources will not be required to provide notice of nondeductible amounts to its members. This exception applies to members that are not subject to the denial of deductions for lobbying expenses under Section 162(e) and the notice requirement of Section 6033(e).

Excepted organizations are Section 501(c)(3) organizations, state governments, local governments, entities whose income is exempt from tax under Section 115, and organizations exempt under Section 501(a) other than those subject to Section 162(e).

Amounts paid in order to be "recognized by the organization as a member for an annual period" as well as "similar amounts" including voluntary payments for basic operating costs and special assessments for lobbying, are included in annual dues.

Members are not limited to persons with voting rights in the organization and are defined very broadly.

The Section 6033(e) notice requirements may not be circumvented by using a complex structure of affiliated organizations.

See also, Hill, Frances R., *The Tax Treatment of Political Organizations, Tax Notes,*
    April 29, 1996.

§403. STATE LOBBYING LAW

Anonymous Campaign Literature

The anonymity of an author is not a sufficient reason to exclude his or her work product from the protections of the First Amendment. There is no form of speech entitled to greater First Amendment protection than the handing out of leaflets that advocate a politically controversial viewpoint. Ohio's statutory prohibition against the distribution of anonymous campaign literature was, therefore, struck down by the U.S. Supreme Court in 1995.

McIntyre v. Ohio Elections Com'n, 115 S. Ct. 1511 (U.S. OH, 1995). *But see Griset below.*

In California, the Supreme Court ruled that a government code section, requiring that candidates for public office identify themselves on any mass mailings, is constitutional and does not infringe on the First Amendment rights of candidates or candidate-controlled committees.

Griset v. Fair Political Practices Com'n., 884 P. 2d 116 (CA, 1994).

Initiative Petitions

A nonprofit association sued to prohibit the Arizona Secretary of State from using a Legislative Council's analysis of an initiative proposal concerning insurance reform. The court held that, under Arizona's statute, the Legislative Council's analysis was not impartial and the Council was ordered to draft an impartial analysis. The court, however, would not order the Council to adopt any particular language.

Fairness & Accountability in Insurance Reform v. Greene, 886 P. 2d 1338 (AZ, 1994).

An initiative petition, barring direct use of corporate funds for the purpose of influencing a ballot question, but allowing a corporation to establish and administer separate funds for that purpose, burdens both corporate expressive activity and corporate associational rights.

Associated Industries of Massachusetts v. Attorney General, 636 N.E. 2d 220 (MA, 1994).

Term Limits

States cannot add to or alter the Constitution's list of qualifications for members of Congress by imposing term limits. There are three qualifications for Congress: (1) age, (2) citizenship, and (3) residency.

U.S. Term Limits Inc. v. Thornton, US SupCt, Nos. 93–1456 & 93–1828, May 22, 1995.

Political Contributions by Corporations

For more information about the power of corporations to make political contributions or expenditures under state law, *see* 79 ALR 3d 491, §8[b].

§405. POLITICAL ACTIVITIES

Voter Education Efforts Must Stay Within Guidelines for Political Activities

Organizations described in Section 501(c)(3) of the Internal Revenue Code are prohibited by the terms of their exemption from participating or intervening, directly or indirectly, in any political campaign on behalf of, or in opposition to, any candidate for public office. Charities, educational institutions, and religious organizations, including churches, are among those tax-exempt under this Code Section.

The final regulations promulgated in T.D. 8628, 60 Fed. Reg. 62209 (Dec. 5, 1995) make few changes to the proposed regulations.

The most significant change in the final regulations is the use of the action organization definition of Treas. Reg. §1.501(c)(3)-1(c)(3)(iii) to define a political expenditure for the purposes of Section 4955. Through Section 53.4955-1(c)(1), the long-standing action organization regulations, the IRS ties the definition of a political expenditure in Section 4955 to existing IRS judicial interpretations of when an organization participates in or intervenes in a political campaign on behalf of, or in opposition to, any candidate for public office in violation of the requirements of Section 501(c)(3). T.D. 8628, 60 Fed. Reg. 62209 (Dec. 5, 1995). The final regulations do not resolve the question of whether Section 4955 operates as an intermediate sanction or as an addition penalty in case of revocation.

Prohibited Political Participation or Intervention

The IRS has ruled that language in an organization's fund raising letter constituted impermissible participation or intervention in a political campaign (PLR 9609007). Encouraging persons to support or oppose a candidate on the basis of nonpartisan criteria constitutes impermissible political activity inconsistent with exempt status. Whether prohibited participation or intervention occurs depends on all the facts and circumstances of each case but does not depend on the motivation of an organization. IR-96-23 (April 24, 1996).

See, Political Activities of Tax-Exempt Nonprofit Organizations: An Overview, John J. Silver, *Colorado Lawyer,* Sept. 1995 24 n9 p2157(4). *See also,* Chapter 4, §26, under Advocacy Societies.

These organizations cannot endorse any candidates, make donations to their campaigns, engage in fund raising, distribute statements, or become involved in any other activities that may be beneficial or detrimental to any candidate.

Whether an organization is engaging in prohibited political campaign activity depends upon all the facts and circumstances in each case. For example, organizations may sponsor debates or forums to educate voters. However, if the forum or debate shows a preference for or against a certain candidate, it becomes a prohibited activity.

The motivation of an organization is not relevant in determining whether the political campaign prohibition has been violated.

The Association of the Bar of the City of New York (a Section 501(c)(6) organization where some political campaign activity is allowed) had requested reclassification as an organization described in Section 501(c)(3). However, the Bar Association had rated and published the ratings of candidates for elective judicial office. The U.S. Court of Appeals for the Second District held that the voter education activities of the association constituted prohibited campaign activities, even though those activities were nonpartisan and in the public interest. The Service, thus, denied the 501(c)(3) reclassification. Therefore, activities that encourage people to vote for or against a particular candidate, on the basis of nonpartisan criteria, were held to violate the political campaign prohibition of Section 501(c)(3).

IRS News Release (IR-96-23) dated April 24, 1996.

Penalties for Prohibited Political Campaign Activity

If the Service finds a Section 501(c)(3) organization engaged in prohibited political activity, the organization could lose its exempt status, and further, could be subject to an excise tax on the amount of money spent on that activity. In cases of flagrant violation of the law, the Service has specific statutory authority to make an immediate determination assessment of tax. The Service can seek a federal district court to enjoin the organization from making further political expenditures. Also, contributions to organizations that lose their status as Section 501(c)(3) organizations because of political activities are not deductible by the donors for federal income tax purposes.

IRS News Release (IR-96-23) dated April 24, 1996.

The Federal "Motor Voter" Law

The national Voter Registration Act of 1993, the "Motor Voter" law, in effect since January 1995, allows community organizations a new tool as an outreach strategy. The law requires states to offer registration at motor vehicle departments, social service organizations, and through the mail. Any 501(c)(3) organization can engage in registration activities.

Useful resources:

Handbook on Tax Rules for Voter Participation Work by Section 501(c)(3) Organizations, by Thomas A. Troyer et al., of Caplan & Drysdale, INDEPENDENT SECTOR, 1828 L St. NW, Washington, DC 20036, (202) 223-8100. ($2.50+$2.50 shipping).

What's Your Last Name: Five Steps to Register a New Voter; Project Vote and Institute for Effective Action, 739 8th St. SE, Washington, DC 20003, (202) 546-3492.

Human SERVE: Various voter registration and educational documents. 622 West 113th St., Suite 410, New York, NY 10025, (212) 845-4053.

Political Forums

An unreleased April 1996 IRS Tax Advice Memorandum (TAM) suggests that the IRS is softening its position on political activities of organizations that sponsor political forums. The TAM appears to acknowledge problems in the Service's mandate that *all* qualified candidates be invited to these forums. Further advice is needed. However, the IRS appears to be willing to exercise discretion in individual cases on these matters.

> Carson, Marlis L., *Exempt Organizations and Politics; New Ruling Has a Few More Hints, Tax Notes,* July 15, 1996.

Fraud in Political Activity

Some say that nonprofits get away with wholesale flouting of the anti-lobbying regulations because enforcement is almost nonexistent.

> *See,* Richardson, R. Randolph, (article), *The Wall Street Journal,* July 5, 1996.

Improper Political Benefits?

House Speaker Newt Gingrich may have received improper political benefits from six nonprofit organizations in the period 1984–1994, according to a June, 1996 *Los Angeles Times* article. The Progress and Freedom Foundation, Kennesaw State College Foundation, Abraham Lincoln Opportunity Foundation, and several other groups were directly tied to Gingrich through his political action committee GOPAC, according to the article. Gingrich's Earning by Learning program and his ties to the American Opportunity Foundation are also being questioned.

> Stokeld, Fred, *Gingrich Improperly Benefited from Charities, Critics Charge, Tax Notes,* July 1, 1996.

IRS Investigation of Newt Gingrich

The IRS will investigate house speaker Newt Gingrich's use of tax-exempt contributions to fund partisan political activities. The investigation could weaken Gingrich's already tenuous hold on the Speakership, regardless of the investigation's ultimate findings. The probe could also give the IRS an excuse to define the acceptable limits of political activities by tax-exempt organizations. Tax-exempt groups have recently been used by political candidates, parties, and special interests for more overtly political purposes. One example of such use is the tax-exempt funding of Newt Gingrich's television programs that aimed to establish a Republican congressional majority.

Koszczuk, Jackie, *All Eyes on the IRS as Agency Looks into Gingrich Case, Congressional Quarterly Weekly Report*, February 22, 1997.

Illegal Political Contributions by Nonprofits?

Several tax-exempt groups received subpoenas, related to G.O.P. gifts, in April of 1997 as the Congressional inquiry widened to both the Republican and Democratic 1996 political campaigns.

Wayne, Leslie, *Tax-Exempt Groups Receive Subpoenas on G.O.P. Gifts: Congressional Inquiry Widens to 2 Parties. The New York Times*, April 10, 1997.

Activist Interference (Abortion Clinics)

"Operation Rescue is a prolife NPO that engages in civil disobedience by using the bodies of its members to block the entrances to abortion clinics. Their stated purpose is to 'rescue' the lives of the unborn children . . . ." However, this violates the civil liability law by being a conspiracy to deprive others of their "equal protection" of law under 42 U.S.C. §1985 (3).

Note, *Operation Rescue Blockades . . .,* 41 *Clev. St. L. Rev.* (1) 145–173 (1993).

A new federal statute, the Freedom of Access to Clinic Entrances Act (FACE) has been held to be within Congress's Commerce Clause power. It does not violate the First Amendment's Free Speech or Religion Clauses. The law, signed into law May 26, 1994, provides criminal and civil remedies against "whoever—by force or threat of force or by physical obstruction, intentionally injuries, intimidates or interferes with" any person who is or has been "obtaining or providing reproductive health services."

American Life League v. U.S., DCEVa, No. 94–700–A, June 16, 1994. *See also American Life League v. Reno,* CA 4, No. 94–1869, Feb. 13, 1995.

The U.S. District Court for the Eastern District of Wisconsin has held that Congress cannot ban or penalize nonviolent obstruction of abortion clinics under the Commerce Clause or the Fourteenth Amendment. Thus, the Wisconsin court found that the Abortion Clinic Access Law, 18 USC 248(b), is an invalid exercise of Congressional power.

U.S. v. Wilson, DC EWis, No. 94–CR–140, Mar. 16, 1995.

A state court may impose a 36-foot buffer zone and noise restrictions around an abortion clinic if the injunction is directed at the protesters' conduct, not their speech. The injunction involved prohibited demonstrations, displaying "images observable" to patients, chanting, singing, or carrying on other noisy demonstrations within 300 feet of a clinic.

Madsen v. Women's Health Center Inc., 62 LW 4686, June 30, 1994.

Women have a claim of action against private actors who blockade abortion clinics under the hindrance clause of 42 USC 1985(3). The hindrance clause applies to conspiracies "for the purpose of preventing or hindering the constituted authorities . . . from giving or securing to all persons . . . equal protection of the laws." There is no action, however, under the deprivation clause of Section 1985(3).

Libertad v. Welch, CA 1, No. 94–1699, Apr. 28, 1995; *Bray v. Alexandria Women's Health Clinic,* 61 LW 4080 (US SupCt 1993). *See also Portland Feminist Health Center v. Advocates for Life, Inc.,* 34 F. 3d 845 (9th Cir., 1994).

Knowing trespass (and intimidation of patients) at an abortion clinic is more than NPO (or religious) activism. It is a violation of the state's (MA) Civil Rights Act, and is enjoined permanently. The test is whether a reasonable woman patient would feel intimidated. If so, such acts go beyond "activism."

Planned Parenthood League of MA, Inc. v. Blake, 417 MA 467 (MA Supr. Ct., April 1, 1994).

Propaganda

Some big corporations organize so-called "Grass Roots" NPOs as fronts for their self-interest. For example, the Beer Drinkers of America was started by a New Mexico beer lobbyist. The members pay less than 10 percent of its revenue.

S. Holton, article, *Orlando (FL) Sentinel,* pp. 1, 16 (Sept. 4, 1993); R. Nader, *Masks of Deception: Corporate Front Groups in America,* 1991.

NPO Free Speech Lobbying

A rule interpreted and enforced by the Rhode Island House of Representatives, that allowed governmental lobbyists onto the floor of the House while denying lobbyists for private organizations the same access, was found by the court to be an improper regulation of time, place and manner of expressive activity, in a limited public forum, where the private lobbyists lacked ample alternative channels of communication.

> *National Ass'n of Social Workers v. Harwood*, 860 F. Supp. 943 (D. RI, 1994). *See also National Association of Social Workers v. Harwood,* 874 F. Supp. 530 (D. RI, 1995).

NPO-sponsored downtown-revitalization festival show is within its rights in refusing permission to a "right-to-life" group to have a booth at the show.

> *Capital Area Right to Life, Inc. v. Downtown Frankfort, Inc., Downtown Frankfort, Inc. v. Capital Area Right to Life, Inc.,* #93–1384, 1994 WL 82867 (May 31, 1994); 862 S.W. 2d 297 (KY 1993).

A state cannot compel the circulators and submitters of petitions, which propose state laws and constitutional amendments, to wear identification badges without violating the political liberty of the circulators and submitters. The state may, however, require the circulators to be registered voters who are eligible to vote on the subject of the petition, require monthly reports on paid circulators, require petitions to be circulated within a six-month period, and require disclosure of the names and addresses of the circulators in an affidavit attesting to the validity of signatures.

> *American Constitutional Law Foundation, Inc. v. Meyer,* 870 F. Supp. 995 (D. CO, 1994).

The Supreme Court of New Jersey held in 1994, that the owners of regional private shopping malls are required to permit distribution of leaflets on societal issues, subject to reasonable conditions. The court reasoned that although the federal Constitution affords no general right to free speech in privately owned shopping centers, regional and community shopping centers involve "public use" that is so pervasive as to include an implied invitation to distribute leaflets. Private owners of property, which serves as a functional counterpart of the downtown business district, cannot monopolize significant opportunities for free speech.

> *New Jersey Coalition Against War in the Middle East v. J.M.B. Realty Corp.,* 650 A. 2d 757 (NJ, 1994) *(rev. denied,* 64 L.W. 3210, Oct. 3, 1995).

A city may not mandate durational limits, lighting bans, and candidate responsibility regulations for political signs. Such regulations violate the Free Speech Clause by being content-based restriction on speech, not adequately supported by the city's interests in aesthetics and traffic safety.

Whitton v. Gladstone, Mo., CA 8, No. 94–1286, May 15, 1995.

Although a policeman has a right to talk politics, he may have to do it out of uniform. Cincinnati police supervisors were recently held to have qualified immunity from a lieutenant's First Amendment challenge to orders barring him from appearing in uniform, displaying his badge, or identifying himself as a Cincinnati officer while appearing at National Rifle Association events.

Thomas v. Whalen, CA 6, No. 93–4129, Apr. 21, 1995.

Homosexual Rights Advocacy

A voter-initiated state constitutional amendment prohibiting local governments from enacting civil rights protections for gay men, lesbians, and bisexuals, violates the Fourteenth Amendment's Equal Protection Clause. *But see* the case below, *Equality Foundation.*

Evans v. Romer, Colo SupCt, No. 94SA48, Oct. 11, 1994.

A Cincinnati law that bars the city council from enacting laws that provide homosexuals with "protected status, quota preference, or other preferential treatment" has been held to be constitutional by the U.S. Court of Appeals for the Sixth Circuit. The amendment was held not to deprive homosexuals of equal protection, or to violate their First Amendment speech, association, or petition rights, or their right to vote.

Equality Foundation of Greater Cincinnati Inc. v. Cincinnati, CA 6, No. 94–3855,
    May 12, 1995. *But see Evans* case above.

Politicking: Gerrymandering

An NPO dedicated to sound political conduct in the area may successfully challenge redistricting only if it shows not only lack of political power and representation in a given group, but also much more than a history of losing elections. If the minority group is not prevented from raising money, organizing and politicking, its mere continued lack of public office is not enough to prove discriminatory unfairness.

Marylanders for Fair Representation, Inc. v. Schaefer, 849 F. Supp. 1022 (D.C. MD, 1994).

Gambling Advocates

In Arkansas, the nonprofit Christian Civic Action Committee challenged a ballot title for a proposed constitutional amendment to allow additional forms of gambling in the state. The court held that the ballot title, which was 709 words long and used hypertechnical terms to describe the forms of gambling, did not provide sufficient information to the voter and was obscure about the amendment's meaning and potential effect.

Christian Civic Action Committee v. McCuen, 884 S.W. 2d 605 (AR, 1994).

§406. POLITICAL COMMITTEES: COMPOSITION AND DUTIES

The Court of Appeals' holding that an independent candidate, then candidate for the 1988 presidential election, lacked standing to challenge the Commission on Presidential Debates' (CPD's) tax-exempt status, collaterally stopped the candidate in her 1992 election and her running mate and campaign committee from relitigating the standing issue in a subsequent action.

Fulani v. Bentsen, 862 F. Supp. 1140 (S.D. NY, 1994).

§407. CAMPAIGN FINANCES

Section 527 Political Organizations

Exempt Function Expenditures

In TAM 9516006, the IRS ruled that salary payments to a candidate for public office by his principal campaign committee were exempt function expenditures, where the salary was less than the candidate had earned before becoming a candidate and less than the salary of the office he was seeking.

Separate Segregated Fund

IN TAM 9616002, the IRS ruled that a separate segregated fund established by a Section 501(c)(5) organization and funded with income from that organization's membership dues did not qualify as a Section 527 political organization, where the political organization performed no political activities during the period in question. The dues were used for general expenses of the Section 501(c)(5) organization. No tax was imposed under Section 527 on these amounts.

Penalty for Failure to Disclose Expenditures and Contributions

In 1986, the Howard Jarvis Taxpayers Association (HJTA) was penalized $600,000 for failure to disclose expenditures and contributions in response to a single letter requesting that information mailed during a state election campaign in 1988. Taxpayer Paul McCauley (who stands to earn a reward of $300,000, or half of the penalty) is also seeking $525,000 in attorney's fees in accordance with the bounty hunter's provision of California's Political Reform Act (PRA). The HJTA is expected to appeal, however.

Holton, Carlotta, (article), 10 *NonProfit Times* (10) 22 (October, 1996).

Christian Coalition Sued (Alleged Violations of Laws on Voter Guides and Campaign Spending)

The Federal Election Commission is suing the Christian Coalition, accusing it of using corporate treasury funds to support Republican candidates (such as Oliver North) and incorrectly reporting expenses from voter guides that advocated particular candidates. The Christian Coalition may be denied its long-sought IRS tax exemption as a social welfare organization, due to its political activity.

Carson, Marlis L., *Christian Coalition in Trouble for Campaign Spending, Voter Guides, Tax Notes,* August 5, 1996. *See also, Collective Politicking,* (Federal Election Commission Files Suit Against Christian Coalition for Supporting Republican Party as Tax-Exempt Organization) (Editorial) *The Wall Street Journal,* August 5, 1996.

Representative Cases

A Minnesota campaign finance reform statute, providing that for each independent expenditure made to advocate defeat of a candidate, the candidate's expenditure limits and eligibility for public subsidy would increase, impairs the political speech of those who make independent expenditures and violates protected associational freedoms by encroaching upon the ability of like-minded persons to pool their resources to gain common political goals. A $100 limit on contributions to and from political committees is so low as to infringe upon citizens' First Amendment rights.

Day v. Holahan, 34 F. 3d 1356 (8th Cir., 1994).

Nonprofit Abuses in Congressional Fund Raising

With the 1997 investigations into Presidential campaign fund-raising, some members of Congress are concerned that abuses may be found at the congressional level. Chaired by Senator Fred D. Thompson, the Governmental Affairs Committee and the House Committee on Government Reform and Oversight, chaired by Dan Burton, are investigating "soft money" and possible abuses by nonprofit groups. Under pressure of investigation, several members of the House and Senate, including Thompson and Burton, have returned approximately $95,000 of contributions from questionable sources.

Carney, Eliza Newlin, *Squirming Under the Lights. National Journal,* April 26, 1997.

Nonprofit Organizations Being Used to Avoid Campaign Finance Laws

More frequently than in the past, nonprofit organizations are being used by political parties and candidates to avoid campaign finance laws. Tax-exempt organizations are able to legally avoid paying taxes, can accept an unlimited number of contributions of any size, and are not required to report either contributor's names or contribution amounts to anyone. Tax-exempt organizations are supposed to avoid certain types of political activity in exchange for the privilege of tax-exemption. Groups affiliated with both major political parties, that are using their status for questionable purposes, will be investigated by Congress.

Carr, Rebecca, *Tax-Exempt Groups Scrutinized as Fundraising Clout Grows.* (includes related articles on attitudes of former IRS commissioner Sheldon Cohen and ex-House member Tony Coelho) (Cover Story), *Congressional Quarterly Weekly Report,* February 22, 1997.

Evasion of Election Laws

See, Wayne, Leslie, and Drew, Christopher, *G.O.P. Tool to Revive Party Instead Results in Scrutiny: Group Accused of Evading Election Laws,* (National Policy Forum), *The New York Times,* June 2, 1997.

Illegally Raised Campaign Funds in the 1996 Democratic Presidential Campaign?

The Democratic National Committee may have used the nonprofit organization, Vote Now '96, to illegally raise money for the 1996 Democratic presidential campaign.

See, Klaidman, Daniel, and Isiskoff, Michael, *Democrats' Charity Shuffle*. *Newsweek*, March 31, 1997.

A company that provided direct-mail fund-raising services to an unsuccessful candidate for U.S. Senator from Pennsylvania brought action against the unincorporated campaign committee, candidate, and the committee treasurer to recover amounts owed. The common law of Texas and Pennsylvania, governing the liability of a member of an unincorporated nonprofit association, was applied to enter a judgment against the committee and candidate.

Karl Rove & Co. v. Thornburgh, 39 F. 3d 1273 (5th Cir., 1994).

Funds solicited by and contributed to a nonprofit charitable organization, that was organized to raise money to celebrate a candidate's inauguration as Governor, are not "campaign funds." After some of the funds were used for the direct personal gain of the candidate or members of his family, such funds can serve as a basis for criminal prosecution under the Code of Ethics for Public Officials.

Ex Parte Hunt, 642 So. 2d 1060 (AL, 1994).

§408. COMMITTEE REPORTS

A nonprofit corporation, whose major objective is to elect a particular federal candidate or candidates, is a "political committee" obligated to register and report under the Federal Election Campaign Act.

Federal Election Commission v. Gopac, Inc., 871 F. Supp. 1466 (D. DC, 1994).

40

AFFILIATIONS

§412. AFFILIATIONS OF ORGANIZATIONS, IN GENERAL

Affiliations; Joint Programs; Sponsorship

Cooperation by a city or county office may be had for the asking in some places. For example, St. Petersburg, Florida, offers "joint operation" to NPO programs that have some general public interest. Application forms for requesting cofinancial sponsorship must be filed well before the city's fiscal year; a processing fee is charged. For details, phone (813) 893–7494.

Disaffiliation

Often, in the disaffiliation process, conflicts arise over who has authority to transfer and take title to the property of the affiliated entities. In a recent case, *First Assembly Church v. Ticor Title Ins. Co.*, the court was asked to determine whether a title insurance company had a duty to defend a church after defects in the title of its property were created by a disaffiliation conflict. The court held that a title insurer has no duty to defend a church that has claims brought against it for a defect in the title to properties, arising from the insured church's violation of duly adopted organizational documents, or if the church takes affirmative action contrary to the supervision and control it authorized in those documents. Such defects are "created" by the insured and were excluded from coverage in the title insurance policy. The *First Assembly* case illustrates well the need to avoid conflicts between an organization and its affiliate.

> *First Assembly Church of West Plains v. Ticor Title Ins. Co.*, 872 S.W. 2d 577 (MO App. S.D., 1994).

Taxation of Cost-Sharing Arrangements

An affiliation of corporations, in an attempt to avoid duplicating expenses, designated one or more corporations to act on behalf of the others in performing certain centralized functions on a nonprofit basis (accounting, administration, lab testing, etc.). Reimbursement for the expenses incurred was accomplished through accounting entries or checks issued between the corporations. The tax court involved held that the affiliated corporations' cost-sharing arrangements did not include pass-throughs of income to reimburse for payments to third parties so as to exclude reimbursed expenses from gross income taxation, whether or not they created agency relationship.

> *Universal Group Limited v. Indiana Dept. of State Revenue,* 642 N.E. 2d 553 (IN Tax, 1994).

§414. AFFILIATES' RELATIONSHIPS ILLUSTRATED

Associations of Associations

Affiliations of nonprofit associations are continuing to grow in number in 1996. One such affiliation, in Florida, is FANO, the Florida Association of Nonprofit Organizations, Inc., 7480 Fairway Drive, Suite 206, Miami Lakes, FL 33014, phone (800) 362–FANO; fax (305) 821–5228. The Florida Association of Nonprofit Organizations, Inc. is a state-wide resource center and professional network for staff and board members of 501, nonprofit organizations in Florida. It was founded by nonprofit leaders to enhance the well-being of all people and communities in the state by building the capacity of the private nonprofit sector. FANO assists Florida's 13,000 nonprofits in strengthening their leadership, management, financial/public policy capacity to reach their missions. *FANO is a 501(c)(3) nonprofit member of the National Council of Nonprofit Associations and the Independent Sector.*

A similar organization, KNPA, the Kansas Nonprofit Association, was started in 1996 to provide services, information, and advocacy to its member nonprofits. The organization will work to influence legislation and public policy affecting nonprofits, and train nonprofit managers and staff, using the Internet and electronic services to write grants and do strategic planning.

> Swarden, Carlotta, (article), 10 *NonProfit Times* (8) 38 (August 1996).

§415. AFFILIATION CONTRACTS

An arbitration agreement, that requires arbitration of disputes between members of an association of personnel consulting firms, does not also necessarily require arbitration in a suit brought by members against the association.

> *Texas Private Employment Association v. Lyn-Jay International, Inc.,* 888 S.W. 2d 529 (TX App. –Houston [1st Dist.], 1994).

In 1994, a franchisee association sued its franchisor for contribution to a fund set up to promote public relations. The court held that the franchisees' rights to financial contribution from the franchisor did not accrue, under the contract, until the franchisor agreed to participate in the campaign in any given year based on its corporate profit.

B-Dry Owners Ass'n v. B-Dry System, Inc., 636 N.E. 2d 161 (IN App. 2 Dist., 1994).

§416. FORMS OF AFFILIATIONS (CONTRACTS)

FORM NO. 172S
Bylaws of an Affiliation of Church Congregations

CONGREGATIONS UNITED FOR ⎯⎯⎯⎯⎯⎯ **BYLAWS**
1/95

ARTICLE I: NAME

The name of the organization shall be Congregations United for ⎯⎯⎯⎯⎯⎯.

ARTICLE II: MISSION STATEMENT

The purpose of Congregations United for ⎯⎯⎯⎯⎯⎯ is to assist pastors and lay leaders to strengthen the internal life of their congregations, and to link congregations together to be a strong grassroots coalition organization capable of negotiating the interests of our community with a special concern for the involvement and issues of low and moderate income people. Having been founded by religious congregations, Congregations United for ⎯⎯⎯⎯⎯⎯ is based on the values of justice and compassion as found in our religious traditions and the moral, spiritual, and democratic ideals of our society.

ARTICLE III: MEMBER CONGREGATIONS

A "Member Congregation" shall be any congregation which subscribes to the Mission Statement of this organization as stated in Article II of these bylaws, demonstrates active participation, and pays membership dues in accordance with the organizational guidelines adopted by the Board and Leadership Team Assemblies.

ARTICLE IV: BIANNUAL CONVENTIONS

SECTION I: AUTHORITY

All powers derive from and ultimate authority is vested in the Founding Convention and subsequently the Biannual Convention, including, but not limited to the authority to:

A. Adopt policies and set action priorities;

B. Elect up to 45 of the members of the member organizations to the Board of Directors;

C. Amend these bylaws in accordance with Article VII, and;

D. Act on any other business of _____ properly brought before it.

SECTION II: DELEGATES

A. Number—Each member congregation of 400 members or less shall be entitled to a maximum of 30 voting delegates, each having (1) one vote. Each member congregation of 401 members or more shall be entitled to a maximum of 50 voting delegates, each having (1) one vote.

B. Certification—A list of delegates certified by the member congregations shall be submitted to the Credentials Committee prior to the convention being called to order.

C. Voting—Only certified delegates present at a convention shall have the right to vote. A delegate shall represent and vote on behalf of only one member congregation. The presiding Chairperson(s) of the Convention may call for a voice vote and/or a show of hands when taking votes. Where more appropriate, by a majority vote the Convention can elect to have a written-ballot vote taken. All actions, other than the amending of these bylaws, will be taken by a majority vote. No absentee or proxy votes shall be cast.

D. Disputes—When in any convention, there shall arise any dispute regarding seat, voice, or vote; the delegates, other than those of the disputing congregations, shall be the final judge in determining, by a simple majority vote of delegates present and voting, the outcome of the issue at hand.

SECTION III: CONVENTION SCHEDULE

A. The Founding Convention shall be the first Biannual convention of _____ and shall be held in 1995 on a date and at a time and place recommended by the Interim Board of Directors and approved by a Leadership Team Assembly.

B. Subsequently, the Biannual Convention shall be held every other year, beginning in 1997, on a date and at a time and place recommended by the Board of Directors and approved by a Leadership Team Assembly.

C. Special Conventions may be called by a ($\frac{2}{3}$) two-thirds vote of a Leadership Team Assembly.

SECTION IV: NOTICE

Notice of any Convention shall be sent, in writing, to all member congregations at least 30 days prior to the Convention.

SECTION V: QUORUM

The delegates present at any properly convened Convention shall constitute a quorum, provided that ($\frac{1}{2}$) one-half of the member congregations have at least (1) one voting delegate present.

ARTICLE V: LEADERSHIP TEAM ASSEMBLIES

SECTION I: REPRESENTATION

Leadership Team Assemblies will occur 2–4 times a year. Each Member Congregation of 400 members or less shall be entitled to a maximum of 15 voting members, each having one vote. Each Member Congregation of 401 members or more shall be entitled to a maximum of 25 voting members, each having one vote. The Leadership Team Assembly shall receive reports and coordinate the work of Issue Task Forces. The Leadership Team Assembly will also take other necessary steps to help build the organization.

SECTION II: VOTING

In keeping with the spirit of the organization a conscious effort will be made to solicit opinions and feelings of all assembled prior to any significant vote, especially from those among the smallest or least vocal Leadership Teams. All action will be taken by majority vote. No absentee or proxy votes shall be cast.

ARTICLE VI: BOARD OF DIRECTORS AND OFFICERS

SECTION I: THE BOARD

The Board shall consist of no more than 50 members, with no more than 45 of whom elected at large by the Convention body and the balance consisting of (1) one representative elected from each Issue Task Force.

A. The Issue Task Force shall meet, elect their representative, and submit the name, address, telephone number and Congregation of said representative to the _____ office prior to the second scheduled meeting of the newly elected Board.

B. The Officers and members of the previous Board or Interim Board shall meet with the new Board in a supportive role until such time as new officers are elected.

C. By or at the time of the Board's third meeting, the Board shall elect the officers required by these bylaws. Such Officers shall be elected by a simple majority of those present and voting provided a quorum, consisting of ($\frac{1}{2}$) one-half of the board members, is present.

D. In keeping with the mission and spirit of the organization, balance and broad representation will be given significant consideration in the election of the Board and its Officers, especially its 2 Co-Chairpersons, in representing wherever possible _____'s racial, ethnic, gender, denominational, income, and geographic diversity. If the Board deems it necessary to add additional Board members in order to achieve this balance and diversity it may nominate up to 10 additional names to a Leadership Team Assembly for election.

SECTION II: THE OFFICERS

There shall be six (6) officers who will constitute the Executive Committee consisting of the following:

A. Two Co-Chairpersons, who shall preside on an alternating basis at Board and Leadership Team Assemblies. The Co-Chairperson shall be responsible for appointing a Nominating Committee of at least 5 Board members at least 3 months prior to any Convention. Said Committee shall prepare a slate of potential Board members and present same to the Assembly prior to the Convention at which time they will seek additional nominations from the floor. All such nominations shall form the slate to be presented to the convention body for consideration and election.

B. Two Co-Secretaries, who shall record the official actions of the Board, Assemblies, and Conventions.

C. Two Co-Treasurers, who shall be responsible for the keeping of the _____ financial records, providing regular financial statements as required by the Board, and for working with the auditors when regular or special audits are required.

SECTION III: MEETINGS

The Board shall meet at least monthly at dates, times, and places set by the Board.

SECTION IV: RESPONSIBILITIES

It shall be the responsibility of the Board to oversee the ongoing work necessary to build and operate the organization, to carry out the mission of _____ , to oversee the work of Issue Task Forces in the periods between Leadership Team Assemblies and to set the Agenda for all Leadership Team Assemblies and Conventions.

SECTION V: TERMS

The Board and its Officers shall serve until the next Biannual Convention.

SECTION VI: ATTENDANCE

All Officers and Board Members shall be expected to regularly attend meetings. Those members not able to attend should notify the _____ office prior to or within 24 hours of a meeting in order to qualify for an excused absence. Any member having more than 3 unexcused absences in any 6-month period shall be contacted by the Chair to determine continued interest in service to _____ and warned that they are subject to removal by the Board. Thereafter, continued absences shall result in the matter being presented to the Board for consideration of removal. Such removal shall require a quorum and a ($\frac{2}{3}$) two-thirds vote of those Board members present and voting.

SECTION VII: VACANCY

A. Board—Any vacancy on the Board shall be filled by election at the next Leadership Team Assembly. Such Board Member will be elected by a simply majority of those present and voting at said meeting.

B. Officer—A vacancy on the Board shall be filled by the Board through an election to be held at the meeting following the announcement of such vacancy.

ARTICLE VII: AMENDMENTS

These Bylaws may be amended by a ($\frac{2}{3}$) two-thirds vote of any of the members present and voting at any properly convened Biannual Convention or Leadership Team Assembly, provided there has been a 30-day written notice of the proposed change(s).

41

ANTITRUST RULES AND NONPROFIT OPERATIONS

§419. STATUTORY EXEMPTIONS

The Robinson-Patman Act/Exemption from Price Discrimination

For information about the construction and application of the provision in the Robinson-Patman Act (15 USCS §13c) which exempts nonprofit institutions from the price discrimination provisions of the Act, *see* 3 ALR Fed. 996.

Antitrust and Charitable Gift Annuities

In January of 1996, President Clinton signed two bills, the Charitable Gift Annuity Antitrust Relief Act of 1995 and the Philanthropy Protection Act of 1995. Both of these acts impact gift annuity arrangements between nonprofits and donors by protecting charitable gift annuities from federal and state antitrust liability and by protecting the rights of charities by codifying the Securities and Exchange Commission (SEC)-recognized exemptions for the collective pooling of charitable donations.

Clolery, Paul, (article), 10 *NonProfit Times* (12) 24 (December, 1996).

§420. JUDICIAL EXEMPTIONS

State and Federal Government Action

When the state of Florida authorized the acquisition of one hospital by another, while reasonably anticipating the anticompetitive effects of the acquisition, the state waived antitrust objections to the acquisition. The hospital was, thus, immunized from federal antitrust liability.

Federal Trade Commission v. Hospital Board of Directors of Lee County, 38 F. 3d 1184 (11th Cir., 1994).

333

The state action immunity doctrine applies to protect a city and a nonprofit against claims of monopoly and restraint of trade when they brought a waste disposal and recycling business under municipal supervision. However, the immunity doctrine does not apply to claims against private competitors who engaged in predatory pricing, wrongful exclusive dealing, and unreasonable restriction of use of containers.

> *Tri-State Rubbish, Inc. v. Waste Management, Inc.,* 998 F. 2d 1073 (1st Cir. [ME], 1993).

Professional Sports

The Sports Broadcasting Act antitrust exemption, for agreements under which a basketball league transferred the rights of its members to telecast games, does not extend to agreements that have the effect of precluding superstations from showing games. A resolution by the league board of governors that prohibits member teams from contracting televised games over superstations is naked restraint of trade.

> *Chicago Professional Sports Limited Partnership v. National Basketball Association,* 874 F. Supp. 844 (N.D. IL, 1995).

National Football League owners, under the nonstatutory labor exemption, have immunity from antitrust liability for fixing the salaries of practice squad players, after bargaining in good faith to impasse. Federal labor policy prevails over federal antitrust policy in a labor market organized around a collective bargaining relationship.

> *Brown v. Pro Football Inc. d/b/a Washington Redskins,* CA DC, No. 93–7165, Mar. 21, 1995.

An alleged conspiracy to prevent the relocation of a baseball franchise is not exempt from antitrust scrutiny. Professional baseball's historic antitrust exemption is limited to the sport's reserve system.

> *Butterworth v. National League of Professional Baseball Clubs,* FL SupCt, No. 82,287, Oct. 6, 1994.

The Learned Professions

Former lawyers who agreed not to advertise in one another's territories violated the antitrust rules of the Sherman Act. However, the lawyers who sued after having signed the agreement cannot reap the treble damages award, under the Act, for successfully challenging the agreement.

> *Blackburn v. Sweeney,* CA 2, No. 94–2737, May 3, 1995.

Interstate Trade Protection

The United States Supreme Court extended interstate trade protection to nonprofits in 1997.

> *See,* Greenhouse, Linda, *Nonprofit Organizations Get Interstate Trade Protection.* (includes other Supreme Court Rulings) *The New York Times,* May 20, 1997.

§422. TRENDS IN ANTITRUST APPLICATION TO NONPROFIT ORGANIZATIONS

Tax-Exempt Tours Sold by Nonprofits

The Small Business Administration (SBA) has asked the Treasury Department to crack down on tax-exempt tours being sold to the public by nonprofit organizations. The SBA claims that the exempt organizations violate the spirit of the law by catering to the richest consumers who can well afford to pay for their travel, and that the exemption cuts into the tourist travel business of small businesses.

> Pina, Michael, *Nonprofit Groups Targeted by SBA; Group Requests Treasury Dept. Crackdown on Tax-Exempt Tours, Travel Weekly,* August 1, 1996. *See also,* Herman, Tom, *Complaints Mount From Travel and Tourism Firms About Tax-Exempt Groups, The Wall Street Journal,* July 10, 1996.

Antitrust and Educational Institutions

The so-called Overlap agreement, permitting elite colleges to fix financial aid levels, was a price-fixing horizontal agreement. "The schools refrained from competing for students by agreeing to fix the tuition rates for any commonly admitted undergraduates while sharing information about the students' financial situations. As an antitrust matter, the agreement hindered fairness, hampered students' choice, created economic inefficiencies such as x-inefficiency and inefficient amenity competition, and fostered transfers of wealth to unchallenged and purportedly nonprofit elite universities."

> Shepherd, George B., *Overlap and Antitrust: Fixing Prices in a Smoke-Filled Classroom, Antitrust Bulletin,* Winter, 1995.

Representative Cases

An internist, whose staff privileges at hospitals were suspended and who was denied membership in a preferred provider organization (PPO), lacked standing to bring an antitrust claim for conspiracy in restraint of trade where he was able to admit patients to several other hospitals while his privileges were suspended and was unable to prove an antitrust monopolization injury.

> *Levine v. Central Florida Medical Affiliates, Inc.,* 864 F. Supp. 1175 (M.D. FL, 1994).

A hospital that denies staff privileges to two doctors because they are said to be inadequately trained is not subject to antitrust laws if the hospital *does not possess enough market power* necessary to commit violations of federal antitrust laws.

> *Flegal v. Christian Hospital,* #92–3775 (U.S. 8th Cir. C.A., Sept. 14, 1993).

A hospital does not per se violate antitrust rules in the Sherman Act by denying hospital privileges to a group of osteopathic physicians if the hospital applies the same admissions standards to all applicants and the exclusion is based on lack of subspecialty training. Such an exclusion falls into the category of "industry self-regulation."

> *Flegel v. Christian Hosp., Northeast-Northwest,* 4 F. 3d 682 (8th Cir. [MO], 1993).

A law school accreditation standard that provided that "compensation paid faculty members at a school seeking approval should be comparable with that paid faculty members at similar approved law schools in the same general geographical area" is not price fixing under the Sherman Act.

> *Massachusetts School of Law at Andover, Inc. v. American Bar Association,* 853 F. Supp. 837 (E.D. PA, 1994).

New York State's Excess Insurance Law violated the federal Liability Risk Retention Act of 1986 by indirectly regulating and discriminating against non-domiciliary risk retention groups (RRGs) and making available free excess insurance to hospital-affiliated physicians who purchased their underlying malpractice insurance from New York insurers. Such laws may also violate antitrust laws.

> *Preferred Physicians Mutual Risk Retention Group v. Cuomo,* 865 F. Supp. 1057 (S.D. NY, 1994).

A plaintiff (trade organization) must prove affirmative acts of concealment by the defendant in order to toll the statute of limitations on a price-fixing claim under antitrust law.

> *Dry Cleaning and Laundry Institute of Detroit, Inc. v. Flom's Corp.,* 841 F. Supp. 212 (E.D. MI, 1993).

There is no conspiracy between an electric company and a telephone company to require a contractor to use union labor, in violation of the Sherman Act, if the legitimate business justification of improving internal relations exists and a conspiracy would not make economic sense.

> *Ehredt Underground, Inc. v. Commonwealth Edison Co.,* 848 F. Supp. 797 (N.D. IL, 1994).

Nonprofit organizations are not entitled to class exemption from antitrust regulation, but are immune from regulation when they perform acts that are the antithesis of commercial activity. The exchange of money for services is a "commercial transaction." Thus, providing aid to students is a commercial transaction. However, the full "rule of reason" must be applied to determine if Ivy League colleges violate antitrust rules when they make an agreement among themselves to offer uniformly determined amounts of student aid to needy students. Such an analysis is necessary due to the nature of higher education and the asserted procompetitive and proconsumer features of the agreement.

> *U.S. v. Brown University in Providence in State of RI,* 5 F. 3d 658 (3rd Cir. [PA], 1993).

A Michigan nonprofit ambulance company, that submits bids that are lower than for-profit ambulance companies, does not use its nonprofit status to engage in predatory pricing in an attempt to establish a monopoly in violation of state antitrust laws. The concept of predatory pricing includes the premise that the actor will eventually raise prices and make a profit. Therefore, a nonprofit cannot have the intent to engage in predatory pricing.

> *ETT Ambulance Service Corp. v. Rockford Ambulance, Inc.,* 516 N.W. 2d 498 (MI App., 1994).

An association of farmers has no standing to pursue antitrust claims under the Clayton Act, and Article III standing does not exist where a causal connection between the defendants' conduct and the plaintiffs' claims depends on speculative review of unknown or unknowable decisions of third parties not before the court.

> *American Agriculture Movement, Inc. v. Board of Trade of City of Chicago,* 848 F. Supp. 814 (N.D. IL, 1994).

Antitrust: Merger "Segments"/Hospitals

Hospital mergers that might violate antitrust law can be changed to legal consolidation-collaborations that will probably be deemed valid by the *"segmented"* approach to analysis of such "mergers." Great cost savings, thus, can be secured by stopping just short of total abandonment of antitrust law enforcement. In one case, after discussion, the parties agreed to a *consent judgment* that substituted for the "merger" a *complicated joint venture,* in partnership form, to control various operations which would be *sold* to the two hospitals at cost, while continuing their "competition." The court approved this.

> *U.S. v. Morton Plant Health Systems, Inc. and Trustees of Mease Hospital, Inc.,* U.S. Dist. Ct., Middle Distr. of FL; June 17, 1994; Geviotzman and Spears, Novel Antitrust Law Analysis . . . , *Natl. L.J.,* B8 (Sept. 5, 1994).

A hospital and a competitor were sued by a medical equipment supplier for alleged antitrust violations related to a joint venture contract. If there is no evidence, related to the joint venture, of a rise in price or reduction in quality of durable medical equipment (DME) and no decrease in the number of firms supplying DME to consumers in a county, there is no anticompetitive effect within the relevant product and geographic market so as to establish unreasonable restraint of trade in violation of the Sherman Act. Willful acquisition or maintenance of monopoly power in an exclusionary or predatory manner must be shown to prove that the joint venture created a "preferred provider" through kickback arrangements. A "monopoly leveraging" claim is not actionable under the Sherman Act. "Denial of access to an essential facility," which is actionable under the Sherman Act, does not exist where patients are presented with a "freedom of choice" form listing all DME options and discharge personnel remain neutral to the patient's choice.

> *Advanced Health-Care Services Inc. v. Giles Memorial Hosp.,* 846 F. Supp. 488 (W.D. VA, 1994).

> *See also, Nonprofit Hospital Mergers and Section 7 of the Clayton Act: Closing an Antitrust Loophole,* Laura L. Stephens, *Boston University Law Review,* March, 1995; *Medical Group Mergers Require Plan Restructure,* (employee benefits plan), Mand and Marblestone, *Taxation for Lawyers,* May–June, 1995.

Hospital Antitrust Safety Zones

The Federal Trade Commission and the Department of Justice, in 1994, issued policy statements clarifying the methods of agency enforcement of antitrust laws concerning joint ventures, networks and other joint activities in the health care industry. Under the new enforcement policy statements, the agencies will not challenge, except in extraordinary circumstances:

1. Hospital mergers where one hospital is more than five years old, has fewer than 100 beds, and fewer than 40 patients a day.

2. Joint ventures among hospitals to purchase or support high-technology or other expensive health care equipment, that involve only the number of hospitals necessary to support the equipment. Additional hospitals, in excess of the number necessary, will not be challenged if they could not support the equipment alone through a competing joint venture. This statement applies to used and new equipment.

3. The collective provision by health care providers of non-fee-related medical data. For example, data about procedure outcomes that help purchasers answer questions about mode, quality, or efficiency of treatment. This statement also includes data relevant to the development of suggested standards for patient management in clinical settings.

4. Collective provision of current or historical, but not prospective, fee-related information to consumers by health care providers. Such activity must meet conditions designed to ensure that there is no sharing of information among providers for the purpose of coordinating prices or engaging in conduct that harms consumers. Information must: (1) be managed by a third party, (2) be more than three months old if shared among providers, (3) be based on information from at least five providers, (4) not consist of more than 25% of information provided by one provider, and (5) be aggregated so that recipients cannot identify prices charged by an individual provider. Further, the provision of fee-related information must not involve any coercive collective conduct or joint negotiation of, or agreement on, price or other competitively sensitive terms by the health care providers.

5. Participation of competing providers in surveys of prices for health care services or salaries, wages or benefits for health care personnel, if activities meet conditions designed to ensure that data is not used to coordinate prices or costs, (1) the activity must be managed by a third party. The data must: (2) be more than three months old, (3) be based on information from at least five providers, (4) not consist of more than 25 percent of information provided by one provider, and (5) be aggregated so that recipients cannot identify the data of an individual provider.

6. Joint purchasing arrangements among health care providers, if conditions are met to ensure joint purchasing arrangements, do not become vehicles for collusive purchasing or for price fixing. (1) Purchases must account for less than 35 percent of the total market for the purchased items, and (2) the cost of the jointly purchased items must account for less than 20 percent of the total revenues of each purchaser.

7. An exclusive physician network joint venture, if the physicians share substantial financial risk and the venture comprises 20 percent or fewer of the physicians in each specialty with active hospital privileges in the geographic market. These ventures restrict the ability of physicians to affiliate with other such ventures or to contract individually with health insurance plans. The venture may include one physician on a nonexclusive basis if, in the market, there are fewer than five of one type of specialist.

8. A nonexclusive physician network joint venture, if the physicians share substantial financial risk, and the venture comprises no more than 30 percent of the physicians in each specialty with active hospital privileges in the geographic market. These ventures do not involve limitations on the ability of participating physicians to affiliate with other ventures or to contract individually with health plans. If there are fewer than four of one type of specialist in the market, the venture may include one of them.

See Statements of Enforcement Policy and Analytical Principles Relating to Health Care and Antitrust, U.S. Department of Justice and the Federal Trade Commission, (Sept. 27, 1994). (The FTC will respond, within 90 days of receipt of all information, to requests for advice from health care plans or providers about matters regarding the "safety zones" or the non-merger enforcement policy statements; and within 120 days to requests for advice about multiprovider networks or matters not addressed by the statements). *See Antitrust Enforcement Policy for Health Care Markets,* Harold E. Kirtz, Assistant Regional Director, Federal Trade Commission, Atlanta, Georgia, *Through the looking Glass: The Health Care System in Transition,* The Florida Bar Continuing Legal Education Committee and The Health Law Section, Course No. 7440R, January 13–February 17, 1995.

See also, Chapter 45, §455.

Health Care "Networks" Regulation

Recent combinations of health care provider organizations to obtain *group bargaining* savings and other advantages and prepaid coverages (for example, physician-hospital *"provider networks"*) are causing increases in government *antitrust scrutiny.* Thus, careful planning is the key to success in these provider networks. "Credentialing" is the chief test factor; as in admission of new providers and retention of incumbents.

> A.J. Demetrion, New Provider Networks Risk External Regulation, *Natl. L.J.*, B10 (Sept. 5, 1994).

Antitrust Damages

A hospital that has an antitrust conspiracy with area anesthesiologists must pay all the damages suffered by a nurse anesthetist whose business in the area is destroyed by that conspiracy.

> *Oltz v. St. Peter's Community Hospital,* 19 F. 3rd 1312 (9th Cir. [MT], 1994).

Educational Institutions

Accreditation

Massachusetts School of Law (Andover, MA) began an antitrust lawsuit against the American Bar Association (Nov. 23, 1993; U.S. Dist. Ct., Phila., PA), charging that the ABA uses its accrediting powers to inflate the cost of legal education, with a small group of deans and professors acting as a dictatorial cartel. MSL was refused accreditation by the ABA.

> *MA School of Law v. ABA,* 93–CV–6206, E.D. PA. *See* Myers, Law Schools, 16 *Natl. L.J.* (14) 4 (Dec. 6, 1993).

The law school in Massachusetts brought action against the American Bar Association (ABA) and members of the accreditation committees for alleged antitrust violations (monopolization of accreditation) stemming from the ABA's denial of accreditation. However, Pennsylvania's District Court had no personal jurisdiction over members of the ABA committees where the members stated in affidavits that they were served outside of Pennsylvania, were not residents of Pennsylvania, and had not consented to the exercise of personal jurisdiction by courts in Pennsylvania. The Clayton Act provides for corporate, not individual, federal court jurisdiction coextensive with the boundaries of the United States in antitrust cases.

> *Massachusetts School of Law at Andover, Inc. v. American Bar Association,* 846 F. Supp. 374 (E.D. PA, 1994).

Financial Aid

See, College Financial Aid and Antitrust: Applying the Sherman Act to Collaborative Nonprofit Activity, (Case Note), Srikanth Srinivasan, *Stanford Law Review,* April, 1994.

42

MANAGEMENT TECHNIQUES IN NONPROFIT ORGANIZATIONS

§423. MANAGEMENT, IN GENERAL

Restructuring of Organizations

There is an increasing trend, in 1997, toward restructuring of nonprofit organizations. Restructuring efforts are generally directed toward becoming leaner and more efficient, following the lead of profit corporations in the 1980s.

> Glovin, Bill, (article), 8 *NonProfit Times* (12) 1, 28–30 (December, 1994).

For example, after a thorough audit, an Arizona Hospital and Health Care Association saw it needed new organizational and communication skills. Such reconstruction is really a continuous process and may invite antagonism from other associations within the same industry for its alleged infringement on their functions and service area.

> Rivers, John R., *Turn Revolution into Evolution, Association Management,*
> August, 1996.

The Internet

Those organizations that wish to use the Internet for marketing need to be prepared with a list of necessary items, changes, and potential problems. Some of the items involve the question of security, such as a fire wall to protect the network from intrusions, an updated disaster recovery plan, and an effective Internet payment method. The Internet market differs from others in that it has a global focus, and that the customer base will change, among other factors.

> Eckman, Mark, *Are You Ready to Do Business on the Internet?, Journal of
> Accountancy,* Jan., 1996.

Problems with the Internet

Internet service providers, including AT&T, ANS, BBN, EarthLink Network, GTE, MCI Communications, Netcom, PSINet, and UUNet, have formed a consortium called Torps.org. The consortium will focus on sharing technical problem reports, preventing router problems, and cutting network outages. The Tops.org group will be run by the Corporation for National Research Initiatives (CNRI, a nonprofit organization based in Reston, Virginia).

Girard, Kim, *'Net Providers Team Up on Problems, Computerworld*, May 26, 1997.

Computer Scientists Criticize the U.S. Government Security Plan for the Internet

Computer scientists at the Center for Democracy and Technology believe that the technical changes the government has planned for unlocking data-scrambling software on the Internet could actually increase the security risks as well as raise the prices of on-line commerce. The study by the nonprofit organization in Washington criticizes the government's plan that would pursue terrorists and criminals on the Internet. The U.S. government plan would require U.S. computer companies to establish a system enabling law enforcement officials to obtain the code with a court warrant before they could export data-scrambling software. The plan has made several foreign governments skeptical and has raised political opposition domestically.

Lohr, Steve, *Study Sees Holes in Internet Security Plan, The New York Times*, May 22, 1997.

Nonprofit Firm to Relieve Congestion on the Internet

The nonprofit firm, CANARIE Inc., is developing a CA*net II, a faster offshoot of the Internet that will be able to carry video and audio transmissions. In the U.S., universities are building "Internet II" to help relieve some of the congestion on the main Internet.

Chu, Showwei, *Surfing at High Speed: A More Powerful Internet is Quickly Approaching, Maclean's*, March 17, 1997.

Internet Training

Training programs offering Internet certification are becoming available to meet the growing demand for Internet and Intranet skills among IT staffs. The programs differ in their approach to certification, making choosing a training program more difficult. International Data Corp. surveyed 253 IS managers and found that the cost savings from increased network availability and help-desk efficiency more than made up for the costs of IT certification. There are three general approaches to Internet training and certification. The approaches are vendor-neutral training, certification from vendor-neutral nonprofit associations, and vendor-sponsored certification. The Internet Training and Certification Consortium (ITCC) offers a program that eliminates redundancies among training programs and cuts the time and cost of training. The International Consortium of Computing Professionals (ICCP) Education Foundation board member, Linda Taylor, says vendor-neutral certification offers broader knowledge than vendor-specific programs.

> Leinfuss, Emily, *Choosing the Right Internet Training.* (includes related articles on Microsoft's absence from Internet Training and Certification Consortium, and on Internet skill certifications), *InfoWorld,* February 17, 1997.

The *NonProfit Times* has entered into an arrangement with EPOCH Networks, which has more than 500 local dial-up numbers in 10 offices across the country to bring discounted Internet services to nonprofits. Another 200 local access numbers are on the way. Call toll-free 1(888)NET-ORGS, ext. 456 to ask about discount and rebate programs for nonprofits. EPOCH networks, Organizations Advancement Group, at www.epochworks.net or (703) 883-9555 or (888) NET-ORGS.

> *See also,* Zeff, Robbin, *The Nonprofit Guide to the Internet,* John Wiley & Sons, Inc., New York, NY, 1996. *See also,* Allen, Mike, *Now, It's Philanthropy Surfing on the Internet, The New York Times,* May 13, 1996.

World Wide Web

The World Wide Web gives organizations and companies the opportunity to bring charitable and philanthropic assistance to the public. The following are a few examples: Prudential Insurance supports a Web page that describes the investments the company has made in particular neighborhoods in order to document its attempts to bring economic revitalization. Impact Online (www.impactonline.org) is a nonprofit group that describes available charities and describes how people can join helpful organizations. The Business Coalition for Sustainable Cities, World Business Forum, United Nations, and Open Text have built the Livelink Commons (LC) Website. LC (www.opentext.com) is a forum that allows people to exchange ideas about technology and resources for building healthy communities.

> Comaford, Christine, *A Click Away from Helping Someone, PC Week,* June 17, 1996.

Freeware

The Independent Sector (IS) is recommending that nonprofits be cautious about using free Web servers. Freeware can be obtained through Apache or the National Center for Supercomputing applications. However, IS warns about the lack of availability of trustworthy support and up-to-date capabilities, and the long wait for services. However, some users say that free software can be especially valuable for a company implementing an intranet with inadequate or nonexistent funding.

Nash, Kim S., *Beware Freeware, Managers Say, Computerworld,* Sept. 16, 1996.

Searching Sites (Sites that have attempted to centralize information and facilitate searches):

1. Deja News, http://dejanews.com
2. Excite, http://www.excite.com
3. Infoseek, http://www.infoseek.com
4. Inktomi, http://inktomi.berkeley.edu
5. Linkstar, http://www.linkstar.com
6. Lycos, http://www.lycos.com
7. Magellan, http://www.mckinley.com
8. Open Text, http://www.opentext.com:8080/
9. Starting Point, http://www.stpt.com
10. WhoWhere white pages, http://www.whowhere.com
11. Yahoo, http://www. yahoo.com
12. Worldwide Yellow Pages, http://www.yellow.com

Sample Starter Sites for Nonprofits

1. The Internet Nonprofit Center, http://www.human.com:80/inc
2. The Philanthropic Initiative (TPI), http://www.tpi.org
3. The Foundation Center, http://fdncenter.org
4. A Grant Getter's Guide to the Internet, gopher://gopher.uidaho.edu:70/11s/e-pubs/grant
5. Guide To Internet Resources for Non-Profits, http://asa.ugl.lib.umich.edu/chdocs/nonprofits/nonprofits.html

6. Frequently Asked Questions About Nonprofits, http://www.eskimo.com/ ~pbarber/npo-faq.html
7. Putnam Barber's Resource for Nonprofit Information on the Web, http:// www.eskimo.com/pbarber
8. The Impact Project, http://www.efn.org/~impact

Nonprofit Websites and Home Pages

The NonProfit Times, http://www.nptimes.com

Library of Congress, http://lcweb.loc.gov/homepage/lchp.html

Thomas Legislative Information on the Internet, http://thomas.govU.S. Bureau of the Census, http://www.census.gov

The White House, http://www.whitehouse.gov

The Legal Information Institute, http://www.law.cornell.edu/

World Wide Yellow Pages, http://www.yellow.com

Department of Health and Human Services, http://www/ps/dhhs.gov

Yahoo Guide to WWW, http://akebono.stanford.edu/yahoo

The John D. and Catherine T. MacArthur Foundation, hearne@macfdn.org

Info on Charities, http://www.human.com/inc.

People for the Ethical Treatment of Animals, http://envorolink.org/arrs/ peta/index.html

American Humanics, http://www.humanics.org

American Ireland Fund, http://misty.com/ulysses/irlfund/

Colorado Association of NonProfit Organizations, http://www.aclin.org/ code/canpo

Father Flanagan's Boys Town, http://www.boystown.org

Habitat for Humanity International, http://www.habitat.org public_ infor@habitat.org

India Gospel Outreach, http://igo.ncsa.com/igo/

Junior Achievement, http://www.ja.org

San Francisco Conservatory, http://www.sfcm.edu

The Civic Federation, http://www.mcs.net/~civicfed/

Toyota USA Foundation, http://www.toyota.com/inside_toyota/ toyota_foundation

U.S. Bureau of the Census, http://www.census.gov/

Best Nonprofit Home Page

One of the best home pages created by a nonprofit is the interactive and educational page created by The Nature Conservancy. The address of the site is http://www.tnc.org

Online Services for Nonprofits

Online information services available to nonprofit organizations continue to grow in number in 1996. A few examples of such services are:

America Online, 8619 Westwood Centre Drive, Vienna, VA 22182, (800) 827–6264.

CompuServe, 5000 Arlington Centre Blvd., P.O. Box 20212, Columbus, OH 43220, (800) 848–8199.

Delphi, 1030 Massachusetts Ave., Cambridge, MA 02138, (800) 695–4005.

GEnie, GE Information Services, P.O. Box 6403, Rockville, MD 20850, (800) 638–9636.

HandsNet, 20195 Stevens Creek Blvd., Suite 120, Cupertino, CA 95014, (408) 257–4500.

IGC Networks (PeaceNet, EcoNet), 18 de Boom St., San Francisco, CA 94107, (415) 442–0220.

MetaNet, 2000 N. 15th St., Suite 103, Arlington, VA 22201, (703) 243–6622.

Women's Wire, 435 Grand Ave., Suite D., South San Francisco, CA 94080, (415) 615–8989.

> 8 *NonProfit Times* (9) 23 (September 1994). *See also,* Chapter 35, §358 for fund accounting software; Chapter 43, §438 for fund-raising software.

Financial and Banking Services for Nonprofits

Banks are starting to develop special programs and financial services especially for nonprofits. The following list is a sample of some services provided:

1. *Wachovia Bank* (800–462–7159), charitable funds management
2. *State Street Bank* (617–654–3338), money-management programs to nonprofits with multiple planned gift accounts, commingling
3. *Meridian Asset Management,* asset management program
4. *Michigan National Bank,* charitable donation through ATMs statewide
5. *Fayette County Bank* (404–631–2265), likely donation charities program

6. *New York Life* (212–576–5145), nonprofit benefits from donor life insurance policies

7. *Philadelphia Insurance Co.* (215–642–8400), nonprofits as beneficiaries of D&O insurance

Mehegan, Sean, (article), 8 *NonProfit Times,* (4) 25 (April, 1994).

Information Sources

A Faculty Presentation Book from Organization Management, Inc.'s (OMI's) 1995 Annual Washington Non-Profit Legal & Tax Conference can be obtained by contacting Organization Management, Inc., 13231 Pleasantview Lane, Fairfax, VA 22033, Phone (703) 968–7039, Fax (703) 818–0259.

> *See,* Bryce, Herrington J., *Financial and Strategic Management for Nonprofit Organizations, 2d ed.,* Prentice Hall, Englewood Cliffs, NJ, 1992; McKinney, Jerome G., *Effective Financial Management in Public and Nonprofit Agencies: A Practical and Integrative Approach,* New York, Quorum Books, 1986; Rados, David L., *Marketing for Non-Profit Organizations,* Boston, Auburn House Pub. Co., c1981; Hopkins, Bruce R., *A Legal Guide to Starting and Managing a Nonprofit Organization,* John Wiley & Sons, Inc., New York, NY, 1993. *See,* Hecht, Bennett, and Stockard, James, *Managing Affordable Housing,* John Wiley & Sons, Inc., New York, NY, 1996. *See also,* Connors, Tracy Daniel, *The Nonprofit Management Handbook,* John Wiley & Sons, Inc., New York, NY, 1993.

Nonprofit Consulting Services

CAMP Inc. is a nonprofit organization that offers low-cost consulting to medium-sized and small businesses.

> Maynard, Roberta, *Putting Manufacturers on the Right Course, Nations's Business,* Oct., 1996.

Nonprofit Health Care Management Groups

HealthGroup of Alabama is a variation on the "hospital network" theme. The organization is a nonprofit management company that functions like a network. It consists of six hospital-based CEOs whose services are leased back to their respective hospitals. One benefit of the arrangement is that a capital investment in a unified ownership system was not required.

Hudson, Terese, *A Virtual Network Get Real, Hospitals & Health Networks*, February 20, 1997.

Restructuring Health Care Institutions Through Nursing Economics

As shown by a study, organizational culture assessments are a valuable tool in health care institutions undergoing change. The study focused on the organizational culture of a 500-bed nonprofit hospital and the effect of a change to patient-focused care. A baseline survey was given to nurses and others prior to changes, followed by a postimplementational survey. The study identified values that might hinder or help the restructuring.

Jones, Katherine R., DeBaca, Vicki, and Yarbrough, Mary, *Organizational Culture Assessment Before and After Implementing Patient-Focused Care, Nursing Economics*, March–April, 1997.

Information Systems

JSTOR is a nonprofit organization that uses digital technologies to preserve and allow access to important academic journals. JSTOR's pilot group is scanning 10 journals and making them available at test sites in a small group of libraries.

Brunet, Patrick J., *CyberHound's Guide to Associations and Nonprofit Organizations on the Internet, Library Journal*, February 1, 1997.

Cable TV and C-SPAN

C-SPAN was created by cable TV in 1979 as a private sector nonprofit company. The industry has put $230 million into C-SPAN in 18 years. However, certain federal laws are undermining the operation. The "must carry" law is one that has forced some stations to drop C-SPAN so that a few commercial shopping channels can be aired.

Lamb, Brian, *An Accidental Victim: Greed Is the Culprit*, (effects of new telecommunications law on C-SPAN and C-SPAN2, nonprofit news and public affairs television networks—Cable Satellite Public Affairs Network) (includes a related article), *Washington Monthly*, March, 1997.

§424. QUALIFICATIONS OF MANAGERS

Leadership Characteristics

A 1994 Seattle University study of NPO leadership effectiveness characteristics led by Dr. Mary Stuart Hall lists the following as core major requirements: effective personal behavior; good humor; long-term thinking; direction selection; builds able and self-confident work force; develops resources; focuses on the client's objectives; cooperates with outside entities; manages the organization. For copies of Dr. Hall's draft report, address her at Seattle U. Institute of Public Service, Seattle, WA 98122.

NPO Management Associations

Persons involved/interested in NPO management procedures practices and developments and their improvement have a forum for study, contribution, and networking in the Nonprofit Management Association, 315 W. 9th St., Suite 1100, Los Angeles, CA 90015.

> [*See also* specific types of NPOs; for example, Condominiums, Trade Associations.]

§425. TRAINING OF NPO MANAGERS

Management Training

An example of NPO training centers and programs is the Support Center of Washington, D.C. It is one of thirteen centers of the Support Centers of America, founded in 1971 to improve the effectiveness of NPOs. They offer a series of workshops, every year, presenting a range of NPO management topics, as well as volunteer and other programs, and consulting services. Address 2001 "O" Street, N.W., Washington, D.C. 20036; (202) 833–0300. Other centers are in Ann Arbor, MI; Atlanta, GA; Boston, MA; Chicago, IL; Denver, CO; Houston, TX; Newark, NJ; New York, NY; Oklahoma City, OK; San Diego, CA; San Francisco, CA; Tulsa, OK; and Providence, RI. The National Office is (415) 552–7660; and International (202) 296–3900.

Seattle University in Washington offers an advanced graduate degree in nonprofit management called the Executive Master of Not-for-Profit Leadership program. Qualified participants are chosen based on personal essays, portfolios, and interviews. For information call (206) 296–5440.

Case Western Reserve University offers a Certificate in Nonprofit Management (CNM) and a Master of Nonprofit Organizations (MNO) degree program. For an application, contact Stuart Mendel, MNO, Director, Graduate Programs Mandel Center for Nonprofit Organizations, Case Western Reserve University, 450 Enterprise Hall, 10900 Euclid Avenue, Cleveland, OH 44106-7235, phone (800) 435–MNO9, fax (216) 368–6624, e-mail sxm30@po.cwru.edu Courses include: Introduction to the Nonprofit Sector; Organizations and Management; Financial Management; Management of Human Resources; and Strategic Planning.

Human Resource Management Practices

The National Organizations Survey found that in 590 for-profit and non-profit firms, human resource management (HRM) practices, such as training and staffing selectivity, resulted in positive associations between HRM and perceptual firm performance measures. The results also suggest methodological issues for consideration in examinations of the relationship between HRM systems and firm performance.

> Delaney and Huselid, *The Impact of Human Resource Management Practices on Perceptions of Organizational Performance, Academy of Management Journal,* August, 1996.

Managing with "Quality Teams"

The Swedish-American Hospital, in evaluating its performance for the 21st century, has created interdepartmental problem-solving/planning teams. The teams stress the importance of communication, consulting with experts, involving physician members of clinical teams, addressing turf issues openly, and encouraging the participation of the people who will implement the solutions developed by the teams. In developing the team approach, Swedish-American has abandoned its "top-down," lightly managed and controlled structure, which was failing to make optimal use of the intellectual ability of each employee.

> *How Teamwork Led Quality Goals at Swedish-American Health, Management Decision,* Sept., 1996.

Risk Management

> *See,* Bergstrom, Robin Yale, *On Quality, Implementing Technology, and Getting to the Future with Reduced Risk, Automotive Production,* July, 1996.

§433. S.E.C. "SECURITIES" TRANSACTIONS

The 1995 Philanthropy Protection Act exempts charitable income funds from SEC registration and regulation. SEC counsel Barry Mendelson and House Commerce Committee Counsel Linda Dallas Rich said, at the May 1996 Tax Section Exempt Organization Committee meeting, that the Act codified existing SEC registration requirements while excluding charitable investment pools. Rich and Mendelson also explained the Act's retained interest disclosure rules.

> Stokeld, Fred, *Gift Annuity Law Gives Exempts Needed Protection, Officials Say, Tax Notes,* May 20, 1996.

43

FUND RAISING

See also, Hopkins, Bruce R., *The Law of Fund-Raising,* Wiley, New York, c1991.

§436. FUND RAISING: INFORMATION SOURCES

Fund Raising in Europe

Information about software, hardware, and database management for fund raising in Europe is available by writing Saturn Corporation, 4701 Lydell Road, Cheverly, MD 20781.

Texts and Articles

McLeish, Barry J., *Successful Marketing Strategies for Nonprofit Organizations,* John Wiley & Sons, Inc., New York, NY, 1995.

See also, Zeff, Robbin, *The Nonprofit Guide to the Internet,* John Wiley & Sons, Inc., New York, NY, 1996.

Events Magazine, Ideas & Resources for Fundraising Events, P.O. Box 19284, Cincinnati, OH 45219-0284.

Greenfield, James M., *Fund-Raising Cost Effectiveness: A Self-Assessment Workbook,* John Wiley & Sons, Inc., New York, NY, 1996.

The NonProfit Times, 240 Cedar Knolls Road, Suite 318, Cedar Knolls, NJ 07927, (201) 734-1700, Fax (201) 734-1777.

§437. NATURE OF FUND RAISING

Fund-Raising Costs

In 1994 state officials in California announced that about 26 percent of funds raised by commercial fund-raising firms in the state in 1993 went to nonprofits. In Massachusetts the attorney general reported that 29 percent of money raised commercially in the state went to charity in 1993.

8 *NonProfit Times* (12) 22 (December, 1994).

Fund-raising Standards

In 1994 the Council of Better Business Bureaus' Philanthropic Advisory Service issued a new set of guidelines designed to "let donors make their own judgment" about joint-cost standards in charitable appeals. The Service wants all nonprofits to include a clear statement explaining that the charity is conducting public education activities in conjunction with fund-raising appeals in its multi-purpose solicitations. Nonprofits should also include a disclosure statement concerning education or advocacy in a prominent position in the same (or larger) type size as the main body of the multipurpose appeal. The Service suggests the following statement: "Some of the cost of this appeal is regarded . . . as a public education program rather than as a fund-raising expense." Of 75 national charities that use joint-cost reporting procedures, 53 percent say that they allocate more than half of the expenses to program services, a percentage that is probably questionable.

8 *NonProfit Times* (4) 4 (April, 1994).

For more information about the right of a member of a nonprofit association or corporation to possession, inspection, or use of membership lists, *see* 37 ALR 4th 1206.

The Council for Advancement and Support of Education (CASE) has issued a set of reporting standards for its members to follow in fund-raising campaigns. CASE will encourage universities to comply voluntarily. CASE's standards were released after several fund-raising associations signed a "Donor's Bill of Rights," and after Independent Sector released a study indicating that donors were angry about fund-raising techniques. Newspapers, faculties, governing bodies, donors, and beneficiaries are all beginning to scrutinize fund-raising campaigns with growing intensity. The standards are available by calling CASE at (202) 328–5900.

8 *NonProfit Times* (6) 4 (June, 1994).

Fraudulent Solicitation

The Foundation for New Era Philanthropy was put into Chapter 7 Bankruptcy liquidation, in May 1995, when the Philadelphia foundation agreed to liquidate its assets and start settling the huge claims of its 300 creditors. It had promised to double donations from charities and philanthropists, with matching donations in six months. Some of the country's most prestigious investors had given it multi-million-dollar grants. They had accepted its president's oral statements that he had a group of seven wealthy donors who would match their gifts, without proof. Many charities were likely to be ruined by this bankruptcy in a seeming Ponzi scheme.

St. Petersburg (FL) Times (article), p. 1A (May 20, 1995).

Nonprofits may be forced to return grants received from the Foundation for New Era Philanthropy. A group of more than 140 organizations have formed an organization called United Response to New Era. The organization cites two reasons why the grants may have to be returned: (1) Payments made by a bankrupt organization up to 90 days before a bankruptcy are ordered back into the pool of money to pay creditors as preferential payments. (2) If money is passed as a fraudulent conveyance, the bankruptcy trustee can go back further than the 90 days to recover assets, even where the receiving party is completely innocent.

See Clolery, Paul, (article), 9 *NonProfit Times* (7) 1, 27 (July, 1995).

A restraining order was issued, by a federal court, against two Las Vegas telefunders for fraudulent telefunding after the companies allegedly falsely represented that donations were tax deductible and promised that consumers would receive large amounts of cash or valuable prizes in return for donations in a prize promotion. Assets of the telefunders were also frozen.

Hesselbein, Francis, (article), 9 *NonProfit Times* (3) 22 (March, 1995).

Attorney/consultant Harriet Bograd has prepared a report on actions by Attorneys General in New York, Massachusetts, and Connecticut in cases of mismanagement, misuse, or selling of assets, abandonments, and excessive debt. The report indicates that investigations are usually prompted by dissenting board members and employees. Registration and reporting rarely lead to investigations. The public plays an important role in initiating investigations related to fund raising. Of 1,600 inquiries received annually, only 150 were *not* related to fund raising. For copies: *The Role of State Attorneys General in Relation to Troubled Nonprofits,* Program on Nonprofit Organizations at Yale University at (203) 432–2128.

8 *NonProfit Times* (7) 10 (July, 1994).

A Pennsylvania fund-raising firm was forced to pay $7,500 to settle a suit brought against it by the state. The firm allegedly failed to identify themselves as professional solicitors and falsely claimed that all money raised would benefit charity, when as little as 10 percent went to charity.

8 *NonProfit Times* (7) 30 (July, 1994).

New Jersey, in 1994, cited a company that sold an illegal gaming device to local businesses. The company fraudulently sold the device by stating that the proceeds would benefit charities and sponsor businesses. Consumer Fraud Act penalties are $7,500 to $15,000 per offense in such situations.

8 *NonProfit Times* (4) 6 (April, 1994).

The International Union of Police Associations (IUPA) (Virginia based) and two professional fund raisers were, in 1994, fined $38,000 in Pennsylvania for misrepresenting the beneficiaries of a telephone solicitation campaign, failing to disclose that their solicitors were paid professionals, and falsely describing the organization as a Pennsylvania-based organization.

8 *NonProfit Times* (4) 4 (April, 1994).

Federal and State Lawsuits Filed Against Professional Fund Raisers and Charities

In April of 1997, the Federal Trade Commission (FTC) and attorneys general from just less than half of this country's states, filed five federal and 52 state civil lawsuits against 40 "professional fundraisers" and charities. The suits involve so-called "boiler room" operators who move quickly into a town and start calling everyone, allegedly on behalf of local police, fire, or public safety organizations. They prey on the elderly and citizens who appreciate law enforcement and fear for their safety. The FTC claims that these so-called "professional" fundraisers bilk the public out of $1.4 billion a year, with little of the money going to charity. The biggest victims are the accredited fundraisers—and their organizations. This type of publicity makes legitimate fundraising efforts even more difficult—and expensive.

McIlquham, John, (article), 11 *NonProfit Times* (7) 17 (May, 1997).

Fund-Raising Contracts

Franchisees of a process for assisting nonprofit organizations through "pizza-make" fund raisers sued the franchisor to rescind their agreement, alleging failure of consideration and fraud. The materials provided to the franchisees, describing a multistep fund-raising process, were used to generate substantial income in a short period of time and were considered by the court to be both consideration and trade secrets.

Pate v. National Fund-Raising Consultants, Inc., 20 F. 3d 341 (8th Cir. [AR], 1994).

Confidentiality of Grant Applications

Under the freedom of information statute, there is a presumption in favor of disclosure. Specific exemptions in the statute are to be construed narrowly. Accordingly, a substance abuse treatment center could not obtain an injunction against the disclosure of their past grant applications. Past grant applications are not exempted "confidential reports" and must be disclosed to competitors if the release serves a public purpose (shows how grant funds have been spent and whether they were properly awarded) and will make the bidding process more competitive.

Northeast Council on Substance Abuse, Inc. v. Iowa Dept. of Public Health, Div. of Substance Abuse, 513 N.W. 2d 757 (IA, 1994).

§438. MECHANICS OF FUND RAISING

Best Cities for Fund Raising

A 1994 *NonProfit Times* study indicated that San Francisco was the most lucrative place to fund raise in 1993, ranking first place in direct mail, special events, and memorial gift donations. New York came in first in foundation support and ranked number three overall. Los Angeles ranked first in business support and fifth overall.

8 *NonProfit Times* (12) 23 (December, 1994).

Software for Fund Raising

Access International, 432 Columbia St., Cambridge, MA 02141, (617) 494–0066.

Blackbaud, Inc., 4401 Belle Oaks Dr., Charleston, SC 29405, (800) 443–9441.

Campagne Associates, Nashua, NH, (800) 582–3489.

Donor Perfect, DOS and Windows, 540 Pennsylvania Ave., Fort Washington, PA 19034, (800) 220–8111.

Fund E–Z Development Corp., 106 Corporate Park Dr., White Plains, NY 10604, (914) 696–0900.

JASK, 11150 Santa Monica Blvd., Ste 1400, LA, CA 90025, (800) 914–JASK.

JSI Fundraising Systems, 210 Lincoln St., Boston, MA 02111, (800) 521–0132.

Master Systems, 1249 Pinole Valley Road, Pinole, CA 94564, (800) 827–7214.

Not-For-Profit-Software, 91 Lukens Drive, New Castle, DE 19720, (302) 652–3370.

Samuelson Computer Services Co., 350 S. Schmale Rd., Carol Stream, IL 60188, (708) 668–1598.

Christensen Computer Co., Inc., Fountain Hills, AZ (800) 222-6102.

GrassRoots / Division of Master Software Corp. (800) 950-2999. 5975 Castle Creek Pkwy. N. Dr., Suite 300, Indianapolis, IN 46250.

Omnium Gatherum Membership Software, 1032 Irving St., San Francisco, CA 94122.

Pledgemaker by Softrek, 606 N. French Road, Amherst, NY 14228 (800) 442-9211.

Donor II / Systems Support Services, (800) 548-6708, 8848-B Red Oak Blvd., Charlotte, NC 28217.

> *See also,* Chapter 35, §358 for fund accounting software; Chapter 42, §423 for nonprofit management software.

Who Is in Charge of Fund Raising?

CEOs should accept ultimate responsibility for development while boards should have ultimate fiduciary responsibility. All board members should also be willing to give financial support to the organization. The board of directors should not be given any power over the development committee. If these procedures are followed, there will be less blame and finger pointing when an organization is in a poor financial position.

> Hendrix and Brustad, *Who's in Charge of Fund Raising?, Fund Raising Management,* August, 1996.

§439. BASIC TOOLS OF FUND RAISING

Telefunding

The 1991 Telephone Consumer Protection Act's ban on automated pre-recorded calls to residences, 47 USC 227(b)(1), does not violate the First Amendment. It is a content-neutral, narrowly tailored restriction on speech, protecting residential privacy, while leaving open ample alternative channels of communication.

> *Moser v. Federal Communications Commission,* 46 F.3d 970 (9th Cir., 1995).

Telefunders who offer token gifts will no longer have to worry about the Federal Trade Commission's telemarketing rule. The FTC, in 1995, exempted all fund-raising solicitation by charities and professional telephone fund-raising firms calling on behalf of charities from all sections of the rule. Sale of items such as tickets and magazines will still be regulated by the FTC as sales, not as solicitations.

See 9 *NonProfit Times* (8) 15 (August, 1995).

New Telemarketing Rule

The new telemarketing rule, effective December 31, 1995, requires telemarketers to make prompt introductions to their products or services while emphasizing that no purchases are necessary in case of promotions. The new rule prohibits calls at the most inconvenient hours before 8AM or after 9PM. The FTC clarified that the purpose of the new regulations is to apprehend fraudulent telemarketers without affecting nonprofit organizations or telemarketing firms contracted by a nonprofit organization.

Gattuso, Greg, *FTC Clarifies New Telemarketing Sales Rule for Non-Profits, Fund Raising Management,* March, 1996.

Telefunding Ethics

In 1994, a group of telefunders organized to create the American Telephone Fundraising Association in order to develop ethical standards for the industry. The standards urge telefunders to conform with the Telephone Consumer Protection Act and to avoid alliance with charities without an independent board of directors or detailed information about finances or programs, on request. Contingent fees are not banned. However, the standards require that charities be offered the option of contingent fees or an hourly fee rate. For information call (703) 734–1234.

Sinnock, Bonnie, (article), 8 *NonProfit Times* (11) 65 (November, 1994).

Management of Fund Raising

See, Worthy Isn't Working, (management of fundraising activities for nonprofit organizations), Simon Caulkin, *Colorado Journal of International Environmental Law and Policy,* Wntr 1995 v6 n1 pB9(1).

Privacy Concerning Donor Lists

Every nonprofit that rents or exchanges donor lists should allow donors a chance to opt out as a matter of privacy. To obtain answers to questions concerning raising money by mail send questions to: The Warwick File, 2550 Ninth Street, Suite 103, Berkeley, CA 94710–2516, FAX (510) 843–0142, e-mail mal@mwa.mhs.compuserve.com on the Internet.

> Warwick, Mal, (article), 9 *NonProfit Times* (3) 20, 22 (March, 1995).

§440. SPECIAL TYPES OF FUND RAISING

Capital Campaigns

In 1995, a survey by the Donor Forum of Chicago indicated that there has been a 36-percent drop in the number of capital and endowment campaigns between 1994 and 1995 and a 15-percent drop in fund-raising efforts during the same time. The study indicates that many nonprofits seem to be spending money on operating costs as opposed to expansions and renovation projects.

> 9 *NonProfit Times* (9) 4 (September, 1995).

Grant Requirement Rules

See: Information on the rules governing applications for (and grants of) federal funds set forth in *Circular A–110* (revised Nov. 1993), titled "Administrative Requirements for Federal Grants," issued by the U.S. Office of Management and Budget (OMB).

> *See* B. Hoersch, (two articles), *Grantsmanship Center* Magazine, pp. 4–7 (Fall, 1994).

Contributions of Nonmonetary Things

See also §84, 1990s Trends in Corporate Giving.

The Support Centers of America and the Support Center of Washington have created a new program, the Support Center TradeBank, that allows nonprofits to accept in-kind donations and turn them into trade dollars. For information, call (202) 833–0300.

> Sinnock, Bonnie, & Nacson, Sharon, (article), 8 *NonProfit Times* (10) 36 (October, 1994).

Unwanted old automobiles (and other vehicles) are collected by some NPOs, such as the American Lung Association (Gulfcoast Florida Program, for example). Such donations are eased by giving the donors simple tax forms for a tax deduction. The proceeds are used for sending asthmatic children to summer camp and so on. Many NPOs can benefit by such collecting of discards.

Article, 2 *Sunset Gazette* (18) 1 (So. Pasadena, FL) July 1, 1994.

Current techniques and materials for fund raising are treated in the *Grantsmanship Center Magazine,* issued frequently by the Grantsmanship Center, 1125 W. 6th St., Los Angeles, CA 90017; (213) 482–9860.

Seminars and conferences on fund raising are many and frequent. For example, *see* Georgetown Univ. Law Center (Natl. Society of Fund Raising Executives) Oct. 28–30, 1993 Seminar. Contact G.U.L.C., CLE Div. (202) 408–0990.

Fund Raising; Affinity Credit Cards

The U.S. Tax Court has ruled, for the third time, that income earned through an affinity credit card arrangement is royalty income, exempt from unrelated business income tax (UBIT). Two of the cases involved the Oregon State University Alumni Association and the Alumni Association of the University of Oregon. The IRS is not happy with the rulings, however, and is still pursuing the issue in two similar cases, which are still pending before the Tax Court, involving alumni associations from Mississippi and California.

Harmon, Gail, (article), 10 *NonProfit Times* (8) 14 (August, 1996).

Deferred Giving Programs

See Chapter 11, §§124–127.

Government Funding

The House of Representatives' plan to cut the budget by $1.04 trillion in the next seven years will leave nonprofits with a $245 billion cumulative funding gap in 1996–2002 according to a national study by Independent Sector (IS). While the federal government provided 32 percent of nonprofit budgets in 1995, it would contribute only 25 percent in 2002 under the House plan. The budget cuts will most affect services to the elderly, nursing homes, housing, community development home health care, legal services, and food services.

McIver, La Vonne, (article), 9 *NonProfit Times* (8) 5 (August, 1995).

Government funding accounted for more than $2 for every $10 of funds raised in 1994 by the top 100 charities. Some of the largest charities reported that, in 1994, government funding accounted for as much as 85 to 90 percent of their yearly income.

McIlquham, John, (article), 9 *NonProfit Times* (5) 12, 14 (May, 1995).

There is no constitutionally protected entitlement to selection as a head start agency or a constitutional right to a discretionary federal contract or grant.

Intercommunity Relations Council of Rockland County, Inc. v. U.S. Department of Health and Human Services, 859 F. Supp. 81 (S.D. NY, 1994).

Organizations that rely heavily on government funding may risk more regulation, less independence, and a decline in public support. They may fail to develop alternate funding sources and become vulnerable to government cutbacks. There is always the risk that such organizations will alter their mission in order to qualify for specific government grants. Donors may begin to think of government-funded organizations as an arm of government. For example, 900 respondents to an American Red Cross survey thought that the Red Cross was part of the U.S. government, even though only 6 percent of the organization's funds come from the U.S. government.

Mehegan, Sean, (article), 8 *NonProfit Times* (6) 1, 36–38 (June, 1994).

A legislature may appropriate money in its budget bill for "services and expenses or for contracts with municipalities and/or private not-for-profit community agencies" without violating a single object or purpose constitution requirement, where the only alternative is to list individually hundreds of programs receiving aid.

Schulz v. State, 610 N.Y.S. 2d 711 (NY Supp., 1994).

Federal Grants on the Internet

Nonprofit organizations looking for resources available from the federal government can get volumes of information from the newly launched Nonprofit Gateway. The Nonprofit Gateway is an Internet Website, constructed by the federal government, that gives online access to 16 federal departments and agencies. This site can link users to more than 300,000 government Web pages. Located at www.nonprofit.gov, the site contains information on grants, budgets, volunteer opportunities, and agency partnerships.

Clolery, Paul, (article), 11 *NonProfit Times* (14) 5 (November, 1997).

Government Funding for Technology

The Department of Commerce is offering about $25 million to companies hoping to develop risky, challenging technologies under its Advance Technology Program (ATP). ATP awards are given to for-profit companies and consortia, although nonprofit independent research organizations, universities, and federal laboratories may also take part as subcontractors or consortia partners.

TIF Solutions, February, 1997.

HUD Now Allowing Funds for Technology

The United States Department of Housing and Urban Development (HUD) is relaxing restrictions on the use of drug-and-crime-fighting funds to allow more money to be used to start and run community technology centers in HUD-funded housing.

McNamara, Don, (article), 11 *NonProfit Times* (7) 37, 38 (May, 1997).

1996 Federal Welfare Reform Law

The 1996 Federal Welfare Reform Law will transfer the federal anti-poverty role to the states. While some predict growth of nonprofit services providers, states and municipalities are largely unprepared for the major changes in store.

Peirce, Neal, *Welfare Reform: Let the Experiments Begin, Nation's Cities Weekly,*
    Oct. 7, 1996.

Solutions to Federal Welfare Reform

In Tulsa, the Industrial Exchange Inc., a nonprofit organization that runs an aggressive welfare-to-work program, is gaining nationwide attention. Its welfare recipients spend an average of six months in the program before moving on to jobs.

Dugan, Jeanne I., *Is This the Way Out of Welfare?, BusinessWeek,* Sept. 23, 1996.

Public Funding Down

In January and February of 1996, the shut down of the federal government caused a panic for nonprofits. Organizations that rely on government checks for operations had no cash flow.

Clolery, Paul, (article), 10 *NonProfit Times* (12) 24 (December, 1996).

See also, Sneider, Julie, *With Public Funding Down, Nonprofits Must Adapt, The Business Journal-Milwaukee,* March 23, 1996.

National Public Radio Facing Government Cuts in Funding

The National Public Radio (NPR) is celebrating its 25th anniversary. NPR programs air on 540 stations and reach 12 million listeners weekly. However, members of Congress are threatening to eliminate $250 million in annual federal funding for the Corporation for Public Broadcasting (CPB) in 1999. In response, CPB is relying on market research to prove its worth, while NPR is using a record label to generate money and is considering the creation of a trust fund.

Speer, Tibett L., *Public Radio: Marketing Without Commercials, American Demographics,* Sept., 1996.

Canadian Government Funding

The Canadian House of Commons, in 1995, is cracking down on government funding of organizations in Canada that promote a specific agenda or viewpoint (advocacy groups). Two bills introduced in 1995 will require such groups to make their tax returns a matter of public record and force government-funded agencies to disclose executive compensation.

See 9 *NonProfit Times* (2) 4 (February, 1995).

Government Donation of Surplus Goods

The U.S. government will sell or donate some surplus goods including furniture, office equipment, and power tools to qualified nonprofits. For information, call 1 (800) 468–8289.

9 *NonProfit Times* (2) 35 (February, 1995).

Low-Income Housing May Lose Government Funding

The government is reviewing the Section 8 low-income housing subsidy program because a majority of the contracts end in the next five years. Opponents object to paying landlords up to 130 percent of market value to provide low-income housing. The nonprofit organizations already involved are overwhelmed. Over 4 million senior citizens, disabled people, and low-income families benefit from Section 8 Housing. If landlords leave the program due to reduced subsidies, where will all these people go?

Wells, Robert Marshall, *Subsidies for Section 8 Program Are on the Chopping Block.* (includes related article on low-income housing in Maryland), *Congressional Quarterly Weekly Report,* March 1, 1997.

Cuts in Federal Spending on Arts and Humanities

The President's Committee on the Arts and Humanities says that cuts in spending on arts and humanities undermines cultural and educational institutions. The Committee is seeking more funds for arts.

> Miller, Judith, *Presidential Panel, Citing Worrisome Trend, Seeks More Arts Funds.*
> *The New York Times*, February 25, 1997.

Relief Agencies and Government Spending Cuts

Relief efforts around the world were stricken by a lack of U.S. government support in 1996. Nonprofits in the relief category were collectively hit with a 16 percent decrease to $445.9 million. That's $86.4 million in actual dollars. CARE was hardest hit with a 22.5 percent drop in government funding. World Vision dropped 19.5 percent to $48.9 million. International Rescue Committee declined in government support 11 percent to $41.15 million.

> Bathchilder, Melissa, (article), 11 *NonProfit Times* (14) 34, 38 (November, 1997).

Recovery of Government Funds

For information regarding the recovery of funds by the United States, pursuant to provisions of the Hill-Burton Act, as amended (42 USCS §291 (i)), of federal funds used in the construction of a nonprofit health facility sold to a profitmaking organization or otherwise ceasing to function as a nonprofit health facility, *see* 60 ALR Fed. 686.

Local Funding by National Organizations

In 1995, a Michigan affiliate of Mothers Against Drunk Driving (MADD) filed suit against its parent organization disputing the use of $500,000 raised by telemarketers. The affiliate alleged that the funds were raised "to prevent drunk driving in Michigan," and thus, should remain in Michigan. MADD National had been taking funds from local chapters in order to offset a deficit it has experienced since 1991. The suit was settled with MADD National agreeing to follow the policies of its volunteer board of directors and to develop a fair procedure for handling disputes. MADD National will also, at its expense, increase volunteer training, drunk driving prevention efforts, and victim assistance measures in Michigan.

> 9 *NonProfit Times* (7) 4 (July, 1995).

Gaming

See also Chapter 12, §142, under Gaming.

Many organizations now use gaming (for example, bingo games) for fund raising. Statutes that allow only a charitable organization or its members to conduct charitable gaming only when *licensed,* barring share in the profits to manufacturers or distributors or lessors of the premises or equipment, are constitutional; not too vague.

> *Devillier v. St. Dept. of Publ. Safety . . ., Div. of Charitable Gaming Control,* 634 S. 2d 884 (LA App., 1994).

In Kansas, the legislature cannot authorize "games of bingo" beyond the limits permitted by the State Constitution. The legislature's definition of bingo must bear reasonable and recognizable similarity to traditional bingo games. Instant bingo or pull tabs exceed the legislature's power to define bingo games.

> *State ex rel. Stephan v. Parrish,* 887 P. 2d 127 (KS, 1994).

Instant bingo, involving a single banded ticket or card with its face covered to conceal one or more numbers or symbols is not "bingo," which is allowed by an amendment to the Alabama Constitution. Such games are "lotteries," prohibited by Constitution.

> *City of Piedmont v. Evans,* 642 So. 2d 435 (AL, 1994); Const. Art. 4, Section 65; Amend. 508.

In Nebraska, telewagering at teleracing facilities is considered to be the functional equivalent of off-track betting and, therefore, is unconstitutional.

> *State Ex Rel. v. Stenberg v. Douglas Racing Corp.,* 524 N.W. 2d 61 (NE, 1994).

An Indian tribal member lacks standing to have a tribal-state gaming compact declared void. A tribe member has no legally protected right to be free from gaming on his/her tribal homeland, where he/she suffers harm no different in kind from the harm which might befall other residents, and the relief sought would only serve to postpone gaming on the reservation, rather than prevent it.

> *Willis v. Fordice,* 850 F. Supp. 523 (S.D. MS, 1994).

Non-Indians may bring qui tam suits under 25 USC 81 and 201 to challenge the validity of contracts with Indian tribes. The government is the real party in interest in such suits.

> *U.S. ex rel. Hall v. Tribal Development Corp., CA 7,* No. 93–3519, Mar. 9, 1995.

<u>Pull-Tab Games, Exemption from Taxation</u>

The IRS has exempted pull-tab games conducted by 501(c)(3) organizations from the federal excise tax on wagers. Lotteries conducted for profit are still subject to a .25% tax on all legal wagers. In pull-tab games the organization purchases a fixed number of tickets from a vendor, containing a set number of winners, under the control of the game operator. Pulling a single tab fixed to the face of the ticket reveals but does not determine the winning status of the ticket, and thus, qualifies the pull-tab game as an exempt "drawing." However, if the player pulls only a portion of the multiple tabs on the ticket, an event not under operator control, the game does not qualify for exemption.

> *See* Harmon, Gail, (article), 9 *NonProfit Times* (6) 48 (June, 1995).

A video display component device, that assists in the play of pull-tab games by permitting the player to watch the game being played, know of the winning ticket before opening it, and use the ticket only as a receipt for redemption, is prohibited under the Local Option Small Games of Chance Act in Pennsylvania.

> *Major Manufacturing Corporation v. Department of Revenue,* 651 A.2d 204 (PA Cmwlth., 1994).

For information about the validity and construction of statutes exempting gambling operation carried on by religious, charitable, or other nonprofit organizations from general prohibitions against gambling, *see* 42 ALR 3d 663.

> [For current fund-raising news/information see *NonProfit Times,* 240 Cedar Knolls Rd., Suite 318, Cedar Knolls, NJ 07927. Telephone (201) 734-1700, Fax: (201) 734-1777.]

<u>Horse Racing</u>

A nonprofit group, the Center to Preserve Racing, will study the management of horse racing in an attempt to preserve it in New York State.

> *Group Will Study Racing. The New York Times,* April 8, 1997.

Nonprofit Executive Donors

A *NonProfit Times* study of nonprofit executives found that nearly all of the responding executives said that they wouldn't respond to a telephone solicitation. However, all but one of the executives use telephone solicitation as a fundraising method at their organization. Some 75 percent of executives do not participate in payroll deductions for the United Way or other federated campaigns.

> Clolery, Paul, (article), 10 *NonProfit Times* (12) 24–25 (December, 1996).

Corporate Sponsorship

The Smithsonian Institution, in 1997, began a new corporate sponsorship program to fund its 150th anniversary traveling exhibition. The Smithsonian has revised its prohibition of corporate logos. However, the museum will be careful to ensure that proprieties are observed.

Heyman, Michael T., *Smithsonian Perspectives, Smithsonian*, February, 1997.

Sale of Names

A Virginia man sued *U.S. News & World Report* alleging improper sale of his name on a list. He might have won the case; however, the name sold was misspelled. The court ruled that the man didn't own the fake name and, thus, had no case. The man, Ram Avrahami, plans to appeal. Apparently, Ram Avrahami spelled his name differently for different lists.

Clolery, Paul, (article), 10 *NonProfit Times* (12) 24 (December, 1996).

Fund Raising Sweepstakes

The Federal Trade Commission (FTC) is targeting sweepstakes and prize promotion contests used by nonprofits to raise donations. The FTC is joining with states' attorney general offices and the United States Postal Inspection Service (USPS), in "Project Jackpot." In one case, the North Shore Animal League of Connecticut has allegedly violated the Connecticut Unfair Trade Practices Act (CUTPA) and General Statute Section 42-110b(a) by stating that the recipient is a "guaranteed winner" of a prize valued at $2.50. The League may have been in violation also for giving the same prize to all who mailed in the entry form. Similar suits have been filed by 15 other states.

Sinclair, Matthew, (article), 10 *NonProfit Times* (9) 5 (September, 1996).

Fund Raising: Registration Fee

An annual fee for the registration of fund-raisers, if not high, is a valid aspect of administration of law as to professional fund-raisers. This is true, even if the fee is not billed to individual fund raisers in proportion to the costs they respectively caused the state.

National Awareness Foundation v. Abrams, (S.D., NY) #91 Civ. 7670; 1994 WL 141266 (April 18, 1994).

Fund-Raising Fee-Caps Laws

Statutes that limit the amount of fund raisers' fees are violations of the First Amendment unless they are "narrowly tailored to the state's interest in preventing fraud." Arbitrary limits would choke off free experimentation with fund-raising methods.

National Federation of Nonprofits case, 1995, Calif. Fed. D.C. (Judge S. Brown) striking down a California statute limiting fees to 50%; citing *Riley v. Natl. Federation of the Blind of NC, Inc.*; described in S. Mehegan (article), *Non-Profit Times*, p. 25 (May, 1995).

Problems with Fund-Raising Registration

The top charity enforcement officials in the nation report that the biggest problems in the fund-raising enforcement arena are: (1) The 1988 Supreme Court decision in *Riley v. National Federation of the Blind* has hindered enforcement efforts in many states. The court held, in that case, that point of solicitation fund-raising disclosure requirements are unconstitutional. (2) Telephone fund-raising scams are numerous and hard to control. (3) Many enforcement officers say that they do not have enough help in doing their job properly. (4) Charity enforcement often must extend across the borders of other states. For example, a Florida telephone fund raiser may call donors in Maine on behalf of a charity in Montana.

Many officials suggest that public education and remedial legislation designed to get around the restrictions of *Riley* may help. Interstate cooperation, such as Utah's new law which gives officials the ability to cross state lines to prosecute unscrupulous fund raisers, in tandem with interstate cooperation, may also help.

Mehegan, Sean, Bush, Betsy, and Nacson, Sharon, (article), 8 *NonProfit Times* (4) 1, 12 (April, 1994).

The question of when the states can force a national charity to register is being debated hotly. Habitat for Humanity International, a home-building nonprofit based in Americus, Georgia, was fighting in 1994 to avoid registration in several states. Habitat says that it is a religious organization, exempt from registration requirements. Habitat also argues that its exemption in Georgia should be extended to other states. The charity withdrew from West Virginia rather than register. Habitat voluntarily registered in Pennsylvania after the state issued a cease and desist order to stop Habitat from fund raising. Pennsylvania's charitable trusts and organizations division defines a religious organization as "one that holds regularly scheduled worship/instruction of a religious nature." Pennsylvania, West Virginia, and Tennessee insist that Habitat is just another nonprofit fund raiser. Habitat argues that registration in all states is a paperwork burden and is duplicative. So, Habitat for Humanity will continue to fight for registration exemption in Pennsylvania.

Mahegan, Sean, (article), 8 *NonProfit Times* (4) 1, 20 (April, 1994).

Challenges of Registration Requirements

In 1995, a coalition of 15 nonprofits met in Washington, D.C. to form a plan to challenge state fund-raising regulations in federal court, alleging that such regulation is an attempt by government to raise revenue, rather than to protect the public from fraud. The coalition will target registration by local, municipal, and county authorities of out-of-state fund-raising consultants, local registration of nonprofit organizations, and the state regulation of fund-raising consultants. The group believes that registration regulations are an excessive burden on the First Amendment Rights of nonprofits, state governments should have no jurisdiction over fund-raising out-of-state consultants, and that local registration is redundant to state registration requirements. By forming an unincorporated association, the coalition hopes to collect and manage a litigation fund to sue for injunctive relief from state and local regulation.

Clolery, Paul, (article), 9 *NonProfit Times* (9) 1, 6 (September, 1995).

Maryland's charitable organizations solicitation law, which requires a sliding scale fee based on an organization's nationwide level of public contributions, is constitutional. The fee is a "user fee," which complies with the commerce clause, rather than a "general revenue tax." User fees must, under the commerce clause, (1) reflect fair, if imperfect, approximation of the cost of using state facilities for taxpayer's benefit, (2) not discriminate against interstate commerce, and (3) not be excessive in relation to the costs incurred by taxing authorities.

Center for Auto Safety Inc. v. Athey, 37 F.3d 139 (4th Cir., 1994).

Regulation of Nonprofits Is Getting More Onerous

A number of states added more registration/solicitation regulations on the nonprofit sector in 1996. Payments in lieu of taxes (PILOTS); the threat of losing property tax exemption; and bounty hunters reporting nonprofits who fail to report campaign expenses challenged nonprofit organizations legislatively, legally, and at the ballot box.

Coloradans for Fair Taxation (CFT) lost its battle to reform taxation in Colorado that would have legally ended the property tax-exempt status for religious and charitable groups. The Colorado Association of Nonprofit Organizations (CANPO) had to wage war against CFT using television advertisements and printed material to reach the voters.

The power of municipalities to collect payments in lieu of taxes was felt from Pennsylvania hospitals to New Hampshire private schools. The Granite State Association of Nonprofits, in New Hampshire, managed to water down a PILOT bill by giving municipalities the ability to ask for PILOTs, without making the contributions mandatory. The proliferation of PILOT programs has incensed the National Society of Fundraising Executives (NSFRE). NSFRE opposes such legislation and expects to have an official position paper out in the near future.

Alabama and Delaware put more regulation on solicitations by nonprofits. Public complaints about solicitors, who would not identify their organizations, prompted the Alabama legislature to charge a mandatory $25 fee in registration and reporting requirements.

The State of Connecticut filed suit against the Sarasota, Florida-based Children's Charity Fund Corporation. The regulation of program expenses is at issue. The nonprofit's primary purpose is to provide medical equipment to handicapped and disabled children. Connecticut claims that only a small part of the money is actually spent on providing this equipment. Consumer complaints prompted the suit. Seth Perlman, who is defending the nonprofit, says the lawsuit tests first amendment rights of the organizations and may be a new strategy by regulators to circumvent the 1980 Reilly vs. North Carolina decision, which bans states from pursuing fundraising issues because fundraising is a form of protected free speech. Some believe that the states are trying to explore fraud found in program earnings.

The bounty hunter, Paul McCauley, is seeking to claim a reward of $300,000—half of the penalty imposed by the court for failure to disclose expenditures and contributions from a single letter mailed during a state election campaign in 1988. The defendants are Butcher-Forde Direct Marketing, and its client, the Howard Jarvis Taxpayer Association (HJTA). Nonprofits, that have to defend such cases, sap resources and moneys intended to fulfill their mission.

Holton, Carlotta, (article), 10 *NonProfit Times* (12) 25–26 (December, 1996).

The Future of Regulatory Statutes

The future of regulation and registration will probably bring more states pushing for charitable solicitation laws. All 50 states can be expected to have some sort of registration requirement. Also, solicitation over the Internet may be at issue. For example, if an organization asks for donations in a state through use of the Internet, will the organization have to register in that state? There may be more class action lawsuits by individuals who think that nonprofits are not properly using donations. Such suits could ruin a medium-to-large organization. Many states are trying to enforce their unfair trade practices acts against nonprofits. Such acts have a private right of action provision to allow individuals to bring cases under the act and allow for damages.

Holton, Carlotta, (article), 10 *NonProfit Times* (12) 25–26 (December, 1996).

Certified Fund-Raising Executives

The National Society of Fund Raising Executives (NSFRE) and the Association for Healthcare Philanthropy (AHP) have become partners in a program to create one baseline credentialing program for fund-raising professionals. Both organizations will use the Certified Fund-Raising Executive (CFRE) Professional Credentialing Program which meets the accreditation standards of the National Commission of Certifying Agencies (NCCA). The criteria for this credential include five years of paid professional experience, meeting the application requirements, and passing the examination. The goal is to credential only those who "possess the knowledge and skills to perform their duties in an effective, conscientious, and professional manner."

10 *NonProfit Times* (9) 4 (September, 1996).

§441. GOVERNMENT REGULATIONS ON SOLICITATIONS (SELECTED STATES)

Registration for Fund Raising in Canada

In 1995, the first Canadian case to deal with the issues in the U.S. Supreme Court's *Riley* decision has resulted in the striking down of Alberta's law requiring Canadian charities to obtain a permit from bureaucrats and prior approval before starting a fund-raising campaign.

For information, Alberta Industry Standards, (403) 422–1588; *see* Clolery, Paul, (article), 9 *NonProfit Times* (8) 5 (August, 1995).

California

In California, the state and over 200 municipalities regulate charitable solicitations. Thus, charity mailers must carefully tailor their letters, disclosures, and information provided to each municipality's requirements.

In California, a federal judge ruled that the state's law, forcing fund raisers to cap their fees at 50 percent, violated the First Amendment. The law "[was] not narrowly tailored to the State's interest on preventing fraud."

> Mehegan, Sean, (article), 9 *NonProfit Times* (5) 23 (May, 1995); *see Riley v. National Federation of the Blind of North Carolina, Inc.* (likening fund raising to a form of protected speech).

Hawaii

On July 1, 1996, Hawaii passed House Bill 3398, an amendment to the state's charitable solicitation law that repeals the sections of the statute concerning filing requirements for charities and exemptions. Hawaii is trying to cut unnecessary red tape out of its regulations. House Bill 3398 still requires registration of fund raising counsel and professional solicitors.

> Swarden, Carlotta, (article), 10 *NonProfit Times* (9) 5 (September, 1996).

Kentucky

Effective July 15, 1994, Kentucky raised its fund-raising registration fee to $50 for consultants and $300 for professional fund raisers. Kentucky is the first state to require that fund raisers pay for their own background checks. There are no charitable registration fees; however, charities must file 990 forms. Kentucky requires a point of solicitation disclosure if solicitors retain 50 percent or more of the donations (which may violate the *Riley* decision rendered by the U.S. Supreme Court).

> 8 *NonProfit Times* (5) 12 (May, 1994).

New Jersey

New Jersey's new charitable solicitation statute requires registration fees of from $30 to $250, depending on contribution levels. Audited financial reports are required from organizations with more than $100,000 in gross revenue. Short-form registration is now required for previously exempt organizations, such as fraternal, patriotic, social, alumni, veterans' organizations, and some historical societies. Religious and educational organizations are still exempt. Written appeals must state that information on charities is available from the state, with a phone number. Fund-raising counsel need not file a $10,000 bond required of professional fund raisers. Fund raisers that have "custody, control, or access" to funds must file a $20,000 bond. Commercial coventurers must file contracts 10 days before a promotion.

8 *NonProfit Times* (5) 12 (May, 1994).

North Carolina

North Carolina's new law for fund-raising solicitations, which became effective on January 1, 1995, requires a verbatim disclosure statement, disclosure of solicitor financial information to the public, an increase of registration fee to $200 for charities with revenues over $200,000, an increase of fund-raising consultants' and solicitors' fees to $200, and written consent from charities for commercial coventures to use a charity's name along with a final accounting of coventure promotions within 10 days of a request.

Bush, Betsy Hills, (article), 8 *NonProfit Times* (10) 10 (October, 1994).

South Carolina

South Carolina's new registration law for fund raisers and charities requires point-of-solicitation disclosure statements, changes registration practices, increases bonds for solicitors from $8,000 to $15,000, changes solicitor registration from biennial to annual, and requires that solicitors, upon request, display a registration certificate. Most significantly, solicitors, upon request, must provide donors with a copy of the charity's financial statement. South Carolina is the first state to require solicitors to deliver charity financial statements.

Bush, Betsy Hills, (article), 8 *NonProfit Times* (9) 10 (September, 1994).

Other States

Nebraska charges paid solicitors only $1 and charities only $10 to register. Charities must also file their articles of incorporation.

New York charges fund raisers $800, charities $25, amd individual paid solicitors $80 to register.

Tennessee requires a professional fund-raising consultant (e.g., copywriter) to pay a $25,000 bond for direct mail solicitation, with 10% of the bond due each year, plus a $250 annual fee as "fund-raising counsel."

North Carolina requires that paid solicitors pay a $50,000 bond.

Pennsylvania fines organizations for late filings and other violations of its regulations. This law may discourage registration while penalizing honest charities that admit to raising money before registration.

North Dakota requires non-North Dakota charities to register as foreign corporations, even though the U.S. Supreme Court has held (*Quill v. North Dakota,* 504 U.S. 298) that a mail order company, whose only contact with the state is by mail or common carrier cannot be required to pay sales or use tax.

Connecticut, Pennsylvania, and Oregon require that contracts between charities and fund raisers be filed with the state. Oregon rebuttably presumes contracts that last for a period of over two years to be entered into with fraudulent intent. Pennsylvania requires that two charity officials sign the contract and file it at least 10 days prior to its effective date, or charities face a fine.

In Pinellas County, Florida, charities must observe an 8 P.M. curfew on telephone charitable solicitations, even though there is no curfew for commercial enterprises.

Utah requires that solicitors be fingerprinted and provide a recent photograph. "In person" solicitations are exempt from registration while mail and telephone solicitations are not.

Tennessee requires that any "control person" in a charity provide personal information including a 10-year employment history, home address and telephone number, date of birth, and Social Security Account Number, all subject to the state's Freedom of Information requirements.

Peters, Geoffery, (article), 9 *NonProfit Times* (6) 62 (June, 1995).

§442. FIRST AMENDMENT IMPLICATIONS IN FUND RAISING

A city may ban solicitation of vehicles from street medians if the ordinance is content-neutral and narrowly tailored to advance the city's significant interest in regulating traffic flow and safety.

Denver Publishing Co. d/b/a Rocky Mountain News v. Aurora, Colo., CO SupCt, No. 94SA36, May 15, 1995.

Charitable nonprofit organizations brought a Section 1983 First Amendment claim seeking a preliminary injunction to enjoin the Nevada Department of Transportation from enforcing licensing requirements limiting the placement of portable tables, chairs, umbrellas, boxes, and signs on public sidewalks in front of hotel and casinos in order to sell message-bearing T-shirts. The court acknowledged that the placement of portable tables was probably entitled to First Amendment protection for the purposes of a preliminary injunction. However, the use of chairs, umbrellas and boxes on public sidewalks was not afforded the same protection.

One World One Family Now, Inc. v. State of Nevada, 860 F. Supp. 1457 (D. NV, 1994).

An injunction was issued by the court after Key West, Florida denied a nonprofit organization permission to sell message-bearing "spiritual ecology" T-shirts from portable tables on public sidewalks. The court reasoned that the public's interest in safeguarding the fundamental rights of the First Amendment outweighed any competing public interest in the preservation of a historical district and in the maintenance of wholly unrestricted public walkways.

One World One Family Now v. City of Key West, 852 F. Supp. 1005 (S.D. FL, 1994).

The private organizers of a St. Patrick's Day Parade in Boston cannot be compelled, under a state public accommodations statute, to include gay rights groups in the parade. The U.S. Supreme Court ruled that the parade organizers have a First Amendment right to choose the content of their own message.

Hurley v. Irish-American Gay, Lesbian and Bisexual Group of Boston, US SupCt, No. 94–749, June 19, 1995.

A state may enforce a statute denying access to the use of criminal records for commercial purposes, but allowing release of records for noncommercial purposes, without violating the First Amendment. Thus, an alcohol treatment center and an attorney were denied access to criminal records for the purpose of direct mail solicitation of DUI drivers.

Lanphere and Urbaniak v. Colorado, State of, 21 F. 3d 1508 (10th Cir. [CO], 1994).

The Federal Communications Commission (FCC) may constitutionally enforce the Telephone Consumer Protection Act, which makes it unlawful to send unsolicited advertisements to telephone facsimile (fax) machines.

Destination Ventures, Ltd. v. FCC, 844 F. Supp. 632 (D. OR, 1994).

A city may not require disclosure of the use of funds solicited by a religious organization without excessive entanglement with religion, in violation of the First Amendment Establishment Clause (matters of ecclesiastical fiscal administration). However, requirements for registering the identity of the person making the solicitation are permissible (e.g., nature and identity of the organization, its tax-exempt status, other cities in which it is registered, and criminal histories of its officers and solicitors). It is constitutionally permissible for a city to require that a refund policy be disclosed, in full, at the time of the offer of a refund. Religious groups that are singled out for discriminatory government treatment by official harassment or conduct resembling defamation have standing to challenge the treatment in federal court.

> *Church of Scientology Flag Service Org., Inc. v. City of Clearwater,* 2 F. 3d 1514 (11th Cir. [FL], 1993).

A statute that prohibits solicitation of the general public for the benefit of law enforcement officers and organizations, while permitting other types of public servants to solicit contributions, is not constitutionally underinclusive, not unconstitutional as applied to a private fund raiser, and does not impose a "prior restraint" on the organization through enforcement through injunctive relief.

> *Auburn Police Union v. Carpenter,* 8 F. 3d 886 (1st Cir. [ME], 1993).

§443. CREATIVE FUND RAISING

Time-Tithing

Time-tithing is a new fund-raising concept developed by Ivan Scheier in *When Everyone's a Volunteer: The Effective Functioning of All-Volunteer Groups* (Energize, 1992). Through time-tithing, volunteers arrange employment for a customer and have the salary amount (sometimes minus expenses) sent to a nonprofit charitable organization. If the check is sent from the customer, and no goods or services are received by the donor, the income amount need not be listed on the donor's tax return.

> Scheier, Ivan, *When Everyone's a Volunteer: The Effective Functioning of All-Volunteer Groups* (Energize, 1992); 9 *NonProfit Times* (7) 17, (July, 1995).

Telecard Fund Raising

Nonprofits in 1995 are turning to telecards as a new method of fund raising. In 1994, telecards generated $325 million in revenue. That figure is expected to rise to between $650 million and $850 million in 1995 according to the editor of *TeleCard World,* an industry magazine. Telecard revenues are expected to top $1 billion in 1996. The cards (similar to debt cards), have a predetermined dollar amount, and are used by callers to access a toll free number. Then the computer deducts the amounts of credits used in each call. Nonprofits that sell the cards receive a few cents for every call and may receive a piece of the point of sale purchase price of the card. Telecards, thus, provide the nonprofit with a continuous base of support and, in addition, give organizations the chance to interact with the user through a prerecorded message played when the access code is dialed.

> Clolery, Paul, (article), 9 *NonProfit Times* (3) 1, 6 (March, 1995) (the article has a list of telecard vendors).

Interactive Television

The Senate Commerce Committee passed an amendment (S–652), in 1995, to help nonprofits gain access to low-cost interactive television technology by prohibiting "video dialtone" carriers from charging nonprofit and governmental entities more than they charge broadcast stations. The reform package must still clear the Senate.

> 9 *NonProfit Times* (5) 4 (May, 1995).

Fund Raising Through the Internet

Boston Children's Hospital is one nonprofit organization that is trying to raise funds over the Internet.

> *See*, Vijayan, Jaikumar, *Nonprofit Attempts Fund-Raising on Web. Computerworld*, February 3, 1997.

Regulators in Pennsylvania, New York, Connecticut, and Massachusetts all agree that nonprofits that send Internet messages, containing an appeal for funds, must comply with state laws regarding registration, financial reporting, and required disclosure statements. Unfortunately, regulators believe that the Internet may become the next tool for fraudulent solicitation.

> Bush, Betsy Hills, (article), 9 *NonProfit Times* (7) 26 (July, 1995).

ReliefNet is an Internet "web site," started in 1994, that offers information about charities and invites users to make a pledge. Though thousands of Internet users have accessed the web site, virtually no pledges have been traced to the service.

> Mehegan, Sean, (article), 9 *NonProfit Times* (2) 4 (February, 1995); A good article on how to connect to the Internet can be found in 9 *NonProfit Times* (6) 31–34 (June, 1995).

In 1995, Internet and commercial service users were largely male, between 20 and 35, well-educated, and employed in a technical job. However, this profile is rapidly changing. Nonprofits are using cyberspace primarily to post job-openings and volunteer opportunities and as an information and research source.

Ellis, Susan J., (article), 9 *NonProfit Times* (9) 18, 20 (September, 1995).

Freenets

Nonprofits are increasingly hitching a ride on community networks and "freenets," in order to communicate on a broader scale. These community networks and "freenets" are local and regional sites that highlight local offerings and often serve as technical support for smaller nonprofits that don't have a technical background. Freenets are usually nonprofits themselves, with volunteer staffs. Some freenets are available at no cost beyond a donation request. Others may charge commercial rates of $20 per month. To find out if there is already a freenet or community network in your area get on the Web and go to City.net (http://www.city.net) or CityLink (http://usacitylink.com) where a listing of sites related to cities all around the world can be found.

Sinclair, Matthew, (article), 10 *NonProfit Times* (8) 1, 6 (August, 1996).

Co-Branding of For-Profit Products

Many nonprofit organizations are co-branding for-profit products for the mutual benefit of both the profit corporation and the nonprofit. Notable examples are the Arthritis Foundation Pain Reliever (marketed by McNeil Consumer Products) and the Veterans of Foreign Wars (VFW) coffee (marketed by Tetley). More recently, the World Wildlife Fund (WWF) and Nabisco entered into an agreement to co-brand and market Barnum's Animals Crackers. In the Nabisco deal, a donation of five cents per 79-cent box of animal crackers, up to $100,000, will be made by Nabisco to the WWF for the preservation of endangered species.

See, 9 *NonProfit Times* (7) 4 (July, 1995).

The March of Dimes, in 1995, finalized an agreement with Kellogg's to put folic acid education messages on three million boxes of Kellogg's Product 19 cereal. Folic acid had been linked with the prevention of birth defects of the spine and brain. In return, Kellogg's will donate $100,000 to the March of Dimes for its promotion. The cereal boxes will also feature the March of Dimes and Kellogg's logo as well as a message concerning the importance of prenatal care and pregnancy tips.

McIver, La Vonne, (article), 9 *NonProfit Times* (9) 5 (September, 1995).

Specialty Beer Co-Branding

Nonprofit organizations are using specialty beer as a promotional tool. For example, Mystic Seaport, a museum in Mystic, Connecticut, partnered with Shipyard Brewing of Portland, Maine, to create a specialty beer. Some other businesses and nonprofits that are developing specialty beers are restaurants, zoos, libraries, bike makers, and home builders.

Khermouch, Gerry, *When Beer Is the Premium, Brandweek,* Sept. 16, 1996.

Partnering vs. Endorsement

Nonprofits are beginning to worry whether co-branding could lead to liability for endorsement of products. For example, The American Cancer Society's (ACS) deal with Smith Kline Beecham, makers of the NicoDerm anti-smoking patch, and the ACS deal with the Florida Department of Citrus (DOC) might be seen by some to be endorsement of products. Lee Cassidy, executive director of the National Federation of Nonprofits believes that the ACS should examine the products and find them to be efficient and as good as similar products. Steven Dickinson, vice president of communications at ACS, answers that, "We are involved in a joint partnership of awareness and education and we are not endorsing it specifically, therefore there is no liability on ACS for the product itself." Most agree that there should, at least, be a link between the organization's mission and the product.

Holton, Carlotta, (article), 10 *NonProfit Times* (10) 42, 44 (October, 1996).

Bartering

Nonprofits are increasingly turning to bartering in order to fill their needs. Two examples of bartering exchanges are Chicago's National Trade Association (NTA) and the Endeavor Group, based in Los Angeles. The sign-up fee for NTA can range from $659 to $1,295 depending on the organizations' number of employees. Other exchanges, such as The Endeavor Group, have no up-front fee at all.

Swarden, Carlotta, (article), 10 *NonProfit Times* 8, 14 (July, 1996).

Innovative Fund Raising

In 1996, the CARE Foundation received more than $1 million from 20 futures and options exchanges and roughly 300 trading firms worldwide when exchanges and firms agreed to give 25 cents for every contract they traded on May 2, 1996 to CARE. Ninety to ninety-five percent of the exchanges had never given to CARE before. Lynn E. Allen, the regional director of CARE's Midwest region, believes that the project could help to expand the organization's revenue from private avenues in international markets.

10 *NonProfit Times* (7) 4 (July, 1996).

Nonprofits and the Olympics

Through Aramark, a leading national food service provider at sports venues, volunteers from nonprofits staffed concessions stands at the Olympic Games. Through Aramark, organizations that worked through the entire Olympics had the opportunity to earn between $5,000 and $10,000.

Sinclair, Matthew, (article), 10 *NonProfit Times* (7) 1 (July, 1996).

900 Numbers

Fund raisers have turned to 900 numbers as a legitimate method of soliciting funds and for other uses by nonprofits.

The development director of the Maryland Public Television (MPT) network, in January of 1996, encouraged people to call a 900 number to join MPT, in a "Resolution Solution," two weeks after their December membership drive. The program generated more than $12,000 of which more than $9,600 went to MPT. Membership was also boosted by more than 350 people.

The Breast Cancer Research Foundation in New York City, in cooperation with *Marie Claire* magazine, is also using a 900 number to offer callers a chance to vote for and win one of three designer outfits, with $2.00 per call going to the Breast Cancer Research Foundation.

Sinclair, Matthew, (article), 10 *NonProfit Times* (10) 31–33 (October, 1996).

Rental of Subscribers' Names

The Circuit Court of Arlington County ruled last month that the names of Virginia residents may in fact be rented and used for commercial purposes. A subscriber had claimed that the inclusion of his name on a list that the *U.S. News and World Report* rented to *Smithsonian* magazine, violated Virginia law, and his property and privacy rights. "*U.S. News* admitted in court that without asking permission from its subscribers it sells their names, addresses, sex, income, occupation, children's age, and other demographic information," to other mailers.

Swarden, Carlotta, (article), 10 *NonProfit Times* (7) 5 (July, 1996).

"The 15-Month Year"

Many organizations experience huge losses in their membership income by allowing a 3-month lag before membership renewal. Often this "15-month year" is a result of unnecessary delays in entering people on file, a renewal strategy that lets contributions be received, even after membership has elapsed. In addition, many organizations have inefficient computer fulfillment services and customer service policies that are too protective of members. To avoid this problem, organizations should enter new members into the file immediately, start reviewing donors early, and rethink their use of fulfillment services.

Dodd, Bill, *The 15-Month Membership Year: The Silent Income Killer, Fund Raising Management,* August, 1996.

44

LAWSUITS AND LITIGATION*

*See, Bachmann, S., *NonProfit Litigation;* John Wiley and Sons, NY, 1992; *Survey of 1993 Nonprofit Case Law.* Orsi, Sakmar, and Schossberger, *University of San Francisco Law Review,* Wntr, 1995. Hopkins, Bruce R., *The Legal Answer Book for Non Profit Organizations,* John Wiley & Sons, Inc., New York, NY, 1996. Hopkins, Bruce R., *The Law of Tax Exempt Organizations,* John Wiley & Sons, Inc., New York, NY, 1992.

§444. CORPORATIONS AS PARTIES IN LAWSUITS

Web Pages Become Evidence

A company's World Wide Web pages are the newest kind of demonstrative evidence. Attorneys with clients in heavily regulated industries should pay close attention to their client's Web pages. The need for examination is constant, since even the finest Web pages are often changed.

Leibowitz, Wendy R., *Home Pages Strikes Back: In Law, Web Sites Are Surprise Weapons. The National Law Journal,* March 17, 1997.

"Truth in Testimony Rule"

The "Truth in Testimony" rule, passed by the House in 1997, may reign in liberal advocacy groups. The rule requires disclosure of federal contributions to groups testifying before the House.

Seelye, Katharine Q., (article), *The New York Times,* January 16, 1997.

Effect of Expensive Litigation on Nonprofit Organizations

The high cost of civil litigation has had significant adverse implications on charitable or nonprofit organizations. Litigation has had a particularly damaging effect on volunteers. The federal government has been trying to evaluate several systemic reforms that would protect nonprofit organizations from frivolous lawsuits. Most important are the reforms which would eliminate the doctrine of joint and several liability and cap punitive damage awards. These reforms have yet to be enacted into law.

> Abraham, Spencer, *Litigation's Stranglehold on Charities. The Public Interest,* Spring, 1997.

Attorney Fees and Attorneys

An attorney, who is the sole contract negotiator for a merchandiser/defendant in a suit for breach of contract brought by a nonprofit religious festival organizer/plaintiff, can be disqualified from the case and precluded from taking or defending depositions in the case if the attorney has firsthand nonprivileged information about the negotiations in which he was involved, and the attorney would be a necessary fact witness in the breach of contract case.

> *World Youth Day, Inc. v. Famous Artists Merchandising Exchange, Inc.* 866 F. Supp. 1297 (D. CO, 1994).

Injunctive relief, statutory damages, and attorney fees and costs are available to environmental organizations, under the Clean Water Act, against the owners and a development limited partnership of an abandoned construction site that continues to discharge solid waste into a navigable waterway, even if the development limited partnership is dissolved.

> *Hudson River Fishermen's Association v. Arcuri,* 862 F. Supp. 73 (S.D. NY, 1994).

A tenant, who prevails against a housing authority in a Section 1983 action, may be entitled to attorney fees even where his or her attorney fails to attempt to resolve the tenant's differences with the housing authority through informal channels, if after settlement of the case the tenant has to reopen the case to enforce the settlement agreement due to the housing authority's noncompliance.

> *Jackson v. Philadelphia Housing Authority,* 858 F. Supp. 464 (E.D. PA, 1994); 42 U.S.C.A. Sections 1983, 1988).

A nonprofit hospital, that seeks payment out of a tort judgment or settlement for medical services provided to a patient under a hospital lien statute, must pay its pro rata portion of legal expenses and costs incurred by the patient against the third-party tortfeasor.

> *In Re Guardianship and Conservatorship of Bloomquist,* 523 N.W. 2d 352 (NE, 1994).

A class of plaintiffs that settles its civil rights claim against Oklahoma's Department of Education, involving the education of severely handicapped school-age children at a residential facility, must prove that its action was a substantial factor or significant catalyst leading to the relief obtained and that the defendant's settlement was required by law and was not wholly gratuitous, in order to receive attorney's fees under the Individuals with Disabilities Education Act (IDEA).

> *Beard v. Teska,* 31 F.3d 942 (10th Cir. 1994); Individuals with Disabilities
> Education Act, Section 615(b)(2), (c), (e)(1,2), (e)(4)(B), as amended, 20
> U.S.C.A. Section 1415(b)(2), (c), (e)(1,2), (e)(4)(B).

An attorney parent may be entitled to attorney fees as the parent of a prevailing party in a suit brought under the Individuals with Disabilities Education Act (IDEA).

> *Miller v. W. Lafayette Community School,* 645 N.E. 2d 1085 (IN App. 2 Dist.,
> 1995).

A homeowners' association is not entitled to attorney's fees from its insurance company, for a suit involving an injunction, if the policy only requires the insurer to bear the cost of sums the insured becomes obligated to pay as damages because of "property damage."

> *Scottsdale Insurance Co. v. Deer Run Property Owner's Association, Inc.,* 642 So. 2d
> 786 (FL App. 4 Dist., 1994).

A defendant's letter, asking the nonprofit Advocacy Center for Persons with Disabilities to provide him with an attorney, is subject to the attorney-client privilege, even where the letter is addressed to a nonlawyer advocate employed by the center, if the center is an entity which provides such assistance.

> *Sanchez v. State,* 641 So. 2d 433 (FL App. 3 Dist., 1994).

Under California's statute that awards attorney's fees for actions brought by groups under the "private attorney general" doctrine, action must be brought for the interests of the association's clients and the general public.

> *California Licensed Foresters Assn. v. California State Board of Forestry,* 35 Cal. Rptr.
> 2d 396 (CA App. 3 Dist., 1994) (suit by forestry association to set aside
> increased requirements of a timber harvest plan).

A prevailing public interest group is usually entitled to reasonable attorney fees.

> *Hickel v. Southeast Conference,* 868 P. 2d 919 (AK, 1994).

In Wyoming, a nonprofit citizen group, that successfully challenges Department of Environmental Quality (DEQ) strip mining permits, is entitled to an award of attorney fees under the Wyoming Environmental Quality Act.

Powder River Basin Resource Council v. Wyoming Environmental Quality Council, 869
    P. 2d 435 (WY, 1994).

Under a Section 1988 civil rights action, a party must "prevail" in order to receive attorney's fees. Where there is no formal judgment, a party can be the "prevailing party" under the "catalyst theory," if the party can prove that the existence of the lawsuit accomplished the original objectives of the lawsuit.

Baumgartner v. Harrisburg Housing Authority, 21 F. 3d 541 (3rd Cir. [PA], 1994).

Prefatory orders granting attorney's fees, without determining the amount of the fees, are not ripe for appellate review until the ultimate order is appealed.

Winkelman v. Toll, 632 So. 2d 130 (FL App. 4 Dist., 1994) (condominium association).

The penalty provision of the Freedom of Information Act, requiring that the violation be "willfully and knowingly made," provides for strict construction of the Act in Virginia. A single violation is sufficient to justify an award of attorney fees.

RF and P Corp. v. Little, 440 S.E. 2d 908 (VA, 1994).

Sanctions may be imposed by the court where litigation is vexatious, or frivolous, or without merit. A professor and his attorney had $8,055 of sanctions imposed against them because they failed to reasonably inquire into the facts of the professor's defamation action against a university president.

Long v. Alost, 637 So. 2d 167 (LA App. 3 Cir., 1994).

Attorneys generally owe a professional obligation to their client only. However, an attorney who drafts a will may owe a duty in contract or tort to remainder beneficiaries, if the beneficiaries can show that they are in the nature of third-party intended beneficiaries of the relationship between the attorney and the client, and the attorney undertook an affirmative duty of advising the testator about estate planning and estate taxes. The law is similar for accountants.

Jewish Hosp. of St. Louis, Missouri v. Boatmen's Nat. Bank of Belleville, 633 N.E.
    2d 1267 (IL App. 5 Dist., 1994).

Bars to Legal Action

Fraud claims brought by the county against the provider of radioactive waste disposal services are barred by the doctrine of res judicata where there are judgments in earlier similar actions brought by the state.

County of Boyd v. US Ecology, Inc., 858 F. Supp. 960 (D. NE, 1994).

Federal citizens suits are barred under the Clean Water Act (CWA) if the state has commenced and is diligently prosecuting an action under comparable state law.

Sierra Club v. Colorado Refining Company, 852 F. Supp. 1476 (D. CO, 1994).

After a highway project is completed, a neighborhood association's challenge to enjoin the construction of the highway before the completion of an environmental impact statement is moot.

Neighborhood Transportation Network, Inc. v. Pena, 42 F.3d 1169 (8th Cir., 1994).

An Illinois nonprofit health care provider (cancer prevention center) does not fall within any of the four categories of health care providers listed in the Illinois malpractice limitation statute. Thus, the four-year malpractice limitation does not apply to such an institution, if it fails to inform a worker of the results of an X-ray.

Solich v. George and Anna Portes Cancer Prevention Center of Chicago, Inc., 630 N.E. 820 (IL, 1994).

In cases involving the National Environmental Policy Act of 1969, actions should be barred by laches only sparingly, where the action is brought to vindicate the public interest. However, in a 1994 case, an Indian tribal coalition waited seven years, after requests for input by the National Forest Service, to challenge the building of a telescope on an Arizona mountain. Their challenge was barred by the court because of expenditures already made by the university building the telescope, possible delays in construction, and possible loss of the project to a foreign site.

Apache Survival Coalition v. U.S., 21 F. 3d 541 (3rd Cir. [PA], 1994).

The Washington Supreme Court may retain and decide a case that is moot if it involves a question of continuing and substantial public interest. The Court must determine whether the issue is of a public or private nature, whether authoritative determination is desirable for future guidance, whether the issue is likely to recur, and whether there is genuine adverseness and quality advocacy on issues.

> *Klickitat County Citizens Against Imported Waste v. Klickitat County,* 860 P. 2d 390
>   (WA, 1993).

Citizens' group challenged the constitutionality of the Wyoming legislature's authority to delegate, to the Game and Fish Commission, the setting of seasons and bag limits for hunting. A challenge to legislation is not moot if it presents an ongoing dispute of public importance.

> *Wyoming Coalition v. Wyoming Game and Fish Commission,* 875 P. 2d 729 (WY,
>   1994).

Discovery

For information concerning what constitutes an agency subject to the application of a state freedom of information act, *see* 27 ALR 4th 742, §§5, 6.

A trial court may impose sanctions on a party that abuses the discovery process. In a 1994 case, a trial court imposed 200 hours of community service on the directors or officers of a cooperative electric company for deliberately scheming to hide material evidence from and midlead the defendant in the trial court.

> *Cap Rock Elec. Coop, Inc. v. Texas Utilities Elec. Co.,* 874 S.W. 2d 92 (TX App.
>   –El Paso, 1994).

When a society of professional journalists filed an emergency motion, requesting the Court of Appeals to unseal all sealed motions and related papers concerning the Final Report of the Iran-Contra Independent Counsel, the court held that its authority to disclose court documents is limited by the requirement that the Court of Appeals protect the rights of individuals named in a Report of the Independent Counsel.

> *In re North,* 21 F. 3d 434 (D.C. Cir., 1994).

Jurisdiction

When an injured guest sued a Mexico hotel and a hotel cooperative, the court held that the availability of a toll-free 800 number, that guests could use to make reservations in Mexico, was not enough contact to establish transactional jurisdiction over the cooperative marketing association, of which the hotel was a member. But, the association's other purposeful contacts with California supported general jurisdiction, including its authorization to do business in California, its designated agent for service of process within the state, its 295 licensed members in California, and its business office in California.

> *Hesse v. Best Western International, Inc.,* 38 Cal. Rptr. 2d 74 (CA App. 2 Dist., 1995).

An action arising under a law providing for "embargo" must be brought before the exclusive jurisdiction of the Court of International Trade. Such a law is the Marine Mammal Protection Act (MMPA) and its ban on importation of yellow fin tuna products.

> *Earth Island Institute v. Brown,* 28 F. 3d 76 (9th Cir., 1994) (action by public interest organizations brought to compel federal government agencies to comply with the MMPA).

If the United States is interested in a case, the case must be conducted and argued in the U.S. Supreme Court by the Solicitor General or his designate.

> *Federal Election Com'n v. NRA Political Victory Fund,* U.S. DC, 1994.

Under the *Younger* abstention doctrine, federal courts may abstain from interference in state proceedings, enforcing important state public policy, where there are ongoing state proceedings, that implicate important state interests, and there is adequate opportunity in the state proceedings to raise the federal questions involved.

> *Fuller v. Ulland,* 858 F. Supp. 931 (D. MN, 1994) (trustee of employee welfare benefit plan brought action under ERISA against Minnesota's Commissioner of Commerce, who initiated proceedings against the plan); *Younger v. Harris,* 401 U.S. 37 (1971).

If a plaintiff sues more than one defendant in a diversity of citizenship action, he/she must meet the requirements of diversity for each defendant. A dissolved nonprofit corporation does not have citizenship with its surviving trustee, but is a citizen where it was incorporated.

> *Omni Equities, Inc. v. Pearl S. Buck Foundation,* 850 F. Supp. 290 (E.D. PA, 1994).

A corporation was held to be not a "citizen" for diversity jurisdictional purposes in a Texas Federal District Court.

> *Tubbs v. Southwestern Bell Telephone Co.,* 846 F. Supp. 39 (D.C. TX, 1994).

Parents of disabled children need not exhaust state administrative remedies when state or local agency procedures are inadequate or futile, or when exhaustion will work severe harm upon a litigant, or when the complaint challenges generally applicable policies that are contrary to law. In such cases, the federal court may take jurisdiction of actions related to the Individuals with Disabilities Education Act (IDEA).

Learning Disabilities Association of Maryland, Inc. v. Board of Educ. of Baltimore County, 837 F. Supp. 717 (D. MD, 1993).

For more information about the Supreme Court's application of the Fourteenth Amendment's equal protection clause to foreign corporations, *see* 49 L. Ed. 2d 1296, §§10[c], 11.

Barring fraudulent joinder, a plaintiff, who states sufficient claims against nondiverse defendants, may defeat federal diversity jurisdiction. Such was the case in a 1993 suit brought by hemophiliacs and their families against a nondiverse school, physician, and foreign domiciled manufacturers of blood clotting factor, after the hemophiliacs contracted the AIDS virus.

Doe v. Armour Pharmaceutical Co., 837 F. Supp. 178 (E.D. LA, 1993).

Forum

The court considers the following factors in deciding to move an action to another forum: (1) convenience of the parties, (2) convenience of the witnesses, (3) relative ease of access to the sources of proof, (4) availability of process to compel attendance of unwilling witnesses, (5) practical problems that make the trial of the case easy, expeditious, and inexpensive, and (6) the interests of justice. The plaintiff's selection of venue is entitled to great, but not dispositive, weight. The existence of a forum selection clause, in a contract, is not entitled to dispositive weight. With a valid forum selection clause, the plaintiff, who set contrary venue must prove that the clause should not be enforced due to convenience of the witnesses, or that the interest of justice demands otherwise.

P and J G Enterprises, Inc. v. Best Western Intern., Inc., 845 F. Supp. 84 (N.D. NY, 1994).

Parties

If a plaintiff erroneously names a nonprofit defendant in his/her slip and fall action, the misnomer may be corrected at any time as long as the defendant (real party in interest) had notice that it was being sued and of the need to respond to the complaint.

> *Borg v. Chicago Zoological Soc.,* 628 N.E. 2d 306 (IL App. 1 Dist., 1993).

A deaf patient, who had trouble communicating with the staff of a hospital emergency room, did not have standing to bring suit to require the hospital to provide sign language interpreters under the Americans with Disabilities Act. The patient could not show that she would be likely to use the hospital in the future.

> *Schroedel v. New York University Medical Center,* DC SNY, No. 92 Civ. 9060 (SWK).

Intervention

A school district does not have standing to intervene as a party-defendant in a taxpayer's suit for declaratory judgment that the taxpayer's real and personal property is tax exempt, based solely upon school district claims that the school district would lose $55,000 in yearly tax revenues if the taxpayer is found to be exempt. That interest is not sufficient.

> *Alexian Brothers Sherbrooke Village v. St. Louis County,* 884 S.W. 2d 727 (MO App. E.D., 1994).

Administrative Review

An unsuccessful applicant for a Head Start grant can bring action to challenge the award of the grant to another organization under the Administrative Procedure Act. To challenge an award, the challenger must prove that agency action was arbitrary and capricious.

> *Head Start Family Education Program, Inc. v. Cooperative Educational Service Agency 11,* 46 F. 3d 629 (7th Cir., 1995).

Bivens claims, predicated upon the maladministration of federally sustained yield units of national forests, are precluded by the Administrative Procedure Act (APA) except for claims that are not characterizable as "agency action," such as postfiling retaliatory conduct on the part of government officials.

> *La Compania Ocho, Inc. v. U.S. Forest Service,* 874 F. Supp. 1242 (D. NM, 1995).

In order to establish standing to seek judicial review of a Department of Health decision that granted permits for geothermal wells and a power plant, the parties have to demonstrate that their interests were injured and that they have been involved in an administrative proceeding in which the result was an unfavorable decision against them. Adjacent property owners, who allege that they fear for their health and request contested case hearings pursuant to Department procedures, have such standing.

> *Pele Defense Fund v. Puna Geothermal Venture,* 881 P. 2d 1210 (HI, 1994).

A routine fiscal disallowance, by the Department of Health and Human Services (HHS), of costs charged to a Head Start grant, is not a "termination" of financial assistance requiring a full hearing before an administrative judge, and need only be heard by the Department Appeals Board.

> *Salt Lake Community Action Program, Inc. v. Shalala,* 11 F. 3d 1084 (D.C. Cir., 1993).

An activist-advocacy NPO charging that a public authority (national forest management/planning authority) was "arbitrary" or "capricious" has the burden of clearly proving that charge.

> *Sierra Club v. Marita,* 845 F. Supp. 1317 (D.C., WI, 1994).

Judicial review of administrative decisions is warranted only where the administrative record is void of the agency's reasoning and judicial discovery is necessary to explain the agency's action. The court may only decide if the agency's decision was "arbitrary and capricious" or had a "rational basis," and not whether the court agrees with the agency's decision. An agency decision may be challenged as being made in "bad faith" if the administrator had an "unalterably closed mind."

> *Organized Fishermen of Florida, Inc. v. Franklin,* 846 F. Supp. 1569 (S.D. FL, 1994). (Fishermen's organization brought action challenging ban on use of fish traps in federal waters.)

Consent of the parties must be obtained before a matter can be referred to a master.

> *Rapaport v. Jewish Federation of Palm Beach County, Inc.,* 627 So. 2d 617 (FL App. 4 Dist., 1993).

The rule-making requirements of the Idaho Administrative Procedure Act (IDAPA) do not apply to the interpretation of an existing rule.

> *Tomorrow's Hope, Inc. v. Idaho Dept. of Health and Welfare,* 864 P. 2d 79 (WA App. Div. 1, 1993) (Medicaid reimbursement).

A nonprofit organization must exhaust its administrative remedies before the Indiana Department of Revenue in seeking to be licensed to begin fund raising before it can seek a declaratory judgment that it is a "qualified organization" from the court.

> *Portland Summer Festival and Homecoming v. Department of Revenue,* 624 N.E. 2d
>   45 (IN App. 5 Dist., 1993).

Under the Michigan NP Health Care Corporation's Reform Act, approval of a medical doctor provider class plan by the Commissioner of Insurance is fairly conclusive. An independent hearing officer's findings are entitled to due deference, but are not per se an overruling decision or a review *de novo.* M.C.L.A. §§24.306 (1) (f).

> *In re 1987–88 Medical Doctor Provider Class Plan,* 514 N.W. 2d 471 (MI App.,
>   1994).

SLAPP Suits (Strategic Lawsuit Against Public Participation)

A neighborhood activist, who claimed that he was sued by a developer to keep him from expressing opinions protected by the First Amendment, does not have an action for malicious prosecution under Illinois law. In Illinois, the plaintiff in such SLAPP suits must suffer some "special injury" such as a seizure of property or other constructive interference with a person or property.

> *Levin v. King,* IL AppCt 1stDist, No. 1–94–2191, Mar. 31, 1995.

Settlements

Settlements of lawsuits, submitted in a consent decree, will ordinarily be approved by the court where there is overwhelming support for the settlement by the class of plaintiffs, completed research and discovery, complex and expensive litigation, and extensive relief granted.

> *Sanders v. U.S. Department of Housing and Urban Development,* 872 F. Supp. 216
>   (W.D. PA, 1994).

§447. DERIVATIVE ACTIONS AND CLASS ACTIONS

Representational Standing

In Maryland, the subscribers to health services, provided by a nonstock nonprofit corporation, have no standing to bring a derivative action on their own behalf against the corporation's former officers and directors to recover losses due to alleged mismanagement, especially where the wrongs described in the complaint are suffered only indirectly by the subscribers and are suffered directly by the corporation. In Massachusetts, only the Attorney General may bring claims of mismanagement against a charitable corporation.

O'Donnell, M.D. v. Sardegna, 646 A.2d 398 (MD, 1994).

An Ohio contractors' association does not have standing to challenge a village's bidding procedure, in a representative capacity, where many of its members failed to submit a bid on the project involved.

Ohio Contractors Association v. Bicking, 643 N.E. 2d 1088 (OH, 1994).

A trade association, whose members were engaged in construction of nonutility generating plants, challenged a Department of Environmental Protection and Energy decision granting an air pollution control permit. The association was given standing to sue because the public interest would best be served by court resolution of the questions presented, even though the organization's interest was speculative and "likened to that of a spoiler."

Independent Energy Producers of New Jersey v. New Jersey Department of Environmental Protection and Energy, 645 A.2d 166 (NJ Super. A.D., 1994).

A nonprofit corporation, that has members who have children attending a public high school, has standing to bring an action against a school board to challenge a board policy that parental consent to distribution of condoms to students was presumed, absent the parent's response to a letter sent by the schools. An organization is the appropriate entity to assert rights held by members if the organization has at least one member who has or will suffer direct, immediate, and substantial injury to his/her interest.

Parents United for Better Schools, Inc. v. School Dist. of Philadelphia Board of Education, 646 A.2d 689 (PA Cmwlth., 1994).

When local condominium boards, tenants, and residents of nearby buildings sought review of the condemnation of a city lot for construction of public housing, the court held that noncondemnees do not have standing to challenge a condemnor's action under Eminent Domain Procedure Law.

East Thirteenth St. Com. Ass'n v. New York, 641 N.E. 2d 1368 (NY, 1994).

A representative association has standing to challenge a city's determination to award a land disposition agreement, for four city-owned buildings, to a developer, where the purpose of the association and its interests fall within the "zone of interests" defined by state and city laws regarding procedures for agency action concerning the adding of low-income housing. The individual members have standing to challenge the city's transfer of property where they are the potential residents of low-income housing.

> *Lee v. New York City Dept. of Housing Preservation and Development,* 615 N.Y.S. 2d
> 592 (Sup., 1994).

A labor union lacked *individual standing* to sue an employer for damages for violating its members' rights under the 1989 Worker Adjustment and Retraining Notification Act (WARN) because the union failed to allege any personal injury that was fairly traceable to the employer's unlawful conduct and was likely to be redressed by the requested relief. The union was also denied *associational standing* based on the requirement that neither the claim asserted nor the relief requested must require the participation of individual members. Under the WARN Act, aggrieved employees must prove their damages on a case-by case basis.

> *United Food and Commercial Workers International Union Local 751 v. Brown Group
> Inc.,* CA 8, No. 94–1929, Apr. 3, 1995.

The court may certify a nationwide class in a product liability action, for the issue of liability, and then permit individual trials on the issues of causation and damages. Such certification is not precluded by the Seventh Amendment right to jury trial or differing state product liability laws.

> *In re Copley Pharmaceutical Inc.,* DC WY, MDL No. 1013, 4/25/95 (concerning
> contaminated bronchodilators). *But see contra In re Rhone-Poulenc Rorer Inc.,*
> 32 F. 3d 851, 63 LW 2579 (CA 7 1995) (concerning hemophiliacs).

A citizens' group has standing, under the National Environmental Policy Act (NEPA), based upon injury to their health, recreational use, and enjoyment of national forests, to challenge the Forest Service's decision to allow herbicide use as a part of a reforestation program.

> *Salmon River Concerned Citizens v. Robertson,* 32 F. 3d 1346 (9th Cir., 1994).

Animal welfare organizations were denied standing to challenge, under the Laboratory Animal Welfare Act, a United States Department of Agriculture (USDA) regulation, allowing individual facilities to set standards for exercising and housing laboratory animals. The organization alleged factual injury was not particularized or concrete, the organization was not in the zone of interests protected by the Act, and the individual members lacked individual standing to bring the action.

Animal Legal Defense Fund, Inc. v. Espy, 29 F. 3d 720 (DC Cir., 1994).

Consumers have Article III standing, under both the Food, Drug, and Cosmetic Act and the National Environmental Policy Act (NEPA), to challenge approval of an application to the Food and Drug Administration (FDA) for the use of bovine growth hormone for dairy cattle. However, nonprofit organizations involved in environmental, economic, and ethical issues raised by the use of the hormone, dairy farmers, and health care professionals could not prove a sufficient "injury" or "threatened injury" to gain standing in the same case.

Barnes v. Shalala, 865 F. Supp. 550 (W.D. WI, 1994).

A lawsuit was brought by an ex utero embryo, an association devoted to Down's syndrome research, and an individual with Down's syndrome, seeking an injunction to stop the submission of an advisory panel's report regarding human fetal tissue research to the Department of Health and Human Services. The court held that an embryo, allegedly representing 20,000 other embryos, had no standing to maintain suit. The nonprofit association devoted to sponsoring research was denied standing after its claim, that resumption of research would reduce funding, was found to be speculative.

Doe v. Shalala, 862 F. Supp. 1421 (D. MD, 1994).

An association of chiropractors had standing to challenge a statutory scheme, under which the State of New Jersey entered into consent agreements with medical practitioners who had been accused of insurance fraud, where some of the members had been injured, the interests the association sought to protect were germane to its purpose of protecting its members from illegal conduct adversely affecting its membership, and participation of individual members was not required for relief.

Chiropractic Alliance of New Jersey v. Parisi, 854 F. Supp. 299 (D. NJ, 1994).

An organization, under the Federal Housing Act, must demonstrate actual or threatened injury in fact that is fairly traceable to the alleged illegal action, and that is likely to be redressed by a favorable court decision in order to show standing.

Ragin v. Harry Macklowe Real Estate Co., 6 F. 3d 898 (2nd Cir. [NY], 1993).

In New Mexico, environmental associations have standing, under the Prehistoric and Historic Sites Preservation Act, to bring action against a city to enjoin planning, funding, contracting, and construction in areas bordering a national monument. Their standing is based on the use of, enjoyment of, benefit from, and substantial interest in protecting the monument. However, a preliminary injunction is not warranted if the association cannot prove an adverse impact on the national monument, from the city's design, that is worse than the impact from the associations' proposed alternatives.

National Trust for Historic Preservation v. City of Albuquerque, 874 P. 2d 798 (N.M. App., 1994).

An advocacy organization has "standing" when its members have standing individually, the interests it protects are germane to its organizational purpose, and the subject matter of the suit does not require individual participation of the members. There is no "standing" if the affected individual is not a member.

Association for Retarded Citizens of Dallas v. Dallas County Mental Health and M.R.C. Board, 19 F. 3rd 234 (C.A. 5 [TX], 1994).

An Immigration Reform and Control Act (IRCA) meant to protect the rights of illegal (undocumented) aliens does not give "standing" to an NPO that is intended to give legal aid to such persons to challenge IRCA regulations. That is not what the statute was meant to do, and such challenges would impose a heavy burden on the Immigration and Naturalization Service (I.N.S.).

I.N.S. v. Legalization Assistance Project, 114 S. Ct. 422 (Nov. 26, 1993); 8 U.S.C. §1255a.

The Wild Bird Conservation Act has an exception to the Act's moratorium on importation of certain birds. An environmental association has "standing" to challenge this, as the members have a valid interest in observing birds, if its enforcement would injure them.

Humane Society of U.S. v. Babbitt, 849 F. Supp. 814 (D.C. DC, 1994).

An administrative decision by the Division of Environmental Protection (DEP) involving the denial of a mining permit may not be reviewed *de novo* by a Circuit Court so that the Circuit Court can substitute its opinion, unless the administrative decision is a clearly unwarranted exercise of discretion or is clearly erroneous.

Francis O. Day Co., Inc. v. Director, Div. of Environmental Protection of West Virginia Dept. of Commerce, Labor and Environmental Resources, 443 S.E. 2d 602 (WV, 1994).

In complex litigation that involves taxation and public matters it is not necessary to join every citizen who might be subject to higher taxes.

> *San Juan Water Commission v. Taxpayers and Water Users of San Juan County,* 860
> P. 2d 748 (NM, 1993).

The members of a class of asbestos victims were denied intervention in a class action suit because the court held that the members would be able to appeal the district court's approval or disapproval of any settlement in the case ("the collateral order doctrine"). They were further denied immediate appeal of the denial of intervention.

> *Carlough v. Amchem Products, Inc.,* 5 F. 3d 707 (3rd Cir. [PA], 1993); *see also Retired*
> *Chicago Police Association v. City of Chicago,* 7 F. 3d 1492 (7th Cir. [IL], 1993).

A nonprofit environmental corporation has standing to compel the Forest Service to promulgate rules governing a recreational area where there is an unreasonably delayed promulgation of final regulations.

> *Hells Canyon Preservation Council v. Richmond,* 841 F. Supp. 1039 (D. OR,
> 1993).

"In sum, a condominium association has a statutory right to file suit on behalf of its unit owners for breach of implied warranty of fitness and merchantability for construction defects affecting the common interest. Such a suit must be filed within the general time limits set out in chapter 95. But, the commencing of this limitations period shall be tolled until control of the association passes from the developer to the unit owners."

> *Charley Toppino & Sons, Inc. v. Seawatch at Marathon Condo. Association Inc.,* #80,
> 872 and 3, FL Supr. Ct., Nov. 10, 1994.

Two associations of residential property owners sued to challenge an ordinance which rezoned nearby property for intensive commercial development. The associations were denied standing because the alleged diminution of value of the property would be suffered by the individual homeowners, rather than the association.

> *Westwood Forum, Inc. v. City of Springfield,* 634 N.E. 2d 1154 (IL App. 4 Dist.,
> 1994).

An environmental activist group, that filed a citizen suit against a city for violations of the state water quality standards and of the Clean Water Act (CWA), has no standing to bring a citizen suit where the National Pollution Discharge Elimination System (NPDES) permit failed to translate water quality standards into end-of-pipe effluent limitations for the combined sewer overflow (CSO) outfalls at issue.

> *Northwest Environmental Advocates v. City of Portland,* 11 F. 3d 900 (9th Cir.
> [OR], 1993).

An association has standing if its individual members have standing and the case does not require individual participation of each injured party. Conflicts of interest in the organization require individual participation of the members. Such conflicts, within a police association, led to a denial of standing for an association that challenged a sergeant promotion procedure.

> *West Valley City Fraternal Order of Police Lodge No. 4 v. Nordfelt,* 869 P. 2d 948
> (UT App., 1993). *See also Retired Chicago Police Association v. City of Chicago,*
> 7 F. 3d 584 (7th Cir. [IL], 1993).

Condo owners may sue, in Florida, over defects in common areas, but must represent the interests of other unit owners, and need not depend solely on corporate action.

> Assoc. Press item, *St. Petersburg (FL) Times* report of FL Supr. Ct. decision,
> (Nov. 11, 1993).

An association for deaf persons does not have standing to seek injunctive relief against a hospital that failed to provide interpreters so that a deaf woman could effectively communicate with a physician about the health of her husband. The association failed to show that its members would have standing to sue in their own right. Associations must also show that the interests they seek to protect are germane to the organization's purpose and that neither the claim asserted nor relief requested requires participation of individual members.

> *Aikins v. St. Helena Hosp.,* 843 F. Supp. 1329 (N.D. CA, 1994).

A class of homeless persons sued a city to prevent the targeting of violation of certain ordinances which they alleged penalized them for their engaging in their life-sustaining activity. The homeless were denied a preliminary injunction against the enforcement of the ordinances because, in their Eighth Amendment claim, they failed to show that they were punished for their "status," and not for their conduct. There is no violation of equal protection if there is no intent by the city to discriminate and the program includes directives for nondiscriminatory enforcement. Such "targeting" is constitutional.

> *Joyce v. City and County of San Francisco,* 846 F. Supp. 843 (N.D. CA, 1994).

Standing Under RICO

A nonprofit corporation that claimed to represent residential real estate owners does not have standing to bring action against a utility, under the Racketeer Influenced and Corrupt Organizations Act (RICO), alleging that the utility schemed to submit false information to an Arizona commission in order to secure higher utility rates, absent facts sufficient to show injury to its "business or property." To invoke the civil remedies of RICO, the plaintiff must show: (1) violation of the RICO section, (2) injury to business or property, and (3) the RICO violation was the proximate cause of the plaintiff's injury. Also, the "filed rate doctrine" bars *taxpayers* from challenging rates approved by a legislatively created agency or utility rate-setting scheme. However, utilities can be sued for antitrust. The *government* can sue utilities for criminal sanctions, RICO violations, and other equitable relief.

> *Sun City Taxpayers' Association v. Citizens Utilities Co.,* 847 F. Supp. 281 (D. CT, 1994).

Groups advocating the rights of the mentally ill have class action standing under the Protection and Advocacy for the Mentally Ill Individuals Act to seek injunctive relief against operators of an adult care facility in an action based upon the Racketeer Influenced and Corrupt Organizations Act (RICO), state law, and federal civil rights law.

> *Trautz v. Weisman,* 846 F. Supp. 1160 (S.D. NY, 1994).

An abortion clinic has standing to bring a Racketeer Influenced and Corrupt Organizations Act (RICO) action against antiabortion groups, where the clinic alleges that the groups conspired to use force to induce clinic staff and patients to stop work and obtain medical services elsewhere, and where there are allegations that the business and/or property interests of the clinic were damaged.

> *National Organization for Women, Inc. v. Scheidler,* 114 S. Ct. 798 (U.S. IL, 1994).

Where each member's injuries would differ, during a 10-year period of alleged RICO schemes, a nonprofit organization, representing residential real estate owners in a city, has no standing to bring a RICO action against water and sewer utilities alleging that the parent corporation was involved in a scheme to submit false information to secure approval of excessive utility rates.

> *Sun City Taxpayers' Association v. Citizens Utilities Co.,* 45 F. 3d 58 (2nd Cir., 1995).

§449. CONSTITUTIONAL PROBLEMS IN NPO LITIGATION

When a nonprofit alliance of Virginia coal producers sued the state of Illinois for discrimination against purchase of its coal, the court held that a state statute may violate the commerce clause by discriminating against out-of-state interests or by benefiting in-state interests, even without demonstrable economic effects.

Alliance for Clean Coal v. Craig, 840 F. Supp. 554 (N.D. IL, 1993).

Minority Organizations Favoritism

A municipal ordinance, giving preference on city contracts to minority organizations (organizations having 51 percent minority members), was attacked as an unconstitutional violation of the 14th Amendment Equal Protection Clause. *Held:* that the complainant has *"standing"* to sue, and "need not allege that he would have obtained the benefit (of getting the contract) but for the barrier" of the ordinance.

Northeast Florida Chapter of Associated General Contractors of Amer. v. City of Jacksonville, 113 S. Ct. 2297 (1993).

A citizens' action group cannot challenge the method of appointing members to the city board of police commissioners by using the Voting Rights Act of 1965. The Act allows challenge to elected officials only where the challenge is based on the inequality of opportunities enjoyed by a class of voters.

African-American Citizens for Change v. St. Louis Board of Police Commissioners, 24 F. 3d 1052 (8th Cir. [MO], 1994).

A state may pass statutes allowing for additional incentives in pension plans for police officers and fire-fighters, in the form of increased retirement benefits, without violating equal protection. The additional benefits are sometimes necessary in order to recruit employees into more dangerous occupations.

Erie City Retirees Association v. City of Erie, 838 F. Supp. 1048 (W.D. PA, 1993).

Free Speech and Constitutional Law

Free speech, picketing, and demonstrations of NPOs or members are not unlimited. Thus, the expressed views of abortion opponents, that are carried to the point of substantial amounts of harassment and name calling against patrons of abortion clinics, may be enjoined by courts, or restricted by court order.

Operation Rescue v. Women's Health Center, Inc., 18 FLW S–559 (FL Oct. 28, 1993); 16 A Am. Jur. 2d Constitutional Law §519 (1993 pocket supp., p. 109).

Standing to Sue

Low-income minority residents of city public housing projects have standing, on behalf of all former, current, and future minority residents of public housing projects, to bring statutory and constitutional claims of discrimination based on alleged racial discrimination and segregation in public housing and assistance programs.

Comer v. Cisneros, 37 F. 3d 775 (2nd Cir., 1994).

The residents of a challenged voting district have standing to bring an equal protection action to challenge redistricting legislation that results in creation of the district.

Miller v. Johnson, 115 S. Ct. 2475 (U.S. GA, 1995).

Workers' compensation claimants have standing to bring action for mandamus and quo warranto relief to challenge the constitutionality of the Workers' Compensation Statute in Kansas.

Sedlak v. Dick, 887 P. 2d 1119 (KS, 1995).

A plaintiff, who resides in a racial gerrymandering district, has been denied equal treatment under the equal protection clause due to the legislature's reliance on racial criteria. Therefore, such plaintiffs have standing to challenge the legislature's action. If a plaintiff does not live in the district and has suffered no special harm through racial classification, there will be no standing granted.

U.S. v. Hays, 115 S. Ct. 2431 (U.S. LA, 1995).

A claim under Section 1983 of the federal civil rights statute must allege that the defendant acted under color of state law and deprived the plaintiff of a right, privilege, or immunity secured by the Constitution or laws of the United States. A nonprofit corporation, that contracts with the state to conduct accreditation services for a penitentiary, is not acting under color of state law unless the state requires or is otherwise significantly involved in its conduct, or if the nongovernmental entity exercises a traditional state function.

Jensen v. Zuern, 517 N.W. 2d 118 (N.D. App., 1994).

Individual members of an organization have to independently meet standing requirements in order to have Article III standing. Those requirements are (1) injury to legally protected interest, (2) causal connection between asserted injury and challenged conduct (fairly traceable to the challenged conduct and not the result of independent action by a third party not before the court), and (3) likelihood that the injury will be redressed by a favorable decision on the merits of the case.

> *Freedom Republicans, Inc. v. Federal Election Commission,* 13 F. 3d 412 (D.C. Cir., 1994).

45

AMENDMENTS, EXTENSIONS, AND MERGERS

§451. AMENDMENTS AND CORRECTIONS OF CHARTERS

Members of a nonprofit credit bureau were able to overturn an amendment to their articles of incorporation, where the minimum requirements set forth in the Louisiana statute for meetings called for amending articles of incorporation were not met. The minimum statutory requirements must be observed where the corporation's articles of incorporation do not sufficiently set forth a "method" (e.g., timeliness of notice, percentage of votes required for a resolution to pass, percentage of members required to constitute a quorum), to be utilized in amending the corporate charter.

Lain v. Credit Bureau of Baton Rouge, 637 So. 2d 1080 (LA App. 1 Cir., 1994).

§452. FORMS OF AMENDMENTS

FORM NO. 184S
Proposed Amendment to a Declaration of Condominium

**PROPOSED AMENDMENT
TO THE DECLARATION OF CONDOMINIUM
_____ CONDOMINIUM
BUILDING B, INC.**

Additions indicated by underlining.
Deletions indicated by ~~striking through~~.

It is proposed that Article XVIII, Section 12 be amended as follows:

> Section 12 Pets. As of the effective date of this provision, only cats and dogs which are presently residing in the condominium in accordance with the provisions of this section heretofore existing, may continue to reside in condominium units, provided, however, that they continue to meet the criteria previously established, and hereafter stated, with respect to their occupancy. After the effective date of this provision

(which shall be the date upon which this language is approved by the membership for inclusion in the Declaration of Condominium) no new pets may be brought upon the condominium property, or kept within a condominium unit. In the event that an existing cat or dog dies, or is permanently removed from the premises, the cat or dog may not be replaced. As to pets presently existing in accordance with this paragraph, the pet:

i) may not exceed 20 pounds at maturity;

ii) may not become a nuisance to any other unit owner;

iii) must be leashed at all times when not in the unit, and hand carried in the hallways, elevators, lobbies and/or garage;

iv) may not be bred or maintained for any commercial purpose; and

v) the owner of the pet must comply with all the rules and regulations which may be adopted from time to time, with respect to the keeping of same in condominium units and as it relates to their access upon the common elements.

~~No pets shall be permitted without the written consent of the Board of Directors and any such consent may be terminated at any time.~~ All pets which ~~are~~ have been, or are hereafter approved, and their owners, shall be subject to such reasonable rules and regulations as the Board of Directors may from time to time promulgate.

FORM NO. 184SS
Proposed Amendment to Rules and Regulations of Condominium

PROPOSED RULES AND REGULATIONS
_____ CONDOMINIUM
BUILDING B, INC.

Additions indicated by underlining.
Deletions indicated by ~~striking through~~.

Pets

1. As of the effective date of this rule, no new pets may be brought upon the condominium property or kept within a condominium unit. As to existing pets, pets are not allowed unless a pet application has been approved in writing by the Board of Directors, and then only one pet, weighing less than 20 pounds, per unit. Pets must be hand-carried when in the hallways, elevators, lobbies or the garage. An exception is a seeing-eye dog for the sight impaired. Failure to observe the rules regarding pets may result in rescinding the pet authorization.

2. When outside in the Building B property areas, the pet must be hand leashed. Do not walk your pet where it might damage the shrubs and plantings.

3. A pet walking area has been designated along the road on the northeast side of the building. Pet waste must be removed from grounds immediately and disposed of properly by the pet owner.

§453. AMENDMENTS OF BYLAWS

Revision of Standards

When the American Kennel Club adopted revised standards for Labrador retrievers, providing for disqualification of dogs from shows for failing to meet height standards, breeders of championship Labrador retrievers brought antitrust action as well as action on other grounds. A preliminary injunction against the implementation of the revised standards was denied by the court after the breeders failed to show the requisite irreparable harm by failing to disclose the height of their dogs, and failed to indicate a total destruction or imminent threat to their business as a whole. The court reasoned that a preliminary injunction prior to a decision on the merits of the case would pose a hardship to the organization through the undermining of their credibility.

Jessup v. American Kennel Club, Inc., 862 F. Supp. 1122 (S.D. NY, 1994).

§455. CONSOLIDATIONS AND MERGERS

See also, Chapter 41, §422.

Hospital Mergers

The FTC has jurisdiction to challenge asset acquisitions of nonprofit hospitals through Sections 7 and 11 of the Clayton Act, 15 U.S.C. §§18, 21.[1]

Incentives to engage in anticompetitive conduct are not negated by nonprofit status. In order to advance goals such as earning additional revenues to further an institution's financial health or to add new benefits for employees, nonprofit hospitals may cause prices to rise through collusion with other hospitals or as a monopoly provider, at the expense of consumer. The FTC's concern in analyzing mergers is consumer welfare. Social goals cannot justify supracompetitive pricing that results in or will result from a merger.[2]

1. *FTC v. University Health,* 938 F. 2d, at 1214–17; *United States v. Rockford Memorial Corp.,* 898 F. 2d, at 1280–81 (dictum); *Adventist Health System/West,* D. 9234 (Order dated August 2, 1991).

2. *See FTC v. University Health,* 938 F. 2d at 1224; *Hospital Corp. of America v. FTC,* 807 F. 2d at 1390–91; *United States v. Rockford Memorial Corp.,* 898 F. 2d at 1285.

The Federal Trade Commission blocked the merger of two hospitals, stating that the merger would have created an anticompetitive situation in the Pueblo, Colorado area. However, the decisions in this antitrust area may seem inconsistent. In January, 1994, the U.S. Department of Justice approved a similar merger in Manchester, New Hampshire. One of the factors considered by the FTC is whether consumers have other alternatives in case of anticompetitive price increases.

8 *NonProfit Times* (4) 4 (April, 1994).

Letters of intent to merge may involve tortious interference with contracts if a nonprofit can prove that execution of the letters prevented another affiliation, which resulted in damages.

See Charleston Area Medical Center, Inc. v. Blue Cross and Blue Shield Mut. of Ohio, Inc., 6 F. 3d 243 (4th Cir. [WV], 1993).

See also, Nonprofit Hospital Mergers and Section 7 of the Clayton Act: Closing an Antitrust Loophole, Laura L. Stephens, *Boston University Law Review,* March 1995 75 n2 p477–503; *Medical Group Mergers Require Plan Restructure,* (employee benefits plan) Mand and Marblestone, *Taxation for Lawyers,* May–June 1995 23 n6 p329–337.

After an unusually public decision-making process, the board of Atlantic Care Medical Center chose to affiliate with the nonprofit North Shore Medical Center/Partners Healthcare in April of 1997. AtlantiCare, the only hospital in Lynn, Massachusetts, worked with a citizens' task force during the effort to choose between nonprofit and for profit bidders. AtlantiCare, with 150 beds, suffered a $2 million loss in 1996. Part of the affiliation deal with the North Shore involves a guarantee of AtlantiCare's debt, which totals $38 million.

Meyer, Harris, *This Hospital For Sale, Hospitals & Health Networks,* May 20, 1997.

Remedy for Failed Hospital Mergers

After the failure of merger negotiations with for-profit provider American SurgiCare, the nonprofit Monument Valley Hospital, in Monument Valley, was forced to close on July 19, 1996. However, Monument Valley Hospital's owner arranged for an agreement with a county health agency, the San Juan Health Care Services, and a federal agency, the Indian Health Service to finance the restoration of emergency care services and the opening of an ambulatory clinic.

> Snow, Charlotte, *Hospital's Closing Doesn't Halt Care, Modern Healthcare,*
>   Sept. 2, 1996.

Areas for Due Diligence Investigation in Mergers

In general, both organizations should inspect the other organization's articles of incorporation, the bylaws, the recent minutes of board meetings, and relevant licenses and permits. In the financial area, audited financial statements for the previous three–five years, contracts (as both buyer and supplier) and leases, debt instruments (if any), annual budget for the past two years and future year, program budgets for the same periods, accounts receivable analysis, accounts payable analysis, information about capital assets, current status of tax obligations, insurance policies, information about restricted funds (if any), information about pending litigation, information about current or recent government audits, regulatory filings, and copies of fundraising material should all be inspected carefully. With respect to personnel, careful inspection should be made of the salary schedule, including full-time equivalencies, a list of active employees, information about benefits packages, personnel policies, collective bargaining information (if applicable), pending claims (overtime, unpaid wages), history of workers' compensation claims, and unemployment claim history.

> McLaughlin, T., *Seven Steps to a Successful Nonprofit Merger,* National Center
>   for Nonprofit Boards, (Washington, DC, 1996).

Mergers in General

The three most important factors to consider in a merger are preserving your mission, maintaining your values, and the constituency you have as well as the potential for an expanded constituency. An ad hoc committee should first discuss options and then take a formal vote to merge. In the next stage, a neutral facilitator and lawyers should be hired to deal with the paperwork. The staff needs to keep focused on the mission.

In response to decreased funding, slow ticket sales, and high costs in renting theater space, one of Chicago's oldest theater companies, Organic Theater, has agreed to merge with Touchstone Theater and become the Organic-Touchstone Theater. Such mergers are becoming more common in the arts community, usually fueled by decreases in federal funding.

Lazare, Lewis, *Marrying for Life: Chi Nonprofs Merge, Variety,* July 22, 1996.

Agricultural Cooperative Mergers

A provision in the articles and bylaws of an agricultural association that entitles the holder of common stock to vote on any question or issue does not require that a shareholder approve mergers in the absence of any language mentioning merger. The Agricultural Cooperatives Act that permits one-member, one-vote approval for a merger supersedes contrary provisions of the Business Corporation Law requiring shareholder approval. Where shareholder approval is not required for merger, shareholders have no dissenters' rights or interest in the association's reserves.

Indiana Farm Bureau Coop Association, Inc. v. AgMax, Inc., 622 N.E. 2d 206 (IN App. 5 Dist., 1993).

Consolidation's Effect on Contracts

Not-for-profit fire companies brought suit against a new consolidated fire district, organized by a municipal ordinance, after the new district demanded new leases for fire-fighting services. The court held that the consolidation into one new fire district did not give the new district power to abrogate the obligations that the dissolved districts had with the not-for-profit fire companies which had served the former districts under leases. A consolidated borough remains responsible for the debts and liabilities of its predecessors.

Cherry Hill Fire Company No. 1 v. Cherry Hill Fire District No. 3, 646 A. 2d 1150 (NJ Super. Ch., 1994).

Conversion to For-Profit Status

New York-based Empire Blue Cross and Blue Shield introduced its plan to go public in September, 1996. As a nonprofit, it has provided insurance for everyone that other insurance companies found too expensive. Many of those who are difficult to insure fear that they will lose their health insurance if Empire becomes a public company. Empire plans to establish a foundation for hardship cases.

Novarro, Leonard, *Empire Strikes Back; New York's Empire Blue Cross & Blue Shield Teetered Near Bankruptcy Before Rebounding. Now It's the Latest Blues Plan Aiming to Go Public, Hospitals & Health Networks,* March 20, 1997.

The 4,200-member New York Macintosh User Group (NYMUG), a nonprofit group that has been threatened with bankruptcy, has been acquired by consulting and services firm, Charles River Computers (CRC). CRC, in an unprecedented move, will turn NYMUG into a for-profit subsidiary. The deal with CRC will allow NYMUG (which had closed its doors) to continue to operate, despite a $100,000 debt. CRC is not tied to any particular third-party vendor. Thus, NYMUG, which had rejected offers of corporate sponsorship in the past, feels less wary that it will become a "mouthpiece" for an Apple-related firm. NYMUG will now be professionally run, and CRC will gain additional support in the Macintosh community and access to expertise.

Picarille, Lisa, *Mac User Group Saved, Computerworld,* January 27, 1997.

Under the Hill-Burton Act, the government may recover funds granted for construction of nonprofit hospitals if the hospital involved changes to for-profit status within 20 years of its substantial completion. However, a transferee, who acquires the hospital after the 20 years has lapsed, is not liable for repayment of the funds to the government, even where the hospital changes its status within the 20-year period.

U.S. v. NBC Bank—Rockdale, 7 F. 3d 63 (5th Cir. [TX], 1993).

For more information regarding the recovery of funds by the United States, pursuant to provisions of the Hill-Burton Act, as amended (42 USCS §291 (i)), of federal funds used in the construction of a nonprofit health facility sold to a profitmaking organization or otherwise ceasing to function as a nonprofit health facility, *see* 60 ALR Fed. 686.

Nonprofit hospital ventures, which end up in a sale to for-profit organizations should be scrutinized for the manner in which they deal with their responsibility to constituents. The sale of Rose Health Care System in Denver, Colorado, was applauded for the directors' decision to convince the buyer to continue Rose's charitable work. A similar sale of HealthONE, also in Denver, was criticized by community groups for failing to provide for charitable efforts.

Meyer, Harris, *The Lure, Hospitals & Health Networks,* June 5, 1996. *See also,* Cain, Carr, and Zacharias, *The Negotiation,* (selling the not-for-profit health care facility), *Hospitals & Health Networks,* June 5, 1996. Meyer,

Harris, *The Deal,* (joint ventures between for-profit and not-for-profit health care companies), *Hospitals & Health Networks,* June 5, 1996. Hudson, Terese, *The Fear Factor,* (not-for-profit hospitals seeking for-profit status may hurt community), *Hospitals & Health Networks,* June 5, 1996.

As more nonprofit health care providers choose to become for-profit companies, it is critical that their public assets be set aside for public benefit instead of executive compensation and venture capital. The public, media, and government should carefully scrutinize such conversions. There should be public notice and hearings. An independent foundation should receive the monetary equivalent of the non-profit provider's assets when a conversion happens. For a discussion of recent conversions in California and Georgia, *see,* Bell, Judith, *Vigilance is Needed to Protect Charitable Assets, Modern Healthcare,* June 17, 1996.

The trend of nonprofit healthcare providers converting to for-profit enterprises leads to questions about how poor people will have access to health care and how the public should be compensated when a nonprofit changes status. More consolidations are likely, partly because of overcapacity. In fact, New York has banned investor-owned hospitals.

Pallarito, Karen, *Hospital Conversions Raise Thorny Issues, Modern Healthcare,*
    June 17, 1996.

The Ocean Federal Savings Bank of Brick Township, New Jersey is using excess profits from its conversion to stock ownership to incorporate the nonprofit Ocean Financial Foundation. This move will help the bank meet the Community Reinvestment Act requirements and foster public good will. Ocean may donate up to $12.5 million to the foundation, which will help community groups and medical or educational facilities.

Epstein, Jonathan D., *N.J. Thrift to Create a Nonprofit to Soak Up Conversion
    Funds, American Banker,* April 2, 1996.

In 1996, Colorado is close to allowing health care nonprofits to convert to stock insurance companies. The condition of conversion is that the companies establish nonprofit foundations to hold the stock. The state's House will consider an amendment that would use "fair market value" rather than "fair value" language to determine the value of the assets being converted. Another amendment would repeal a law that allows nonprofits to mutualize.

Niedzielski, Joe, *Colorado For-Profit Conversion Bill Pending, National Underwriter
    Life & Health-Financial Services Edition,* March 18, 1996.

For-Profit hospital chains that acquire nonprofit hospitals must set up charitable foundations, according to federal law. In some places this trend has increased hospital care for indigent patients, such as in Alexandria, Louisiana, where the Rapides Hospital was acquired by Columbia HCA Healthcare Corp.

> Page, Leigh, *For-Profit Conversions Spawn New Sources of Charity, American Medical News,* April 22, 1996. *See also, For-Profit Conversions Must Come With a Commitment to Community, Modern Healthcare,* April 15, 1996.

In 1996, Nebraska passed legislation aimed at regulating the acquisition of a nonprofit hospital by a for-profit hospital company. Nebraska is mandating public interest criteria that must be met to make an acquisition valid. All sales will be reviewed and approved by the Nebraska health department and attorney general. The law also established public disclosure of acquisition-related data and documents.

> Burda, David, *Neb. Wages War on Hospital Takeovers, Modern Healthcare,* May 20, 1996.

Faced with huge government cuts in funding, the National Public Radio is looking into the possibility of transforming itself into a money-making profit enterprise.

> Tolan, Sandy, *Must NPR Sell Itself?, The New York Times,* July 16, 1996.

Florida regulators are challenging the National Council on Compensation Insurance's (NCCI) plans to convert to a for-profit entity. The NCCI has issued a rate filing which would drop workers' compensation rates by an average of 3 percent in 1997. That rate reduction could affect carriers who are stockholders in the NCCI.

> Adams, Michael H., *NCCI Profit Plans May Cause Interest Conflict: Regulators, National Underwriter Property & Causality Risk & Benefits Management,* Sept. 23, 1996.

Empire Blue Cross, which is suffering from deregulation of hospital rates in New York State, is asking the state to become a for-profit company.

> Freudenheim, Milt, *Empire Blue Cross is Asking New York State to Become A For-Profit Company, The New York Times,* Sept. 26, 1996.

§456. FORMS FOR MERGERS AND CONSOLIDATIONS

FORM NO. 200S
Report on Proposal for Conversion from Business to Nonprofit Organization
(Condo-Coop Golf Club Development)

SUMMARY OF PRINCIPAL ACTIVITIES
RE PROPOSED PURCHASE OF _____ C.C. FROM _____
BY RESIDENTS/LOT OWNERS/CLUB MEMBERS ("Community")
FALL, 1990 TO SUMMER, 1991

Determination of Community Interest/Support

Three broad actions were taken in the Fall of 1990 after indications from _____ in the Summer of 1990 that it might be interested in selling the Club:

1—General meeting of _____ CC Community was called for 9/10/90. More than 200 people overflowed dining room at Club. Support appeared to be virtually unanimous. About 20 individuals across all main categories of residential subsections and classes of membership were nominated to serve on an advisory group to launch studies/make recommendations.

2—Follow-up mini-survey was sent to entire Community (889 addresses at the time). More than 50% responded, of which 70% were "very" or "somewhat" interested, with most of the rest awaiting more information.

3—Request was made of Community for contributions to operating fund for advisory group. More than $70,000 was received. (Details following.)

Organization of Advisory Group

Planning Committee of 27 people was formed at meeting 9/25/90. The title incorporated was _____CC, Inc. Of the 27, 9 were elected as Trustees. Of the 9, 4 were elected as Officers: President, Vice President, Treasurer, Secretary.

Six subcommittees were formed—capitalizing on those with particularly-pertinent backgrounds where possible: Finance; Property Evaluation; Membership; Bylaws; Communications; Transition.

Mission/Goals of _____ CC, Inc.

Simplified Mission was set: "To establish a financially sound private Club owned and operated by the members for their benefit and enjoyment." In support of the Mission, 12 discrete goals were set, having to do with keeping everyone informed, conducting special studies, defining equity shares, etc.

Legal Counsel

A most critical goal was to assure experienced legal counsel. Attorney _____ was lead counsel to _____ members in their successful conversion to equity membership, and has acted in the same capacity for several other Florida clubs. He and his firm of _____ , _____ represented _____CC, Inc. throughout the project.

Membership Data

We received from _____ lists of current residents and vacant lot owners; golfing members (including off-site); yachting members, social members. Initial total was 889, including out-of-state and international addresses.

All names were compiled into our own master list on computer, sorted by residential subsections (_____, etc.), classes of membership (golfing, yachting, etc.), responses to survey, contributors to fund, etc.

Independent Studies

Three major studies were conducted by outside experts. Major issues included classes of future memberships; cost of equity shares; annual dues; cap on golf memberships; governance of club; needs for course repairs and improvements; values of comparable clubs; ultimate financial offer to _____ .

1–<u>Fair market value of property</u> _____ <u>was expected to sell</u> (Golf course, club house, marina, tennis courts, driving range, swimming pool, and grounds). Study/ appraisal was conducted by country club experts in Atlanta office of national auditing firm, _____ . Cost for this Study was split equally with _____ .

2–<u>Financial condition of Club</u>. Also performed by _____ . _____ provided Club financial records/forecasts, confidentially, to the 9 Trustees only.

3–<u>Physical condition of Golf Course</u>. Analysis/deficiencies described by _____ from headquarters at West Palm Beach.

In addition, the Bylaws Committee of _____CC, Inc. obtained from various members copies of bylaws of other clubs to which they belong, conducted an extensive review as each item might pertain to equity-owned _____CC, and drafted a "Proposed Constitution and Bylaws."

Operating Funds/Expenses

Almost 300 individuals contributed $71,750 to fund Committee expenses. The request for $250 contained three stipulations: (1) If our effort was unsuccessful, all unused funds would be returned on a pro rata basis; (2) Contributors would be <u>charter</u> members of the _new_ _____CC—and if the equity issue was oversold, priority for membership would be set by postmarks related to the contributions; (3) If the purchase goes through, contributors would be credited with the $250 if they bought an equity share.

Actual expenses came to about $40,000, or approximately $140 of each $250 contribution. Charges were for consultant studies, the survey by _____ , legal fees, printings and multiple mailings, etc. All remaining money was returned pro rata to contributors—about $110 each.

Communications/Meetings

The initial Community-wide meeting and other early actions as described previously were central to measuring interest and engendering support—and to providing impetus for a group to organize and embark on the project.

Once the work was underway: "_____CC, Inc." letterhead was produced and progress reports (7) were sent to the Community over the ensuing months; a hot-line phone number was set up (courtesy of a member); Trustees attended homeowner group meetings to give updates/answer questions; etc.

The full Planning Committee met once a month, for reports by the Trustees and for input and decisions. Trustees met at least once a week. Members of subcommittees met at various times aside from the other regular meetings.

Administrative Items

A resident who is a computer expert volunteered to set up the mailing lists, run off labels, conduct sophisticated cross-referencing of demographics, assure proper records on contributions, etc. Printing of newsletters, etc., was done by a St. Pete printer—and assembly of materials/stuffing of envelopes was done by volunteers, usually in the club room of the Building-A condo. Other needs included a postage meter (provided by _____); bulk rate permit; arrangements for Committee meetings (usually in the lower level of the Club); a mailing address (donated by a member); etc.

2/7/95

February 7, 1995

TO: Residential Association Presidents/Representatives—_____
     Country Club (_____CC)

A meeting was held January 31, 1995, at a resident's home to discuss two general issues of importance to the _____CC Community:

1– What are the legal rights of the Community regarding the possible future sale by _____ of the Club, course, grounds, etc.

2– Should the Community organize a group to update prior studies conducted in our effort to purchase the Club, and to prepare to deal with any eventuality that may occur re a sale by _____ .

Representatives of all residential sectors of _____CC, of the _____ and _____ , and of the Yacht Club were present (total of 15–list enclosed).

Leading the discussion was _____ , former President of the group of nine Trustees which managed the studies and subsequent negotiations with _____ in 1991–92. Also attending were Attorney _____ , who represented the Community in that effort; and _____ , one of the former Trustees and head of Communications during the earlier project.

The following decisions/actions were taken:

- A letter to _____ will be drafted for the group's signatures by _____ regarding our legal standing in the event _____ proposes to sell the Club.

- Attendees will report to their individual Boards on this meeting, and obtain approval of proposed actions. They also will raise $100 from each of their groups to underwrite initial legal expenses (escrow account to be set up at _____ firm).

- Respective heads of the Associations (or their designees) should now organize as a Review Board to oversee a possible purchase of the Club. This special Board, in turn, should promptly conduct a "skills inventory" of _____CC residents qualified and available to direct a possible future acquisition program–and mobilize them for appropriate action.

   (Discussion also was held regarding the possible permanence of such a Review Board to serve in deliberations on other major matters affecting the entire _____CC Community. Further study of this proposal is suggested.)

- _____ agrees to continue serving the Community in leading the early stages of preparing for a possible acquisition program–but he asks that his involvement be only temporary. The Review Board should begin its search at once for another leader who has strong business experience.

- _____ agreed to prepare background material which summarizes for a possible future working team all that took place the last time–and which outlines the optimal background suggested for serving on the team. A "package" of three documents is enclosed:

   –"Summary of Principal Activities" engaged in by the previous advisory Trustees and Planning Committee from 1990 to '91;

   –"Report on Negotiations . . ." to the Community by the Trustees 9/4/91, describing our studies, our offer to _____ , and the _____ rejections;

- "Profile of Ideal Representatives" suggested for use in identifying leadership for a possible future effort.
- There will be a second meeting of Community representatives to approve the _____ letter and possibly begin to organize for an upcoming effort.

Next meeting of homeowners' representatives on this matter:

Tuesday, February 14, 1995–7 p.m.

February 16, 1995

TO: Association Presidents/Representatives–
_____ Country Club (_____CC)

A second meeting of the above group was held at a resident's home February 14, 1995 to discuss further the possible change of ownership of the _____ Club, course, etc. (First report 2/7 contains names/associations.)

Actions taken/decisions made at the 2/14 meeting were as follows:

- A draft letter to _____ regarding the Community's position on possible attempts by _____ to sell the Club was edited and approved. The letter, prepared by Legal Counsel _____ , was sent to _____ 2/16 with signatures of all association heads. Copy is enclosed.
- The group voted unanimously to organize as a unified body to help assure coordination on this matter by the Community at large. A temporary name was picked, then changed to the _____ United Community.
- All members of the group will begin an immediate talent search for candidates to head and to comprise a small working committee which would manage a possible acquisition program. Names should be submitted within 10 days–or by Friday, February 24–to _____ , who is serving as interim head of the group. Emphasis should be on residents/Club members with business/corporate backgrounds . . . on those who are active in the Club . . . and on those who will dedicate the time that may be needed for studies, analyses, negotiations with _____ , etc. List of suggested specifications for individuals on acquisition team is enclosed.
- _____ and maybe a couple others will serve as an informal sub-group to meet with potential candidates and propose to the full group recommendations for: (1) Mission/Objectives of the working committee; (2) Organization, including subcommittees; (3) leader of the working committee and other members. The goal will be to have all this ready for the next group meeting, expected by mid-March.

- Each member of the group will survey his/her association members to determine their types of Club memberships (if any). Association address lists should be submitted to _____ with a notation of member type aside each name. This should be completed by <u>mid-March</u>.

- Checks for $100 were submitted by each association (or are on the way) to cover initial legal costs associated with this effort.

PROFILE OF IDEAL REPRESENTATIVES TO LEAD THE EFFORT
ON POSSIBLE PURCHASE OF _____ C.C. FROM _____

Experience of four years ago in attempting to purchase _____CC demonstrated the imperative of having a <u>leader</u> and <u>senior advisory group</u> with a wide range of experience and certain other characteristics.

Purchase of _____CC is a multi-million-dollar proposition with long-term implications for the personal and financial interests of the Community.

While it has golfing and yachting and other social-life overtones, this is, above all, a <u>business</u> matter. If the effort is begun again, it will involve not only disciplines of the law, finance, etc.—but negotiations with the 24th largest industrial corporation in America, _____ , and with its legal counsel.

Against this background the following "Job Description" has been prepared for possible use in recruiting the <u>ideal</u> representative to <u>head</u> the team. It is difficult to find all this in one person, but the incumbent is, by far, the Community's single most critical representative, and the standards are high:

LEADER/PRESIDENT OF TRUSTEES

- <u>Business/corporate background</u>—Professional experience in financial analysis, negotiation, legal affairs, marketing, market research, real estate, and communications.

- <u>Personal leadership skills</u>—Able to develop multi-faceted goals, direct a wide range of tactics, coordinate a diverse committee, build consensus, tolerate dissent, drive the team to action/decisions, evaluate results.

- <u>_____CC dedication/country club background</u>—Resident on the property, active in _____CC (preferably including golf), experience with other clubs.

- <u>Significant availability</u>—Year-long resident free to devote considerable time, probably over many months, to the effort.

To the greatest extent possible, these specifications also should be applied in the naming of other project-team members who would represent the entire Community and spearhead the project.

46

FOREIGN ORGANIZATIONS AND ACTIVITIES

§459. LICENSING AND REGISTRATION IN OTHER STATES

A nonprofit incorporated trust, that accepts contributions in Tennessee from member employers nationwide and administers an employee welfare benefit plan for health, dental, hospital, life, accidental death, and workers' compensation benefits, is entitled to challenge the validity of a cease and desist order that precluded their conducting business in Minnesota. The District Court must consider the Dahlberg factors of the issuance of injunctive relief. *See Dahlberg Bros., Inc. v. Ford Motor Co.,* 137 N.W. 3d 314 (1965).

> *State v. International Association of Entrepreneurs of America,* 527 N.W. 2d 133
> (MN App., 1995).

For information about the Supreme Court's application of the Fourteenth Amendment's equal protection clause to foreign corporations, *see* 49 L. Ed. 2d 1296, §§10[c], 11.

Captive Insurance Income from Controlled Foreign Corporations

A 1996 Small Business Job Protection Act provision, which carves out certain universities' and hospitals' captive insurance income from unrelated business income tax (UBIT) liability would allow insurance income from a controlled foreign corporation (CFC) to avoid UBIT. The Clinton Administration and the insurance industry have attacked the provision. In Clinton's 1997 budget, an alternative way of handling captive insurance income from CFCs will be presented.

> Burstein, Emanual, *Tax Burden on Captive Insurance Income Eased in Small-Business Act, Tax Notes,* Sept. 2, 1996.

§462. WHAT IS "DOING BUSINESS"?

The spouse, heirs, and legal representatives of employees who suffered brain damage from exposure to mustard fumes, allegedly due to a defective safety standards sheet used by the employer of the victims, sued the trade association that produced the safety sheet. The court held that it had no in personam jurisdiction over the association, which was a nonresident of the state without continuous, substantial or systematic contacts with Louisiana. Contact between the injury and the association's act of producing the safety sheet was too tenuous for the association to expect to be hauled into court in Louisiana.

Fricke v. Owens-Corning Fiberglass Corp., 647 So. 2d 1260 (LA App. 4 Cir., 1994).

Connecticut's long-arm statute cannot reach a nonstock foreign corporate hospital, whose sole contact with Connecticut is involvement in a purported joint venture with an entity that allegedly developed defective surgical implants, and over which Connecticut does have jurisdiction. The nonstock corporate hospital was not part of the joint venture under Texas law, where the purported joint venture was formed.

Bensmiller v. E.I. Dupont De Nemours & Co., 47 F. 3d 79 (2nd Cir., 1995).

An artist sued a carrier and the governing body of a territorial subdivision of France when his sculptures were damaged following the closing of an art exposition in France. The court held that the art exposition was not "commercial activity" within the meaning of the exception to the Foreign Sovereign Immunities Act (FSIA). The test is whether the activity is of the type an individual would customarily carry on for profit.

Aschenbrenner v. Conseil Regional de Haute-Normandie, 851 F. Supp. 580 (S.D. NY, 1994); 28 U.S.C.A. Sections 1603(d), 1605(a)(2).

Forum Selection Clauses

A forum selection clause in an equipment lease is not a sufficient basis for a Michigan court to exercise personal jurisdiction over an incorporated Georgia nonprofit hospital. Thus, in a 1994 case, a default judgment for alleged breach of contract to lease certain equipment, entered in Michigan was denied domestication (unenforceable) in Georgia.

American Financial Service Group, Inc. v. Minnie G. Boswell Memorial Hospital, 447 S.E. 2d 333 (GA App., 1994).

47

INTERNATIONAL NONPROFIT ORGANIZATIONS

§466. WHAT IS AN "INTERNATIONAL NONPROFIT ORGANIZATION"?

Public Interest Groups

In some countries, nonprofit organizations are called *Nongovernmental Organizations* if they are actually *public interest groups,* such as consumer protection organizations. In recent years (for example, since the 1980s) they have become important in areas where no such organization had any substantial effect before, such as in Malaysia.

> *See* Andrew Harding, Public Interest Groups, Public Interest Law and
>   Development in Malaysia, *Third World Legal Studies* 1992, p. 231 (issued
>   July 1994).

British Nonprofit Organizations

For information about the taxation of British nonprofit organizations, *see Taxation of Non-Profit Organisations: Towards Efficient Tax Rules,* (United Kingdom) Yishai Beer, *British Tax Review,* March–April 1995 n2 p156–172.

Czech Nonprofit Organizations

For recent developments in the privatization of Czech Social Welfare Organizations, *see The Czech Republic's Law on Nonprofit Organizations: The Next Step in Privatization,* Milton Cerny, *Tax Notes International,* Jan. 9, 1995 10 n2 p143–149; *Local Financing Reform, Nonprofit Organizations, and the Czech Economic Transition,* Pavel Pelant, *Tax Notes International,* Jan. 9, 1995 10 n2 p150–151.

Korean Nonprofits

The nonprofit Federation of Korean Industries (FKI) was founded in 1961 to promote growth and internationalization of the Korean economy through private sector initiatives and exchanges. The International Management Institute (IMI), one the FKI's subsidiaries, has trained many Korean managers through various programs. The IMI recently instituted the International Management Exchange program (IMEX) to enable Korean business leaders to meet and share information with their foreign counterparts.

Ortiz, Elizabeth, *Networking for Asian Prosperity, Business Korea,* Sept., 1996.

Europe Online

Europe Online S.A. has returned as a nonprofit organization acting as an Internet navigation service.

The New York Times, Oct. 10, 1996.

International Volunteers

An example of international volunteer work is the work of the Flying Doctors of America. The group traveled to Peru in June, 1996 to provide medical and dental care in the village of Huilloc in the Andes mountains. Over 5 days, the 18 physicians, dentists, nurses, and chiropractors treated 1,200 Quechua Indians, who live without electricity or running water. Flying Doctors of America, formed in 1992, seeks to share US medical expertise with the less fortunate.

Krause, Karen Culotta, *A House Call in the Andes, American Medical News,*
    August 26, 1996.

Federal Aid to NGOs

See, Edwards and Hulme, *Too Close for Comfort? The Impact of Official Aid on
    Nongovernmental Organizations, World Development,* June, 1996.

48

INSOLVENCY, BANKRUPTCY, AND REORGANIZATION

§472. WHAT IS INSOLVENCY LAW?

Insolvency—Distribution of Assets

A Chapter 7 trustee is entitled to a full two years to bring a preference proceeding, even where the Chapter 11 debtor-in-possession has administered the estate for seven years before conversion and appointment of the Chapter 7 trustee.

In re California Canners & Growers, 175 B.R. 346 (9th Cir. BAP, 1994).

§475. RECEIVERSHIP

The Federal Deposit Insurance Corporation (FDIC) may not be restricted judicially in the exercise of its powers or functions, as a conservator or receiver, if it decides to sell a historic building over the objections of historic preservation societies, even where there are allegations that the sale would violate the National Historic Preservation Act.

National Trust for Historic Preservation in U.S. v. FDIC, 21 F. 3d 469 (DC Cir., 1994).

For information about the distribution of funds by nonprofit corporations absent dissolution, *see* 51 ALR 3d 1318.

§477. PRESENT (NEW) BANKRUPTCY LAW

Eligibility for Relief

An Illinois HMO is a "domestic insurance company" ineligible for bankruptcy relief and is subject to the state liquidation and rehabilitation scheme.

Matter of Estate of Medcare HMO, 998 F. 2d 436 (7th Cir. [IL], 1993).

A lessee, that had filed for Chapter 11 relief, brought suit against its lessors to recover $500,000 in damages based on the lessors' alleged interference with its subtenants' use of the premises during renovation of the building. The court held that the bankruptcy court committed abuse of discretion in denying the lessors' motion for relief from default due to the willfulness of the lessors' default and the lack of a "meritorious defense" of the lessor.

In re Rymsbran Continental Corp., 177 B.R. 163 (E.D. NY, 1995).

Bankruptcy Fees

Granting of attorney fees and costs in an interpleader action in a bankruptcy proceeding is a matter of equity, and is a matter of discretion of the bankruptcy court. [Bank action (interpleader) to settle various parties' claims to funds on deposit.]

In re Mandalay Shores Coop. Housing Association, Inc., 21 F. 3rd 380 (11th Cir., [FL], 1994).

Religious Tithing

The extent of charitable contributions and church tithing may be considered in determining whether a Chapter 7 filing is substantial abuse, without burdening the free exercise of religion. Under the Religious Freedom Restoration Act, a debtor who tithes may not receive Chapter 7 discharge when another similarly situated nontithing debtor cannot receive such discharge. Tithing, under Chapter 7, is not a reasonably necessary expenditure for maintenance and support of a debtor. But, a nominal amount of charitable contributions may be permissible. Neither state nor federal law exempts assets intended for tithing from the claims of creditors. If a reduction of tithing from 10 percent to 3 percent of the debtor's income will result in the debtor's ability to pay 73 percent of his/her unsecured debt under Chapter 13, a Chapter 7 case can be dismissed for substantial abuse.

In re Faulkner, 165 B.R. 644 (Bankr. W.D. MO, 1994).

Creditors' Rights

A class proof of claim for a debtor hospital's former employees, that would effectively extend the bar date for employee creditors who had not yet filed claims, is inappropriate where the putative class has not been certified as appropriate by the nonbankruptcy court, the debtor's plan in bankruptcy is before the court for imminent confirmation, employees had clear notice of the bankruptcy, and the class proof of claim is filed 11 days before the bar date and just prior to the holiday season.

In re Sacred Heart Hospital of Norristown, 177 B.R. 16 (Bkrtcy, E.D. PA, 1995).

A van purchased by a nonprofit corporation established to provide mental health and counseling services to low-income individuals is not included in the corporation's Chapter 7 estate where there are significant governmental restrictions on the use of grant funds used to purchase the van and where the granting agency is authorized to repossess the van. The bankruptcy trustee acquires only the rights of debtor, prepetition. Restricted grant funds, received from the state, and segregated from the corporation's funds, are not "property of the debtor" for fraudulent transfer avoidance purposes, unless they are commingled and untraceable as trust assets.

In re Alpha Center, Inc., 165 B.R. 881 (Bankr. D. SC, 1994). *See also In re Community Associates, Inc.,* 173 B.R. 824 (D. CT, 1994).

Where intercompany debts place three interrelated Chapter 11 debtors in possession into a creditor/debtor relationship, there are conflicts among the debtors. Thus, the debtors cannot be represented by the same law firm.

In re Interwest Business Equipment, Inc., 23 F. 3d 311 (10th Cir. [UT], 1994).

Under Nevada's alter ego doctrine, a Chapter 7 trustee is entitled to the turnover of all estate assets, including real estate held by a debtor's corporation and assets of a debtor's foundation, if the corporation and foundation are the debtor's alter egos and were used by the debtor to avoid payment of taxes.

In re Towe, 173 B.R. 197 (Bkrtcy. D. MT, 1994).

A debtor may negotiate with its nonprofit creditor for acceptance of its contemplated plan, before the debtor has presented the final version of its disclosure statement to the court for approval. Such a debtor is not guilty of "solicitation" of the nonprofit's vote for the plan, in violation of statutory requirements, if the nonprofit creditor receives no "special consideration" for voting to accept the plan.

In re Kellogg Square Partnership, 160 B.R. 336 (Bankr. D. MN, 1993).

A nonprofit cannot pay the debts of a related Chapter 7 debtor nonprofit and then recover the funds under the doctrine of money had and received, if the payor nonprofit disregards corporate form and indiscriminately uses the debtor's assets as its own. This is true even where the payments in question conferred benefit on the debtor.

In re Mission of Care, Inc., 164 B.R. 877 (Bankr. D. DE, 1994).

The board of trustees of a debtor nonprofit corporation is not a "class of interests" that is entitled to vote on confirmation of bankruptcy plans. Under Ohio law, the board is neither an equity security holder, nor creditor, nor indenture trustee holding an allowed claim against the corporation. There is no interest in a nonprofit equivalent to a stockholder that stands to profit from the success of the enterprise.

In re Lincoln Ave. and Crawford's Home for the Aged, Inc., 164 B.R. 600 (Bankr. S.D. OH, 1994).

The Fraternal Order of Eagles, a nonprofit fraternal society, filed a proceeding to determine the dischargeability of expenses which it incurred in obtaining completion of a construction contract after a debtor failed to perform. For the purposes of dischargeability, the creditor's speculation that the debtor intentionally underbid the job in order to obtain it, and then demanded that he be allowed to submit a higher bid, was not sufficient to show fraud. Technical embezzlement through progress payments was insufficient to establish embezzlement nondischargeability. The evidence presented to show fraudulent intent was insufficient to show embezzlement.

In re Mercer, 169 B.R. 694 (Bkrtcy. W.D. WA, 1994).

Debts to Nonprofit Educational Institutions

Student loans may be dischargeable in bankruptcy if there is "undue hardship" to the debtor. "Undue hardship" must not be created, either willfully or negligently through the debtor's own default, but rather, the condition must have resulted from factors beyond his/her reasonable control. The *Johnson* test or the *Brunner* test for undue hardship may be used. However, the court adopts a case-by-case approach and usually does not use a bright line method for finding "undue hardship." For example, a debtor received discharge where his loan was $20,000, which was to be paid back over 20 years in exchange for two and one-half weeks of useless flight training. The court reasoned that the flight school closed before the debtor received any financial benefit from his bargained-for education.

In re Law, 159 B.R. 287 (Bankr. D. SD, 1993).

Student loans, extended by nonprofits, may be discharged in bankruptcy on grounds of hardship. The court looks to the debtor's present and future needs, the debtor's good faith, and whether the policies of the Bankruptcy Code are met. Where the debtor has present and future income sufficient to pay expenses and the loans, makes no voluntary loan payments, fails to pursue administrative remedies, and files bankruptcy for the sole purpose of discharging student loans, discharge is not proper.

> *In re Bethune,* 165 B.R. 258 (Bankr. E.D. AR, 1994); *see also Matter of Sands,* 166 B.R. 299 (Bankr. W.D. MI, 1994).

The bankruptcy court can reduce, in its discretion, the amount of nondischargeable student loan debt to a level that will not inflict "undue hardship" on the debtor, rather than discharging the entire amount of the loan.

> *In re Woyame,* 161 B.R. 198 (Bankr. N.D. OH, 1993).

The fraud exception to discharge applies to debt (1) that is obtained through representations that the debtor either knew were false or that he made with reckless disregard of the truth, (2) where the debtor intended to deceive the plaintiffs, (3) where the plaintiffs relied on misrepresentations to their detriment, and (4) where the plaintiff's reliance was reasonable.

> *In re West,* 163 B.R. 133 (Bankr. N.D. IL, 1993).

A Federal Credit Union is not a "nonprofit institution" for the purpose of an exception to the discharge for educational loans made under a program funded by a nonprofit institution, if the credit union has shareholders and is authorized to pay dividends on shares of its members.

> *In re Delbonis,* 169 B.R. 1 (Bkrtcy. D. MA, 1994).

If students consolidate their debts by way of a new consolidation loan, the 7-year nondischargeability period for student loans begins to run from the date that the new consolidation loan is first due, rather than from the due date of the original student loan.

> *In re Hesselgrave,* 177 B.R. 681 (Bkrtcy. D. OR, 1995).

Post default agreements between a nonprofit lender and a student loan debtor do not toll the 7-year repayment period for discharge of student loans in bankruptcy. Suspension of the repayment period is not achieved by voluntary cessation by the lender of its collection efforts (i.e., "forbearance") during a time when increased monthly repayments were to have been made by the debtor.

> *In re Marlewski,* 168 B.R. 378 (Bkrtcy. E.D. WI, 1994).

For more information about the discharge of student loans in bankruptcy and nonprofit institutions, see the following:

> *In re Garelli,* 162 B.R. 552 (Bankr. D. OR, 1994); *McCullough v. Brown,* 162 B.R. 506 (N.D. IL, 1993) (unsecured student loans would be paid in full while other unsecured claims would be paid between 10 and 20 percent of their allowed amount); *In re Bachner,* 165 B.R. 875 (Bankr. N.D. IL, 1994); *In re Healey,* 161 B.R. 389 (E.D. MI, 1993); *In re Plotkin,* 164 B.R. 623 (Bankr. W.D. AR, 1994); *In re Kellogg,* 166 B.R. 504 (Bankr. D. CT, 1994); *In re Raymond,* 169 B.R. 67 (Bkrtcy. W.D. WA, 1994); *In re Simmons,* 175 B.R. 624 (Bkrtcy. E.D. VA, 1994); *In re Joyner,* 171 B.R. 759 (Bkrtcy. E.D. PA, 1994); *In re Joyner,* 171 B.R. 762 (Bkrtcy. E.D. PA, 1994); *In re Ridder,* 171 B.R. 345 (Bkrtcy. W.D. WI, 1994); *In re Eiland,* 170 B.R. 370 (Bkrtcy. N.D. IL, 1994); *In re McLeod,* 176 B.R. 455 (Bkrtcy. N.D. OH, 1994) (debtor owned half-interest in house with non paying tenants and could sell the house or collect rent); *In re Stebbins-Hopf,* 176 B.R. 784 (Bkrtcy. W.D. TX, 1994); *In re Wilson,* 177 B.R. 246 (Bkrtcy. E.D. VA, 1994).

Chapter 11 [Condo Conversion Plan] "Fairness"

A bankruptcy judge in Chicago rejected a Chapter 11 debtor (real estate developer) plan to reorganize by converting an apartment house complex into condominiums in order to restructure a $30 million loan. That would not satisfy the Bankruptcy Act's "fair and equitable" requirement. The mortgage holder was Met Life Insurance Co. The developer (Michael R. Sparks) was trying to retain ownership of a 468-unit complex worth $27 million. In effect the ruling said that a mortgage holder of a condo is not in as good a risk situation as is one holding a mortgage on an apartment complex. The two are not "indubitable equivalents"—on the "fairness" basis.

> *In re Michael R. Sparks,* 92 B 21692 (Sept. 14, 1994); contra held in *In re Monarch Beach Venture, Ltd.,* 166 B.R. 428 (C.D. CA, 1993). M. Middleton, report, *Natl. L.J.,* p. B1 (Oct. 3, 1994).

Bankruptcy Act 1994 Revisions

Approved by House and Senate (and awaiting presidential signature) in October 1994, Bankruptcy Act Amendments imposed new restrictions on big corporations' lengthy blockages of their creditors' claims. *Savings and loan associations* (and banks) claims thus will be better protected in Chapter 11 cases. *Condo associations* may require debtors to continue paying association fees after they file for bankruptcy if they occupy or rent a condo unit. Fraudulent conduct by debtors (such as buying expensive cars and then filing in bankruptcy) will be harder to justify.

Washington News item, *The New York Times* (Oct. 8, 1994).

50

EFFECTS OF DISSOLUTION AND TRANSFER OF PROPERTY

§485. EFFECTS OF DISSOLUTION

Statutes concerning the survival period of a nonprofit corporation after dissolution may affect the nonprofit's ability to be used. In New Mexico, in 1994, a nonprofit hospital's survival period was tolled by the corporation's fraudulent concealment of the cause of a patient's death. However, the survival period began to run again when the plaintiff discovered the true cause of the patient's death.

Quintana v. Los Alamos Medical Center, Inc., 889 P. 2d 1234 (NM App., 1994)

A new nonprofit corporation is liable for the debts of a dissolved nonprofit if there is identity of management and control. Former volunteer officers who serve the new nonprofit and served the old dissolved corporation, under Wisconsin's volunteer immunity statute, are not liable for the debts of the dissolved entity, absent "willful misconduct." Willful misconduct includes a dishonest role in either the dissolution of the old nonprofit or formation of its successor or a primary motivation, in organizing the successor corporation, to avoid payment of debt.

IGL-Wisconsin Awning, Tent and Trailer Co., Inc. v. Greater Milwaukee Air and Water Show, Inc., 520 N.W. 2d 279 (WI App., 1994).

Asset Transfers That Could Result in Tax Liability

The IRS has proposed regulations to make transfers from taxable corporations to tax-exempt corporations taxable events if the proposed regulations are finalized in their current form. Three of the asset transfers that would trigger the IRS imposition of tax are (1) the transfer of assets from a for-profit to a nonprofit corporation (2) dissolution of a for-profit subsidiary and transfer of substantially all of the assets to the exempt parent organization and (3) the transformation of a taxable corporation into an exempt organization.

Harmon, Gail, (article), 11 *NonProfit Times* (7) 40–41 (May, 1997).

For information about the distribution of funds by cooperative associations *absent dissolution, see* 51 ALR 3d 1318.

§486. DISPOSITION OF PROPERTY (*CY PRES* DOCTRINE)

Illustrative Cases on Property Transfer

A water association has no enforceable real property right against the purchaser of a well based on the association being a third-party beneficiary of a service portion of a prior contract to use the well. This is true, even where the purchasers had notice of the association's use of the well before purchase.

> *Bear Island Water Association Inc. v. Brown,* 874 P. 2d 528 (ID, 1994).

A mortgage foreclosure sale and certificate of sale may be set aside by the court, where there is a gross inadequacy of the foreclosure sale price (less than 5% of the property's appraised value), and where the bidders cooperated to submit a joint bid indicating that they were not "good faith" purchasers.

> *RSR Investments, Inc. v. Barnett Bank of Pinellas County,* 647 So. 2d 874 (FL App. 2 Dist., 1994).

The unauthorized transfer of property by a local church is invalid if the transfer is governed by provisions contained in a constitutional document setting forth the internal structure of the church's denomination, in which written permission from the national church is required for transfer.

> *Bethany Independent Church v. Stewart,* 645 So. 2d 715 (LA App. 3 Cir., 1994).

A sub licensee, under a licensee's agreement with the foundation of a deceased artist's estate (Andy Warhol Foundation for the Visual Arts), is not a third party beneficiary of the licensee's agreement with the estate. Where the agreement does not permit enforcement by third parties, the sub licensee has no enforcement rights against the estate and no action for tortious interference with contractual relations against the estate.

> *Artwear, Inc. v. Hughes,* 615 N.Y.S. 2d 689 (AD. 1 Dept., 1994).

In a recent case, agreements between a nonprofit corporation and a developer were extinguished when the developer lost the development site through foreclosure. A lease between a developer and nonprofit corporation is not valid where the lease was subordinate to a deed of trust to the development site, the developer lost title to the site through foreclosure and a sale at the trustee sale, and the developer never reacquired the property.

San Francisco Design Center Associates v. Portman Companies, 38 Cal. Rptr. 2d 270
(CA App. 1 Dist., 1995).

A land developer may be required to discharge or obtain release on obligations on common lands that are already identified and encumbered, and to convey the lands to the landowners' association, where an order incorporating the terms of a settlement agreement directs the land developer to act.

Gannon v. Quechee Lakes Corp., 648 A. 2d 1378 (VT, 1994).

INDEX

political contributions by corporations, **S313**
political finances, 1221, **S321–324**
propaganda, **S318**
rating of candidates, 1211
regulation of, federal, **S311–312**
by social welfare organizations, **S310**
state laws on, 257, 1213–1215, **S312–313**
  anonymous campaign literature, **S312**
  corporate political contributions, **S313**
  initiative petitions, **S313**
  term limits, **S313**
tax on lobbying, **S308–309**
tax deduction for, **S308–309**, **S310**
by trade associations, **S310**
See also, Political committees; Political
    activism; Tax-exemption, federal
Lobbyists, definition of, 214
Louisiana:
  officer liability in, 934
  proxy rules in, 858
  right to vote in, 830
  unincorporated associations in, 150

M

Maine:
  annual reports in, 936–941
  charitable immunity in, 548
  forms for:
    Articles of Consolidation (Domestic)
        form, 1426–1429
    Articles of Consolidation (Foreign and
        Domestic) form, 1433–1436
    Statement of Intent to Dissolve,
        1513–1514
  charitable immunity in, 548
  proxy rules in, 858
  statutory classifications in, 90
  tax-exemption statutes in, **S133**, **S135**
Management techniques, 1277–1308,
    S342–352
  charitable funds management, 1278
    software for, **S268–269**
  consulting services, **S348**
  courses/seminars on, 4–5, 1278, **S2**,
    S350–351
  definition of, 1277–1278
  elements of, 1294–1295
  forms for:
    guide forms and tables, 1296

management contract, 1286–1294
Outline for Objective and Investment
    Policy Statement for Investment
    Managers, **S217**
staff policies/manuals, 1302–1304
financial services, **S347–348**
health care groups, **S348–349**
human resources management, **S351**
information sources for, 1278–1279, **S348,**
    S349
Internet II, **S343**
Management techniques *(continued)*
  websites, home pages for, **S346–347**
  freeware, **S345**
  online services, **S347**
  sample starter sites, **S345–346**
  World Wide Web, **S344**
investments, **S215–217**
  "prudent investor" rule, **S215–216**
IRS standards for, 1298
management associations, **S350**
pessimism for 1997 and the future, **S350**
problems in management, **S343**
"quality teams" management, **S351**
restructuring, **S342**
risk management, 1282, **S351**
securities transactions and, 1298, **S352**
staff policies, 1301
support centers for, 4, 1282, **S350–351**
systems approach to management, 1295
    Management Information System (MIS),
        1295–1296
    Management by Objectives (MBO),
        1296–1297
training for, 4, 1280–1284, **S350–351**
    Master's Degree curriculum for,
        1282–1284
    seminars for, 1281–1282, **S350–351**
    suggested curriculum for, 1280–1281
    workshops for, **S350**
volunteer background checks, **S251**
women as, **S219–220**
See also, Officers; Agents; Management
    techniques; Employees; Volunteers;
    Directors
Manuals, forms for employee, 1296,
    1302–1303, **S240**
Maryland:
  fund raising in, 1328–1329
  proxy rules in, 858
  registration for solicitation in, **S370**